MOVING BOXES BY AIR

Moving Boxes by Air
The Economics of International Air Cargo

PETER S. MORRELL
Cranfield University, UK

ASHGATE

Published by
Ashgate Publishing Limited
Wey Court East
Union Road
Farnham
Surrey, GU9 7PT
England

Ashgate Publishing Company
Suite 420
101 Cherry Street
Burlington
VT 05401-4405
USA

www.ashgate.com

British Library Cataloguing in Publication Data
Morrell, Peter S., 1946-
  Moving boxes by air : the economics of international air
  cargo.
  1. Aeronautics, Commercial--Freight. 2. Aeronautics,
  Commercial--Freight--Economic aspects.
  I. Title
  387.7'44-dc22

Library of Congress Cataloging-in-Publication Data
Morrell, Peter S., 1946-
  Moving boxes by air : the economics of international air cargo / by Peter S. Morrell.
      p. cm.
  Includes bibliographical references and index.
  ISBN 978-1-4094-0252-7 (hbk.) -- ISBN 978-1-4094-0253-4
(ebook) 1. Aeronautics, Commercial--Freight. I. Title.
  HE9788.M67 2011
  387.7'44--dc23

2011012353

ISBN   978-1-4094-0252-7 (hbk)
ISBN   978-1-4094-0253-4 (ebk)

Printed and bound in Great Britain by the
MPG Books Group, UK

Contents

List of Figures		*ix*
List of Tables		*xi*
Preface		*xv*
Abbreviations		*xix*

1	**Air Cargo Traffic and Capacity**	**1**
	1.1 Air Cargo Traffic Trends	1
	1.2 Air Cargo and the Economic Cycle	10
	1.3 Airport Traffic	12
	1.4 Hub Transhipment Traffic	14
	1.5 Air Cargo Traffic Variation within a Year	16
	1.6 Air Cargo Capacity	18

2	**Air Cargo Market Characteristics**	**23**
	2.1 Commodities Carried	25
	2.2 Special Handling Items	31
	2.3 Humanitarian Aid	35
	2.4 Defence Support	36
	2.5 Modal Choice	37
	2.6 Bimodal Shipment	44

3	**Economic and Technical Regulation**	**49**
	3.1 Licensing of Airlines	50
	3.2 Regulation of International Air Services	55
	3.3 Mail Regulation	68
	3.4 Future Air Cargo Liberalisation	69

4	**Supply: Passenger and Freight Airlines**	**73**
	4.1 Introduction	73
	4.2 Network Carriers	74
	4.3 Low-Cost Carriers	75
	4.4 Regional Carriers	76
	4.5 Major Domestic Carriers	76
	4.6 Passenger Flights of Combination Carriers	77
	4.7 Freighter Flights of Combination Carriers	77
	4.8 Freighter Flights by Freight-Only Carriers	80

4.9 Charter and ACMI Operators   82
4.10 Air Cargo Carriers by Region   84
4.11 Conclusion   94

5   Supply: Integrated Carriers, Post Offices and Forwarders   97
5.1 Courier Companies   98
5.2 Integrated Carriers   99
5.3 The Post Offices   109
5.4 Freight Forwarders and Consolidators   109
5.5 Maritime Operators   115

6   Air Cargo Alliances and Mergers   117
6.1 Air Cargo Alliances   117
6.2 Air Cargo Mergers and Acquisitions   126

7   Aircraft and Flight Operations   131
7.1 Passenger Aircraft: Lower Deck   131
7.2 Freighters: Converted from Passenger Aircraft   134
7.3 New Production Freighters   139
7.4 'Combi' and Quick Change Aircraft   144
7.5 Unit Load Devices for Aircraft   145
7.6 Aircraft Operations   146
7.7 Future Freighters   148

8   Airport and Ground Operations   153
8.1 Information Flows   154
8.2 Physical Facilities   161

9   Distribution and Marketing   173
9.1 Marketing Environment   175
9.2 Air Cargo Marketing Strategies   181
9.3 The Air Cargo Product   183
9.4 Air Cargo Promotion   186
9.5 Air Cargo Distribution   186

10   Pricing and Revenues   189
10.1 Cargo Revenue and Yield Trends   189
10.2 The Structure of Yields by Major Region and Type of Service   192
10.3 Air Freight Pricing   192
10.4 Revenue Management   200

11	**Airline Costs**	**207**
	11.1 All-Cargo Airline Costs	207
	11.2 Freighter Aircraft Costs by Aircraft Type	218
	11.3 ACMI/Wet Lease Aircraft Operating Costs	224
	11.4 Problems of Joint Production on Passenger Services	227

12	**Air Cargo Financial Performance**	**235**
	12.1 Cargo Airline Profitability	235
	12.2 Nippon Cargo Airlines Case Study	239
	12.3 Federal Express Case Study	247
	12.4 Network Carrier Cargo Subsidiaries	254

13	**Air Cargo and the Environment**	**259**
	13.1 Background	259
	13.2 Aircraft Noise	259
	13.3 Air Transport's Existing Contribution to Global CO_2 Emissions	265
	13.4 Environmental Taxes and Charges	272
	13.5 Emissions Trading Schemes and Air Cargo	274
	13.6 Air Cargo and Food Miles	279
	13.7 Conclusions	280

14	**Air Cargo Forecasting**	**283**
	14.1 Air Cargo Forecasting Approaches	284
	14.2 Airline Forecasts	288
	14.3 Airport Forecasts	289
	14.4 Air Traffic Management Forecasts	291
	14.5 Aircraft Manufacturer Forecasts	292
	14.6 ICAO Forecasts	296
	14.7 OAG Forecasts	298
	14.8 Other Industry Forecasts	298
	14.9 Conclusions	300

15	**Air Cargo Issues and Prospects**	**303**
	15.1 Air Cargo Issues	303
	15.2 Air Cargo Prospects	305

Definitions		*309*
Bibliography		*319*
Index		*325*

List of Figures

1.1   Passenger versus freight traffic trends, scheduled international
      services, 1995–2009   2
1.2   Growth rates for international freight versus mail traffic, 1995–2009   3
1.3   Distribution of world international freight tonne-km traffic by trade
      lane, 2009   6
1.4   US inventory to sales ratio vs. scheduled air freight traffic   11
1.5   Air freight tonne-kms traffic variation by month, Hong Kong
      Airport, 2007   16
1.6   Air freight tonne-kms traffic variation by month, AEA airlines, 2007   17

2.1   Recent trend in the air share of world containerised trade   23
2.2   Air trade by commodity, 2007: Europe to/from Asia   26
2.3   Air trade by commodity, 2007: North America to/from Asia   28
2.4   Air trade by commodity, 2007: North America to/from Latin America   29
2.5   Air trade by commodity, 2007: North America to/from Europe   30
2.6   Air exports of fresh flowers from Latin America to US, 2007   33
2.7   US air share of trade value (excluding North America), 1965 to 2004   38

3.1   Freedoms of the Air (air traffic rights)   57

4.1   Air cargo carried on freighter aircraft and share in total traffic IATA
      international services   78
4.2   Lufthansa Cargo management structure   79

5.1   Operators in air cargo/parcels market   97
5.2   Global freight forwarding market size, 2003 to 2008   110

7.1   Freighter aircraft conversions, 2000 to 2009   135
7.2   Payload-range trade-off   147

8.1   Example of air waybill   156
8.2   Cargolux containers   163
8.3   Forklifting packages at Hong Kong International Airport   164

9.1   Example of multinational off-shoring of production   177
9.2   Total distribution cost model   179

10.1   World airline passenger versus cargo yields, US dollars in real terms   190
10.2   Lufthansa reported cargo revenues per RTK, and €/US$ exchange
       rate, 1999 to 2009   190
10.3   Quarterly index of French freight transport prices   194
10.4   British Airways fuel surcharge versus jet kerosene price (September
       2003 to May 2010)   195
10.5   Spot market rates by product and advance booking   204
10.6   Overbooking cost optimisation   205

11.1   All-cargo airline unit costs versus average sector distance, 2008   208
11.2   Trends in spot crude and jet kerosene prices, 2005–2008   213
11.3   Cost allocation on passenger/cargo flights: cargo by-product   231
11.4   Product profit allocation on passenger/cargo flights   233

12.1   Airline profitability by type of carrier, average for 2006–2009
       inclusive   236
12.2   Return on invested capital by value chain participant   237
12.3   Nippon Cargo Airlines traffic and load factor trends, 1985 to 2008   242
12.4   Nippon Cargo Airlines Organigram   244
12.5   Nippon Cargo Airlines margin developments, 1988–2008   246
12.6   Nippon Cargo Airlines yield and unit cost developments, 1988–2008   247
12.7   Federal Express traffic and load factor trends, 1985 to 2008   250
12.8   Federal Express margin developments, 1988–2008   253
12.9   Federal Express airline yield, unit cost and break-even load factor,
       1990 to 2008   253

13.1   EU-25 CO_2 emissions by sector, 2004   266
13.2   Impact of benchmarking on B737-400 flight with hypothetical
       average at 1,850 km sector length   276

14.1   Forces and constraints for air cargo growth   293
14.2   ICAO methodology for forecasting air freight   297

List of Tables

1.1 International world cargo traffic by type of service, 1999, 2008 and 2009 — 4

1.2 World cargo traffic, domestic services, 1999, 2008 and 2009 — 5

1.3 Intra-EU air cargo tonnes (000) carried between top 10 countries, 2008 — 9

1.4 Freight tonne-kms by region of airline registration, 2008 — 10

1.5 Air freight throughput for top 10 world airports, 2009 — 13

1.6 Top 12 world airports in terms of international air cargo tonnes, 2009 — 15

1.7 Traffic breakdown at Amsterdam Schiphol hub airport — 15

1.8 Published freighter flights from Europe to Asia, January 2010 — 20

1.9 Integrator flights from East Midlands to Western Europe, summer 2010 — 21

2.1 Value to weight ratio for UK extra-EU international trade by mode of transport — 24

2.2 Special handling air tonnages by category, 2003 — 31

2.3 WFP Aviation operations, 2001 to 2008 — 35

2.4 US Civil Reserve Air Fleet (CRAF) allocations, April 2010 — 37

3.1 Air Services Agreements and cargo provisions, 1980 to 2005 — 58

3.2 Analysis of ASAs in APEC countries, 2005 — 64

4.1 International air freight by type of carrier, 2008 — 73

4.2 World low-cost carrier cargo acceptance policy — 75

4.3 International scheduled air freight by freighter-only airline, 2008 — 81

4.4 Top 10 US airlines by total FTKs carried, 2008 — 85

4.5 Cargo share of total revenue for US combination carriers, 2008 — 86

4.6 Top 10 European airlines by total FTKs carried, 2008 — 87

4.7 Top 10 Asian/Australasian airlines by total FTKs carried, 2008 — 91

4.8 Top 10 Africa/Middle-East airlines by total FTKs carried, 2008 — 93

4.9 Top seven South and Central American airlines by total FTKs carried, 2008 — 94

5.1 International air freight by integrator, 2008 — 99

5.2 Total courier, express and parcels market volume in 2007 — 100

5.3 Deutsche Post world net revenue by division (€m) — 101

5.4 Deutsche Post world net revenue by geographic area (€m) — 102

5.5   DHL Express long-haul air service provision, 2008   102
5.6   DHL regional operating companies, 2009   103
5.7   UPS US and international hub airports, 2009   107
5.8   Global freight forward value share by top 10 forwarders, 2008   111

7.1   Typical payload, volume and density for lower deck cargo   132
7.2   Top 10 most popular freighters   133
7.3   Wide-bodied aircraft conversions to freighters, 2004–2008   138
7.4   Medium-sized freighter aircraft: out of production in 2010   140
7.5   Medium-sized freighter aircraft: in production in 2010   140
7.6   Large freighter aircraft: out of production in 2010   141
7.7   Large freighter aircraft: in production in 2010   142
7.8   Combi, converted combi and Quick Change aircraft   144
7.9   Description of most commonly used ULDs   146

8.1   DHL Express hub at Leipzig/Halle Airport   166
8.2   Major third party cargo handling companies   169

9.1   Air freight rate structure for UPS, June 2010   185

10.1   Lufthansa forecasts of yield by type of cargo (€ per kg), 2003
       to 2009   191
10.2   US cents yield per RTK by type of service, 2005   192
10.3   German air freight price index by region/country   193
10.4   Traditional air freight rate structure   197
10.5   Charges reduced by consolidation   199
10.6   UPS Air and International selected fuel surcharge calculations 201

11.1   ICAO reporting form for collection of financial data, part 1   209
11.2   Cargolux asset depreciation policy, 2009   214
11.3   Freighter values (US$ million), April 2010   215
11.4   Cargolux operating cost breakdown, 1999 versus 2008   216
11.5   UPS unit cost trends by cost item, 1999 to 2008   217
11.6   Cargo aircraft capital conversion costs, 2007   218
11.7   Short-/medium-haul freighter aircraft operating costs, 2008   220
11.8   Long-haul freighter aircraft operating costs, 2008   222
11.9   Large freighter operating costs, 2007   224
11.10 Atlas Air segment contributions, 2008   226
11.11 ACMI rates by cost category and long-haul aircraft type, 1999   226
11.12 Costs assumed by lessor/charterer   227

12.1   All-cargo airline profit margins in 2008 and previous years   238
12.2   NCA route development, 1985 to 2000   241
12.3   Key Federal Express highlights   249

12.4	FedEx Express fleet, end May 2009	251
12.5	Federal Express fleet productivity, 2008	252
12.6	Lufthansa Cargo financial and operating data, 2005 to 2009	255
12.7	Lufthansa Cargo operating cost breakdown, 2008 and 2009	255
12.8	Singapore Airlines load factors by product and type of flight, 2008–2009	256
12.9	SIA Cargo financial and operating data, 2005/2006 to 2009/2010	257
13.1	Quota Count (QC) for selected aircraft types at Brussels Airport, 2010	265
13.2	Freighter flights by region of major airline base, 2002	266
13.3	Global aviation fuel used by type of flight, 2002	267
13.4	Jet freighter aircraft, estimated fuel consumption, 2002	268
14.1	BAA forecasts of air cargo tonnes with and without Terminal 5	290
14.2	FAA air cargo traffic (ton-mile) forecasts, 2010–2030	291
14.3	Boeing air cargo forecasts (RTKs), average annual change	294
14.4	Airbus air cargo forecasts (RTKs), average annual change	295
14.5	Boeing and Airbus freighter aircraft delivery forecasts	296
14.6	OAG medium-term air cargo traffic forecasts	298
14.7	Short-term forecasts by main region/routes, 2008–2012	299

Preface

The first air cargo or air mail flight is a highly contentious issue. Mail is said to have been first carried from Albany to New York in May 1910 and cargo first carried from Dayton to Columbus, Ohio, in November of the same year (Wensveen, 2007). The first flight by a hot air balloon carrying cargo (a cockerel, a sheep and a duck) was much earlier. The third distinct type of traffic, air express, owes its rapid development to the ending of the Railway Express Agency in 1975, a couple of years after the founding of Federal Express. The airline deregulation act of 1978 further removed any obstacles for the growth of air express operators such as FedEx and UPS, at least within the US.

Air cargo is closely linked to international trade whose expansion has been fostered by the removal of physical restrictions and growth of commercial opportunities through improved communications and international contacts. It has benefited from freer transfers of funds, stability of exchange rates and easier access to credit. Above all the reduction and removal of duties has also encouraged the growth in trade, as has the outsourcing of manufacturing to lower cost firms in other countries.

Air cargo also plays a key role in humanitarian aid. Airlift is provided by both military and civil aircraft often through hostile airspace and to below standard airports. Probably the most famous example of this was the Berlin airlift after the Second World War. In 1948, Berlin was jointly controlled by the Allies and Russians, although the Russians held the area surrounding the city and thus land access. This access was closed and thus an airlift remained the only option to get increasingly urgent deliveries of food, coal and other supplies to what became West Berlin. Over 330 days to 12 May 1949 a total of 2.26m tonnes of cargo were airlifted into Berlin, an average of 6,800 tonnes a day, 80 percent by the US and 20 percent by the UK. Almost three-quarters of the payload was coal, vital in heating the city especially over the winter period. The aircraft used were initially mostly C-47s with 3.5 tonnes of payload, but these were gradually replaced with C-54s and Avro Yorks with 10 tonnes. An assortment of other aircraft was also pressed into service. The peak day involved a total of almost 13,000 tonnes supplied by 1,383 flights, an average of 9.4 tonnes per flight. Only three runways were available and techniques had to be developed for efficient loading, unloading and air traffic control. Maintenance had to be adapted to schedules that gave high utilisation with often ageing planes. More recent examples of international aid have been in response to the devastation caused by earthquakes or floods: here surface transport is either too slow or impossible and air transport is the only means to supply food and clothing to the homeless.

In spite of the importance of air cargo in international trade, aid and relief operations, it has remained the poor cousin to the more glamorous passenger side of the business. This has been reflected in the dearth of air cargo books, with the topic usually dealt with as one chapter in books on air transport. It also receives little attention in books on logistics and the supply chain. Hence this book, which for the first time gives the industry its own up-to-date and comprehensive analysis of air cargo.

Individuals and firms assume that income will continue to grow indefinitely every year and economies will continue on their expansion path. Thus the upswings of economic cycles are fuelled by spending and investment supported by bank lending, whether consumer credit or company debt. Bubbles form, especially in popular sectors such as IT and housing. At some point expansion can no longer be sustainable, the bubble bursts and the downturn starts, triggered or reinforced by a world event or crisis, as well as high prices and shortages of key inputs. As this gathers pace, investment plans are shelved, consumers cut back spending and pay off some of their debt, and companies start to build depleted cash reserves.

The air cargo business fits this story well, with the pattern driven more by international trade and inventory levels than GDP alone. With increased outsourcing to third countries, exports and imports become more volatile: changes in final demand impact inventory levels which lead to a multiplier effect on trade from decisions made by exporters and importers of intermediate goods. This seems to affect air trade more than other modes of transport since consumers often cut back first on the high-tech goods that are shipped by air. In the upward part of the cycle, airlines invest in new and especially converted freighter aircraft, the extra capacity justified by forecasts that often disregard the expansion plans of others. Where these are taken into account an increased market share is assumed, but then the assumption on yields may not be realistic. Many airlines have ordered aircraft towards the end of the upturn and delivery and final payments are timed to coincide with the bottom of the downswing when no airline needs the capacity, causing further financial distress and perhaps bankruptcy. Airlines invest in other airlines on the basis that they need to position themselves in emerging markets, for example China. Forwarders and integrators strive to become more 'global' by buying the pieces of the jigsaw that they lack. These decisions, unlike aircraft, are more likely to be justified by long-term trends, and a short duration downswing has to be suffered to gain longer-term expansion and profitability. This the background to the world of air cargo which this book intends to examine in some detail.

Most recently the global banking crisis that gathered pace in the middle of 2008 had a dramatic impact on international trade and thus air trade. Banks were forced to cut lending and credit in the inter-bank markets almost dried up. Trade credit was affected in addition to the sharp reduction in demand that was also fuelled by a cutback in consumer debt. While this book looks at the evolution of the air cargo industry over a much longer period, the recent downturn gets perhaps a disproportionate amount of space. This is not just because it is still in most readers' memories but because it is a convenient time to take stock of how the various participants have reacted and fared.

The challenge of air cargo is that it offers a premium product that competes with surface transport on the basis of speed and reliability. However, the average time for consignments to reach their final destination is around five days, of which only 20–25 percent is accounted for by the flight time. The rest is attributed to delays in ground handling, customs inspection and collection (Groenewege, 2003). Passengers are often referred to as 'self loading freight', and while they sometimes challenge the seat they are allocated they do not have the very different weights, shapes and sizes of goods and documents. These can also change shape, such as when several parcels are combined into a single pallet, and they can have different requirements in terms of speed of delivery, security and point of delivery. They can have very different distance characteristics ranging from domestic to cross-border to intercontinental. These challenges and others will be explored in the following chapters, sometimes contrasting cargo with the passenger side of the business, sometimes comparing it with surface transport modes.

Abbreviations

ACMI	Aircraft, Crew, Maintenance and Insurance
AEA	Association of European Airlines
AOC	Air Operator's Certificate
APEC	Asia-Pacific Economic Cooperation
ASA	Air Services Agreement
ATA	Air Transport Association of American
ATK	Available Tonne-Kilometres
AWB	Air Waybill
Cargo-IMP	Cargo Interchange Message Procedures
CASS	Cargo Accounts Settlement System (IATA)
CCS	Cargo Community System
CEO	Chief Executive Officer
CLI	Composite Leading Indicators
CMV	Current Market Value
CPA	Capacity Purchasing Agreement
CSC	Cargo Services Conference
CTK	Cargo Tonne-Kilometres
e-AWB	Electronic Air Waybill
EASA	European Aviation Safety Agency
ECAC	European Civil Aviation Conference
EDI	Electronic Data Interchange
EEA	European Economic Area
EZFW	Estimated Zero Fuel Weight
FAA	Federal Aviation Administration
FF	Freight Forwarder
FFA	Freight Forwarders' Association
FWB	Forwarder Air Waybill
GATS	General Agreement on Trade in Services (WTO)
GCA	Guaranteed Capacity Agreement
GDP	Gross Domestic Product
GHA	Ground Handling Agent
GSA	General Sales Agent
HAWB	House Air Waybill
IATA	International Air Transport Association
ICAO	International Civil Aviation Organisation

IPCC	Inter-Governmental Panel on Climate Change
IRR	Internal Rate of Return
JAR	Joint Airworthiness Requirements (EASA)
KPI	Key Performance Indicators
LTL	Less than Truck Load
MALIAT	Multilateral Agreement on International Air Transport
MAWB	Master Air Waybill
MTAW	Maximum Taxi Weight
MTOW	Maximum Take-off Weight
MZFW	Maximum Zero Fuel Weight
NPV	Net Present Value
OAG	Official Airline Guide
OECD	Organisation for Economic Co-operation and Development
RCS	Ready for Carriage Shipment
RFID	Radio Frequency Identification
RFS	Road Feeder Service
RM	Revenue Management
RTK	Revenue Tonne-Kilometres (also RTKM)
SLA	Service Level Agreement
SSC	Security surcharge on air freight rates
T or t	Metric tonne
TACT	The Air Cargo Tariff (IATA)
TDC	Total Distribution Cost
TEU	Twenty-foot equivalent unit
TIACA	The International Air Cargo Association
TSA	Transportation Security Administration
ULD	Unit Load Device, usually either a pallet or container
UNCTAD	United Nations Conference on Trade and Development
VAN	Value added network
WACC	Weighted Average Cost of Capital
WATS	World Air Transport Statistics (IATA)
WCO	World Customs Organisation
WFP	World Food Programme
WTO	World Trade Organisation (formerly GATT)
ZFW	Zero Fuel Weight

Sources: www.aea.be/glossary; Groenewege (2003); IATA, www.iata.org/whatwedo/cargo.

Chapter 1

Air Cargo Traffic and Capacity

1.1 Air Cargo Traffic Trends

In this chapter trends in both international and domestic air cargo traffic will be analysed, focusing on cargo tonne-kms as a traffic measure but also using tonnes carried where appropriate. Freight and express will be distinguished from mail and trends on passenger and freighter flights will be identified. The main trade routes will be examined, also moving to a country level where warranted. More detailed data at the airline level will be discussed in Chapter 4. Mention will also be made of trucking, in cases where it is used as a cheaper alternative to aircraft on an airport-to-airport basis.

The second section will compare trends in air cargo traffic and economic indicators, exploring correlations at the global level. This is followed by an analysis of the freight handled at airports to see how the importance of major hubs is changing, finishing up with indications of traffic flows by season, month and day of week. While annual traffic is the most usually reported metric, variations within a year are useful in planning schedules and airport capacity.

1.1.1 Global Traffic

International freight traffic, excluding mail, has grown at an average rate of 3.7 percent a year between 1995 and 2009 (Figure 1.1). This period spanned one major downturn and the beginning of a second, and suggests greater volatility in traffic compared to passengers. Generally, freight turns down before passengers and recovers first and often faster. Contrary to popular belief, freight tonne-kms have grown at a slower average rate than passengers over this period: 4.9 percent versus 5.9 percent for passengers. Perceptions are probably based on a longer period than this and going back further, especially to the time when large amounts of lower deck capacity were introduced to the market (the 1970s and 1980s).

Freight tonne-kms are usually preferred to tonnes as a traffic measure for aggregate analysis since this captures both the weight and distance travelled. The trends for each are in fact very similar, since the average distance each tonne of freight was carried has remained fairly constant at between 5,200 km and 5,600 km. This reflects the preponderance of traffic carried on the long-haul trade lanes between Asia on the one hand and Europe and North America on the other.

Domestic freight traffic accounted for 16 percent of total world traffic in 2008, much of it carried within the US. Trends in domestic traffic were distorted by a major change in reporting traffic in the US: the United States Department

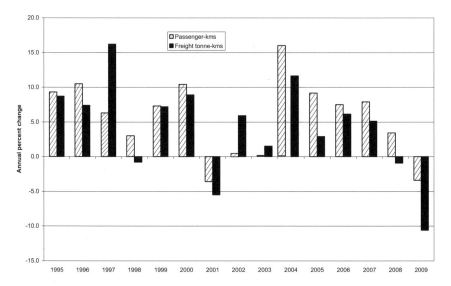

Figure 1.1   Passenger versus freight traffic trends, scheduled international services, 1995–2009

Source: ICAO.

of Transportation implemented new air traffic data reporting rules whereby previously reported non-scheduled freight traffic was reported as scheduled traffic from 2003 onwards. Consequently there was a discontinuity in US Department of Transportation (DOT) traffic. The International Civil Aviation Organisation (ICAO) obtains its data from member governments and thus its data contain the same change. This resulted in very high (20 percent) increases in annual growth in 2002 and 2003.

The above would distort the comparison of average annual growth of world ICAO freight and passenger traffic, with the reported figures showing freight to have grown by 1.5 percentage points faster than passengers. The average length of haul for domestic freight was, as expected, much shorter than international: around 1,600 km compared to 5,200 km for international in 2008.

Total world scheduled international mail revenue tonne-kilometres (RTKs) declined from 68 percent of total cargo traffic in 1938 to 21 percent in 1970 and 2.5 percent in 2008, reflecting both the rapid growth of freight and the success of the integrators whose express traffic is recorded under 'freight'. In 2008, domestic mail accounted for 5.3 percent of total cargo tonne-kms. This might be surprising given the expectation that more mail would move by surface transport overt the shorter domestic distances. However, the domestic data includes a large weight from the US (as mentioned above) and the integrators' data has been reported under domestic traffic. The US integrators, especially FedEx, had a contract to carry mail within the US, and most of this would be carried by air via their Memphis hub.

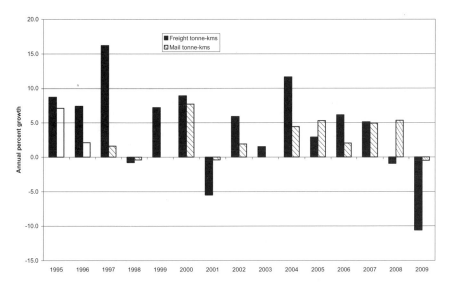

Figure 1.2   Growth rates for international freight versus mail traffic, 1995–2009

Source: ICAO.

Figure 1.2 compares the growth rates of mail and freight on international routes. Over the period 1995 to 2009 freight has increased at an average rate of 3.7 percent compared to 2.4 percent for mail. One reason for the lower growth rate of mail may have been the diversion of smaller parcels to the integrators as they expanded internationally, and this traffic would be reported under freight (and express). Mail has historically not been immune to the sharp downturns that have hit freight, but it has avoided years of negative growth (apart from a small decline in 2001).

The share of international cargo traffic carried on freighter flights has increased over the past 10 years from 42.9 percent in 2008 to 52 percent in 2008 before falling back sharply in 2009 (Table 1.1).[1] The sudden downturn in traffic at the end of 2008 resulted in a widespread grounding of freighter aircraft without such a removal of the capacity offered on passenger flights. This led to the greater share on passenger services, with part of this lost in 2010 as some of the freighters were brought back into operation.

As might be expected a negligible amount of international mail goes on freighter aircraft. Mail is almost all carried under contract with combination carriers with international wide-bodied passenger flights to a large number of destinations worldwide. While the integrators carry domestic mail, they carry next to no international mail, a market that is distinct from international express in which they are the dominant form of transport.

---

1   It was 83 percent in 1949 and continued to take a high share until the introduction of wide-bodied passenger aircraft in the 1970s.

Table 1.1   International world cargo traffic by type of service, 1999, 2008 and 2009

	1999	2008	2009
Cargo tonne-kms carried (m)			
All-cargo flights	39,010	74,345	62,516
All flights	90,882	142,858	128,763
% all-cargo	42.9	52.0	48.6
Flights (000)			
All-cargo flights	282	456	410
All flights	5,062	6,491	6,175
% all-cargo	5.6	7.0	6.6
Average tonnes carried per flight			
All-cargo flights	54.0	55.9	47.0
Passenger flights	5.3	4.8	4.6
Cargo weight load factor (%)			
All-cargo flights	70.7	67.6	68.2
Passenger flights	45.4	42.1	42.0

Source: IATA World Air Transport Statistics.

The large difference in the loads carried on passenger and cargo flights is reflected in the lower share of flights that are accounted for by all-cargo operations, each one offering a much larger capacity. The average load on freighters did not increase greatly between 1999 and 2008, and dropped in 2009. The average capacity offered by freighters in tonnes dropped from 83 tonnes in 2008 to 69 tonnes in 2009, suggesting that more larger B747s were grounded (and retired) than smaller freighters (see Chapter 7 for typical capacities of the various freighter aircraft). The average load carried on passenger flights declined over the past 10 years to just under 5 tonnes, falling further in 2009. One reason for this is the rapid expansion and increasing importance of low-cost airlines which carry little or no cargo in the lower decks of their passenger flights. The other reason is the higher load factors and longer sectors operated by long-haul passenger flights which add more checked baggage to the lower deck holds, thus displacing cargo, and the increasing fuel loads which also reduce the cargo payload available. Declining and low load factors in the lower holds of passenger flights is another consequence, although the level may be due to the reporting of theoretical rather than actual capacities.

Table 1.2   World cargo traffic, domestic services, 1999, 2008 and 2009

	1999	2008	2009
Cargo tonne-kms carried (m)			
All-cargo flights	11,492	15,295	13,568
All flights	20,677	23,788	22,146
% all-cargo	55.6	64.3	61.3
Flights (000)			
All-cargo flights	440	417	371
All flights	10,790	9,592	9,620
% all-cargo	4.1	4.3	3.9
Average tonnes carried per flight			
All-cargo flights	26.8	32.7	29.0
Passenger flights	1.0	0.9	0.9
Cargo weight load factor (%)			
All-cargo flights	57.5	57.5	58.7
Passenger flights	19.8	20.0	20.2

Source: IATA World Air Transport Statistics.

Table 1.2 shows a similar trend for domestic services, but with a larger share of traffic on freighters. This is heavily influenced by US domestic operations where integrators (operating only freighters) take a much larger share of the market. This is also evident in the lower average loads per flight, since the integrators operate smaller aircraft domestically to feed their hub operations. Also the absence of wide-bodied aircraft on domestic services means that the capacity available is limited to narrow-bodied holds, often offering less than 1 tonne for cargo. Load factors on domestic freighters tend to be less than on international flights, but this is compensated by higher yields. The average load factor in the lower decks of passenger flights has remained extremely low, again reflecting the policy of many low-cost airlines not to carry lower deck cargo.

1.1.2 Regional Route Traffic

Major international trade lanes
Figure 1.3 gives a picture of world international freight traffic by trade lane. Flows which are close to zero have been omitted. Because this is international traffic the large market within the US has not been included, and even trans-border flows within North America do not amount to much since most cargo is trucked.

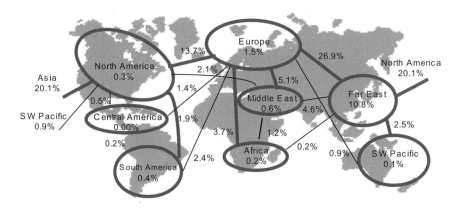

Figure 1.3   Distribution of world international freight tonne-km traffic by trade lane, 2009

Source: IATA World Air Transport Statistics, 2009.

Over the past 10 years freight tonne-kms carried in short-haul markets have increased slightly faster (+4.7 percent a year) compared to long-haul markets (+4.4 percent a year). The former were also slightly less badly hit by the 2009 slump. The three main air trade lanes are discussed next, accounting for just over 60 percent of total international freight tonne-kms in 2009. These are followed by the two largest intra-regional markets. The next largest routes between Europe and Africa grew by only 3.4 percent a year between 1999 and 2008 and now account for just under 3 percent of the world total.

Transpacific
In 2007, air exports from Asia to North America were estimated to have been 57 percent higher in terms of tonne-kms than imports from North America. This poses problems for achieving high return trip load factors, and often results in excess capacity in one direction and/or a shortage in the other. This in turn leads to lower yields where demand is lower and vice versa. MergeGlobal reported a larger imbalance in 2005, with eastbound transpacific route air cargo traffic estimated to be almost twice the westbound flow.[2] Individual countries often display even more extreme imbalances, and this is worse at the city-pair level. In 2007 the air freight carried between Taipei and Los Angeles amounted to 7,568 tonnes while only 1,941 tonnes were carried in the opposite direction, a ratio of 3.9:1.

Transpacific air cargo has increased by 6.6 percent a year between 1999 and 2008 compared to world growth of only 4.5 percent. However, it suffered a larger setback of 25 percent in 2009 compared to 2008 (the world market fell by 16 percent). Its share of world international traffic rose from 18.2 percent in 1999 to 22.3 percent in 2008 before falling to 20.1 percent in 2009.

---

2   MergeGlobal in *Aviation Strategy*, October 2005.

North Atlantic

In 2007, air exports from North America to Europe were broadly similar to imports from Europe. Boeing reported that the dollar/euro exchange rate was a key factor in westbound flows, but its influence overall had diminished with greater EU integration. At the city-pair level, traffic flows were well balanced on New York/London, with around 80,000 tonnes moving in each direction in 2007. In the same year New York/Frankfurt displayed some directional imbalance with 26 percent more freight carried westbound from Frankfurt to New York.

Traffic across the Atlantic in 2009 was 17 percent below its 1999 level, all of the drop occurring in the year 2009. However, the maturity of this market is indicated by the fact that it has stagnated over the 10 years to 2008. This means that its share of world international traffic dropped from 21.4 percent in 1999 to 14.4 percent in 2008, and 13.7 percent in 2009.

Europe/Asia

In 2007, air exports from Asia to Europe were estimated to have been 74 percent larger than imports from Europe. Individual countries can be even more unbalanced, and at the city-pair level worse still. For example, in 2007 freight traffic carried from Tokyo to Amsterdam was 42 percent higher than the flow in the opposite direction, with this magnitude of imbalance far from atypical. Sometimes, imbalances are worse for some carriers on a particular route. For example, British Airways' exports from London Heathrow to Tokyo in 2006 were 6,160 tonnes, not too different from their imports from Tokyo of 6,776 tonnes (a 10 percent difference). However, in the same sector, Japan Airlines carried 64 percent more exports to the UK than imports to Japan, and All Nippon 63 percent more. Virgin Atlantic had a 19 percent imbalance on the same route.

Europe/Asia air cargo has increased by 6.2 percent a year between 1999 and 2008 compared to world growth of only 4.5 percent. Surprisingly its traffic fell by only 13 percent in 2009 over 2008, compared to the world downturn of 16 percent. Its share of world international traffic increased from 22.0 percent in 1999 to 25.9 percent in 2008 and to almost 27 percent in 2009.

Intra-Europe

Most airport-to-airport 'air cargo' in Europe is carried on trucks. These are operated by airlines (usually contracted out to firms such as Rutges or DVS) and most of this traffic feeds their long-haul flights at their hub airports. Boeing estimated that the number of weekly flights of this nature rose from 3,870 in 2002 to 11,497 in 2007 (Boeing, 2008). This would amount to 600,000 trips a year in 2007. Each truck might average three or four ULDs or around 10 tonnes of cargo giving a total of 6 million tonnes a year. It is hard to verify this figure since few airlines or airports report such data. Some of the non-hub German airports handle significant amounts of trucked cargo, accounting for 70 percent of total cargo at Stuttgart Airport (Horst, 2006). At another German airport, Hanover, most of the air cargo is consolidated on-airport and trucked to a major air cargo hub.

Table 1.3 shows how the total of 2,127,000 unduplicated tonnes of intra-EU cargo is flown between the major member countries. The table ranks the countries in terms of exports from left to right (Germany being the largest). Most of this will be carried on integrator feeder flights, usually with small aircraft, in the lower decks of the few passenger wide-bodied aircraft flights operated or on the first sector of a long-haul freighter flight.

According to the IATA traffic flow data, intra-European international air cargo declined by 1.5 percent a year between 1999 and 2008, with a 20 percent drop in 2009. It now only accounts for only 1.5 percent of total international traffic.

Intra-Asia

Air cargo carried on routes within Asia rose by 7.8 percent a year over the 10 years to 2008, with a below average fall of 13.6 percent in the year 2009. It accounted for 10.9 percent of the world total in 2008 up from 7.7 percent in 1999. The country flows within Asia with the most air freight connect Japan with large trading centres in Hong Kong, Taiwan and Korea, and more recently China. Most of these international routes are relatively long sectors and over water such that the opportunities of shipping goods by truck are limited. However, the two airport cargo terminal operators at Hong Kong International Airport operate a bonded truck service to and from the Chinese mainland covering 17 destinations.

By region/country of airline registration

Table 1.4 shows the distribution of freight tonne-kms by region of registration of airline, split into international and domestic operations. The Asian carriers take the largest share of international traffic, led by large cargo operators such as Korean Air, China Airlines and Singapore Airlines. This share is likely to increase further as the Chinese airlines take a larger share of their markets. European airlines take second place, with their larger freighter operators such as Air France-KLM, Lufthansa and Cargolux. The North American combination carriers tend not to operate freighters, and the integrators' share of both the express and general cargo market is quite low. This depresses the international share taken by North American markets. The US is, however, still the largest country of registration in a ranking of international freight tonne-kms, followed by Hong Kong,[3] Germany, Singapore, Japan and Korea.

Middle Eastern carriers such as Emirates have increased their regional share of international air cargo from 4.4 percent in 2000 to 8.4 percent in 2008.

From the IATA CASS reporting system, the top five country markets from the US in 2008 were London, Tokyo, Frankfurt, Amsterdam and Hong Kong. London was the largest flow with over 160,000 tonnes transported. From the UK, Dubai, New York, Hong Kong, Tokyo and Singapore were the largest with around 30,000 tonnes to Dubai. Hong Kong (with just under 100,000 tonnes), Taipei,

---

3   Data is reported separately for mainland China and Hong Kong. Together they still are a long way behind the US, in second place in the international ranking.

Table 1.3   Intra-EU air cargo tonnes (000) carried between top 10 countries, 2008

	Germany	UK	France	Italy	Belgium	Spain	Sweden	Netherlands	Austria	Luxembourg
Germany	-	186	139	102	63	97	68	27	43	1
UK	146	-	43	40	60	23	13	26	4	4
France	126	45	-	30	15	28	6			
Italy	93	44	34	-	44	13	0	16	1	36
Belgium	62	80	35	45	-	35	29	1	11	1
Spain	77	19	15	6	23	-	1	5	1	2
Sweden	39	11	3	0	13	1	-	5	3	2
Netherlands	19	39	6	9	0	7	5	-	4	0
Austria	29	4	5	1	8	1	0	2	-	1
Luxembourg	1	29	0	28	0	6	3	2	3	-

Source: Eurostat.

Table 1.4   Freight tonne-kms by region of airline registration, 2008

	International	Domestic	Total
Europe	30.6	4.0	26.3
Africa	1.6	0.4	1.4
Middle East	8.4	0.4	7.1
Asia and Pacific	38.3	23.1	35.8
North America	18.0	67.6	26.0
Latin America and Caribbean	3.2	4.5	3.4
Total	100.0	100.0	100.0

Source: ICAO.

Shanghai, Seoul and Chicago were the largest from Japan. The only other flow that approached the level of US/London and Japan/Hong Kong was Germany to Shanghai with just under 80,000 tonnes (increasing to almost 100,000 tonnes in 2009 contrary to the downward trend on the other routes).

Domestic markets are dominated by the US and some carriers in Asian countries. Japan and China have relatively large domestic markets which are always reserved for carriers registered and based there. Europe's domestic markets are limited to the larger countries such as France, Germany and the UK and here almost all cargo is trucked.

1.2 Air Cargo and the Economic Cycle

The ratio of trade growth to GDP growth remained close to 1.5 between the 1950s and the end of the 1980s, increasing to 2.0 during the 1990s and the second half of the 2000s. Furthermore, containerised maritime trade rose faster than maritime trade overall, with the former growing by 9.5 percent a year between 1987 and 2006, and the latter by only 4.1 percent a year. On the other hand air trade expanded more slowly than world trade and certainly than containerised maritime trade. Between the mid-1990s and the end of the 2000s, air freight traffic has on average risen 2 percent a year less than world trade, but a cyclical pattern can be observed around that longer-term relative decline. Air trade tends to fall faster than world trade at the start of the economic downturn, but starts to increaser faster on the up-cycle (IATA, 2009).

Total world scheduled freight tonne-kms were closely correlated to both world trade and GDP over the period 1972 to 2008. Taking logarithmic values of both freight traffic and economic activity gives a very good statistical fit, with an adjusted R^2 of 0.99, and high t-ratios for the explanatory variables. The coefficient for both GDP and trade was just above 2, which means that air traffic has increased by 2 percent for each 1 percent increase in economic activity.

The slower growth of air cargo versus ocean containerised shipping seems to indicate a longer-term loss of market share to surface transport. IATA points out that this can partly be explained by faster handling at ports and the increasing speed of ocean liners, but it may also be due to the use of tonne-kms to measure the relative trends. As the nature of shipments carried by air changes to lighter capital and especially electronic goods the growth of air trade expressed in tonnes or tonne-kms slows.

Air trade data is usually published before global GDP or trade data. It is thus often used as a proxy for turning points in the world economic and trade cycle. This is not to say it is a leading indicator, since it tends to move together with international trade. However, in the 2008 cyclical downturn air cargo did lead the downturn in international trade by four to five months. Another attempt to identify turning points in the economic cycle is the 'Composite Leading Indicator' published by the OECD. This is essentially the index of industrial production that is available on a monthly basis earlier than other national statistics. For the OECD Europe region this index was 100 in May 2008, falling over the next months to 96.7 in December 2008. This 3 percent point fall occurred at the same time as air cargo volumes were falling, but it did not predict the magnitude and severity of the downturn in international trade.

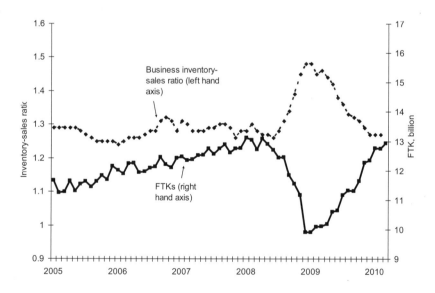

Figure 1.4   US inventory to sales ratio vs. scheduled air freight traffic

Source: IATA.

Purchasing managers' confidence is sometimes used as an early indicator of air freight upturns or downturns, leading by two or three months. Manufacturers' inventory to sales ratio reductions are often associated with increases in air freight traffic and vice versa (Figure 1.4). This makes sense since when inventory gets too low re-stocking takes place and this might initially be best done by using air freight. However, over the period 2006 to 2008 the two indicators seems to have been positive correlated. It should be added that the US sales to inventory ratio declined from 1.6 in 1980 to 1.3 at the end of the 1990s, a period that coincided with strong cargo growth, especially from express shipments. Lower inventory levels were possible through the provision of more reliable air cargo services. The recent turbulent period upset this trend, but it would appear that the 1.3 level to which the ratio has returned is the longer-term minimum level.

The onset of the 2008/2009 recession led to the emergence of a huge inventory overhang with manufacturers and retailers, as consumers of finished goods cut their expenditure sharply. Air trade tumbled since inventory levels rose fast and there was little need to air freight final or intermediate goods until the ratio had fallen to more sustainable levels. In this respect it is surprising that air freight made such a rapid recovery.

The WTO puts forward four possible factors that could explain the 2008/2009 trade contraction:[4]

- demand slowdown in all world regions simultaneously;
- recent declines magnified by global supply chains;
- shortage of trade finance;
- trade protection.

The first is driven by consumer and investment sentiment both of which have been affected by the banking crisis. The second is due to the recording of one consumer purchase of a manufactured item as a number of separate exports, as it crosses various borders at each stage of its production. Exports need to be financed up to the value tied up in the cost of manufacture and distribution and warehousing before cash is generated from the final sale. This trade finance has also been hit by the banking crisis. The last reason is less likely since trade barriers take more time to erect (or dismantle).

1.3 Airport Traffic

The airports with the largest amount of total international and domestic air cargo handled tend to be either Asian hubs or the major hub of a US integrator. Thus Memphis, the home of FedEx, and Louisville (UPS) are in the top 10, but do not feature if domestic traffic is excluded (Table 1.5). Anchorage in Alaska is one the

---

4   WTO Press Release, 24 March 2009, PRESS/554.

Table 1.5   Air freight throughput for top 10 world airports, 2009

	International and domestic (tonnes)		International (tonnes)
Memphis	3,697	Hong Kong	3,350
Hong Kong	3,385	Seoul (Incheon)	2,268
Shanghai	2,539	Dubai	1,846
Seoul (Incheon)	2,313	Tokyo Narita	1,810
Anchorage	1,990	Paris CDG	1,785
Louisville	1,949	Shanghai	1,775
Dubai	1,928	Frankfurt/Main	1,758
Frankfurt/Main	1,888	Singapore	1,634
Tokyo Narita	1,852	Taipei	1,345
Paris CDG	1,819	Miami	1,332
Top 10	23,359	Top 10	18,904

Source: IATA World Air Transport Statistics.

world's largest cargo airport but three-quarters of its traffic is in transit (neither loaded nor unloaded in Anchorage), a useful refuelling stop on the very long transpacific routes.

The largest international airports are all mainly combination carrier hubs, most operating a large fleet of freighters in addition to carrying cargo on their passenger flights. Some such as Dubai International Airport have grown dramatically over the past years: 12.6 percent a year in the 1990s and 13.1 percent in the 2000s to reach almost 2m tonnes in 2009. Dubai is well positioned on the Asian trade lanes and a high share of the airport's cargo is transhipped and not originating from or destined to the United Arab Emirates. The airport also handles a small amount of sea-air cargo that moves from the Port of Jebel Ali to air services at Dubai.

Paris Charles de Gaulle and Frankfurt/Main are the only two European airports in the top 10, and Miami is the only one in North America, capitalising on its strategic position on the trade lanes between North and South America, and Europe and Central and South America. At Hong Kong Airport, freighters accounted for 14 percent of total air transport movements in 2009, up from 10 percent in 2000. Tokyo Narita had a similar share of freighters in its total international movements in 2009. Data from airports on the share of air cargo on passenger and freighter flights is rarely published, and many airports do not show the split of flights between passenger and freighter that the Asian airports provided.

A new airport, Guangzhou Baiyun, was opened in 2004 and became FedEx's intra-Asian hub in February 2009. Its traffic for the full year 2009 was 48 percent higher than the previous year, reflecting the integrator's move. Another south Chinese airport nearby, Shenzhen Baoan, was chosen by UPS in 2008 to be its new intra-Asian hub, transferred from Clark Base in the Philippines. It was expected to become operational in 2010. The third large integrator, DHL, decided to make Shanghai Pudong Airport its North Asian hub in 2007, and cargo traffic there jumped by 38 percent between 2005 and 2008, before levelling off in 2009. Shanghai's other airport, Hongqiao, also handles around 400,000 tonnes of air cargo and is the main base of freighter operator Yangtze River Express. This airline flies long-haul freighters (e.g. to Luxembourg in Europe) and operates within China for UPS and DHL.

Hub concentration has been increasing especially in Europe. In 2008, between midnight and 5 a.m., 82 percent of cargo flights in the Eurocontrol area were concentrated at 25 airports, with cargo traffic dominated by just four airports: Frankfurt/Main, Amsterdam, Paris Charles de Gaulle (CDG) and London Heathrow. Paris CDG is the main FedEx hub in Europe, and not far from Paris is the former military airfield at Vatry, an airport that has had little success in developing as a cargo airport: its air cargo traffic declining from 38,000 tonnes in 2005 to only 23,000 in 2009. Cargo traffic at Brussels National Airport has declined 32 percent between 2005 and 2009 as a result of DHL moving its main hub to Leipzig Airport (and the 2009 downturn). Leipzig, on the other hand, has seen cargo traffic grow from a mere 1,000 tonnes in 2005 to 507,000 tonnes in 2009, even increasing its traffic in 2009 by 18 percent. The number of freighter aircraft flights reached 27,000 in 2008 (averaging 37 departures a day), almost equal to the number of passenger flights at the airport (and just above the number at runway constrained Frankfurt/ Main). Liège Airport, the TNT hub, averaged around 33 departures a day in 2008.

1.4 Hub Transhipment Traffic

Table 1.6 shows the dominance of air cargo hubs, especially on international sectors. Almost all of the top 12 air cargo airports are also major hubs, and these accounted for 44 percent of total international cargo tonnes in 2005. If domestic traffic is included two very large hubs at Memphis and Louisville in the US move into the top 12. These are the major hub airports of FedEx and UPS respectively.

Combination carriers that operate hubs at their main base airport need to know the breakdown of traffic through the hub for purposes of planning ground handling facilities. These might involve landside access for trucks, cargo terminal areas for breakdown and building of loads or transhipments between one passenger flight and another, sometimes in sealed containers.

Table 1.7 shows the distribution of traffic handled at KLM's cargo terminal at Schiphol. This data is not up-to-date but would not be atypical of a European cargo hub airport. The relative importance of truck feed may be higher than some of the

Table 1.6   Top 12 world airports in terms of international air cargo tonnes, 2009

Airport	Tonnes (000)	Hub carrier(s)
Hong Kong	3,350	Cathay Pacific
Seoul	2,268	Korean Air
Dubai	1,846	Emirates
Tokyo	1,810	Japan Airlines
Paris	1,785	Air France, FedEx, La Poste
Shanghai	1,775	China Eastern, UPS, Great Wall
Frankfurt	1,758	Lufthansa
Singapore	1,634	Singapore Airlines
Taipei	1,345	China Airlines, Eva Airways
Anchorage	1,307	Transpacific transit point
Amsterdam	1,284	KLM
Miami	1,332	South American gateway
Top 12 total	21,494	

Source: IATA WATS 2010.

other hubs due to Amsterdam's distance from major manufacturing and population centres. British Airways also had just under 60 percent of the total being transhipped, but its truck feeder share was much lower. Air-to-air transfers are also a large part of the total traffic, some of these on through containers, with less than full loads in order to minimise handling costs at the hub. Interline (between airline) transfers have declined considerably and only account for a small share of total traffic.

Table 1.7   Traffic breakdown at Amsterdam Schiphol hub airport

	Tonnes	%
Air terminating or originating	123,895	16.9
Air to air transfer	261,977	35.7
Air to truck or truck to air	343,227	46.8
Truck terminating or originating	3,745	0.5
	732,844	100.0

Source: KLM Cargo.

1.5 Air Cargo Traffic Variation within a Year

1.5.1 Monthly Traffic

Monthly variations in cargo traffic can be viewed from the airport or airline perspective. Hong Kong has been selected as representative of the Asian freight market, having only international services. The year 2007 was chosen in preference to 2008 because there was no major downturn in the last three months of the year. The monthly variation in both all freight traffic and that carried on freighters is shown in Figure 1.5.

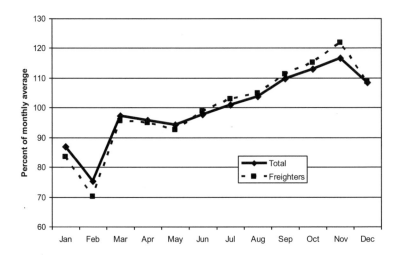

Figure 1.5   Air freight tonne-kms traffic variation by month, Hong Kong Airport, 2007

Source: ICAO.

First there is little difference between the total and freighter service traffic. The share of traffic carried by freighters remained constant throughout the year (at around 60 percent). After the low months in January and February there was a gradual build-up in throughput to a pre-Christmas peak in November.

The year 2007 has also been chosen to examine the monthly airline traffic levels. The freight traffic carried by Association of European Airlines (AEA) members includes both passenger and freighter flights, and is shown separately for the two major long-haul flows in Figure 1.6. Both the North Atlantic and Europe/ Far East have a distinctive peak in the pre-Christmas months of September, October and November, especially the Far East which is the manufacturer of many of the presents that will be purchased at that time. Easter also appears to coincide with a smaller peak on both trade lanes. The beginning of the year is traditionally less busy, as well as the European summer holiday months of July and August, when in the past some factories have even closed down.

The monthly pattern of freight traffic contrasts with that of passenger traffic which in Europe has a peak in the summer months and over the Easter and Christmas holiday periods. A low month for passengers is the second half of November and the first half of December, just the time that cargo is busy.

The monthly variation discussed above is for total traffic. For planning and forecasting purposes it is sometimes necessary to break this down into by direction and type of shipment. An example of the peak month to year ratios that might be experienced at a typical cargo hub airport is as follows:

	Peak Month	**Percent Annual**
Total imports and exports	October	9.3
Total imports:	October	9.3
Import terminating	December	9.6
Import transhipments	October	9.1
Truck transhipments	October	10.6
Truck terminating	October	11.1
Total exports:	October	9.2
Airport originating	October	9.0
On-line transhipments	October	9.3
Interline receipts	February	11.2

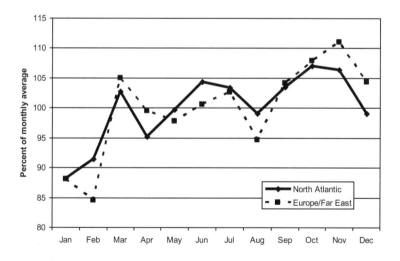

Figure 1.6   Air freight tonne-kms traffic variation by month, AEA airlines, 2007

Source: AEA monthly traffic data.

The variation is not large, with October featuring in almost every flow. It should be added that although the cargo traffic peaks in the last months of the year, the number of freighter flights is generally fairly constant over the year.

1.5.2 Weekly and Daily Traffic

Traffic data for air cargo at the weekly or daily level is not usually published but a typical peak week to year ratio (percentage) might be 2.2 percent, occurring perhaps during November. There is very little variation by day of week, with the ratio of peak day to average day of the peak month (month divided by 31) little above 1.0.

A study of cargo flights in the Eurocontrol area found that during the week, Wednesdays and Thursdays are the busiest days, linked to business weekday activity. Other figures also show Fridays as busy days. The traffic distribution pattern throughout the week did not change significantly in four years to 2007: weekdays are at least twice as busy as weekend days.

The weekends are generally quiet for freighter activity but in Europe between 2004 and 2007, there was a higher than average increase in daily cargo movements from Fridays to Mondays. This was because cargo operators increasingly needed extra lift on weekends to serve their key points and to provide second day delivery, especially from Europe to Asia.

1.6 Air Cargo Capacity

1.6.1 Short-/Medium-Haul

Short/medium-haul routes generally have high frequency service with passenger aircraft, but most of the timings are not suitable for air cargo. The normal pattern of flights between medium to large cities would be a morning peak between 7–9 a.m., another around the middle of the day and a third evening one. That would give four aircraft return flights or 'rotations' a day (low-cost airlines might achieve five). Of these only the early evening one might be suitable for feeding long-haul flights, but the schedule lacks a later evening departure to give a next day delivery possibility for intra-regional express cargo.

Freighter aircraft tend to be expensive to operate on shorter haul routes, especially if its utilisation is limited to night flights. These can be justified by higher yield traffic carried by integrators, and these tend to operate most of the shorter haul freighters at least in Europe and North America.

Road Feeder Services (RFS) are operated instead of freighters between airports by the combination carriers, especially in Europe. These offer around 20 tonnes of capacity per trip, and frequencies can be daily or higher on routes between the main cargo hubs. Some airlines consolidate truck loads at a central point before trucking aircraft compatible ULDs to the airport hub. British Airways operated a truck hub at Maastricht Airport.

1.6.2 Long-Haul

Long-haul passenger flights are usually operated with wide-bodied aircraft with up to 20 tonnes or more of cargo capacity in the lower deck. Some of them depart late evening, which suits the pattern of freight delivery. They can handle all but certain categories of cargo (e.g. dangerous items) and outsized cargo shipments. The frequencies of service are often once a day, with at least three or four times weekly operated as a minimum. This allows express operators the possibility of a two- or three-day delivery commitment.

Freighter flights are operated where there is not sufficient passenger capacity, and particularly from major manufacturing centres to consumers in North America and Europe. The busiest routes are Europe/Asia and Asia/North America. Published flights for the former are shown in Table 1.8 for January 2010. One integrator (TNT) is included but DHL's joint services from Leipzig (with Lufthansa) have been omitted. The first destination is given, often in Russia or neighbouring countries to reduce sector length to maximise payload and combine traffic to achieve higher load factors. For example, Cargolux's Kazakhstan route continued to Shanghai on certain days of the week. The most popular destinations are Shanghai with 268 flights per month (almost nine per day), followed by Seoul with 211 flights (just under seven per day) and Beijing and Hong Kong each with around four per day.

Overall there were 42 flights a day operated with a variety of aircraft. The B747-400F accounted for 16 of these, either the B747-400F or -200F another 13[5] and MD-11Fs 11 a day. The older B747-200F itself only operated just over one flight a day, with a few of the 13 unspecified B747 freighters, indicating the withdrawal of this less efficient aircraft by most operators. The capacities of these freighters is discussed in Chapter 7. Frequencies were reduced by around 10 percent in February 2010, a somewhat slow reaction to the traffic slump that had started just over a year previously. DHL's exit from the intra-US market has resulted in its moving from its US hub at Wilmington, Ohio, to Cincinnati in Northern Kentucky.

None of the integrators were included in the published timetables of routes between Asia and North America. The freighter flights that were published for January 2010 totaled just over 27 per day, 21 of them making an intermediate stop in Anchorage and only four going non-stop to Los Angeles. The main origins in Asia were Shanghai with eight flights a day, Seoul with six and Taipei and Hong Kong, each with around four. Almost all the flights were with B747-400F aircraft with a few remaining B747-200Fs.

Multi-sector routes are common for freighters in order to consolidate loads and improve load factors. European flights may have two stops, for example Lufthansa's westbound flights to North America stop at East Midlands to pick up its UK originating cargo. Other carriers have used Prestwick in Scotland en route from North America to Luxembourg or Paris. Asian carriers sometimes stop in central Europe on the way to UK.

---

5   The published schedule does not specify which model will be operated.

Table 1.8   Published freighter flights from Europe to Asia, January 2010

Airline	Major European origin	First destination in Asia (flights per month)
AirBridge	Moscow	Shanghai (40), Hong Kong (27), Beijing (22), Tokyo (4), Kazakhstan (4), Kabul (4)
Cargoitalia	Milan	Kazakhstan (4), Mumbai (9), Chennai (5), Osaka (9)
TNT	Liège	Hong Kong (13), Singapore (14), Shanghai (4)
ACG Air Cargo	Frankfurt/Hahn	Kazakhstan (13), Hong Kong (5)
Air France	Paris CDG	Shanghai (18)
British Airways	London	Taipei (10), Osaka (9), Hong Kong (5)
Eva Air	Brussels	Delhi (9)
Air China	Frankfurt/Main	Beijing (36), Shanghai (21)
China Airlines	Luxembourg	Taipei (33), Bangkok (5), Colombo (4)
China Cargo	Luxembourg	Beijing (44), Shanghai (49)
Cathay Pacific	Paris CDG	Mumbai (13), Delhi (9), Hong Kong (13)
China Southern	Amsterdam	Shanghai (40)
Ethiopian Air	Brussels	Hong Kong (5)
Grandstar	Frankfurt/Main	Shanghai (18)
Great Wall	Amsterdam	Tianjin (14), Shanghai (34)
Jade Cargo	Frankfurt/Main	Delhi (5), Shenzhen (4), Shanghai (4), Lahore (4), Seoul (18)
Japan Airlines	Moscow	Krasnojarsk (9), Tokyo (41)
Korean Air	Frankfurt/Main	Seoul (119), Uzbekistan (8)
KLM	Amsterdam	Kazakhstan (8), Hong Kong (8)
Nippon Cargo	Milan	Tokyo (32)
Lufthansa	Frankfurt/Main	Bangalore (13), Mumbai (16), Delhi (11), Krasnojarsk (36)
Malaysian	Frankfurt/Main	Tashkent (22), Colombo (5)
Martinair	Moscow	Kazakhstan (9), Hong Kong (10)
Asiana	Brussels	Seoul (79)
Polar Air	Leipzig	Seoul (5), Hong Kong (14)
Cargolux	Luxembourg	Kazakhstan (8), Taipei (5), Komatsu (Japan) (5), Singapore (10), Shanghai (9)
Singapore	Brussels	Singapore (19), Kolkata (9), Bangalore (13), Mumbai (9), Chennai (9)
Aeroflot	Moscow	Novosibirsk (36), Kazakhstan (9), Hong Kong (22), Khabarovsk (9), Beijing (22), Shanghai (31)

Source: OAG Aviation Solutions.

1.6.3 Integrator Hubs

The largest integrator hub is at Memphis in the US. In 2008, cargo airlines operated an average of 177 departures a day, almost all of those by FedEx. FedEx's departures are highly concentrated during the hours 7 a.m. to 10 a.m. when just under 80 percent of the daily flights depart, with around 100 flights between 8 a.m. and 9 a.m. This is the time that allows the sorting of the night arrivals to have taken place. The transatlantic MD-11F flights to Paris CDG and London Stansted both go in the morning peak, as do the transpacific departures. There is a much smaller departure window between 8 p.m. and 10 p.m. to take the early evening arrivals at the hub. Louisville, UPS's main US hub, is a much smaller operation by contrast, with just under 100 departures on average in 2008.

DHL's joint venture airline, AeroLogic, initially started operating routes from Leipzig to Bahrain, Singapore, Delhi and back to Leipzig on weekdays, primarily, for express shipments. At weekends it served Leipzig-Tashkent-Hong Kong-Tashkent-Leipzig for the general cargo market. These were flown by Lufthansa Cargo with MD-11F aircraft offering up to around 100 tonnes of capacity. UPS

Table 1.9   Integrator flights from East Midlands to Western Europe, summer 2010

Destination	Integrator	Flights/week	Day of week	Aircraft type
Barcelona	DHL	4	Tue–Fri	B757
Bergamo	DHL	5	Mon–Fri	All types
Brussels	DHL	6	Mon–Fri, Sun	A300/B757
Cologne	DHL	4	Tue–Fri	ATP-F
Cologne	UPS	6	Mon–Sat	B767
Frankfurt	DHL	4	Tue–Thu, Sat	B757
Leipzig	DHL	7	Daily	A300/B757
Liège	TNT	6	Mon–Fri, Sat	A300/B757
Madrid	DHL	2	Sat, Sun	B757
Munich	DHL	4	Tue–Thu, Sat	B757, Metroliner
Paris CDG	DHL	4	Tue–Fri	B757
Paris Vatry	DHL	4	Tue–Fri	B757
Shannon	DHL	5	Mon–Fri	B757
Vitoria	DHL	4	Tue–Fri	B737-400

Source: East Midlands Airport website.

Moving Boxes by Air

operated regular flights from its European hub at Cologne-Bonn Airport to its US base at Louisville, Taiwan, Hong Kong, Shenzhen, Manila and later added Shanghai. Its transpacific routes serve Shanghai and Qingdao in China, Manila, Nagoya, Tokyo, Osaka and Seoul.

Comprehensive integrator flight schedules for integrators are not published and difficult to obtain. Table 1.9 gives an example of the flights operated by an integrator from one of its European bases. East Midlands Airport showed data by destination and frequency but not departure times, although these tend to be in the late afternoon, evening and nighttime. This airport is one of DHL's hubs, another being Leipzig which has the highest frequency and largest aircraft designated of any intra-European route. Most of the routes have a daily frequency during week days, few of them having weekend flights.

Chapter 2
Air Cargo Market Characteristics

The previous chapter discussed the size of the air cargo market in terms of traffic. This is usually described in tonnes or tonne-kms, with integrators also reporting numbers of shipments. This data may be collected for freight, mail and express traffic but these segments are subject to more and more overlap and do not give much useful market information. In this chapter a more detailed look will be made of the types of shipment and their characteristics.

Air takes a relatively small share of total international trade by weight, but considerably more in terms of value (40 percent plus). Seabury estimates that the share of tonnage going by air has declined recently from 2.8 percent in 2000 to 1.8 percent in 2008 (see Figure 2.1). The largest part of this decline (0.5 percentage points) came from the fact that faster growth was recorded on routes that have low air penetration; a smaller part (0.2 percentage points) was the result of slower growth in the commodities that air takes a large share of, such as 'high-tech'; third, there was some shift mode selected from air to sea (0.3 percentage points) (de Jong, 2010). One reason for the modal shift was the relative cost impact of higher fuel prices on the less fuel efficient mode of transport.

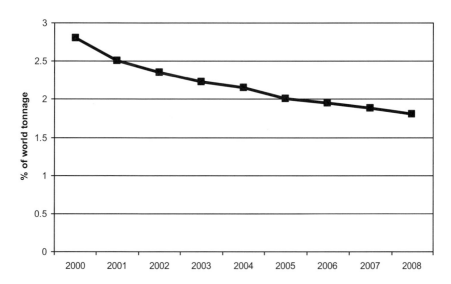

Figure 2.1   Recent trend in the air share of world containerised trade

Source: Seabury Global Trade Database.

Based on nine months of 2009, Seabury estimated that some recovery of the air share had taken place, partly as a result of re-stocking of high-tech products.

Given the fact that air rates are some 10–15 times those for sea transport (Shaw, 2007), only higher value to weight items are likely to be able to support the cost of going by air in the final price of the product. Boeing suggests that products that have a value to weight ratio of greater than US$16 per kg have a high likelihood of being carried by air (Boeing, 2008). However, motor vehicle bodies with a value of $9.14 per kg are almost all shipped by surface modes while specialty chemicals with a similar value to weight ratio go by air (Kasarda et al., 2006). The average value for US freight shipments carried by air was estimated by DOT to have been US$59 per kg, compared to $44 for parcels, mail or courier, and $0.92 for truck. The air and parcels shipments consisted mainly of electronic and other electrical goods, precision instruments and pharmaceutical products. Those carried by air totalled US$209,611 million compared to $1,597 trillion for parcels, mail and courier. Together they accounted for 3 percent by weight and 15 percent by value.[1]

Table 2.1 shows that the average value-to-weight ratio of cargo shipped by air from the UK is nearly 75 times greater than that of goods shipped by sea. At 2008 exchange rates, air exports would be around US$49 per kg and imports US$17 per kg lower than the US estimates above, especially for imports.

Table 2.1   Value to weight ratio for UK extra-EU international trade by mode of transport

	Value per kilogram (UK£)		
Transport mode	**Exports**	**Imports**	**Total**
Air	90.93	30.77	42.78
Channel Tunnel	14.76	20.29	16.11
Miscellaneous	1.23	1.43	1.26
Sea	1.20	0.47	0.58

Source: UK DfT, 2009.

In addition, certain shipments benefit from the fast transit times for air cargo because of their perishability. Fresh flowers, fruit and vegetables generally need the number of days between harvesting and availability on the shelves to be minimised. Some products such as bananas can be transported by sea or land, since they can be picked unripe and ripened slowly in transit. Ships can also handle refrigerated containers which allow products such as fish and other fresh items to support longer transit times.

---

1   Bureau of Transportation Statistics Special Report based on 2007 Commodity Flow Survey, September 2009.

The other form of perishability is more economic than physical. For example newspapers and magazines can be physically transported by sea and arrive in good condition but by that time the market has disappeared. However, even with fast delivery these items will not support a high air cargo rate and are only likely to be viable using marginal cost or fill-up rates on passenger flights.[2] Other items in this category are textiles, especially those with a high fashion content. These need to appear in world markets in time to satisfy demand following fashion shows in trend-setting centres and subsequent promotions.

The world air freight market was estimated to have totalled 15.8 million tonnes in 2003, of which 11.3 percent was express, 25.3 percent was items requiring special handling and the remainder general air cargo. A more detailed breakdown by commodity is discussed in the next section followed by a look at the express and special handling market segments.

2.1 Commodities Carried

The breakdown of air trade by commodities varies according to the categories selected and whether tonnes or tonne-kms are used as measures of traffic. MergeGlobal use freight tonne-kms, and its 2007 breakdown was:

- high-tech products (27 percent);
- capital equipment (19 percent);
- apparel, textiles and footwear (17 percent);
- consumer products (16 percent);
- intermediate products (12 percent);
- refrigerated foods (5 percent).

Refrigerated foods do not account for a large part of world air trade, but for Latin America to North America they take 41 percent of the total, with a further 8 percent for non-refrigerated foods. Asia is the big generator of high-tech products and this and other regions will be discussed below. This will use a different breakdown, with documents and small packages one of the categories not found in the MergeGlobal analysis.

2.1.1 Asia to/from Europe

According to the Boeing (2008) analysis, 74 percent more air cargo was carried from Asia to Europe than in the opposite direction. The tonnage taken from Asia to Europe increased from 1.72 million in 2003 to 2.51m in 2007, or by 46 percent. European air exports grew more slowly by 25 percent to 1.44m tonnes. The

---

2   Technology now allows the simultaneous printing of newspapers in regional centres, considerably reducing the need for air freighting from one national printing facility.

directional imbalance worsened considerably in this period, reflected in a scarcity of westbound capacity by 2007 and higher yields than in the other direction.

It can be seen from Figure 2.2 that European exports consisted more of industrial and electrical machinery than any other commodity, with small packages the second largest. These provide the manufacturing capability in China and other East Asian countries to manufacture consumer and office goods that feature in

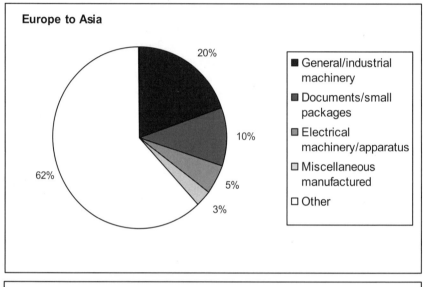

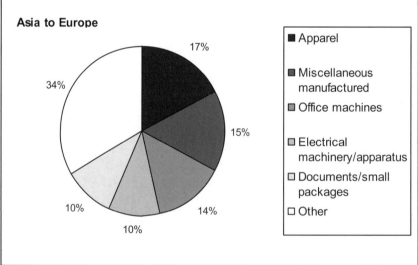

Figure 2.2   Air trade by commodity, 2007: Europe to/from Asia

Source: Boeing, 2008.

Asian exports to Europe. Apparel and textiles also account for a large part of Asian exports, especially for India and a lesser extent China.

High-tech exports from Asia are also a part of the miscellaneous and electrical goods category from the Boeing analysis. China and Taiwan are large exporters of these goods, mainly laptops, integrated circuits and LCD displays. These are transported primarily by air.

2.1.2 North America to/from Asia

According to the Boeing (2008) analysis, 57 percent more air cargo was carried from Asia to North America than in the opposite direction. The tonnage taken from Asia to North America increased from 1.62 million in 2003 to 2.21 million in 2007, or by 36 percent. North American air exports also grew strongly by 33 percent to 1.40m tonnes. As a result, the directional imbalance did not change very much. This trade imbalance, not just for air shipments, has been the cause of concern in the US government with calls for a revaluation of the Chinese currency, thus making Chinese exports less competitive.

It can be seen from Figure 2.3 that North American exports consisted mostly of industrial and electrical machinery in the same way as for European exports, with chemicals and scientific instruments also significant. Apparel/textiles also account for a large part of Asian exports, with telecommunications equipment, mainly mobile phones, also a large Asian export market. The air share of many of these commodities exported from Asia to the US has declined between 1999 and 2007, especially apparel/textiles where ocean transport increased its market share from 16.7 percent to 8.7 percent (MergeGlobal, 2009). Machinery exports accounted for a higher total tonnage (8,600 versus 3,800 tonnes) and the air share of the total only fell by just under 2 percentage points over this period. Toys were another significant export (3,800 tonnes in 2007) where air lost ground, 2 percentage points down in market share.

2.1.3 Latin America to/from North America

According to the Boeing (2008) analysis, 51 percent more air cargo was carried from Latin America to North America than in the opposite direction. The tonnage taken from Latin America to North America increased from 0.72 million in 2003 to 0.82 million in 2007, or by 13 percent. North American air exports advanced strongly by 36 percent from a low base of 0.40 million tonnes. As a result, the directional imbalance improved significantly.

It can be seen from Figure 2.4 that over half of North American imports consisted of flowers, fish and vegetables. Fish imports dropped slightly as more was carried on refrigerated ships from countries like Peru, while imports of fresh flowers by air increased by 30 percent.

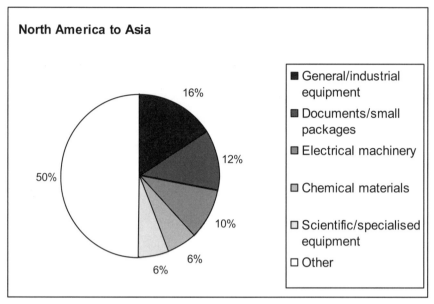

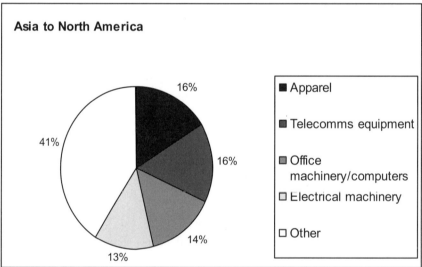

Figure 2.3   Air trade by commodity, 2007: North America to/from Asia
Source: Boeing, 2008.

2.1.4 Europe to/from North America

Trade in each direction on the North Atlantic was almost identical in 2007, compared to a marked imbalance in 2003, when 34 percent more was exported from North America to Europe. Machinery features strongly in trade in both

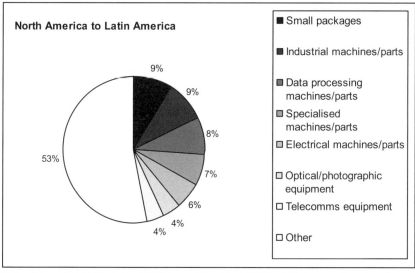

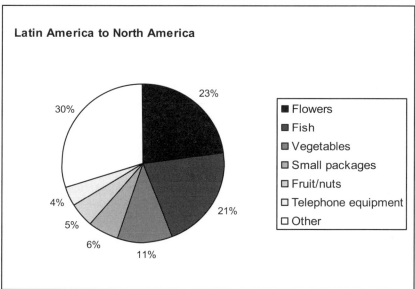

Figure 2.4   Air trade by commodity, 2007: North America to/from Latin America

Source: Boeing, 2008.

directions, with transport equipment a significant export to the US (for railways and aircraft). Documents and small packages tend to be around 10 percent of air trade flows in most regions, with a higher share than this from North America and somewhat lower from Europe (see Figure 2.5).

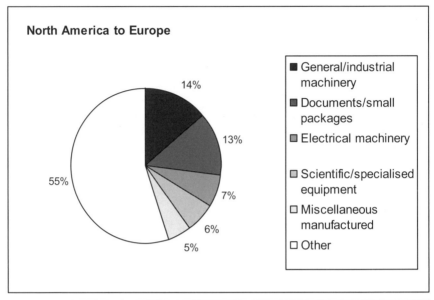

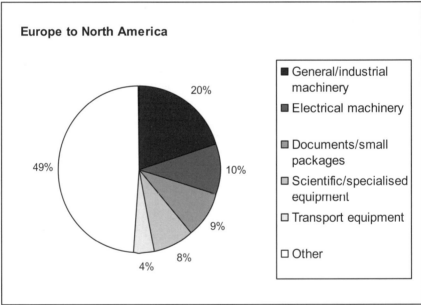

Figure 2.5   Air trade by commodity, 2007: North America to/from Europe
Source: Boeing, 2008.

2.1.5 Africa to/from Europe

Europe is Africa's main air trading partner although 17 percent is with Asia and the Middle East. Southbound air cargo consists mainly of printed material, pharmaceuticals, equipment and machinery. Some northbound flows have been growing quite fast, notably flowers and perishables from Kenya. Vegetables were the largest single food item imported by air into the UK from Africa, for example, green beans, baby corn and mangetout from countries such as Kenya, the Gambia and Egypt. Fresh fruit was also imported but tonnages were less than from Asia.

2.2 Special Handling Items

Forecasts prepared by MergeGlobal for Lufthansa in 2004 gave the split of the world air freight market by segment. Special handling items accounted for 25.3 percent of the 2003 world market, with the fresh produce or perishable market taking almost half of that (see Table 2.2).

Table 2.2   Special handling air tonnages by category, 2003

	2003	Percent share
Temperature controlled	328,927	8.3
Fresh produce/perishables	1,799,884	45.2
Shock sensitive	244,094	6.1
Theft endangered	887,647	22.3
Highly valuable	88,032	2.2
Animal transport	109,658	2.8
Dangerous goods	527,245	13.2
Total	3,985,487	100.0

Source: Global AirFreight Outlook, Lufthansa Cargo Planet, 2004.

All these types of shipment have been growing faster than general air cargo and are targeted by Lufthansa and other cargo airlines (see Chapter 9 on marketing strategies). Shock sensitive goods are those that require careful handling, such as some chemicals, but are not on the list of items that need to be treated as dangerous goods (see Chapter 8, section 8.2.5). Lufthansa now includes them under the same 'care' product as dangerous goods.

Theft endangered and valuable items can clearly support the relatively high air rates, but do need special treatment. Valuable items such as works of art, gold, jewellery and bank notes are carefully packed in the centre of containers to minimise the opportunities for theft. Lufthansa Cargo groups fast-growing items such as computers and their components, and mobile phones in the theft endangered category. These are discussed below (section 2.5.4). Temperature controlled shipments will be those that need to kept within a certain temperature range, such as fresh produce and other perishables, pharmaceuticals and medical supplies. These are examined in the next section.

2.2.1 Perishables

From the Boeing analysis in the previous section the largest import market for perishables in 2007 was North America from Latin America. However, these figures leave out Africa and some perishables may be included under 'other'. Jansen (2008) shows that in 2007 Africa was the largest exporter to Europe:

Latin America to North America:	474 tonnes
Africa to Europe:	376 tonnes
Middle East to Europe:	317 tonnes
Latin America to Europe:	222 tonnes
North America to Europe:	121 tonnes

The above flows accounted for 1.5 million out of the total perishable air exports of 2 million in that year. This compared with perishables going by sea of 90m tonnes. A less recent 2005 estimate for imports of perishables by air gave the three largest markets as:

Europe:	858,000 tonnes
US:	523,000 tonnes
Asia:	501,000 tonnes

Europe recorded the fastest growth between 2000 and 2005 of 8 percent per annum, followed by Asia with 2 percent and the US 1 percent a year respectively.[3] Flowers and plants were the fastest growing segment. European countries with the largest imports were the Netherlands and the UK. There was evidence of some switch to surface transport, especially by sea, with better control facilities available on refrigerated containers carried by ships. For example, the Peru to US asparagus market changed in the past 10 years from 80 percent by air to 80 percent by sea. Bananas and frozen fish are the two largest perishable markets carried by sea in 2007 (Jansen, 2008). While neither of these may be potential air commodities, the fastest growing segment of perishables going by sea between 2000 and 2007 were those with a value of between $2–5 per kg, accounting for around 20 percent of the total.

---

3   *International Freighting Weekly*, 11 December 2006, p. 10.

Flowers

The major flower exports by air are from South America, Africa and Asia. Ecuador is one of the largest South American producers that has until recently relied on North American markets but diversified towards Europe and Russia between 2006 and 2009. The two largest African countries that export flowers by air to Europe are Ethiopia and Kenya, with over 50,000 tonnes a year flown out of Nairobi by one carrier alone. Zimbabwe has also been a large exporter until its economy collapsed. Israel has also been a large exporter to Europe, as have Colombia and Ecuador. Thailand has been a large exporter in Asia, but tending to focus on orchids, whereas other regions offer a wider range of blooms such as carnations and roses.

The European and Asian markets are still predominately distributed through flower shops, which are supplied from wholesalers that often deal through the Aalsmeer flower auction in the Netherlands. Supermarkets, on the other hand, dominate North American and UK flower distribution, often obtaining their supplies direct from overseas companies.

Some air cargo shippers fly to Amsterdam or nearby gateways to reach the Dutch auction warehouse quickly. However, flowers can be viewed electronically by auction participants at other warehouses in Europe. Roses feature strongly in air exports, particularly from Kenya to the Netherlands, which grown at an annual average of 12 percent between 1998 and 2007 (Seabury, 2009).

In addition to being unidirectional, air exports of some flowers are also highly peaked with a surge in demand just before Valentine's Day and Mother's Day in

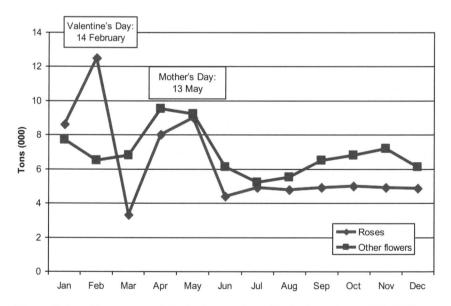

Figure 2.6   Air exports of fresh flowers from Latin America to US, 2007

Source: Adapted from Bloemen, 2009.

the US (see Figure 2.6). A similar pattern would also be expected in Europe as retailers exploit the same opportunities.

Other perishables
Europe's major suppliers of tropical fruits in the early 2000s were Ghana, Brazil, Ivory Coast, Pakistan and South Africa (Jansen, 2004). Spain gets its fish (hake) from Chile, while Peru is a major supplier of fresh asparagus. Argentina was one of the first countries to export perishables: meat in the form of 'corned' beef. In those days it would have gone by sea, mostly to Europe. Today, Argentina exports horse meat to Europe by air, in addition to fresh beef.

Much of the above exports of perishables have only been possible when air freight rates have been low enough to be supported by the final prices to the consumer. Most of the export countries have low labour costs, which mean that the air freight cost is a large part of the final price. Often low rates can be offered in the lower deck of passenger flights. These flights are usually operated with wide-bodied aircraft with up to 20 tonnes' capacity. However, they are sometimes supplemented by freighters, for example between Peru and the US (Miami). In this case the heavy directional flow is from the US to Latin America or Europe to Africa, and so low rates encourage the use of capacity that would otherwise be empty.

2.2.2 Animal Transport

The largest part of the live animal market is horses, mostly racehorses that are bought and sold and raced at international venues. The Middle East is one of the biggest customers here, but Hong Kong is also home to the rich with an interest in horse breeding and racing. Polo is an international sport for the wealthy and countries such as Argentina have a long history of playing this game, with international matches in Europe and North America. Special regulations were introduced to make sure animals were transported in appropriate conditions, and there are also some animals that cannot be exported or need a licence to do so.

Other animals that require air freighting are zoo animals such as tigers, lions and farm animals that are imported for breeding purposes. The latter has been affected by moves to ship the embryos rather than the live animals.

Documentation is more complicated than for normal cargo with import licences and veterinary checks, in addition to the normal security screening processes. The spread of avian flu has resulted in a tightening of the regulations on the movement of farm animals even within individual countries. Special containers are available for the transport of horses and other animals.

2.3 Humanitarian Aid

The air cargo industry provides a ready source of lift for emergency food aid and medical supplies. Governments and aid agencies, such as USAID, EuropAid and Oxfam, charter freighter aircraft from the industry at short notice to meet emergencies, and some have their own aircraft. Without a flourishing air freight industry these flights would cause much greater disruption to scheduled flights and international commerce.

One of the largest agencies, the World Food Agency, through its World Food Programme (WFP), relies heavily on airlifts to get food into some of the world's most hostile and inaccessible places, or to remote areas where much of the infrastructure has been damaged or destroyed, for example in the wake of the December 2004 Indian Ocean tsunami.

At the beginning of 2006, WFP/UNHAS (the UN's Humanitarian Air Service) was itself operating some 103 aircraft on missions ranging from food airdrops to transporting relief workers to remote and dangerous locations. Its division WFP Aviation charters both passenger and cargo aircraft and also operates on behalf of other agencies such as the United Nations, donor countries and non-governmental organisations (NGOs).

Table 2.3 shows that its traffic varies over time according to emergency needs, with passengers generally having a greater weight than cargo.

Table 2.3   WFP Aviation operations, 2001 to 2008

Year	Hours	Passengers	Cargo (tonnes)
2001	54,000	91,000	110,000
2002	56,000	116,000	95,300
2003	59,000	150,000	100,600
2004	64,000	176,000	140,000
2005	89,000	368,000	154,000
2006	64,000	383,000	32,700
2007	50,000	321,000	11,000
2008	47,000	361,000	15,200

Source: WFP Aviation Annual Report, 2009.

The WFP Aviation budget for providing Special Air Operations in 2008 was US$193 million but its income for that year fell short at $170 million. The largest individual donor country specifically to these operations was the US with US$15 million (with the UK a close second with $14 million) and the European

Commission (ECHO) gave $25 million. Many of the aircraft it charters are small turbo-props such as Cessna Caravans and Twin Otters, reaching more remote airstrips that the larger jets cannot get into, in countries like the Sudan and Chad. It uses helicopters where no airstrips exist and roads are poor or non-existent.

The earthquake in Haiti in January 2010 was described by the UN General Secretary as 'one of the worst humanitarian crises in decades'. It required the immediate airlift of supplies followed by further flights with items such as earthmoving equipment and trucks for longer-term reconstruction work. Many airlines offered capacity at cost for these flights, which occurred at a time when there was spare capacity available as a result of the economic downturn. The main port of Haiti was still closed a week after the earthquake and so air was the only mode of transport possible. However, the airport came under strain and could not handle the number of flights that were chartered over the first few days.

2.4 Defence Support

Commercial airlines are often used by a government's military to support operations in various parts of the world. This can take the form of chartering passenger aircraft for troop movements, for example flights from the US via Shannon in Ireland to the Middle East. They are more likely to involve freighter aircraft in support of logistics needs in foreign countries. The largest of these has been the US Department of Defense contracts to fly equipment and supplies to Iraq and Afghanistan.

This is a profitable business for an airline or freight forwarder, but it cannot be depended on to support its fleet in the longer term. Atlas Air generated about a quarter of its 2008 revenues from military charters which produced over half of its profits for that year (see section 11.3). It makes more sense for the government to outsource much of its air freight needs, many of which are of a shorter term nature. The US has since 1951 had the Civil Reserve Air Fleet (CRAF) programme which signs up US passenger and cargo carriers to make aircraft available. The intention was to provide a more orderly system of allocating aircraft than had been the case during the Berlin Airlift.

The CRAF supports Department of Defense (DOD) airlift requirements in emergencies when the need for airlift exceeds the capability of the military aircraft fleet. Participants must be US airlines and must meet the relevant Federal Aviation Administration regulations (Bolkcom, 2006). To join CRAF, a carrier must commit at least 30 percent of its CRAF-capable passenger fleet, and 15 percent of its CRAF-capable cargo fleet.

There are international long-range and short-range sections for both passenger and cargo aircraft. As at April 2010 there were nine aircraft allocated to the short-range cargo section, five of them from ABX Air (B767-200Fs), three from Northern Air Cargo (B737-200F) and one from Lyndon Air Cargo (L100-30). The long-range cargo allocation is shown in Table 2.4.

Table 2.4   US Civil Reserve Air Fleet (CRAF) allocations, April 2010

Aircraft type	Allocation	Carriers
DC8-62CB	6	Air Transport Internat. (ATN)
DC8-63F	2	Murray Air
DC8-70F series	13	DHL, ATN, Murray
DC10-30F	12	FedEx, Arrow Air
B747-100F	5	Kalitta Air, Evergreen
B747-200F	38	Kalitta Air, Evergreen, Atlas
B747-300F	3	Atlas, Southern
B747-400F	34	Kalitta, Atlas, Polar
B767-200SF	10	ABX
B767-300	12	UPS
B767-400ER	2	World Airways
MD10/11-CF	95	FedEx, UPS, World
Total	232	

Source: US DOT, Office of the Secretary of Transportation.

Air carriers volunteer their aircraft to the CRAF programme through contractual agreements with the Air Mobility Command (AMC), a part of the US Air Force located at Scott Air Force Base, Illinois. In return for having aircraft and crews available at 24–48 hours' notice the AMC guarantees certain levels of contract for participants, although they tend to favour long-haul cargo types such as the B747 rather than smaller short-haul aircraft.

2.5 Modal Choice

Hummels (2009) noted that air trade had increased rapidly up to 2000 but had declined relative to sea transport since then. He identified two key factors in this change: the changing nature of international trade and the cost of shipping by air relative to the value or final price of the goods. Air transport was helped by the fact that 'from 1960–2004, the real value of trade in manufactures grew about 1.5 percent per year faster than the weight of non-bulk cargoes'. Seabury estimated that the air share had risen from 18 percent in 2004 to 24 percent in 2008. It had then dropped sharply over the first half of 2008 to 21 percent. This was short-lived since it resumed its upward trend at the end of 2008 to reach almost 27 percent in the first quarter of 2010.

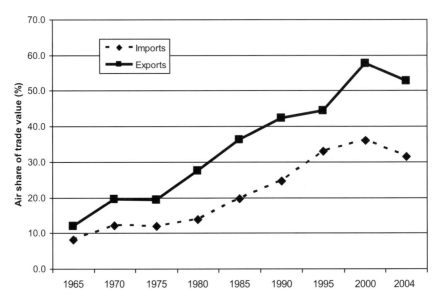

**Figure 2.7   US air share of trade value (excluding North America), 1965
            to 2004**

Source: Hummels, 2009.

The decline in the share of both exports and imports since 2000 can be seen from
Figure 2.7 for the US alone, but anecdotal evidence from airlines and forwarders
suggests that this trend has been global. The greatest modal shift occurred between
1980 and 2000, coinciding with the growing use of wide-body aircraft offering a
large increase in capacity on freighters and passenger flights.

The decline in value share in the 2000s is confirmed by European data
(Hummels, 2009): between 2000 and 2007 the value share for air transport
declined by 4 percentage points for German exports compared to an increase of
1.2 percentage points for sea transport. Road (truck) transport accounted for the
rest of the gain. The figures for the UK were a fall of 4.2 percentage points for air
and an increase of 1.1 percentage points for sea respectively.

It was noted above that ocean freight rates could be one-tenth or less of air
freight rates, and the value to weight ratio was important in modal choice. Air
freight's rapid growth in the 1990s and into the twenty-first century has been
helped by the marketing of high-tech products for both the consumer and industry.
These have had a relatively short life cycle, with significant improvements in their
successors justifying continued high prices.

However, towards the end of the 2000s it was impossible to maintain higher
prices. This was both because of strong supplier competition and the maturity
of some products such as mobile phones and laptops. Products from the older
industrial countries such as the US and in Europe had tended to maintain prices
by adding new features such as improved software or a larger screen. On the other

hand, newly industrialised countries tend to target the huge markets (and not just their own) of lower spending power with cheaper high-tech products. The other factor that caused some switch from air to sea was the impact of high oil prices on air freight rates, which was much greater than on ocean rates. As shown above, some perishables such as fresh fish exports from South America could no longer afford air freight and moved to sea. Datamonitor predicted a modal shift between 2010 and 2013 with 'air freight losing ground to rail, road and sea' because of cost effectiveness and sustainability.[4]

Another way of looking at this is to split air cargo into planned and emergency shipments. MergeGlobal estimate that the split is about 50:50. It goes further to suggest that planned shipments are gravitating to surface transport modes, while emergency ones have been increasingly captured by integrators (Tirschwell, 2007). Their analysis may be based more on North American trends, but similar threats to air cargo carriers are also likely to affect other parts of the world.

The following factors that affect modal choice will be examined in turn:

- cost;
- delivery time;
- frequency;
- security;
- quality of service.

2.5.1 Cost

The cost of shipping a consignment is determined by the rate charged to the shipper together with the various charges and surcharges that have become commonplace in recent years. The rates are discussed more fully in Chapter 10. Here it is necessary to look at relative trends in air and surface rates, especially taking into account fuel and security surcharges.

As we will see in Chapter 5, ocean container freight rates fell by 17 percent in 2009 for eastbound transpacific sailings while Far East to Europe dropped by 32 percent. These trends were similar to those experienced by air cargo operators at least on transpacific routes. It is difficult to compare air and sea freight rates since ocean rates do not quote fuel surcharges separately as is the case with air (see Chapter 10, section 10.3). But ocean rates had risen very rapidly between 2002 and 2008 before they collapsed, especially between Asia and Europe where the decline was largest. This also supports the air share analysis above.

Airlines often complain of the very low rates that they get from the forwarder, but not all of this is passed on to the shipper. Forwarders may have a need to meet monthly volume targets and pass on more of the rate advantage that they have negotiated with a particular airline.

---

4   *Air Cargo World*, 26 April 2010.

2.5.2 Delivery Time

Delivery time from the shipper's standpoint is the time from collection from the factory to delivery to the consignee or distributor in the destination country. This is where air has a distinct advantage, some of which is often lost in delays along the route. These could be because of customs clearance, late pick-up at the destination airport, or offloading onto the next flight.

The longer the route the greater the time advantage for air. Conversely on shorter routes, air is less well placed since flying takes a much smaller percentage of total time than for long trips, and has less scope for influencing door-to-door delivery time. This is one reason why most intra-European freight goes by truck.

2.5.3 Frequency

Frequency of service and choice of non-stop flight destinations is clearly an advantage for emergency shipments. Passenger services generally score better than freighters in this respect, but larger consignments may not fit into lower deck compartments. Air would also usually win over sea and even truck, with greater than daily air services reducing the time waiting for the next departure.

Planned shipments also benefit from higher frequency, especially where Just-in-time (JIT) methods of inventory management are used. Here the cost disadvantage of smaller shipments is offset against the lower cost of holding a large inventory.

2.5.4 Security

Air freight operators have long promoted their mode as being more secure than surface transport. One reason may be the shorter time that the shipment is at risk, although a limited number of people would have access to cargo during a sea voyage. Pirate raids, however, have become commonplace in certain sea lanes, such as off the Somalian coast and in the Straits of Malacca. On the other hand air freight is not entirely risk-free and there have been notable cases of theft in airports, although most have targeted passenger baggage.

Valuable items are often packed at the centre of containers that are sent by air. This in itself suggests that the risks are not insignificant. Pallets are thought to be more risky. An Australian government police initiative in 2007 was designed to reduce air cargo theft at Perth Airport. However, in many cases the air cargo shipment is stolen on its way to or from the airport. For example, in 2005 Eli Lilly sued FedEx when a shipment of pharmaceuticals was stolen en route to a customer in Japan from the company's factory in São Paulo, Brazil. The theft occurred when a truck taking the shipment from the factory to São Paulo Airport was hijacked. With a large share of air cargo controlled by freight forwarders and consolidators, theft may also occur at the off-airport premises of these companies.

The question here is whether air cargo is inherently more risky than surface transport. This is impossible to answer, but there are also numerous examples of theft from cargo carried by sea or trucks. In 2009, DHL launched a Europe-wide secure Less than Truck Load (LTL) road service for small- and medium-enterprise (SME) shippers of high-value goods up to 2,500 kgs. It cited such losses from the shipment by all modes of €8 billion a year.

It is estimated that direct losses due to cargo theft across all transportation modes total between $10 and 25 billion annually in the United States (US General Accounting Office, 2002). The large range in this estimate reflects the fact that cargo theft is not a specific crime category and therefore reliable statistics on cargo theft are unavailable. Furthermore, many experts believe a large percentage of cargo theft is unreported. The large estimated level of cargo theft and other cargo crimes is indicative of potential weaknesses in cargo security including air cargo security. Specific weaknesses in air cargo security have been highlighted in several high profile investigations of cargo theft. Major cargo and baggage theft rings have been uncovered at JFK International Airport in New York, Logan International Airport in Boston, and at Miami International Airport in the US and at London Heathrow in the UK. A large portion of cargo crime is thought to be either committed by or with the assistance of cargo workers. This is not restricted to handling staff: Dallas/Fort Worth Airport police convicted a UPS pilot for stealing iPods and laptops in 2009. Another example, this one from Europe, indicates access to the supposedly secure airside area of the airport: a series of robberies took place at Brussels Airport in 2001, thieves stealing $160 million in diamonds from the holds of Lufthansa jets.

Solutions proposed have included conducting more stringent or more frequent background checks of cargo workers and enhancing physical security of cargo operations areas. A review of transportation security needs for combating cargo crime identified the following four key issues regarding cargo security:

- a lack of effective cargo theft reporting systems;
- weaknesses in current transportation crime laws and prosecution;
- a lack of understanding regarding the nature of cargo crime by governments and industry;
- inadequate support for cargo theft task forces.

After 9/11 the focus was on screening against terrorist acts, which has more to do with introducing material (explosives etc.) into containers or pallets than removing them through theft. However, tighter security is expected to reduce both these threats. Their implication for airport handling is further discussed in Chapter 8.

2.5.5 Quality of Service

Airline service has a number of elements stretching from initial enquiries from shippers, or more likely forwarders, through to post delivery follow-up. Twenty years ago or more the integrators set the standards for the industry which the combination carriers have been slow to follow. Part of the reason was their legacy systems and the difficulty to move forward without taking their partners with them. Part of the reason was their limited role in the supply chain and impossibility to improve the quality of service to the shipper. Integrators also charged a premium price and were expected to match this with a high quality service. For example, their call centres have for many years monitored calls on a daily basis to ensure that each inquiry is answered within a defined number of 'rings'.

Forwarders were not happy in the past with airline standards, particularly on aspects that tended to delay shipments. One of these was putting consignments on the flight on which they were booked, something that is taken for granted on the passenger side. Airlines in response argued that forwarders often delivered shipments of dimensions that differed significantly from those on the booking system, which meant they did not have space on the flight for which they were booked. Ten years ago airlines, under the auspices of the IATA, decided to set up Cargo 2000 to improve service and streamline the physical and information flows involved with shipping by air. By attracting both forwarders and airlines Cargo 2000 was designed to respond to the high service standards set by their integrator competitors. As discussed below the number of members is not large, although many of the larger companies participate. A large number of smaller forwarders, however, cannot see the benefits outweighing the administrative burden and often do not have the necessary IT systems to fully benefit.

The Cargo 2000 Master Operating Plan was developed based on detailed customer research. It is designed to address deficiencies in and improve the air cargo industry-wide process control and reporting system.

By reducing the number of individual processes in the air cargo supply chain from 40 to just 19, Cargo 2000 is less labour intensive and improves the processes for managing shipments in a paperless environment. It substantially reduces time spent managing irregularities, such as service failures, cuts the time required for manual track and trace procedures and leads to a reduction is service recovery costs.

Cargo 2000's quality management system is being implemented in three distinct phases. The key to the Master Operating Plan is the creation of a unique 'route map' for individual shipments that is monitored and measured throughout the delivery cycle of each shipment.

- Phase 1 manages Airport to Airport movements – shipment planning and tracking at Master air waybill level. Once a booking is made, a plan is automatically created with a series of checkpoints against which the transportation of every air cargo shipment is managed and measured. This enables the system to alert Cargo 2000 members to any exceptions to the plan, allowing them to respond proactively to fulfil their customers' expectations.
- Phase 2 is responsible for shipment planning and tracking at House air waybill level and provides interactive monitoring of the door-to-door movement.

- The third and final phase of Cargo 2000 manages shipment planning and tracking at individual piece level plus document tracking. This provides for real-time management of the transportation channel at piece level. It will also control the flow of information which will be vital for current and future security requirements. In Phase 3 the control of information is most important, as the necessity for paper will be limited to the bare minimum – as required by law. In the attempt to operate in a paperless environment, the IATA e-freight initiative and Cargo 2000 are complementing each other.

As of mid-2010 Cargo 2000 had the following active full members:

Airlines
American, United, Delta Airlines, Cathay Pacific, Korean, Singapore, Swiss, Austrian, Air France-KLM, Alitalia, Cargolux, SAS, Lufthansa, British Airways, Turkish, Etihad, and Air Canada.

Freight forwarders
Agility Logistics, CEVA, DHL Global Forwarding, Geodis-Wilson, Kuehne + Nagel, Schenker AG, SDV International Logistics, and Yusen Air and Sea Service.

The following were active associate members:

Ground handling
Aviapartner, SwissPort, TAT, and International Cargo Centre Shenzhen.

IT providers
British Telecom, CCN, Descartes Global Logistics Network, GLS, Riege Software, Traxon and Unisys.

The move to tracking individual shipments at the house air waybill level still looks some years away. In the meantime service standards have improved considerably: the percentage of shipments flown by airlines as planned (and booked) has risen from 53 percent in September 2004 to 90 percent in June 2009, still just short of the target of 96 percent. The percentage of Forwarder Master Air waybills (FWB) correctly received by airline rose from 79 percent in December 2004 to 92 percent in June 2009, just below the target of 96 percent. These two measures confirm that forwarders are much better at providing correct information to airlines, and that airlines are putting more shipments on the flight they are booked on, something that is taken for granted on the passenger side of the business.

2.6 Bimodal Shipment

Forwarders have always been keen to offer their customers a choice of delivery times and rates and this can sometimes mean using two modes of transport (in addition to the short delivery and collection segments by truck or van). Of relevance here are air transport combined by first sea and second rail transport.

2.6.1 Sea-Air

The freight forwarder offers the shipper fast, more costly air transport or much slower and cheaper ocean transport. Over shorter distances trucks are used. However, on the longer haul trade routes from Asia to Europe and North America, an intermediate option has been offered which combines air and sea transport. This pitches the cost somewhere between the two modes, depending on the relative distance travelled by air and sea, and delivery times that are significantly faster than by sea. The traffic is bimodal rather than inter-modal since through containerisation is not possible and the shipments need to be transferred to air containers or pallets for the second leg of the journey. This requires an efficient handling operation from ship to aircraft.

The origins of this go back to the 1950s when forwarders used ocean ships from Europe to North America and then air to take the consignments on to South America. Kuehne + Nagel offered a 13–16-day delivery time by taking an ocean sailing from Hamburg to New York, and air transport to the final destination in South America (Al-Hajri, 1998). This was slower than a direct air service taking between three and four days, but this may not have been available, or limited in payload, and of course more expensive. Ocean transport was also used from Antwerp to the Belgian Congo and onwards to various African destinations by air. Sailings from Marseille to French possessions in Africa also used similar air connections.

This early use of sea-air transport was based more on the fact that no alternatives existed than the attraction of the cost/time combination. Flights to various destinations in Africa or South America with passenger aircraft had very limited lower deck capacity and freighters were not viable for the volumes on offer. It was not until the 1970s that wide-body passenger aircraft made cargo capacity available to many destinations at a reasonable price. From the 1980s sea-air became attractive to the fast-growing export markets of Asia, for example from Japan, Korea and more recently Taiwan and China. For these exporters sea-air also offered attractive prices and speeds that were adequate to stock warehouses in the US and Europe. But often cargo capacity on aircraft flying from Asia to the markets of Europe and the US was in short supply and prices were high. Sea-air provided additional capacity at a price that combined cheap sea transport with not so expensive carriage by air. The latter often depended on making use of a directional imbalance and a need to fill an aircraft's return leg.

There are numerous possible combinations of sea-air shipment between Asia and Europe but the main eastbound ones that are or have been used are:

1. North-east Asia to Vancouver by sea; Vancouver to Europe by air.
2. North-east Asia to Seattle by sea; Seattle to Europe by air.
3. North-east Asia to Los Angeles by sea; Los Angeles to Europe by air.
4. North-east Asia to San Francisco/Oakland by sea; San Francisco to Europe by air.

A modification of the above is the use of trucks to move shipments from the west to the east of North America, and then flown from east coast airports such as New York or Boston to Europe. A more recent addition has been shipments from China to Korea by sea and from Korea to North America or Europe by air. Another combination is Hong Kong to Los Angeles by sea and LA to São Paulo by air, giving a 10-day saving over sea.

In the westbound direction, the following are used:

1. North-east Asia to Singapore by sea; Singapore to Europe by air.
2. North-east Asia to Dubai by sea; Dubai to Europe by air.
3. North-east Asia to Sharjah by sea; Sharjah to Europe by air.

By the 2000s eastbound sea-air had decline to almost nothing while the westbound routes were dominated by Dubai and Sharjah. The latter was not so dependent on the air capacity situation out of Asia and had an on-going direction imbalance which favoured attractive rates for onward shipment to Europe. These points had the advantage of having frequent sea and air connections, and fast connection times (which were reported to be as little as four hours).

In the early 1990s sea-air tonnages were probably higher than they are today, although it is difficult to obtain reliable data. At that time, around 15,000 tonnes was going to Vancouver by sea and by air on to Europe. Another 10,000 tonnes transferred at Seattle, and smaller amounts through Los Angeles. In the westbound direction almost 100,000 tonnes went by sea from Japan to Vladivostok and then by air to Europe, with Singapore taking a further 10,000 tonnes. The Middle Eastern routes were estimated to take around 25,000 tonnes.

Following the sharp downturn in international trade in late 2008/early 2009, the sea-air market collapsed as rates tumbled out of Asia and plenty of capacity was available at low rates. This left sea-air priced no lower than air freight with longer transit times. However, by the end of 2009 capacity from Asia was once again tight with some airlines having retired or grounded a major part of their freighter fleet. This made sea-air once again a competitive proposition.

The transhipment points need sufficient air cargo capacity at relatively low rates and a nearby container port. Seattle has an advantage in that both the seaport and airport are divisions of the same organisation, the Port of Seattle. Shipments will arrive in sea containers and need to be transhipped into smaller aircraft compatible containers. Facilities will also be needed to transport the containers in bond between the port and airport to avoid customs inspections. Dubai International Airport is 30 km from the Port of Jebel Ali, and Emirates Airlines has put considerable effort into making sure goods move rapidly between the two, with up to six hours possible for the transfer.[5] One problem is the need to break down the sea containers and re-build them in air compatible containers or pallets.

Sea-air in 2010 was around 30–35 percent cheaper than direct air service but took around 13 days compared to two to three days for non-stop air or slightly longer for air services involving transhipment en route.[6] It would take 18–22 days by sea. Evidence of slow steaming by ocean ships has added around two days to an Asia/Europe voyage compared to only a day for sea-air via the Middle East, giving the latter a small advantage. However, in mid-2008 sea transport rates for Asia to Europe were around US$0.07 per kg compared with $2.95 per kg for sea-air and $4.25 per kg for air.[7]

Sharjah Airport is a major sea-air transhipment point in the Middle East. Typically, cargo routed by sea-air from Tokyo to Frankfurt via Sharjah can cut 40 percent off the cost of pure air freight, while slashing a third of the time taken by ship-only mode. Sea-air cargo volumes handled by Sharjah Airport exceeded 20,000 tonnes in 1995. It also handles more than 60 percent of the United Arab Emirates' (UAE) sea-air business, and is thought to be second to Seattle in world rankings. However, the volumes are still very small relative to the 1.8 million tonnes handled by another UAE airport, Dubai. Emirates Airlines flies a large part of this business to European destinations, and its head of cargo cited an example of the type of product that might use sea-air.

According to Ram Menen, Senior VP for air cargo at Emirates Airlines, mobile phone hand-sets might only have a market for six months before a new model comes along and makes it obsolete. Previously that meant air freight would be used for the whole six months. Now, he suggested, the first batch goes by air, the second by sea-air and the third by sea.[8]

2.6.2 Rail-air

Rail can be used for the regional distribution of air cargo if the hub airport has freight rail access. Amsterdam Schiphol Airport conducted a feasibility study for putting in a rail link to the Alkmeer flower market (see section 2.2.1) but it was not viable. On the other hand, Fraport has invested in a rail link to Frankfurt Airport and this is used by hub carrier Lufthansa to distribute and collect air cargo from countries like Italy, which face environmental restrictions and charges for trucking

---

5   The new international airport at Jebel Ali will be much closer to the port.
6   *Lloyd's List*, 16 April 2010, p. 7.
7   *International Transport Journal*, 6 June, p. 15.
8   Paraphrased from Andrew Doyle in *Airline Business*, September 2009.

through Switzerland. A rail terminal in Northern Italy at Novara, west of Milan, allows the final distribution of cargo by truck.

One forwarder which also uses sea-air via Dubai, Panalpina, is developing Urumqi in Chinese Mongolia as a rail-air interchange point, with rail feed to a weekly flight to Luxembourg. Five rail origination cities are used including Guangzhou in the south. Another option considered is moving goods by air to Vladivostok in Eastern Siberia and using the rail connection to Europe.

Chapter 3
Economic and Technical Regulation

International air transport, unlike shipping, is governed by a web of bilateral agreements which restrict traffic rights to specified carriers. Shipping, on the other hand, benefited from a 1609 treatise by a Dutchman, Hugo Grotius, whose *Mare Liberum* put forward the principle that the sea was international territory and all nations were free to use it for international trade (Grotius, 1609). The Netherlands at that time was vying for supremacy of world trade and commerce with the British who opposed the principle. Britain's view was that ownership of the land could easily be extended to cover the sea. Subsequently a compromise was reached whereby each country's control or ownership of the sea would only extend within the range of a cannon's shot from its coastline, which evolved into the three-mile limit.

The carriage of cargo by air has a much shorter history than sea or land transport with the growth of the industry in the first half of the twentieth century mostly restricted to domestic routes with few international implications. By the time of the Second World War, however, international flights had grown to the point where a legal framework for their operation was thought essential. To a greater degree than ocean shipping, safety and security issues were considered to present sufficient risk to give rise to the need for international regulation. This emerged from the Chicago Conference of 1944 and its effect on air cargo flights is discussed in this chapter.

Setting up a cargo or a passenger/cargo airline requires an operator's licence as well as the necessary traffic rights to pick up and set down cargo. The airline will need to apply for this from the country in which it is to be domiciled. This generally means that the country will be its principal place of business and, crucially for obtaining international traffic rights, majority owned and controlled by nationals of that country. The Civil Aviation Authority or Department of Civil Aviation will be responsible for maintaining a register of aircraft of all airlines that it licenses and also undertake the continuing technical and financial oversight of the carriers it has licensed.

This chapter will first address the technical and safety aspects of regulation before covering the economic and financial side. The latter will include traffic rights that are negotiated in Air Services Agreements between the country and other countries.

3.1 Licensing of Airlines

3.1.1 Technical Regulation

The Chicago Conference resulted in the Chicago Convention of December 1944, agreed by 52 countries. This had 15 annexes that set standards and recommended practices (SARPs) for civil aviation covering both technical and commercial or economic aspects. Three more have been added since then:

Annex 1:   Personnel Licensing
Annex 2:   Rules of the Air
Annex 3:   Meteorological Service for International Air Navigation
Annex 4:   Aeronautical Charts
Annex 5:   Units of Measurement to be used in Air and Ground Operations
Annex 6:   Operation of Aircraft
Annex 7:   Aircraft Nationality and Registration Marks
Annex 8:   Airworthiness of Aircraft
Annex 9:   Facilitation
Annex 10:   Aeronautical Telecommunications
Annex 11:   Air Traffic Services
Annex 12:   Search and Rescue
Annex 13:   Aircraft Accident and Incident Investigation
Annex 14:   Aerodromes
Annex 15:   Aeronautical Information Services
Annex 16:   Environmental Protection
Annex 17:   Security: Safeguarding International Civil Aviation against Acts of Unlawful Interference
Annex 18:   The Safe Transport of Dangerous Goods by Air.

The most relevant of the above to the licensing of an airline and its aircraft are Annexes 1, 6 and 8. But all will have relevance to air cargo, especially Annex 18. Over time these are modified as new issues arise, for example the most recent edition of Annex 9 to the Chicago Convention contains SARPs that encourage the development of electronic data interchange systems for cargo facilitation.

The Convention had no legal status and so its standards needed to be incorporated into the aviation legislation of each country. These may vary between countries but the essential elements of the Convention and its annexes are included in the laws of its signatory (and other) countries. This forms the basis for the technical regulations that are imposed on flights that carry passengers and cargo. An example of how these work in practice is shown below for the countries of the European Union, the UK in particular.

As mentioned above, any UK-domiciled airline needs to obtain the relevant licences, an Air Operator Certificate (AOC), and place its aircraft on the UK register. The licences are granted and the register kept by the Civil Aviation

Authority (CAA) in the UK. The CAA is a separate governmental body responsible for aviation, similar to the Federal Aviation Administration (FAA) in the US or in Japan the Civil Aviation Bureau in the Ministry of Land, Infrastructure and Transport. The UK CAA implements various UK legal instruments, not just those related to aviation, but its aviation licensing functions are now governed by European Union legislation, specifically Commission Regulation 1008/2008.

The requirement for an air operator to hold an Operating Licence granted by the state in which it is based extends to virtually all carriage by air anywhere in the world of either passengers or cargo for remuneration, irrespective of whether the sale is made to the general public or to a charterer. Flights within the European Economic Area (EEA) are authorised by the European Council Market Access Regulation, which allows Operating Licence holders to operate on most routes in the EEA without needing a further license or permit from any state. There is no restriction on flights being either scheduled or charter (that is, selling seats direct to the public or selling them to a tour operator).

The granting of an Operating License depends on satisfying the authority that the airline:

- has its principal place of business and company's registered office in the country;
- must be majority owned and effectively controlled by nationals of its country (or nationals of the European Economic Area for countries in that agreement);
- has sufficient financial resources;
- has the necessary insurances to cover accidents involving passengers, cargo and third parties;
- has an Air Operator's Certificate.

A route licence is also issued, and some countries have separate categories of these such as scheduled, charter, and other. These may restrict operations to particular international routes or cover any routes, but in either case the airline would need to be designated as the sole or one of a number of airlines for whom the country seeks to negotiate traffic rights with another country.

In some countries such as the UK and US, the authority may hold a hearing to decide how to allocate a limited number of routes and frequencies agreed in negotiations with another country, where more than one airline has applied for traffic rights. An example of this was the UK CAA's hearing in November 2004 to decide how to allocate the 21 frequencies newly available for UK airlines to serve various points in India under the UK/India bilateral Air Services Agreement. British Airways already operated between UK and India, and bmi and Virgin Atlantic wished to start operations to India, but with a reasonable number of frequencies to make the routes viable. Where an Air Service Agreement contain no such restrictions such hearings are unnecessary.

The US TransPacific case was another example where the Chinese government wished to liberalise traffic rights on routes between the US and China gradually. The US had a number of airlines that wanted to enter the Chinese market or expand their operations there.

A US based air cargo operator would be regulated by the following:

- the US Department of Transportation (DOT);
- the Federal Aviation Administration (FAA);
- Transportation Security Administration (TSA).

The DOT would primarily deal with the economic aspects of air transport described in the next section. The FAA's main responsibility is air safety, including aircraft operating procedures, the movement of hazardous materials, record keeping standards and aircraft maintenance and the licensing of technical staff and ground facilities. The FAA issues an operating licence subject to compliance with their regulations and standards. The TSA regulates various security aspects of air cargo transport. Its regulations cover staff, facilities and procedures.

More specifically, under Title 49 of the United States Code, anyone who wants to provide air transportation service as a US air carrier or foreign air carrier must first obtain two separate authorisations from the Department of Transportation: 'safety' authority from the Federal Aviation Administration and 'economic' authority from the Office of the Secretary of Transportation. Economic authority for US carriers may be in the form of a certificate for interstate or foreign passengers and/or cargo and mail authority, an all-cargo air transportation certificate, or authorisation as a commuter air carrier. Economic authority for foreign carriers may be in the form of either a foreign air carrier permit or an exemption.

Leasing allows airlines in one country to operate aircraft that are registered in other countries; if such aircraft are also crewed and maintained by airlines or companies based in other countries the arrangement is called a 'wet lease'. This means that the licensing authority of the first country has little control over the standards imposed by the other country. In most cases this would not be a problem, but in some cases the safety oversight exercised by other countries over their airlines, specifically those involved in wet leasing, is considered inadequate. For this reason wet-leased aircraft are only permitted for a limited duration,[1] in the case of the EU up to seven months. Article 13 of Commission Regulation 1008/2008 includes a section on wet leasing:

> 3. A Community air carrier wet leasing aircraft registered in a third country from another undertaking shall obtain prior approval for the operation from the competent licensing authority. The competent authority may grant an approval if:

---

[1]   The US is a notable exception in not allowing its airlines to wet lease aircraft from companies registered outside the US, a significant bone of contention in EU/US ASA negotiations.

a) the Community air carrier demonstrates to the satisfaction of the competent authority that all safety standards equivalent to those imposed by Community or national law are met; and

b) one of the following conditions is fulfilled:

i. the Community air carrier justifies such leasing on the basis of exceptional needs, in which case an approval may be granted for a period of up to seven months that may be renewed once for a further period of up to seven months;

ii. the Community air carrier demonstrates that the leasing is necessary to satisfy seasonal capacity needs, which cannot reasonably be satisfied through leasing aircraft registered within the Community, in which case the approval may be renewed; or

iii. the Community air carrier demonstrates that the leasing is necessary to overcome operational difficulties and it is not possible or reasonable to lease aircraft registered within the Community, in which case the approval shall be of limited duration strictly necessary for overcoming the difficulties.

Wet leasing is usually likely to be a short-term measure to provide peak season capacity or replace an aircraft that is temporarily grounded. However, it has been used for longer-term requirements for freighter capacity in cases where it is not economic for an airline to own (or dry lease), crew and maintain its own small fleet of aircraft. A number of specialist airlines such as Atlas Air, Kalitta, Southern, Evergreen and Air Atlanta Icelandic have filled this niche market and provide freighters on a wet lease or ACMI (Aircraft, Crew, Maintenance, Insurance) basis to airlines such as British Airways, Qantas and Emirates cargo divisions.

However, the regulatory problem remains and where a longer-term wet lease contract is signed it may be necessary to satisfy the regulator that the aircraft meets its technical requirements.

British Airways operates three B747-400F aircraft, which are ultimately owned or leased by US carrier Atlas Air. All three aircraft are leased by Atlas Air to Global Supply Systems Ltd (GSS), a UK company that is owned by GSS Employee Benefit Trust (51 percent) and Atlas Air Worldwide Holdings (49 percent). GSS is a UK licensed airline with its 100 or so pilots, technical and administrative staff, and its three B747-400F aircraft have been placed on the UK register. GSS then wet leases the aircraft to British Airways, the contract renewed for a further five years in September 2007. This means that the British Airways wet lease is now from a UK licensed airline and no longer falls under article 13.3(b) of the EU Regulation 2407/92. Following UK CAA concerns, Global Supply Systems Ltd. was set up in 2001 as a British all-cargo carrier whose principal business was providing aircraft on long-term leases to other airlines on an ACMI basis. This followed complaints to the UK CAA that the wet lease should not be allowed to continue under 2407/92. Operations commenced, or continued under the new structure, in June 2002 using a B747-400F leased from Atlas Air. A second similar aircraft joined the fleet in October 2002 and a third arrived in August 2003. Its major and probably only customer is British Airways, on whose behalf it operates scheduled freighter services to the Far East, India, the Middle East, Europe and the US. It reported 2009 freight tonne-kms (FTKs) of 822 million compared to British Airways all-cargo traffic of 752 million, or 91 percent; this compared with FTKs carried on BA's passenger services of 3.5 million in the same year. The new company structure for the wet-leased aircraft surprisingly seemed to satisfy the CAA in terms of compliance with the EU Regulation, and furthermore it rather looked as though control of the UK company might have effectively been by US rather than EU interests.

3.1.2 Financial Fitness

The granting of air operator's licences, whether for passenger or cargo airlines, involves the assessment of the technical and financial fitness of the airline applying for the licence. The technical fitness is assessed to ensure that the airline operates safely in conformity with international standards. This would include the airworthiness of the aircraft that the airline intends to operate, the licensing of its personnel, provisions for maintenance, etc. The ICAO's annexes lay down recommended practices for these but do not include financial and economic matters.

Financial fitness is required to make sure, as far as possible, that the airline has sufficient capital at the outset to continue trading at least for the first year and in some cases for two years. Monitoring continues this financial oversight based on the submission of financial statements for subsequent periods. This process of assessment is generally carried out by the country's DCA or Ministry of Transport. It varies considerably in strictness from country to country. Countries like the US and UK that have above average new entrants and airline failures tend to have stricter hurdles to meet. This may seem contradictory, but the failures occur more amongst charter and cargo operators that face large seasonal and cyclical variations in demand.

Setting the financial hurdles too high risks deterring new entrants. These airlines help to ensure a competitive industry and are often the best source of innovation and change. Setting the hurdles too low leads to failure and disruption, as passengers are stranded at their destinations, often in the peak period when seats on alternative flights are not available.

Thus more stringent financial fitness tests would have a cost of lower efficiency and higher operating costs for existing operators. This would be offset by less airline failures. However, given the likelihood of failure (see next section) these risks might be better covered by some kind of insurance. Airline failure is more common amongst charter, cargo and low-cost operators than network carriers. On the other hand most new entrants fit into one or other of these business models.

Network carrier failures can occur especially at times of major economic downturn. Examples of this are the bankruptcy of Sabena and Swissair after 9/11. In the US, bankruptcy is often avoided by reorganising under Chapter 11 or acquisition by another carrier. In both cases passenger contracts are honoured and disruption is negligible.

Once an airline enters bankruptcy or liquidation it ceases trading and passenger contracts can no longer be fulfilled. Assets are sold and secured creditors reimbursed. Most of the assets are already pledged against loans or leases and there is usually little money left for unsecured creditors, which include the air traffic liabilities (passengers and cargo shippers). Credit and some debit card companies will be in touch with bankruptcy administrators (and bonding scheme administrators) to check whether they will become liable for passenger, cargo shipper or forwarder reimbursement.

In some countries, an airline that is approaching bankruptcy might be administered by a court or firm appointed by its creditors. This ensures that the airline continues to operate and honour its air traffic liability commitments. The administrator tries to get agreement for a recovery plan, while the airline has certain protection in terms of deferring certain payments or seizing of assets. The best known of these procedures is Chapter 11 in the US. At the end of the protection period the airline more often emerges as a slimmed down more efficient airline that has some chance of continued existence. Occasionally, the recovery plan cannot be agreed and the airline is liquidated (Chapter 7 in the US).

In Europe schemes that are similar to the US Chapter 11 are the German *Insolvenzordnung* of 5 October 1994 and its amendments. Delays in payments of debt are also possible in the Netherlands (*surcéance van betaling*) and in the UK such proceedings are termed *Moratorium of Payments* (Booz & Company, 2009). Countries that have this possibility (e.g. the US, the UK, Germany, the Netherlands and France) should have less disruption to customers and thus less need for cover from insurance or bonding. However, in practice administrators are often too slow to prevent the grounding of aircraft and the termination of operations.

3.2 Regulation of International Air Services

Over the past two decades, international air transport liberalisation has been gathering pace. The process was largely started by the US through their re-negotiation of many of its key bilateral Air Services Agreements between 1977 and 1985. These were initially with European countries but their 'open skies' formula was subsequently applied both in Latin America and Asia. The process started in the lead up to US domestic deregulation that became law in 1978. Deregulation inside the European Union had to wait until 1993 when Regulation 2407/97 was introduced that completed this process in 1998. This replaced all ASAs that previously governed air services between each EU country, which were then treated as domestic flights.

3.2.1 Air Services Agreements

Air Services Agreements (ASAs) have generally been negotiated on a bilateral basis between two countries and are thus often called 'bilaterals'. These agreements usually cover the carriage of both passengers and cargo by air, including both passenger and freighter flights. Although a significant amount of air cargo is carried on passenger flights some countries have signed separate ASAs for all-cargo flights only. An example of this was the US–Japan 1996 cargo agreement, which was designed to clarify a number of technical problems such as Federal Express's fifth freedoms it had acquired with Flying Tigers.

All flights within the EU were gradually liberalised from the late 1980s, with the final third 'package' introduced at the end of 1992, and completely implemented by 1998. It had been hoped that the EU style liberalisation, described as an open aviation area, might be extended to include the US and perhaps Canada. However, little progress has so far been made, with major sticking points being the ownership and control clauses and a number of points including environmental issues.

In addition to the above, Australia and New Zealand have signed an open aviation area between their countries, and other initiatives are underway through multilateral forums such as Mercosur and ASEAN. So far, multilateral approaches have had limited success. More recent encouraging signs have come from two of the world's largest markets: India and China. India has recently signed a number of significantly liberalised agreements, and China is moving in a similar direction, albeit slowly.

Most ASAs include broadly similar clauses or articles, going back to the original model 'Bermuda I' agreement between the US and UK. One of these is a statement that the airlines designated by each country should have a 'fair and equal opportunity' to compete. This has not always been adhered to in the past, for example when one country decrees that the national flag carrier should be used for air trips by government employees. The next covers the traffic rights permitted by route and in some cases frequency restrictions applied to the airlines of each country. There are articles on designation of airlines and also safety and security. Customs duties and charges are also covered, and it is here that the uplift of fuel for international flights is given tax-free status. Pricing, airport fees and government subsidies are also addressed, as are the mechanisms for dealing with disputes and notice of termination of the agreement.

3.2.2 Air Services Agreements: Air Traffic Rights

Worldwide
Air traffic rights for the carriage of freight and mail can be exercised both on passenger and freighter flights. Those related to passenger flights, which also carry cargo, depend on the carriage of passengers and the negotiations are mainly concerned with factors that are governed by passenger markets. Thus airline

Freedom	Air cargo examples
FIRST FREEDOM To overfly one country en-route to another	Lufthansa Cargo: Germany over Russia to China
SECOND FREEDOM To make a technical stop in another country	Lufthansa Cargo: Germany over Russia to China
THIRD FREEDOM To carry air traffic from the home country to another country	Lufthansa Cargo: air cargo from Germany to China
FOURTH FREEDOM To carry air traffic to the home country from another country	Lufthansa Cargo: air cargo from China to Germany
FIFTH FREEDOM To carry air traffic between two countries by an airline of a third country on route with origin / destination in its home country	Lufthansa Cargo: air cargo from Australia to China en route for Germany
SIXTH FREEDOM* To carry air traffic between two countries by an airline of a third country on two routes connecting in its home country	Cargolux: air cargo from North America to/from points in Africa via their Luxembourg base/hub
SEVENTH FREEDOM To carry air traffic between two countries by an airline of a third country on a route outside its home country	DHL's regional hub at Bahrain. Flights operated using B727, A300 and other smaller freighters based there to/from points in the region
EIGHTH FREEDOM OR CONSECUTIVE CABOTAGE To carry air traffic within a country by an airline of another country on a route with origin / destination in its home country	Cathay Pacific Cargo: air cargo from Atlanta to Dallas/Fort Worth (within USA) with flight continuing to Hong Kong
NINTH FREEDOM OR 'STAND-ALONE' CABOTAGE To carry air traffic entirely within an airline's home country	Tiger Airways Australia's traffic within Australia (no freighter airline examples)

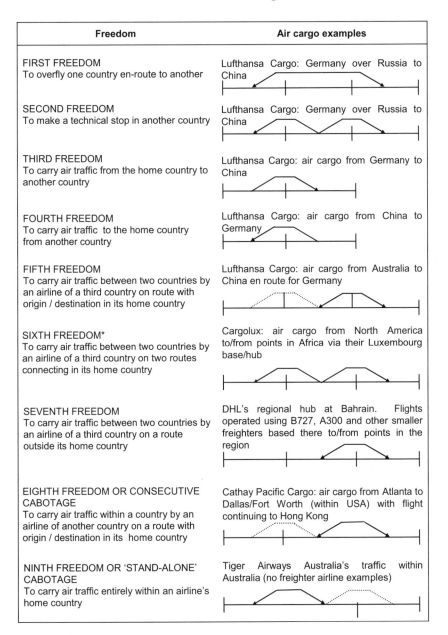

Figure 3.1   Freedoms of the Air (air traffic rights)

Note: * The term 'sixth freedom' was coined to describe the combination of two sets of third and fourth rights, reflecting the reality of hub and spoke networks (it is not usually recognised in air services agreements).

Source: Author based on Manual on the Regulation of International Air Transport (Doc 9626, Part 4).

designation and routes will be passenger airlines seeking rights and the demand potential for passengers. These have been liberalised over the past 20–30 years, especially with regard to designation of national airlines permitted to operate, ranging from single to multiple designation. The number of third and fourth freedom routes has also been opened up, with the addition of some fifth freedoms (see Figure 3.1). Some airlines have been able to expand their hub airport in their country of registration by combining two sets of third/fourth freedoms to carry sixth freedom traffic. Examples of this were Singapore Airlines and more recently Emirates Airlines. Flying wide-body passenger aircraft they have also been able to carry significant amounts of cargo on these routes, mainly from Australasia to Europe.

Air cargo traffic rights are generally also granted under the same Air Services Agreement as passengers, and thus have benefited from the gradual opening up of rights that was evident for passengers. In a few cases (e.g. US/Japan) separate agreements were signed for all-cargo or freighter routes. These are often more liberal than their passenger counterparts, since they provide less of a threat to national or flag carriers that depend on passengers.

Table 3.1   Air Services Agreements and cargo provisions, 1980 to 2005

Years (inclusive)	Number signed	% with all-cargo seventh freedom rights	% with general sixth freedom rights	% with specific all-cargo routings	% containing all-cargo clauses
2001 to 2005	234	10	16	46	29
1996 to 2000	294	10	17	33	45
1991 to 1995	678	0	2	5	14
1986 to 1990	477	0	0.2	2	8
1981 to 1985	294	0	0	3	4
1976 to 1980	538	0	0	2	6

Source: Aero-Accords in *Airline Business*, January 2006.

Table 3.1 focuses on the cargo-specific provisions in ASAs signed between 1976 and 2005. It shows that liberalisation worldwide only really took off in the 1990s, with an increasing number having all-cargo clauses and specific cargo routings. Sixth freedoms can be operated without specific provisions and so seventh freedoms are a better indicator of a genuine wish to move to open skies. These are still only granted in a small number of cases.

Various attempts have been made to evaluate the degree of liberalisation has taken place. Listing the number of liberal ASAs or provisions in ASAs (as in Table 3.1) does not give a representative picture that takes into account the importance of the bilateral relationship. This could be measured by the actual or potential passengers and freight carried between the two countries. An attempt to remedy this was proposed by the WTO Secretariat through its QUASAR work (WTO, 2006). This used the ICAO World Air Services Agreement database on CD-ROM (WASA). Its approach for each ASA was to:

- assess the main market access features (e.g. designation, traffic rights, etc.);
- categorise each agreement by type;
- weight the agreements by traffic covered;
- check the results against commercial data.

An index (ALI) was constructed by assigning points to each of the market access provisions of the agreement. For example, approval for tariffs required by the governments of both countries would get no points, while unrestricted pricing with no approval would get eight points. Multiple designation gets four points and single designation zero. ALI is the sum of all the points assigned and can range from zero to 50. It does not, however, differentiate between passengers and freight. A World Bank study that examined the air cargo provisions in ASAs concluded that liberalisation of these (by replacing them with an 'open skies'[2] regime) would reduce air transport costs by 8 percent, implying an increase in trade of 10 percent. Its econometric approach included various explanatory variables including 'regulatory quality' and a dummy for 'open skies'. The latter is fairly well defined but the difficulty remains in knowing what the starting position was.

In order to obtain a better picture of progress, the following sections examine developments on a regional basis, starting with the multilateral agreement between EU countries and the US, focusing on the US and EU separately and concluding with key Asian markets.

EU/US Air Services Agreement of 2007[3]

Many expected the EU/US agreement of 2007 to result in an 'open aviation area' but what emerged, at least for the first stage, was 'open skies'. The agreement contained a proposed second stage 'open aviation area' largely dependent on the US government being able to deliver the necessary change to the ownership and control clause. As an 'open skies' agreement all restrictions on third/fourth freedoms rights were lifted and any number of carriers could be designated by either side. US carriers had unlimited fifth freedom rights between EU countries and carriers from both sides had generous beyond rights. All this applied to

---

2   Which essentially means the full freedom to airlines designated by each country to use third, fourth and fifth freedom traffic rights.

3   Council Decision 2007/339/EC, Official Journal L.134, 25 May 2007.

both passenger and cargo flights, but cargo was mentioned specifically in the following two articles:

Article 3:1

(c): the right to perform international air transportation between points on the following routes:

> i. for airlines of the United States (hereinafter US airlines), from points behind the United States via the United States and intermediate points to any point or points in any Member State or States and beyond; and for all-cargo service, between any Member State and any point or points (including in any other Member States);

> ii. for airlines of the European Community and its Member States (hereinafter Community airlines), from points behind the Member States via the Member States and intermediate points to any point or points in the United States and beyond; for all-cargo service, between the United States and any point or points; and, for combination services, between any point or points in the United States and any point or points in any member of the European Common Aviation Area (hereinafter the ECAA) as of the date of signature of this Agreement;

Article 10:10

Notwithstanding any other provision of this Agreement, airlines and indirect providers of cargo transportation of the Parties shall be permitted, without restriction, to employ in connection with international air transportation any surface transportation for cargo to or from any points in the territories of the Parties, or in third countries, including transport to and from all airports with customs facilities, and including, where applicable, the right to transport cargo in bond under applicable laws and regulations. Such cargo, whether moving by surface or by air, shall have access to airport customs processing and facilities.

Airlines may elect to perform their own surface transportation or to provide it through arrangements with other surface carriers, including surface transportation operated by other airlines and indirect providers of cargo air transportation. Such inter-modal cargo services may be offered at a single, through price for the air and surface transportation combined, provided that shippers are not misled as to the facts concerning such transportation.

United States

Until 1977, air cargo carried within the US was regulated by the Civil Aeronautics Board (CAB), as was the carriage of passengers. Route entry and pricing were controlled, with air fares and rates having to be justified to the CAB on a cost plus reasonable profit basis. However, there were growing pressures for liberalisation, and it was recognised that air cargo could be opened up as a first stage. Most of the incumbent airlines involved in carrying both passengers and freight were not vocal in the support for change with the exception of two all-cargo carriers, Flying Tigers and Federal Express.

The result of this was the enactment of the Air Cargo Act in 1977 which totally deregulated air cargo flights within the US, subject to some safeguards. The Airline Deregulation Act in the following year did the same for airlines that carried both passengers and cargo. Any licensed carrier could now enter the US market, and indirect carriers such as freight forwarders were now allowed to charter their own flights. Examples of this were Emery Air Freight and Airborne Express. Rates were considered legal unless found to be 'unjustly discriminatory, or unduly preferential, or unduly prejudicial, or predatory'. Rates no longer had to be filed with governments or justified in relation to costs.

Grandfather rights were offered to 70 all-cargo carriers in 1977, and after the one-year grace period a further 20 licences were granted (OECD, 1999). Flying Tigers rapidly expanded its domestic network to become the largest US all-cargo carrier.[4]

DHL Airways provided the US domestic airlift for the worldwide network of DHL Worldwide Express (DHLWE). After DHLWE was acquired by the German Post Office (Deutsche Post), FedEx and UPS challenged the citizenship of DHL Airways. Without designation as a US citizen, the airline could not provide the service for DHLWE that it did. This would force DHLWE to find alternative arrangements for serving its customers within the US. An administrative law judge (ALJ) was appointed to examine the citizenship question regarding DHL Airways in April 2003. However, the subject of the citizenship challenge changed in the midst of the proceeding because the ownership of DHL Airways changed in July 2003. At that time, a group of investors (including the president of DHL Airways) purchased DHL Airways, renamed it ASTAR Air Cargo and changed its senior management and ownership structure. Following the change and agreeing with the decision of the law judge (ALJ) the DOT rejected the petition and confirmed that ASTAR was controlled by US citizens. In its decision DOT said that 'although ASTAR obtains most of its business from the DHL network of companies' DHL did not have any 'potential ability to exercise substantial influence over ASTAR's decisions'.[5] Subsequently DHL decided to withdraw from the domestic US market and contract out its international flights to and from the US to Polar Air (see Chapter 5) with its international packages distributed using the flights of ASTAR Air Cargo from its Cincinnati, Ohio, hub (as an entirely independent US airline).

---

4   It was subsequently acquired by Federal Express (see Chapter 5).
5   Docket OST-2002-13089, 13 May 2004.

The European Union (EU)
The EU also experienced pressures to liberalise air services (as in the US) but with its international air routes it was inherently more complex to achieve this. As in the US there was little pressure to liberalise from existing air carriers, with the driving force provided by the EU institutions that were pushing for a 'level playing field' within the EU. Certain countries, notably the UK and the Netherlands, were also keen to open up EU aviation.

The regulation that liberalised air cargo entered force one year ahead of the so-called Third Package that liberalised all intra-EU air services published in 1992 (and which replaced it). The one-year lead time was similar to the process that had taken place in the US almost 15 years earlier in 1978. The 1991 air cargo regulation (294/91) introduced five important principles:

1. national ownership replaced by EU ownership;
2. unrestricted third, fourth and fifth freedom rights on all intra-EU routes;
3. no restrictions on frequency, capacity and aircraft type;
4. complete rate setting freedom, subject to regulatory intervention on predatory grounds;
5. no distinction between scheduled and charter services.

A sixth on full flexibility to operate truck feeder services was agreed but excluded from the Regulation due to complications with other legislation. On the first point very little change occurred since ownership was now only important for ASAs between EU and third countries. Here the changes had to wait for another 15 years until the EU negotiated 'horizontal' agreements. On the second point no seventh freedoms were permitted but these had limited relevance to the intra-EU markets.

Compared to the US deregulation, EU liberalisation had a very limited impact on the air cargo market. This was hardly surprising since the distances are much shorter and trucking had already replaced flights on many intra-EU routes. Of much greater importance were routes between the EU and Asia and North America which were still governed by separate ASAs negotiated by each EU state.

India
A policy of 'open skies' for air cargo was adopted in 1990, initially for a three-year period and extended in 1992 on a permanent basis.[6] Under this new policy any airlines, whether Indian or foreign carriers which met specified operational and safety requirements, were allowed to operate scheduled and non-scheduled cargo services to/from any airports in India where custom/immigration facilities were available. In addition, regulatory control over cargo rates for major export commodities had been abolished so that carriers were free to set their own rates.

The government would also give favourable consideration to applications by foreign airlines for additional passenger flights operated by mixed passenger/

6   Indian Aeronautical Information Circular AIQ No. 18/1992.

freight aircraft. These new policies were implemented on a unilateral basis without requiring comparable rights for Indian carriers from bilateral partners in return.

According to Indian government statistics, the period since the adoption of an 'open skies' policy has seen a strong growth in international air cargo traffic, which increased from about 300,000 tonnes in 1991 to over 420,000 tonnes in 1998. The traffic increase was mainly due to a sizeable growth in scheduled services operated by foreign airlines (about 80 percent increase for the same period), most of which were permitted to inaugurate under an 'open skies' policy. For example, Lufthansa, Air France and KLM doubled their capacities to India, while most foreign airlines adopted a strategy of selective entry in peak periods without long-term commitments. Carriage on foreign airlines' non-scheduled services also doubled for the first three years, but sharply declined to less than the 1991 level by 1998 because of a marked shift to scheduled services and sea cargo. The boom in air cargo was propelled by the progress of the country's economic liberalisation, although infrastructure bottlenecks including a shortage of warehousing facilities have gradually hampered potential cargo business opportunities.

Faced with stiff competition from foreign airlines, Air India, a state-owned national carrier, has seen its market share of international cargo tonnage reduced from 23 percent in 1991 to 16 percent in 1992 and has remained around that level since. To recover its market share and augment its capacity, Air India submitted a fleet acquisition programme, for which the government had expressed support, and new wet-leased freighter operations. Indian Airlines, another state-owned carrier serving domestic and short-haul international routes, tripled its cargo operation from 1991 to 1998. The revenue from cargo reached about 10 percent of Indian Airlines' revenue, but its market share for international cargo was still about 3 percent, compared to 10 percent for passengers.

Despite this liberal policy, traffic rights can still be a limiting factor as these also require approval from the national authorities of the airline's home country and, in case of fifth or seventh freedom, traffic connecting two foreign countries. As several carriers, including British Airways, Lufthansa and China Airlines, use fifth freedom traffic rights to and from India, these restrictions can be overcome.

Asia Pacific Economic Community (APEC)
Other countries in Asia have pushed for further liberalisation and open skies, notably Singapore and Brunei. Both have no domestic services, relatively small home markets and international 'flag' carriers. These airlines rely on liberal traffic rights to survive, especially fifth freedoms. For example Singapore Airlines unsuccessfully tried to negotiate fifth freedom traffic rights from the UK (Heathrow) to the US, so as to allow it to continue its Singapore/London flight to New York or other points in the US on a viable basis. Both countries are signatories to the Multilateral Agreement on the Liberalisation of International Air Transport (MALIAT), in addition to Chile, New Zealand and the US. Signed in 2001, this agreement offers 'open skies' between these countries and unlimited

fifth and seventh freedoms to third countries. It also provides for other countries to join on an all-cargo basis only (Geloso Grosso and Shepherd, 2009).

A 2007 study of ASAs in APEC countries confirmed the notion that cargo was treated more liberally than passengers (see Table 3.2). Less bilaterals had route restrictions and the granting of seventh freedom traffic rights was more prevalent for cargo than for passengers. On the other hand third/fourth freedoms appeared less open and fifth freedoms broadly comparable to passenger rights in relation to total ASAs examined.

Table 3.2   Analysis of ASAs in APEC countries, 2005

	Passenger	Freight
Open route schedule		
ASAs included	293	274
Number of ASAs	52	56
% of total assessed	16.8	20.4
Restricted route schedule		
ASAs included	310	275
Number of ASAs	239	115
% of total assessed	77.1	41.8
Open third/fourth freedom		
ASAs included	310	274
Number of ASAs	170	74
% of total assessed	54.8	27.0
Open fifth freedom		
ASAs included	310	254
Number of ASAs	85	66
% of total assessed	27.4	26.0
Open seventh freedom		
ASAs included	286	221
Number of ASAs	7	25
% of total assessed	2.4	11.3

Source: Thomas and Tan, 2007.

The situation since 2005 has improved further with some progress achieved through the smaller group of Association of South-East Asian Nations (ASEAN) countries and also on a bilateral basis between the US and a number of Asian countries. ASEAN countries are generally more protective at least on the passenger side. Its members signed a Memorandum of Understanding on Air Freight Services in 2002, which opened up third/fourth freedom rights with no restriction on frequency or aircraft type, but with a maximum permitted capacity first of 100 tonnes per week; this was increased to 250 tonnes in 2007 (Geloso Grosso and Shepherd, 2009).

3.2.3 Air Services Agreements: Ownership and Control

According to the US General Accounting Office, in July 2003 no US airlines had any significant shareholding held by foreign interests (GAO, 2003). Two US majors had stakes held by a US subsidiary of a French-based insurance company but these amounted to only 18 percent (Northwest Airlines) and 13 percent (Delta Airlines). However, around the late 1980s 'a number of foreign airlines had invested significant amounts of capital in US airlines, only to later disinvest due in part to US policies concerning airline control' (GAO, 2003). Examples of this were KLM in Northwest, British Airways in US Air (44 percent of equity and 21 percent of voting rights), and Lufthansa in United Airlines. Most recently Virgin America's licence was under threat when the US DOT found in December 2006 that the airline had failed to establish that it was a US citizen, and that it would be owned by and remain under the actual control of US citizens. Virgin America subsequently changed its financial arrangements, management and corporate governance. These changes, notably the establishment of a voting trust to ensure that control was exercised by US citizens, subsequently satisfied the DOT. Of relevance here is the DHL Airways case discussed above.

In the early 1990s DOT had proposed that the US foreign ownership limit be raised from 25 percent to 49 percent, mainly as a result of the dire financial state of many large US airlines, but this was not adopted. The issue was raised most recently during the EU/US Air Services Agreement negotiations in response to the EU request to bring it in line with the 49 percent applied by EU states. However, the US did not give way and an 'open skies' was agreed rather than an open aviation area which many had desired.

3.2.4 Competition Regulation

Together with progress on moving to a more open market has been the increasing intervention by competition authorities. Proposed mergers and alliances often need approval but most of these are principally concerned with passenger markets. The other area of scrutiny is concerted practices, in particular the collusion in the setting of air fares and rates which is illegal in the US, EU and many other countries. The most active of these types of investigation have been by the US (Department of Justice) and by the EU (the Directorate for Competition). Investigations have also been initiated by similar authorities in Australia, New Zealand, Canada and Korea. It is difficult to distinguish in some of these cases between a genuine desire to foster fair and open competition and the bandwagon effect following initial US concerns. The potential for raising not insignificant sums of money for the exchequer from fines should not be overlooked. For example, the South Korean Fair Trade Commission fined 19 airlines a total of 120 billion Won (US$98m) for fixing air cargo fuel surcharges by holding joint meetings.

The setting of air cargo rates had historically been agreed through IATA conferences, where most airlines met to agree their rates and interline arrangements. These rates were then submitted for approval by governments (see Chapter 10). Following liberalisation the tariff conferences were deemed to restrict competition, initially given a block exemption (in the EU until June 1997) and finally outlawed. Following the withdrawal of the block exemption by the Commission, the IATA notified its cargo tariff consultation system under Council Regulation 3975/87 and applied for an individual exemption. The system notified by the IATA is similar to that for which the block exemption was withdrawn. According to the IATA, the tariff conference system facilitates cargo interlining. Interlining occurs when cargo is carried for part/all of the journey by an airline other than the airline which sold the ticket. The cargo tariffs fixed by the tariff conferences are then used to calculate the participating carrier's compensation.

In liberalised markets, cargo rates were set by individual carriers and no longer required to be submitted for approval by government. However, with the introduction of fuel surcharges, a major part of the tariff charged to forwarders and shippers, the possibility of collusion arose. An indication of this is given by identical fuel surcharges introduced on the same day by a number of carriers. Collusion was then confirmed by anti-trust authorities finding evidence of such contacts between airlines from their so-called 'dawn raids' on airline offices. The following investigates took place:

February 2006
The US Department of Justice and the European Commission begin probes into suspected price-fixing activity by air cargo carriers.

September 2006
Lufthansa offers $85 million to settle class action claims (civil lawsuits) relating to the cargo price-fixing case in the US and is accepted into the DoJ's leniency programme.

August 2007
BA fined $200 million and Korean Air fined $100 million by the US DoJ for their parts in the air cargo affair. BA fined a further £121.5m by the UK authorities for similar anti-competitive activity.

November 2007
Qantas fined US$61m by DoJ in connection with breaches of antitrust laws related to fuel surcharges imposed on its air cargo services between 2000 and 2006.

December 2007
The EC sends letters to several carriers alleging they took part in cargo price-fixing.

British Airways chief executive Willie Walsh was reported as saying that 'fuel surcharges are a legitimate way of recovering costs and when set independently do not breach competition law. I want to reassure our passengers that they have not been overcharged'. The decisions by the various authorities claim that customers were overcharged, although they do not provide supporting analyses or data. The US DoJ seemed to jump from fuel surcharges to rates without recognising the possibility that collusion on rates might have been accompanied by independent reductions in underlying rates. This is very difficult to prove.

The EC's investigation (which had not been concluded by mid-2010) and claims allege a price-fixing conspiracy involving cargo surcharges. They did not raise any issues about passenger surcharges, although one of BA's settlements included claims about passenger fares. Conversely, and contrary to earlier suggestions, the cargo claim is not limited to an alleged agreement among airlines to stick with the fuel surcharges posted on Lufthansa's website. The allegations apparently extend to other surcharges to cover the added costs of anti-terrorism measures and war-risk insurance after the outbreak of war in Iraq.

The case also concerns the provision of freight forwarding services. The offices of various international freight forwarders were inspected through 'dawn raids' by the European Commission in October 2007. Their investigation was in response to allegations from shippers that various forwarders fixed prices by colluding on the imposition, level, timing and application of various surcharges, in breach of Article 101 of the Treaty. This was related to freight forwarding services in four different global markets during 2003 and 2004.[7] Deutsche Post DHL was given immunity by the EU Commission's competition authorities in return for cooperation. Such arrangements generally follow 'whistle-blowing' by one player to gain advantage. While this system generally helps correct a situation of asymmetric information, there have been cases where whistle-blowers were selective in the information they provided and gave the regulators a false picture of the situation. The freight forwarders have themselves got in on the act by filing civil damages claims against the airlines in the US and Australia, with shippers suing forwarders and airlines.[8] Air New Zealand, BA, Cathay Pacific, Japan Airlines, Lufthansa, Qantas

---

7 No ruling on this case had been made by mid-2010; this is typical of such cases and means that forwarders (and airlines) often make provisions in their financial statements for estimated future liabilities (fines).

8 American Airlines settled a class action claim by paying US$5 million without admitting fault.

and Singapore Airlines have been named in a civil class action filed by freight forwarders in Australia, and Malaysian Airlines in the US suit. Most of the price-fixing cases concerned air cargo, but the US also fined British Airways US$100m for collusion on fuel surcharges imposed on North Atlantic air fares with Virgin Atlantic.[9]

All this makes cargo mangers very cautious about who they talk to and when they change their market prices and by how much. Price leadership is not illegal, but if an airline follows another one by raising fuel surcharges by the same amount albeit a week later, the authorities might ask questions if the second airline has fully hedged fuel at a much lower price.

3.3 Mail Regulation

Since air mail is a key part of air cargo traffic, the regulations concerning the carriage of mail are also relevant. These apply to postal services in each country which up to now, at least for letter post, have largely been provided by government agencies. Mail also includes parcels, however, and the integrators have been taking an increasing part of this market.

The EU Postal Directive of February 2008 stated that the main part of the market should be liberalised by 2011, with a fully liberalised market throughout the EU by 2013 at the latest. By 2009, the United Kingdom, Germany and Finland had formally liberalised their mail markets although in practice it was still difficult for new players to enter these markets. The previously government-owned incumbent mail operators are protected from competition in most EU countries, especially for mail rather than parcels business. These operators have been privatised in Germany and the Netherlands and are now owned by large integrators in both countries.

The process of liberalisation of the postal market within the Netherlands, which began in the late 1980s, is continuing. Pursuant to the EU Postal Directive, as of 1 January 2006 the restriction that reserved the provision of letters up to 100 grams exclusively to TNT (the reserved postal services) was reduced to 50 grams. On 13 April 2006 the Dutch government decided to fully liberalise the postal market in the Netherlands in 2008 on the condition that there is a 'level playing field' with the British and German postal markets (which was by 2010 not yet the case). The Dutch government also agreed upon the proposal for a new Dutch Postal Act and fully liberalised their postal services in 2009.

---

9   Virgin Atlantic was not fined because it revealed the price-fixing to the authorities.

3.4 Future Air Cargo Liberalisation

ICAO report in their 2008 annual report to Council that 17 new 'open skies' agreements were concluded by 21 states, bringing the total to 153 agreements involving 96 states. These bilateral agreements provide for full-market access without restrictions on designations, route rights, capacity, frequencies, code-sharing and tariffs. At the regional level, at least 13 liberalised agreements or arrangements were in operation, with another country joining MALIAT, and an agreement between nine countries in the Caribbean. The Association of South-East Asian Nations (ASEAN) also concluded the ASEAN Multilateral Agreement on Air Services and the ASEAN Multilateral Agreement on the Full Liberalization of Air Freight Services.

The Organisation for Economic Co-operation and Development (OECD) has focused considerable resources on proposals for further liberalisation of international air cargo on a worldwide basis. It has put forward a draft multinational agreement that would allow considerable freedom for freighter operators to fly the most economical routes and greater flexibility in ownership and control. Market entry would be facilitated by unlimited fifth and seventh freedoms allowed on a multilateral basis. Fifth freedoms that allow the most economical routings of freighter flights (see Figure 3.1) need a larger number of countries to agree to them. Seventh freedoms are less useful on the major trade lanes for general air cargo and more appropriate to integrators. The latter would then have more flexibility to base aircraft in third countries and establish regional hubs without having to rely on local airlines.

Traditional ASAs require that the air carriers designated by a contracting party be substantially owned and effectively controlled by nationals of that contracting party. This is done to safeguard essential safety requirements in order to avoid the emergence of substandard air carriers. Such requirements impede the flow of inward investment to contracting states and thus inhibit the development of the air cargo industries: precisely the opposite of the results the proposed principles are meant to encourage. For international air cargo services to become more efficient, restrictions on inward investment should be eliminated, and air carriers should be able to determine their ownership and control structures freely, based on capital and strategic business needs. The OECD proposed that this aim could be achieved by changing the standard ownership clause to:[10]

- a designated air carrier has to be incorporated and is required to have its *principal place of business* in the territory of the Contracting Party that designates it;
- and second, it is required that the designated air carrier be appropriately licensed by the Contracting Party that designates it.

---

10   OECD Workshop on the Principles for the liberalisation of air cargo. Paris, 4–5 October 2000.

The same Workshop also suggested the scope should not be limited for air cargo operators to diversify into related businesses such as trucking and freight forwarding, and that ground handling should be opened up (as it has, to a large extent, in the EU).

The ICAO summarised one way forward at a worldwide air transport conference held in Montreal in March 2003. It proposed a possible way to liberalise the ownership and control clause in ASAs in the same way as the OECD above by moving to the 'principal place of business plus a strong link' approach which had already been endorsed by the ICAO's Council. This put forward a new designation article to be inserted in ASAs:

Article X: Designation and Authorization

1. Each Party shall have the right to designate in writing to the other Party [an airline] [one or more airlines] [as many airlines as it wishes] to operate the agreed services [in accordance with this Agreement] and to withdraw or alter such designation.

2. On receipt of such a designation, and of application from the designated airline, in the form and manner prescribed for operating authorization [and technical permission,] each Party shall grant the appropriate operating authorization with minimum procedural delay, provided that:

   a) the designated airline has its principal place of business [and permanent residence] in the territory of the designating Party;

   b) the Party designating the airline has and maintains effective regulatory control of the airline;

   c) the Party designating the airline is in compliance with the provisions set forth in the articles on safety and aviation security; and

   d) the designated airline is qualified to meet other conditions prescribed under the laws and regulations normally applied to the operation of international air transport services by the Party receiving the designation.

This would allow air cargo operators to set up regional feeder airlines, provided they met the above conditions. These were expanded on in a footnote to the ICAO proposal, specifically noting that the airline should have a 'substantial amount of its operations and capital investment in physical facilities in the territory of the designating Party, pays income tax, registers and bases its aircraft there, and employs a significant number of nationals in managerial, technical and operational positions'.

The Word Trade Organisation (WTO) is an international governmental body committed to multilateral trade liberalisation. It has in the past considered the inclusion of air transport in such efforts but decided to restrict it coverage to only three ancillary services:

- aircraft repair and maintenance;
- selling and marketing of air transport services; and
- computer reservation system services.

The WTO's General Agreement on Trade in Services (GATS) contains an annex on air transport but this specifically excluded anything on traffic rights. *Traffic rights* were defined to include routes, capacity, pricing and the criteria for the designation of airlines (i.e. ownership and control requirements). They are sometimes referred to as *hard rights*, meaning the basic authorisation needed to operate services to and from another country as distinct from *soft rights* that include the ancillary services mentioned above. Ground handling was also going to be included in GATS but was later left out. The main reason for leaving out the hard rights was the fact that involvement of WTO might hinder efforts already made under the auspices of ICAO. However, the position was to be reviewed periodically.

The world's airline association, IATA, is also putting pressure on governments to 'eliminate archaic rules that prevent airlines from restructuring across borders'. This was one of the key points that emerged from the Istanbul declaration at their 64th Annual General Meeting and World Air Transport Summit held on 2–3 June 2008. This was followed on 26 October by the Agenda for Freedom Summit, also held in Istanbul, where airlines and government officials discussed how this might be achieved. The Statement of Policy Principles emerged as the best compromise to move forward with this idea. The Statement of Policy Principles is a declaration of intention from the parties to signal their willingness to waive restrictions on a reciprocal basis with like-minded states but does not create a legal obligation for them to do so. Governments would still need to implement a change in market access and ownership rules through traditional tools such as an exchange of letters, Memorandum of Understanding, or Air Services Agreement.

The case for further liberalisation of air cargo was presented by Airport Council International (ACI), the International Air Cargo Association and the International Federation of Freight Forwarders Associations to the ICAO Assembly in 2007. It called for a shift in current regulation by proposing an agreement between like-minded countries that support the principle of severance of cargo from passenger rights, as an initial step in a long-term strategy. Under this approach, a new generic all-cargo agreement would grant the same rights and privileges, on a reciprocal basis, to all signatories.

In summary, the technical regulation of the industry continues to work well, with a strong ICAO lead and good cooperation between many countries. Safety assessments have been implemented worldwide and airline blacklists have been introduced in the EU and elsewhere, often affecting cargo operators in developing countries. Security has been tightened up more recently for cargo operations. The economic regulation has changed in advanced countries from restrictions on traffic rights and operations to preventing anti-trust infringements and protecting consumer interests. Mergers and alliances have been investigated, especially in the US and EU, but these do not often concern air cargo operators. Liberalisation is always a slow process and an initial breakthrough with the 2007 EU/US bilateral agreement was not followed up by a second stage agreement on, *inter alia*, more liberal ownership and control rules. The ICAO's 2008 annual report said that bilateral 'open skies' Air Services Agreements and regional liberalised agreements and arrangements now covered about 31 percent of country-pairs with non-stop international passenger services and almost 57 percent of the frequencies offered. It is difficult to see any removal of the foreign ownership restrictions on airlines in the short to medium term without a change in US policy. This is because the present position of the US government is that foreign control of US airlines would need legislation and this is not required because the US market is already well-served by airlines, there is not pressure from unions or airlines to change things (quite the opposite) and concern has been expressed on whether safety standards would be maintained. Some relaxation of foreign ownership rules might be possible, however, with perhaps a move from allowing up to 49 percent foreign control, as is the case in the EU.

Chapter 4
Supply: Passenger and Freight Airlines

4.1 Introduction

The air cargo carriers discussed in this chapter have been limited to those companies that fly cargo from one airport to another using aircraft. It should, however, be noted that there are truck operators that carry 'air cargo' between airports under air waybills, usually as feeder services to long-haul cargo flights. These are common in Europe and North America.

Table 4.1 shows the types of airlines flying international air cargo in 2008. The largest part was carried on freighter aircraft operated by combination carriers, i.e. those airlines that offer both passenger and cargo services. This was closely followed by the passenger flights of the same type of airline, most of it in the lower deck of the aircraft and some on the main deck of aircraft that have been configured to take both types of traffic on the main deck ('combi' aircraft).

Table 4.1   International air freight by type of carrier, 2008

	Freight (tonne-kms (m))	% total
Freighter flights of combination carriers	74,071	44.8
Passenger flights of combination carriers	65,364	39.5
Integrators	13,133	7.9
Freighter-only airlines	12,745	7.7
Total international	165,313	100.0

Source: IATA WATS, 2009 and airlines.

A much smaller share of the world's international cargo traffic is carried by the integrators and specialist airlines that only operate freighter aircraft. These will be discussed in the next two chapters. Before examining in more detail the share of cargo on passenger and freighter flights, the degree to which each of the airline business models focuses on air cargo will be addressed. These are currently split into network, low-cost and charter and regional.

4.2 Network Carriers

Network carriers operate a network of scheduled air services to and from their main or secondary hub airports. These hubs are usually one of the major airports in their country of registration since that maximises the air traffic rights that they can use. Passengers and cargo can be carried between any two points on their network using single or multiple flights. Alliance partners may fly one or more leg of a multi-sector trip, and may sell sectors that they do not operate using the code of their partner airline.

Passengers choose the network airline based on a variety of factors including standard of service and frequent flyer awards, and often trade off convenience in terms of trip time for a lower price. Thus they could fly a circuitous multi-sector route via the network airline's hub airport to obtain an attractive fare. Air cargo is even more suited to such circuitous routings in return for an acceptable end-to-end delivery time and price. This is because the shipper or forwarder does not need to know the routing (or even the precise flights taken) as long as the carrier delivers on the contract.

Most network carriers use a major hub airport through which they schedule short- and long-haul flights, as many as possible connecting with each other without too long connection times. Long-haul passenger flights are generally operated with wide-bodied aircraft with a sizeable lower deck hold for cargo. These are supplemented by freighter aircraft flights serving the denser air cargo markets. The loads on the long-haul flights are, wherever possible, increased by connecting with short-/medium-haul passenger feeder flights, usually using narrow-bodied aircraft with little lower deck cargo capacity. This means that connecting cargo has to be fed into the hubs by trucks, at least in Europe and North America where this is possible. These are cheaper to operate than freighter aircraft, although some time advantage might be lost on the longer sectors. These trucks are also able to feed the long-haul freighter aircraft. For example, it was estimated that the cost of road haulage between Glasgow and London Heathrow Airport was only around 7 percent of the total cost of carrying a shipment between Glasgow and Hong Kong, the second sector by aircraft (MDS Transmodal et al., 2000).

Those combination carriers that have a sizeable freighter operation will downsize the latter at times of a major drop in demand (as occurred at the end of 2008). Given that cargo capacity on passenger and combi flights is a by-product of the passenger services the axe tends to fall on their freighter flights. For example, in 2009, Air France-KLM reduced their freighter fleet from 25 to 14 (two leased to AirBridge Cargo), most of the parked aircraft awaiting an economic recovery before being returned to service. Its sister airline KLM transferred all its freighters to its charter subsidiary Martinair.

4.3 Low-Cost Carriers

Almost all low-cost carriers (LCCs) have up to now operated on short-/medium-haul routes with narrow-bodied aircraft such as the B737-700 or A319/A320. These aircraft have very limited lower deck cargo capacity once their usually full passenger loads and their checked bags have been taken into account. This often leaves as little as 0.5–1 tonne for cargo.

Table 4.2 shows which low-cost carriers accept cargo on their passenger flights. Few that adhere strictly to the LCC model do so, mainly because it might compromise the short turnaround times, but some are now reassessing this policy. Southwest Airlines in the US was the first LCC and now the longest lasting. It originally declined to take any cargo but with the advent of slightly larger aircraft changed this, subject to a per piece limit of 150 pounds. This was raised to 200 pounds in August 2006. A number of LCCs are now also accepting cargo (Table 4.2).

Table 4.2   World low-cost carrier cargo acceptance policy

Europe		North America		Asia/Middle East	
Ryanair	No	Southwest	Yes	AirAsia	Not initially
easyJet	No	AirTran	No until 2006	Jetstar Asia	No
Air Berlin	Yes	JetBlue	No	Lion	No
SkyEurope	No			Orient Thai	No
Vueling	No			Tiger	No
Norwegian	No			Jazeera	Yes

Air Berlin is one of the LCCs that do accept air cargo. In 2009 it attempted to sell its cargo unit but two of its bidders withdrew and the third failed to raise the necessary finance, so it decided to take it off the market.

easyJet introduced a pilot scheme on a number of its flights from London Gatwick Airport in 2010. It hired a third party cargo service company to handle the project, dealing with marketing and airport handling. This could be rolled out across its network if the trial was successful in terms of net ancillary revenue generated and impact on its short turnaround times. AirAsia did not initially accept cargo, but now sells lower deck space on its bulk loading A320s. Its long-haul sister company, AirAsia X, is selling its A330/A340 lower hold capacity, reportedly at 30 percent lower rates than incumbent airlines out of Kuala Lumpur. For 2009, however, it had not been that successful. Taking its three weekly Kuala Lumpur/Melbourne flights as an example: flights to Melbourne carried an average of 1.9 tonnes per flight with the return leg only taking 0.4 tonnes.

It is worth mentioning an unusual type of airline that had sizeable charter operations carrying passengers and freight but on separate services: Martinair operated a fleet of four B747-400F, one B747-200F and seven MD-11Fs on the cargo side and a further six B767-300ERs for passengers. In 2008 it carried 305,563 tonnes of cargo and 850,000 passengers. At the end of 2008 Air France-KLM were allowed by the EU competition authorities to acquire the remaining 50 percent of the shares that it did not already hold, and in 2009 the KLM part of the group's freighter operations were transferred to the wholly owned subsidiary.

4.4 Regional Carriers

Regional airlines are defined as those that operate passenger services within a region or from regional airports. Thus they generally operate turbo-prop or smaller jet aircraft. This gives them very little cargo capacity, especially those with the regional jets. In the US they are often owned by or franchised or contracted to large network carriers. In Europe they tend to be subsidiaries of large network carriers such as Air France or Lufthansa. British Airways sold their remaining regional airline operations to FlyBe in 2007 and retained 15 percent of the shares in the enlarged FlyBe operation.

Given the limited cargo capacity on regional flights, there are a number of airlines that offer smaller freighter aircraft on regional sectors. These can be contracted to Post Offices (especially for night flights) or to feed integrators' own flights.

4.5 Major Domestic Carriers

Most of the domestic air cargo that has its true origin and destination within one country is transported overland. The exceptions are when surface transport is not well developed or unreliable, or where the distances between major cities is large, as in North America, Russia, China and India. Most carriers that offer domestic flights for cargo thus tend also to operate internationally. An exception to this is where an integrator has a domestic feeder airline for flights from its international hub: Astar Air Cargo in the US operated for DHL International and carried 93 percent of its total of 186,000 tonnes of air cargo on domestic routes.

An airline that operated solely within the Japanese domestic express market, Galaxy Airlines, went bankrupt towards the end of 2008. This occurred after only two years of loss-making operations on four domestic routes with two A300-600F freighters.

4.6 Passenger Flights of Combination Carriers

Apart from LCCs, almost all airlines that carry passengers also carry air cargo in the lower deck holds of their passenger aircraft. This is particularly true of long-haul flights operated by wide-bodied aircraft that offer up to 30 tonnes of such cargo capacity. In the UK, over 80 percent of all long-haul cargo was carried on passenger flights in 2006, in contrast to short-/medium-haul where passenger services carried only 20 percent of the tonnage. Lower deck cargo at the largest UK cargo airport, London Heathrow, amounted to 3.5 tonnes per 100 passengers on long-haul and only 0.4 tonnes per 100 passengers on short-haul. This would be around 14 tonnes on cargo on long-haul and only 0.5 tonnes on short-haul.[1]

4.7 Freighter Flights of Combination Carriers

Some, but not all, the passenger airlines also operate freighter aircraft that carry only air cargo.[2] This is to supplement their capacity on routes operated by passenger aircraft; to operate routes that do not justify passenger services; and to accommodate consignments and loads that cannot be carried in the restricted space on passenger flights (or is constrained by the size of the cargo loading door).

The share of IATA airline cargo carried on freight-only flights has increased particularly during the 1990s (see Figure 4.1). Integrators such as UPS and FedEx are included in the figures, and these expanded internationally during that period. Boeing 2008–2009 cargo forecasts predict the share to increase marginally between 2008 and 2027, resulting from a 6 percent annual growth compared to only 5 percent a year for the cargo carried on passenger flights.[3]

MergeGlobal estimated that the largest freighter share of tonne capacity was on transpacific routes, increasing from 73 percent in 2000 to 78 percent in 2005 and forecast to reach 81 percent in 2010 (MergeGlobal, 2006). The share was a little lower on Asia/European routes increasing from 61 percent in 2000 to 70 percent in 2010. Transatlantic routes had the highest share of tonne capacity on passenger flights, with freighters only offering 43 percent in 2010, up from 37 percent in 2000.

Within the US, only 22 percent of freight is carried on passenger aircraft, the larger freighter aircraft share resulting from the success of the integrators in competing in this market. However, 70 percent of intra-US air mail is still carried on passenger flights.

---

1 'Connecting the Continents – Long-haul Passenger Operations from the UK', CAP771, UK Civil Aviation Authority, 31 July 2007.

2 Some freighter aircraft such as the B747 or Antonov 124 do offer a number of passenger seats adjacent to the cockpit, but do not generally sell these to the public.

3 Boeing, 2008.

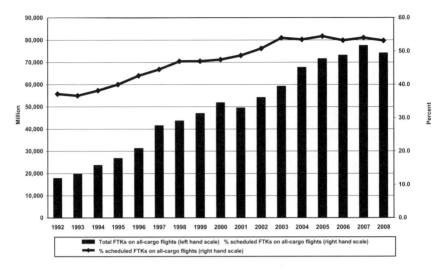

Figure 4.1   Air cargo carried on freighter aircraft and share in total traffic IATA international services

Source: IATA WATS.

In 1994, Lufthansa decided to form a separate air cargo subsidiary company that was 100 percent owned by Lufthansa Group. This had the advantage of giving the previous air cargo division a greater control of and responsibility for their business. It also made financial reporting and planning more focused. Three divisions were established within Lufthansa Cargo AG (see Figure 4.2):

*   Global cargo net;
*   Global cargo handling services;
*   Global freighter operations.

The 'Global cargo net' was responsible for marketing across the network, and crucially negotiating with the passenger part of the group on the purchase of capacity in the lower decks of passenger flights. This was supposed to lead to an internal 'market' for such space, with the cost determined by arm's-length negotiations. In reality, a situation whereby Lufthansa Cargo walked away and the passenger side marketed the space to third parties was unthinkable. However, in the event, Lufthansa Cargo managed to avoid purchasing capacity on domestic sectors, where trucks already provided most of the feeder traffic. Costs could be set using the allocation method described in Chapter 11.

'Global handling services' covered the ground handling staff and operations that were dedicated to cargo traffic, while the 'Global freighter operations' division took responsibility for the all-cargo aircraft operations, crewing and maintenance.

The advantages of the new company such as greater customer focus, cost and financial transparency, and improved planning were only offset by small

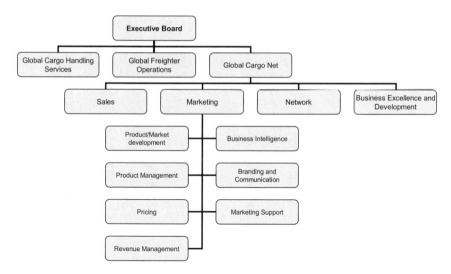

Figure 4.2   Lufthansa Cargo management structure

Source: Hellemann, 2002.

disadvantages of loss of economies of scale from the need to have its own human resources, finance and IT departments that were previous combined with the other parts of the Lufthansa Group. As a result other Star Alliance members followed Lufthansa's lead (e.g. Singapore Airlines and SAS).

Lufthansa's cargo subsidiary also became the holding company for a number of related companies in which it had majority or minority stakes. Examples of the former are the 100 percent owned Lufthansa Cargo Charter Agency GmbH and 67 percent owned Handling Counts GmbH. Associates included AeroLogic GmbH (the 50 percent owned partnership with DHL, operating freighters based at Leipzig Airport), air cargo terminal operations companies at Shenzhen, Tianjin and Shanghai airports, and Jade Cargo International, Shenzhen (25 percent).

Singapore Airlines also set up a separate cargo subsidiary in 2001 (described in more detail in Chapter 12, section 12.4), as did another Star Alliance member SAS. Lan-Chile's cargo operations have been in a separate subsidiary since the airline was acquired by the all-cargo carrier, Fast Air.

Japan Airlines planned to hive off its air cargo division and merge it with Nippon Cargo, the air cargo subsidiary of Nippon Yusen Kaisha (NYK) (see next section). This followed a code-sharing agreement between the two in March 2009. Neither company had been profitable, even prior to the major slump in world trade and it was felt that the combined operations were thought to have a better chance of profitability. NYK is involved in air, land and sea transport services, but it may decide to focus on sea transport and sell its air cargo subsidiary. This was subsequently considered less likely since NYK acquired further shares in the airline and took control of the company.

Air India reached the same conclusion in 2007, but with a plan to split the airline into six Strategic Business Units: the main airline business, its low-cost carrier operation, cargo, engineering and maintenance, ground handling, and related businesses like IT and security. It envisaged these operating independently each with its own cost centres and accountable for its own profitability. By the beginning of 2010 this plan had not been implemented, but it announced that it was part of the 'accelerated' implementation of a restructuring plan.

Aeroflot is an airline that set up an air cargo subsidiary and subsequently reversed the decision in 2009 following a number of loss-making years. It was announced that the freighter services of the Russian carrier would be terminated and cargo operations revert to its parent company. The freighters previously flown by the cargo subsidiary would re-enter Aeroflot service in March 2010.

4.8 Freighter Flights by Freight-Only Carriers

In addition to the stand-alone cargo subsidiaries discussed above, a number of companies are dedicated to providing services with freighter aircraft with no involvement in the passenger business. These have no financial ties with the integrators which are described in Chapter 5. One of the first of the large all-cargo airlines was Flying Tigers that eventually ran into severe financial problems and was acquired by Federal Express.

Table 4.3 shows the majority of the air cargo specialists in terms of traffic carried in 2008. By far the largest was Cargolux, 52.1 percent owned by Luxembourg's government-owned airline, Luxair. The Luxembourg government directly holds 8 percent and the rest of the shares are held privately by financial institutions. In 2009, the 33.7 percent stake held by the receiver for the bankrupt SAirlines (the Swissair holding company) were finally sold to existing shareholders, giving Luxair control. Its main base and country of registration is Luxembourg, which generally enjoys relatively liberal air traffic rights with non-EU countries. The airline operates a fleet of 13 B747-400F aircraft with the same number of B747-8Fs on order. In December 2008 it set up a subsidiary, Cargolux Italia, in Italy to capitalise on the reduced operations of Alitalia. Cargolux has been consistently profitable over its many years of operations, in contrast to the financial results of many of its competitors.

The next largest scheduled carrier was Polar Air Cargo, based in New York and owned by ACMI specialist Atlas Air. The airline operates scheduled and charter services with a fleet of six B747-400Fs and a further two B747-200Fs in storage in 2009. In 2007, DHL took a 49 percent stake in the airline (only 25 percent of its voting rights to comply with US regulations) and has a block space agreement on flights from the US to eight destinations in Asia. It made an operating loss in both 2007 and 2008 financial years, but the group as a whole was profitable.

The third largest freight-only airline was Nippon Cargo, based in Japan. This is owned by the Japanese shipping company, NYK Line (83.8 percent), with

Table 4.3   International scheduled air freight by freighter-only airline, 2008

	Freight (tonne-kms (m))	Share of total (%)
Cargolux	5,334	41.8
Southern Air*	2,290	18.0
Polar Air	2,090	16.4
Nippon Cargo	1,796	14.1
Volga-Dnepr	1,046	8.2
Evergreen*	999	7.8
Jade (China)	934	7.3
Great Wall (China)	706	5.5
CAL Israel	373	2.9
Air Hong Kong	358	2.8
Astar*	300	0.3
Cielos Peru	71	0.6
Total international	12,745	100.0

Note: * Charter flights only.

smaller holdings by Nippon Express (2.7 percent), Yamato Group (2.6 percent) and Suzuyo (2.5 percent). It incurred large operating losses in its 2006 and 2007 financial years (22 percent and 21 percent of total revenues respectively), but returned to just above breaking even in 2008 after rationalisation that included discontinuing its New York flights. Two of its eight B747-400Fs were in storage in 2009, and it had ordered 14 B747-8F aircraft. Some of its US operations were code-shared with the integrator UPS. In 2009 it seemed possible that Nippon Cargo would be sold by its majority owner or merged with the cargo division of Japan Airlines (see section 4.7).

Volga-Dnepr is a Russian all-cargo airline owned by an assortment of individuals and companies, none of them with overall control. Just under 3 percent was held by the Ukraine part of Antonov, the aircraft manufacturer. It had grown rapidly between 2004 when its annual revenues were US$309m to $1,177m in 2008. It operates a fleet of 10 very large Antonov 124 aircraft, each with up to 150 tonnes capacity, six Iluyshin76s (with up to 50 tonnes) and some smaller aircraft. A former competitor in the outsize shipment market, the UK based Air Foyle HeavyLift, ceased trading in July 2006. Another UK freighter operator trading under the name of Air Bridge Carriers for many years in the 1970s and 1980s became part of the Hunting aviation group and was sold off to Air Contractors which moved its base to Ireland. Air Bridge Carriers began life in the 1970s carrying fresh produce from the Channel Islands to the UK using Argosy and later Merchantman freighters, and in the 1980s operated night flights for the major integrators that were fast expanding in Europe at that time. Both these markets subsequently expanded rapidly in many parts of the world.

The fifth and sixth largest were the relatively recent entrants based in China: Jade in Shenzhen and Great Wall in Shanghai. Jade (China) is a joint venture between Lufthansa and Shenzhen Airlines, established in October 2004 but operations only commencing in 2008. Great Wall China is partly owned by Singapore Airlines. Both these are covered in greater detail in section 4.10.3 below.

Of the other smaller cargo specialists, CAL Israel is now controlled by Israel's Organisation of Agricultural Cooperatives, having previously been 49 percent owned by the country's national carrier, El Al. Its single B747-200C facilitates exports from Israel, especially fresh produce. Cielos Peru is also active in flying fresh produce while Astar has been reduced in size following severing its connection with DHL.

Two US freighter-only carriers operated only charter flights in 2008: Southern Air with 2,290m FTKs and Evergreen International with 999m. Another independent air cargo specialist is Transmile Air Services of Malaysia, operating six B727-200F aircraft mainly for integrators but also started scheduled flights between Kuala Lumpur and Singapore via Kuching and Labuan in East Malaysia in 2010. Its associate airline, K-Mile Air of Thailand, also operates to Singapore from Bangkok and Jakarta. It has four long-haul MD11F in storage in 2010. It made significant operating losses in each of the five years to 2009, and has been in financial trouble since buying the four MD11Fs which it has been trying to sell to pay off debts.

The Central and South America to/from US market has supported a number of cargo specialist airlines in the past such as Arrow Cargo. These often operate for a number of years and then cease trading or re-emerge with a different owner and name. The Africa/European market has done the same with Affretair and MK Airlines. Both markets are relative low volume, low yield and cannot justify entry by the major operators with larger aircraft. However, the emergence of fresh produce markets from countries such as Kenya and Peru has improved the fortunes of some operators, assuming they can achieve a balance in air cargo flows.

4.9 Charter and ACMI Operators

Operators of charter flights differ from the regular services that carry cargo in providing tailor-made capacity to meet ad hoc demands. These could be to support the construction of a major new manufacturing plant in a foreign country, as was the case with General Motors in Italy. Similar requirements for a limited time period such as disaster relief or military support are also ideally suited for charter flights. Many of the airlines mentioned in the previous section operate a mixture of scheduled and charter flights, some such as Volga-Dnepr mostly charter and others such as Cargolux mostly scheduled.

Whatever the need, outsourcing freighter flight operation to a specialist company is often a more economic proposition. This is because of the complex and often costly licensing procedures for aircraft and personnel, as well as the high costs of operating small fleets of freighters. The growing trend to greater manufacturing outsourcing leads to the need for regular and frequent freighter flights to feed components to a production line. Both Boeing and Airbus own their own special freighter aircraft for this, the Airbus one the result of combining the bodies of two A300 aircraft. Boeing has four Dreamlifter freighters, the operation of which was first outsourced to Evergreen and subsequently by Atlas Air Worldwide.[4]

Some of the freighter operators introduced in sections 4.7 and 4.8 lease their aircraft on an ACMI basis. Some of them such as Atlas Air operate their own scheduled and charter flights in addition to providing aircraft to other airlines on an ACMI basis. In Atlas Air's case its own flights are operated by 100 percent owned subsidiary, Polar Air, now partly owned by DHL. Atlas's ACMI customers over the years have included Air France, Alitalia, British Airways, Cargolux, China Airlines, El Al, Emirates, Korean Air, Thai International and Cathay Pacific. In 2008, Emirates was its largest customer with 7.8 percent of total revenues and 34.9 percent of ACMI business. Others such as Cargojet Canada (formerly Canada 3000) combine the two types of business in one company mostly employing B727-200F freighters on an ACMI and night charter basis. Many ACMI operators such as Southern Air, Kalitta, Evergreen and Air Atlanta Icelandic offer older and less efficient B747-200F aircraft. However, Air Atlanta will upgrade to B747-400Fs and Southern is to acquire B777F freighters. Another ACMI specialist, World Airways, is adding B747-400Fs to its MD-11 fleet. Some such as World and Air Atlanta market both passenger and cargo aircraft on an ACMI basis, but the remainder only offer freighters.

ACMI gets its name from the first letters of the operating costs that are the responsibility of the lessor: *A*ircraft, *C*rew, *M*aintenance, *I*nsurance. In the case of cargo aircraft 'crew' refers to cockpit crew. ACMI is a specific type of wet lease, which can have varied cost responsibilities depending on the contract. For example, some passenger wet leases operate with cabin crew provided by both the lessor and lessee (sometimes called a 'damp' lease). 'CMI' is also a growing market where the lessee owns the aircraft, perhaps for tax reasons, and the operation is outsourced to the lessor.

It was generally thought that a major recession would have a severe impact on carriers that depended too much on short-term ACMI contracts, such as Atlas Air. However, Atlas Air Worldwide Holdings reported an increase in net earnings in the third quarter of 2009, and finished the year with good results considering the industry downturn and its significant ACMI presence.

---

4   It was suggested that the contract was switched to Atlas Air as part of a compensation package for delays to the delivery of Atlas's six new B747-8F freighters.

4.10 Air Cargo Carriers by Region

The nationality of an airline still largely determines its principal place of business (apart from liberalised regional country groupings such as the EU). This dictates its main hub or base airport and the traffic rights available to it. Given that the main air trade flows are between North America and Europe, Europe and Asia and Asia and North America, it is likely that the main air cargo carriers will be located in one of these three regions.

However, those countries located between the main regions may also take advantage of sixth freedom rights to build up hub traffic more than commensurate with the country's size. Singapore and Dubai are two examples of this. The following sections look at the cargo airlines in each region, highlighting the largest operators both within the region and to/from the region. New entrants will also be identified and the market position that they achieved, as well as those that have been acquired by other airlines or gone bankrupt.

4.10.1 North America

The US and Canada cover large geographical areas and offer a large domestic market to potential air cargo operators. In the distant past, combination carriers such as American and United dominate the US air cargo market, supplemented by charters and truck services. However, with the introduction of the integrator model, these carriers expanded, first taking a large part of the small parcels market and later all consignment sizes. From 1978 the combination carriers began to compete more strongly with each other using high frequency flights with smaller narrow-bodied aircraft. With less cargo capacity on their passenger services these airlines' focus shifted more towards the passenger side of the business and they had little need to operate freighter aircraft.

Federal Express (FedEx) carried the greatest amount of air cargo in 2008, 57 percent of which was on scheduled domestic flights (see Table 4.4). The other US integrator, United Parcel Service (UPS), was the second largest with 52 percent of its total 2008 traffic on international routes. Together they accounted for almost 60 percent of the air cargo market.

Next come three of the US majors (combination carriers), all carrying similar amounts. The recent merger of Delta Airlines and Northwest would put their combined total above the other two but still well behind the integrators. Table 4.5 shows the very low share of air cargo in the total revenues of those US carriers that focus on passengers.

Three freighter-only airlines also feature in the top 10 (some already discussed above). Polar Air Cargo is the operating arm of Atlas Air, which focuses on cargo aircraft leasing. Kalitta Air specialises in regular charter flights, 78 percent of which were on international routes in 2008. It currently operates a New York Kennedy-Liège-Bahrain-Hong Kong route eastbound and Newark-Chicago-Anchorage-Nagoya route westbound, although its main base is at Detroit's Willow

Table 4.4   Top 10 US airlines by total FTKs carried, 2008

	Total FTKs (m)	Share of regional total (%)
FedEx	15,463	36.3
UPS	10,024	23.5
American Airlines	2,940	6.9
United Airlines	2,805	6.6
Northwest Airlines	2,391	5.6
Polar Air Cargo	2,096	4.9
Southern Air	2,044	4.8
Delta Airlines	1,778	4.2
Kalitta Air	1,715	4.0
Continental Airlines	1,388	3.3
Top 10 airlines	42,644	100.0

Source: IATA World Air Transport Statistics, 2009.

Run Airport. Southern Air's traffic in 2008 was largely international (74 percent) and was supplemented by the wet leasing of cargo aircraft.

Polar Air Cargo is one of the carriers that had a contract with the US military's Air Mobility Command (AMC) to provide charters using various B747 freighter aircraft. It would also have had priority in additional flying that the military needed at times of increased overseas involvement, for example in the Gulf and Afghanistan.

Another freight-only airline, Evergreen International, only carried 892m FTKs in 2008, but would have made the top 10 US air freight carriers in 2006. Its fleet of nine B747-200F freighters became much less economic with the jump in fuel prices in 2008 and it cut back its operations which had included scheduled flights to Hong Kong and Taipei.

Two US air cargo specialists ceased operations in the early part of the century: Airborne and Gemini Air Cargo. Airborne Express emerged from the long-established Airborne freight forwarding company in 1980 moving into the door-to-door express parcels and logistics businesses. Its aircraft base was Wilmington, Ohio, an airport it also owned. It was acquired by DHL's Belgian subsidiary in 2003, as a means to compete more effectively in the US market. DHL separated Airborne's ground operations and airline, the latter becoming ABX Air. ABX's traffic reached 943m FTKs in 2007, before it was wound down by DHL. The acquisition caused considerable opposition because of DHL's ultimate control by foreign (and government) interests, Deutsche Post (see Chapter 3 for a more detailed discussion of the regulatory aspects of this change).

Table 4.5   Cargo share of total revenue for US combination carriers, 2008

Airline	Cargo as % of total revenues
Northwest	6.3%
United	3.6%
American	3.3%
Continental	2.9%
Alaska	2.7%
Delta	2.3%
Southwest	1.2%
US Airways	1.1%
Airtran	0.2%

Source: Air Transport Association of America.

Gemini Air Cargo started life in 1996 initially as a freight forwarder that wet leased freighter aircraft. In 1999, it was acquired by the Carlyle Group (with a minority held by Lehman Brothers). Its traffic peaked at 1,206m FTKs in 2004. It went into Chapter 11 bankruptcy in 2006 and again in 2008 when it went into liquidation and ceased operations. During its better days it had hubs in Miami and New York Kennedy, and operated four MD11F and nine DC10-30F aircraft. The main reason for its final demise was the very high price of fuel in 2008 combined with the fact that the majority of its fleet was not very fuel efficient. The name was purchased late in 2008 and the new owner planned to start operations in 2009. The most recent casualty of the 2008/2009 banking crisis was all-cargo airline, Arrow Air. It had previously gone into Chapter 11 bankruptcy but was reported to have made losses in both 2008 and 2009, mainly on flights between the US and Central and South America.

Two large air freight forwarders have in the past attempted to operate profitable freighter networks in the US: Emery and BAX Global. In 2002, BAX wet leased McDonnell Douglas DC-8 freighters from sister company Air Transport International (ATI) and Boeing 727s from Capital Cargo International Airlines. Emery had its own fleet of DC8-70F aircraft that it operated within the US, but its fleet was grounded in 2001 after a crash and poor maintenance, and never recommenced operations.[5]

Mention should be made of one Canadian freighter operator, Cargojet Canada. This airline is based in Winnipeg, its hub for overnight freighter flights throughout Canada and to Bermuda, via New York. The airline was spun off from Canada

---

5   The forwarding part of its business, Menlo Worldwide, was sold to UPS in 2006.

3000 cargo, the cargo arm of the charter carrier Canada 3000 that collapsed in 2001. The airline's fleet of B727-200F and B737-200F aircraft, together with turbo-prop feeder planes, was updated in 2008 with the addition of B767 and B757 freighters. The carrier's revenues come from selling block space on its own flights together with ACMI contracts.

4.10.2 Europe

The European region consists both of the EU countries that now extend across to Eastern Europe, Iceland, Norway and Switzerland, Russia and other countries that were part of the USSR, the former Yugoslavia and Turkey. Air transport has been liberalised within the EU and larger European Aviation area countries, although this has benefited passenger markets more than cargo. The largest of the European based air cargo carriers were Air France-KLM and Lufthansa Cargo, capturing over 50 percent of the traffic, with Cargolux and British Airways some way behind (see Table 4.6).

Table 4.6   Top 10 European airlines by total FTKs carried, 2008

	Total FTKs (m)	Share of regional total (%)
Air France-KLM	10,217	28.3
Lufthansa Cargo	8,283	23.0
Cargolux	5,324	14.8
British Airways	4,638	12.9
Virgin Atlantic	1,581	4.4
Alitalia	1,574	4.4
Swiss	1,231	3.4
Iberia	1,156	3.2
AirBridge	1,102	3.1
Global Supply Systems	942	2.6
Top 10 airlines	36,048	100.0

Source: IATA World Air Transport Statistics, 2009.

Global Supply Systems is a company set up to operate the three freighter aircraft originally wet leased to British Airways by Atlas Air of the US. To comply with UK Civil Aviation Authority requirements of leasing, 51 percent of the company is owned by UK interests through a trust and 49 percent by Atlas Air. The company could lease to other operators but so far operations are limited to the three B747-

400F aircraft leased by British Airways for five years from 2007.[6] Adding the traffic of Global Supply to the British Airways traffic in Table 4.6 would put it in third position, still well behind Lufthansa. The only other UK freighter operator of any size is DHL Air which operates sub-charters for DHL and carried 232m tonne-kms in 2009 with its fleet of B757-200F aircraft.

Another UK freighter operator lasted only a couple of years before ceasing operations and eventually becoming bankrupt: launched in late 1999, the UK charter company initially commenced scheduled services to New York with a single 747-200F but was later forced to suspend its scheduled operations after an earlier deal for a second aircraft fell through. It subsequently operated to Hong Kong and wet leased its aircraft to Cargolux and other airlines. It was unusual in operating from a Heathrow Airport base. Another UK freighter airline, Air Bridge, had focused on very large shipments and was eventually sold to the Russian Volga-Dnepr Airlines and renamed AirBridge Cargo (see Table 4.6). AirBridge operates a fleet of six B747 freighters including three B747-400Fs, with orders for five B747-8F aircraft. Its main base is at Moscow's Sheremetyevo Airport with flights to points in Asia and Western Europe. Its parent, Volga-Dnepr Airlines, carried 621m tonne-kms in 2008 with its Russian-built fleet, which included 10 120-tonne payload Antonov 124 aircraft. The expansion of this Russian airline was the main cause of the cessation of trading in 2006 of another UK cargo airline: Air Foyle HeavyLift, the result of a merger back in 2001 of two separate cargo airlines (HeavyLift and Air Foyle).

Another unusual air cargo operation based in the UK was Channel Express, which flew flowers and other cargo mainly from the Channel Islands to UK markets. Its cargo business was acquired by Ferryspeed in July 2006, resulting in a switch in the mode of transport from air to sea. What is now another UK registered cargo airline, MK Air Cargo, was originally set up in Ghana by a South African entrepreneur and in 1995 transferred to Nigeria. The founder went into partnership with a British company in 2006 having spent 18 months in obtaining UK registry and a British AOC. With rapidly increasing fuel prices and inefficient aircraft, it went into administration in 2008, emerging in 2009 with additional funding.

Two European cargo airlines planned to start operations in 2009 – unfortunate timing given the major downturn – Cargoitalia and ACG Air Cargo Germany. Cargoitalia had received its AOC early in 2009 but deferred its first operations until September of that year. By 2010 it will have taken delivery of three MD-11 freighters, with eight A330 freighters ordered for 2012. The new Cargoitalia is the result of a combination of the original Cargoitalia (which suspended operations in 2008) with the recently purchased Alitalia cargo business. Cargoitalia's new owners are ALIS (66.7 percent) and Intesa SanPaolo (33.3 percent). ALIS in turn is controlled by the family of the chief executive officer (62 percent) with other private investors (including Benetton) each having 8–10 percent.

---

6   These will be replaced by B747-8Fs in 2011.

Uncertainty over the future of Alitalia and its cargo operations provided the catalyst for Cargolux's Italian venture. Its wholly owned subsidiary, Cargolux Italia, commenced operation in June 2009 and in 2010 operated a schedule of three weekly services from Milan Malpensa to Dubai and Hong Kong and back to Milan via Baku. The carrier also operates weekly services to Luxembourg. All flights are operated on B747-400F aircraft.

Lufthansa Cargo is expected to withdraw its two MD-11Fs from Milan by the end of 2009, after finding that its Italian operation could not operate at a profit. The aircraft would be re-assigned to the Frankfurt base. The airline commenced direct services from Italy after identifying a gap in the market following the demise of Alitalia Cargo. Italy has been known for having the second strongest air export market but following the 2008 downturn demand has declined significantly and rates have plummeted.

ACG Air Cargo Germany also has its AOC and has arranged leases on two B747-400SF freighters to be based at Frankfurt/Hahn Airport. This airport is around 75 miles from Lufthansa's main base at Frankfurt/Main and has the advantage of no night curfew or slot restrictions imposed by the larger airport. Equity finance came from the founder with a majority and an Irish leasing company a minority. The airline was planning initially to offer two scheduled routes: Frankfurt Hahn-Moscow-Shanghai and Hahn-Istanbul-Bombay-Hong Kong. This might seem a bold move given Lufthansa's nearby stronghold, but the new entrant argues that German shippers and importers need a choice. Around 70 percent of the capacity from the two aircraft would be used for scheduled flights, the remainder for charters. One year later, the airline was, surprisingly, surviving and a third aircraft was to be leased from Martinair to enable frequencies to Shanghai to be increased to five a week, and a new flight to Seoul operating three times per week.

A Belgian cargo airline that started flights in late 2007 (Cargo B) hit turbulence first with the rapid increase in fuel costs in 2008 and then with a major downturn in demand in 2009. Its fleet of two B747-200Fs was not very fuel efficient and by the time they had been replaced by more efficient B747-400s in 2009 the recession was starting to bite. The new aircraft were taken on dry lease from Nippon Cargo Airlines whose owners, NYK, also injected new capital into the airline to keep it afloat. Services were started to South America and these were linked to Nippon Cargo's Europe/Asia flights through an interline agreement. This northbound traffic, much of which was fresh flowers, had been moving on an interline basis to Eastern Europe and Russia. The airline also moved its European base from Brussels Airport to Liège and had hoped for some financial support from its new airport base. This was not forthcoming and it ceased operations and entered bankruptcy proceedings in July 2009, when its two B747-400Fs were put into storage.

Many European cargo airlines, both combination and freighter operators, use trucks for airport-to-airport feeder services. These link the various European markets with each carrier's long-haul hub, where the cargo is transferred to passenger or freighter aircraft. The cargo is transported under air waybills using air freight rates. Sector times are not too long, even cross-channel, and operating costs are much lower than short-haul freighters. Combination carriers operate few wide-bodied aircraft within Europe and so there is little lower deck capacity available. One trucking company has operated on behalf of British Airways, KLM and others and in 2008 published a schedule of services to/from Amsterdam Schiphol, Paris Charles de Gaulle, Frankfurt/Main and London Heathrow airports. These would be up to daily frequencies, generally leaving in the late afternoon or early evening. Their standard vehicle would take up to four Q7 pallets (around 17 tonnes), and capacities ranged from 15–20 tonnes per trip.

4.10.3 Asia and Australasia

Asia and the countries of the South and Mid Pacific differ from those in the two regions addressed above in being generally separated by large distances. This rules out trucking and feeding hubs by truck. The exceptions to this are Singapore and Hong Kong, both of which have established large cargo hubs by feeding cargo across the border in Malaysia and China respectively. Hong Kong gained most from this since it has good surface transport connections to the manufacturing region of south China.

Of the top five in Table 4.7, Korean Air and China Airlines are both based in countries with strong exports of high-tech air-freightable products: China and Taiwan. Cathay Pacific and Singapore Airlines both feed traffic from these and other Asian countries through their hubs. Japan Airlines is also based in a country that has a large export industry, although not one that has shown high growth in the past few years. The other major Japanese combination carrier, All Nippon Airways (ANA), established a joint venture airline in 2006 called JP Express (AJV). ANA took the majority stake, with minorities from the national Post Office, Nippon Express (Japan's largest global logistics firm) and the shipping company Mitsui Lines. The airline did not own or operate aircraft: these were wet leased from ANA on an ACMI basis (three B767-300F freighters) later to be replaced by a similar arrangement from ABX Air of the US. In 2010, ANA bought out the minority stakes and merged the airline with its low-cost passenger subsidiary.

Notable absentees from Table 4.7 are two of the three major Chinese combination carriers: China Eastern and China Southern with 2,379m and 1,709m freight tonne-kms respectively. The first Chinese all-cargo airline was formed by China Eastern in conjunction with China Ocean Shipping in 1998. China Eastern's stake was originally 70 percent but it was reduced to 55 percent when both founders sold 25 percent to China Airlines from Taiwan for an estimated sum of US$82m in 2001. The airline is based at Shanghai's Hongqiao Airport. It operates domestically and to other Asian countries, the US and Europe, carrying 1,455m freight tonne-kms in 2008. It made a sizeable operating loss in 2007.

Early in this century a number of foreign airlines identified opportunities for setting up joint venture freighter aircraft operations in China. Chinese carriers had focused on the passenger side of the business and acquiring freighters required the

Table 4.7   Top 10 Asian/Australasian airlines by total FTKs carried, 2008

	Total FTKs (m)	Share of regional total (%)
Korean Air	9,005	17.9
Cathay Pacific	8,842	17.5
Singapore Cargo	7,299	14.5
China Airlines	5,384	10.7
EVA Air	4,077	8.1
Japan Airlines	3,946	7.8
Air China	3,487	6.9
Asiana	3,340	6.6
Qantas	2,569	5.1
Thai Airways	2,490	4.9
Top 10 airlines	50,439	100.0

Source: IATA World Air Transport Statistics, 2009.

agreement of the government, a lengthy process. At the same time cargo traffic was growing strongly on the back of Chinese manufacture and export of relatively high value goods. A joint venture between a Chinese and foreign carrier seemed the obvious way forward with the Chinese holding the majority to protect air traffic rights.

The first was an investment by various Taiwanese interests including China Airlines in a new airline, Yangtze River Express, based at Shanghai's Hongqiao Airport. China Airlines took 25 percent of the airline with Taiwan based shipping companies taking a further 24 percent and the majority owned by Hainan Airlines. Operations started in 2003, with a Shanghai-Anchorage-Los Angeles service opened in late 2006. Luxembourg was added in 2007. The airline operates three long-haul B747-400F freighters and six B737-300QCs for short-/medium-haul domestic feeder flights. Traffic reached 393m tonne-kms in 2007, with a fall to 352m in 2008. This was followed by Lufthansa and Shenzhen Airlines forming Jade Airlines in 2004 to operate A300 freighter services from Guangzhou base (Shenzhen Airlines taking 51 percent, Lufthansa 25 percent and a German government agency, KfW, 24 percent).

In May 2005 Singapore Airlines Cargo took a 25 percent stake in Great Wall Airlines, based in Shanghai, with a Singapore government subsidiary (a subsidiary of Temasek Holdings) holding 24 percent and China Great Wall Industry with 51 percent. The new airline was incorporated and based in Shanghai and SIA Cargo's investment in the joint venture over the next three years was projected at RMB 250m. Great Wall Airlines planned to begin operations in the first half of 2006 to destinations within China as well as serving the major cargo markets in the US, Europe, North-east Asia and South-west Asia. The airline suspended operations in August 2006 after its parent company, China Great Wall Industry, had sanctions imposed on it by the United States government for allegedly supplying missile technology to Iran. All aircraft were returned to Singapore Airlines Cargo. In December 2006, it was announced that sanctions against Great Wall Airlines had been lifted following the sale of the Great Wall Industry shares in the airline to Beijing Aerospace. The airline resumed services in February 2007 and expanded traffic from 543m freight tonne-kms in 2007 to 706m in 2008.

Another joint venture started operations in June 2008: Grand Star Cargo International was set up by a Chinese logistics company, Sinotrans Air (see section 5.4.5) controlling 51 percent, with Korean interests taking the remainder (led by Korean Air with 25 percent). The cargo airline is based at Tianjin Airport near Beijing and started a Frankfurt service with a B747-400F. In December 2009, Sinotrans expressed an intention to sell some or all of its stake in the airline due to lack of profitability and the fact that it had not expanded beyond its Tianjin/Frankfurt route. Selling the shares to another Chinese airline would be in line with Civil Aviation Administration of China (CAAC) policy that encouraged the merger and reorganisation of domestic airfreight companies to consolidate the market.

Finally, Cathay Pacific has a 17.6 percent stake in Air China and its wholly owned subsidiary, Air China Cargo, operating five B747Fs. In turn, Air China holds just under 30 percent of Cathay Pacific Airways. In August 2009 the two airlines decided to launch a joint venture all-cargo airline, with operations planned to start at the end of 2009. Cathay Pacific also has a joint venture with DHL in Air Hong Kong. Cathay now has 60 percent and DHL 40 percent, the latter's stake increasing from 30 percent in 2003. Air Hong Kong operates A300-600F aircraft from its Hong Kong base to cities in China, Indonesia, Japan, Singapore, Thailand and Taiwan. It carried 410 million FTKs in 2009, part of which is under a Services Agreement with DHL, whereby DHL pay Air Hong Kong for capacity based on an arm's-length pricing deal and an annual revenue cap. This agreement runs at least until 2018.

4.10.4 Africa and the Middle East

The Middle East region has a geographical advantage over Africa in lying between the potentially lucrative Asia/Europe air cargo markets. Countries in this region have huge financial resources from their oil wealth to establish competitive hub airports and set up airlines with modern aircraft. African airlines, in contrast, have very limited exports by air of manufactured goods and small markets for air imports. Some such as Kenya have made some headway in developing exports of fresh flowers, fruit and vegetables by air, using cheap space on passenger flights.

Table 4.8 Top 10 Africa/Middle-East airlines by total FTKs carried, 2008

	Total FTKs (m)	Share of regional total (%)
Emirates	6,156	49.2
Qatar Airways	1,657	13.2
Saudi Arabian	1,413	11.3
El Al	771	6.2
South African	748	6.0
Gulf Air	447	3.6
Ethiopian Airlines	365	2.9
Maximus Air Cargo	348	2.8
CAL Cargo	336	2.7
Kenya Airways	279	2.2
Top 10 airlines	12,520	100.0

Source: IATA World Air Transport Statistics, 2009.

It is no surprise that the four largest airlines in these regions are from the Middle East, with Emirates capitalising on their passenger and cargo hub at Dubai International Airport.

Two freighter-only airlines are included in the top 10: CAL Cargo, whose purpose is to facilitate fresh produce exports by air from Israel, and Maximus Air Cargo (see Table 4.8). The latter is based in Abu Dhabi and operates an Airbus A300-600F and various Russian built freighters. In 2008 it was acquired by Abu Dhabi Aviation, which is partly owned by the government investment arm and has a small commuter aircraft fleet and a large number of helicopters used in construction and offshore oil support. Another all-cargo airline from the region that was a global player in the 1970s, Trans-Mediterranean Airlines, re-started services in 2010, having been suspended since 2005. Its first route under new ownership from renovated cargo facilities at Beirut Airport was to London Heathrow with an A300 freighter.

Another African cargo airline is the Zimbabwe registered Avient Aviation. This was set up in 1993 to fly charters from its European hub to/from Africa and the Middle East. Vatry in France was originally chosen as the hub but this was later switched to Liège in Belgium. Its fleet consisted of one Iluyshin 76 and two DC10-30F freighters, later to be joined by an MD-11F. This aircraft had been in its fleet for little more than one week when it crashed during take-off from Shanghai's Pudong airport in November 2009. A previous cargo airline based in Zimbabwe, Affretair, was a 100 percent owned subsidiary of Air Zimbabwe. It was liquidated in 2000 under a $511m debt that had grounded its only aircraft for close to two years.

4.10.5 South and Central America

South and Central America is dominated by the Chilean national carrier, LAN, with only seven airlines large enough to include in Table 4.9. This is both through its main, Santiago-based, airline Lan-Chile but also through the subsidiaries it owns in Peru, Brazil and Argentina. These offshoots are controlled by the LAN Group, but sometimes not majority owned to safeguard international air traffic rights. One would expect Brazil to be the base of a larger cargo carrier. In fact one of the top cargo airlines in South America, Varilog, was originally the cargo division of Brazilian flag carrier Varig, but it ceased trading in 2000. The cargo part was sold off by the liquidator as a stand-alone business and in 2006 was acquired by a US investment company that itself went bankrupt in early 2009 following the rapid decline in air cargo markets. Later in 2009 it was sold to Colombian airline Avianca's parent company together with the airline's CEO also taking shares. Avianca also has an indirect control of another Colombian airline, Tampa Cargo. Each had 50 percent with the former having an option to increase his stake to 90 percent. It serves mostly domestic points with two Boeing 757s and two B727s, much reduced from the 20 aircraft it operated prior to bankruptcy.

Table 4.9   Top seven South and Central American airlines by total FTKs carried, 2008

	Total FTKs (m)	Share of regional total (%)
LAN Chile	2,907	67.2
Tampa Cargo	365	8.4
ABSA	357	8.3
TAM Brazil	202	4.7
VarigLog	192	4.4
Aeromexico	153	3.5
Avianca	151	3.5
Top seven airlines	4,327	100.0

Source: IATA World Air Transport Statistics, 2009.

4.11 Conclusion

It was shown above that a large part of international air cargo is still carried on passenger flights. If domestic air cargo was included this share would be much less owing to the large share of integrator freighters in the huge US domestic market.

The integrators themselves do not yet have a large presence on international routes, choosing to contract with the combination carriers or regional freighter specialists.

Looking at the various regions, Asia stands out as having a number of large carriers but these are almost all combination carriers, but cargo accounts for a much larger share of their total traffic than, say, the Europe-based airlines. China's airlines were slow to enter international cargo markets initially but have remedied this more recently, mainly through joint ventures with European or other Asian airlines.

North America and Europe are regions where there has been no shortage of start-ups over the years, but also many bankruptcies. A new German-based all-cargo airline even started up in middle of the recent economic crisis, although this is sometimes preferred due to it being a good time to acquire aircraft cheaply or at low lease rates. In Asia new entry is more difficult due to some designation restrictions in Air Services Agreements, and new airlines have tended to be limited to low-cost passenger business models. However, Africa and South America tend to have the highest turnover rate, many start-ups poorly capitalised and targeting small and variable volumes of air cargo.

Chapter 5
Supply: Integrated Carriers, Post Offices and Forwarders

This chapter discusses integrated carriers, the extent of their involvement in air cargo and their evolution from the 1970s to the present day. Other players in the air cargo market will be introduced, especially those involved in the shipment of letters and small parcels. Transport of the latter used to be described as 'air mail' although this now overlaps with 'express' traffic. It will be seen that two of the largest integrators have acquired the air mail business of the national Post Offices and have positioned themselves to benefit from future privatisation and outsourcing by these national authorities. Freight forwarders will also be covered because of their key position in air freight distribution and consolidation.

Figure 5.1 gives a good approximation of the roles played by the various operators in the air cargo markets. All of them will use air transport for their long-haul shipments and some (the integrators and to a lesser extent the Post Offices) own, lease or charter aircraft.

The y-axis describes the degree to which the shipper is offered assurance as to the number of days (or even hours) taken to deliver the shipment to the final destination. A major integrator advantage used to be delivery time guarantees,

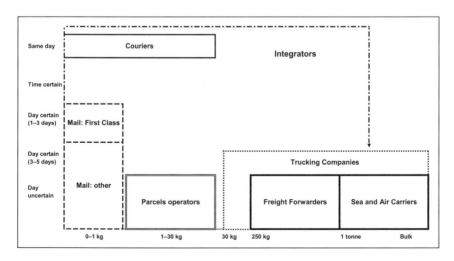

Figure 5.1   Operators in air cargo/parcels market

Source: Baird, 2007, in TNT Annual Report 2008, Chapter 2.

but these have become less cast-iron especially for international shipments. The x-axis gives the range of shipment weights applicable to each type of operator. Thus the traditional mail services offered by Post Offices handle mainly letters and small packages, with larger parcels carried by their own parcel offshoots or independent parcels operators. Trucking companies will carry larger units, generally consolidated into containers for easier handling by freight forwarders or consolidators.

The chapter will deal with those operators that are involved in transport, whether it is for the entire door-to-door trip (integrators) or for part of the trip (parcels operators or freight forwarders). Air carriers were covered in the previous chapter. It concludes with a brief look at maritime carriers that compete for the lower value to weight, less urgent and bulkier shipments. These can also operate in conjunction with air transport to provide 'sea-air' connections. This provides a slower but cheaper service than air.

5.1 Courier Companies

Courier companies emerged in the 1960s and 1970s to meet the demand for the fast delivery of documents and small packages. Their customers were often investment banks, management consultants or lawyers that needed to deliver prospectuses, consultant reports and deeds as quickly as possible. Loss or delay could result in large financial loss for these companies and so they were prepared to pay a premium price for the service. Their customers were located in many different countries and so the scheduled network of passenger flights with relatively high frequency provided the best means of transport.

The early courier companies made use of this network and also the availability of up to 20 kg of free baggage allowance (and some cabin bags) that the airlines offered. All the courier company needed to do was to book the cheapest fare and a member of their staff would pick up the document, take it to the airport and check-in on the flight. At the destination it could be delivered to the customer or handed to an agent for the final delivery. After a while, they even dispensed with the cost of time of their own staff by using students or others that wished to take the particular flight and who had no or little baggage of their own. This meant that the courier company's costs were limited to handing the bag and ticket to the passenger, paying for the ticket and arranging for collection at the destination.

As this type of traffic developed, the airlines began to enter the market themselves. The courier bags could be carried in the cargo hold at premium cargo rates and the seat could be sold to another passenger. Delivery and collection could be arranged at the two ends of the route. Furthermore, the collection of the courier bags could be moved from the passenger terminal, where they might have slowed the passenger check-in process, to the cargo terminal.

5.2 Integrated Carriers

5.2.1 Market Overview

Integrated carrier origins lie with both the courier model described in the previous section (and a key part of the earlier years of DHL) and the hub/feed model invented in the US by Federal Express. The integrated carrier business model was based on the following main elements:

- door-to-door transport;
- fast and reliable transport;
- guaranteed delivery times;
- tracking systems.

In addition, parcels would be delivered to hub airports by small aircraft or trucks and sorted using automated handling systems before being flown to a destination airport or another regional hub for final distribution.

Over time four companies have come to dominate the integrated market. So-called integrators exist at a national or regional level but entry into the truly global market now requires a very large investment in aircraft, vehicles, IT systems and handling infrastructure in many different countries. These are formidable barriers to entry, even for those companies already having some of the necessary investments in place. Airlines, for example, lack the surface transport infrastructure, and freight forwarders the airport facilities and aircraft.

The two largest integrated carriers in terms of air cargo flown on international routes also have large domestic operations in the US (see Table 5.1). DHL is not a US owned company and has been trying to enter the US domestic market for a number of years. On international routes, DHL (and other smaller integrators) make significant use of the combination carriers as well as local charter airlines in various countries.

Table 5.1   International air freight by integrator, 2008

	Freight tonne-kms (m)	Share of total (%)
FedEx	6,582	50.1
UPS	5,289	40.3
DHL (incl. EAT)	775	5.9
TNT Belgium	487	3.7
Total international	13,133	100.0

Source: IATA World Air Transport Statistics, 2009.

Table 5.2 shows estimates of market shares by region. This data, provided by the parent company of DHL, does not cross-check with estimates from other interested parties. For example, according to TNT, it carried 18 percent of European CEP market in 2007, DHL 16 percent, UPS 9 percent and FedEx 2 percent. However, the key points here are:

- the traditional Post Offices have very small shares of the market;
- FedEx is not strong in Europe;
- neither DHL nor TNT is strong in the US.

Federal Express had intended to become a major player in Europe but has retrenched after a number of years of financial loss.

Table 5.2   Total courier, express and parcels market volume in 2007

	Europe	US	Asia/Pacific
Total volume (€ billion)	€15.3	€7.5	€5.9
Market share (%):			
DHL Express	25	9	34
UPS	18	17	12
FedEx	0	24	24
TNT	15		
La Poste (France)	4		
Royal Mail (UK)	2		
USPS (US)	0	2	

Source: Deutsche Post World Net Annual Report, 2008.

The four major integrators will be examined in the following sections, focusing on their involvement in air cargo.

5.2.2 DHL

DHL is one of the two main brands of Deutsche Post DHL, which until 2009 was known as Deutsche Post World Net. This company has four operating divisions:

- Mail
- Express;
- Global Forwarding/Freight;
- Supply Chain/CIS.

The group was formed from the acquisition by Deutsche Post (now essentially the mail division) of DHL, the express division, and three freight forwarders (Danzas, Exel and Air Express International or AEI). The large Swiss forwarder Danzas, and the largest US international freight forwarder AEI were acquired in 1999, and the UK based Exel followed in 2005. Deustche Post went on a shopping spree in the late 1990s and, in addition to buying DHL and these large forwarders, it acquired around 50 other national parcels companies, such as Securicor in the UK, Parcelogic in Canada, Global Mail in the US and Ducros in France. The freight forwarders became the forwarding and supply chain divisions. As shown in Table 5.3, each division accounted for a roughly similar share of total turnover in 2008.

Table 5.3   Deutsche Post world net revenue by division (€m)

Division	2008	% share
Mail	14,393	25.7
Express	13,637	24.4
Global forwarding/freight	14,179	25.4
Supply chain/CIS*	13,718	24.5
Total above	55,927	100.0

Note: * Corporate Information Solutions.

Source: Deutsche Post World Net Annual Report, 2008.

DHL was founded in 1969 in San Francisco by three entrepreneurs: Adrian Dalsey, Larry Hillblom and Robert Lynn. The first shipment of documents was by air from San Francisco to Honolulu. This involved the carriage of the documents by one of the founders as personal cabin baggage, a business that became known as 'courier' (see section 5.1). It was the first air express operator to serve Asia from the US, with the Philippines in 1971, Japan, Hong Kong, Singapore and Australia in 1973 and Europe in 1976. DHL added parcels to its document service in 1979. In 2000 it signed an alliance agreement with Lufthansa Cargo and Japan Airlines that resulted in each airline taking a 25 percent stake in DHL (and a Japanese trading company a further 7.5 percent). Deutsche Post took a minority (22.5 percent) stake in DHL in 1998 and in July 2002 took its stake to 75.67 percent with the purchase of Lufthansa's 25 percent stake. In between it had bought 6 percent of DHL from Japan Airlines in 2000 (Japan Airlines having sold 20 percent to German controlled investment trusts the previous year).

Deutsche Post was still majority owned directly or indirectly by the German federal government at the time it assumed sole control of DHL. Up to then major decisions could only be taken jointly with Lufthansa. So DHL, having started life as a US owned company, was now German-owned, a change that was to make difficulties for its US airline, DHL Airways (see section 3.2.2). Germany accounted for 30 percent of turnover in 2008, mainly through its monopoly provision of domestic mail in Germany. However, Europe accounts for almost two-thirds of revenues with the Americas and Asia/Pacific taking a further 30 percent.

Table 5.4   Deutsche Post world net revenue by geographic area (€m)

Area	2008	% share
Germany	16,765	30.0
Rest of Europe	19,129	34.2
The Americas	10.171	18.2
Asia/Pacific	6,292	11.3
Other	3,570	6.4
Total above	55,927	100.0

Source: Deutsche Post World Net Annual Report 2008.

The 'Express' division will be covered in this section and 'Global Forwarding' in section 5.4.1. Each of these two operating divisions had broadly the same turnover in 2009, just above €10,000 million, while 'Express' generated a profit on operations before non-recurring items of €238 million, compared to the forwarding division's €272 million.

Table 5.5   DHL Express long-haul air service provision, 2008

Region	
Transpacific	Connecting the US with AsiaPacific Strategic partnership with Polar Air Cargo Six B747-400s in operation since 27 October 2008
Transatlantic	Connecting the US with all of Europe, the Middle East, and Africa Stand-alone operation by DHL Air Ltd. Improved transit times and next-day capabilities Six new B767-300 ERFs introduced from 2009 through 2012 First commercial flight September 2009, three aircraft operational as of 23 October 2009
Europe–Asia	Connecting Europe with Asia Pacific, the Middle East, and Africa Joint venture with Lufthansa Cargo: AeroLogic Heavily improved transit times and non-stop service capabilities Eight new B777-200Fs introduced commencing 2009 through 2011

Source: www.investors.dp-dhl.de Investors Factbook, Express.

Table 5.5 shows DHL's involvement in long-haul air services. These are operated between major hubs, with shipments distributed to and from other regional points by truck or aircraft. These may use airlines owned by DHL (see Table 5.6) or chartered from independent operators under contract. Other long-haul air services are provided by scheduled airlines.

The major trade routes across the Pacific and between Europe and Asia are operated by partner airlines under medium term contract: the latter by a large ACMI and freighter aircraft operator and the former through a joint venture with a major combination carrier. Both are operated with modern economic freighters. The transatlantic flights are operated using DHL's own fleet of B767-300 freighters, registered with its UK airline.

Table 5.6   DHL regional operating companies, 2009

Airline name	Country	Region
ASTAR Air Cargo	United States	North America
DHL Aero Expreso	Panama	South America
DHL Air Ltd	United Kingdom	Europe
DHL de Guatemala	Guatemala	South America
DHL Ecuador	Ecuador	South America
DHL International	United States	North America
DHL International Aviation ME	Bahrain	Middle East
European Air Transport	Belgium	Europe

Source: DHL website, accessed 28 August 2009.

Four of the airlines in Table 5.6 are owned by DHL: European Air Transport, based in Brussels, provides capacity for DHL's European network as well as long-haul services to the Middle East and Africa, using Boeing 757SF/PF and Airbus A300B4 aircraft; DHL Air UK, based at East Midlands airport in the United Kingdom, offering services on DHL's European network using Boeing 757SFs and transatlantic flights with B767 freighters; DHL's Middle East airline, based at Bahrain International Airport, serving Middle East destinations including Afghanistan and Iraq, using a variety of regional aircraft; and DHL's Latin American airline, based in Panama City, flying to a wide range of destinations in Central and South America using Boeing 727 aircraft.

In addition to the above, ASTAR Air Cargo is 25 percent owned by DHL and was operating both within the US market and internationally. However, in November 2008, the group announced that it would withdraw from the domestic express business in the US at the start of 2009. The international express business to/from the US would be kept. Total costs for restructuring the US express business amounted to around €3 billion.

Over 70 percent of DHL's Chinese shipments are routed through DHL's hub in Hong Kong, where in 2004 it handled over 22 million shipments, over 60 percent of which were intra-Asia shipments. In 2005 the hub traffic totalled more than 30 million shipments. DHL has a services agreement with Air Hong Kong, a carrier based there (in which it has a 40 percent stake), to provide capacity within Asia.

5.2.3 Federal Express (FedEx)

The company started overnight operations in April 1973 with 14 Dassault Falcon 20s that connected 25 cities in the United States. With the deregulation of domestic aviation in the US in 1977, Federal Express was allowed to operate freighter flights with larger aircraft and purchased seven B727-100Fs. It focused on the express product until 1998 when it purchased Caliber and started offering trucking, forwarding and other services.

In an interview with *Business Week* (20 September 2004), the founder of the company dispelled some of the myths surrounding his success story. First, while the idea came from a paper he wrote at Yale University for his undergraduate degree it was further developed and launched after time with the Marines. Second, he did not invent the hub-and-spoke system of air services whose main pioneer was Delta Air Lines, and only made possible by deregulation.

FedEx, as it was later called, invented the system of feeding overnight packages into a hub airport, sorting it and delivering it across the network. Feed used mostly small (and later larger) aircraft and some trucks. The network was gradually expanded, with 90 US cities added in 1980.

International flights were started in 1981, with Canada linked to the Memphis hub. Eight years later, the acquisition of Flying Tiger, a major international air cargo carrier, enabled FedEx to further expand overseas. In 1995, air routes were purchased from Evergreen International to start services to China with the acquisition of Evergreen International Airlines' all-cargo route authority, and in the same year an Asia and Pacific hub in was launched at the former US Air Force base at Subic Bay in the Philippines. FedEx's planned Indian operations were a direct response to DHL starting a similar service earlier (using BlueDart, Deccan 360 and the planned QuickJet air services). Initially it was to focus on 14 major cities. Apart from North America, FedEx only provides domestic services in Mexico, China and the UK.

The company originally started by carrying spare parts and documents exempted from the US postal monopoly. That changed with deregulation in 1978 and FedEx soon began offering overnight letter and document deliveries. Its ZapMail fax service was introduced in 1983 although this was later undermined by a rapid fall in the price of individual and company fax facilities. SuperTracker, a hand-held bar code scanner which brought parcel tracking to the shipping industry for the first time was introduced in 1986.

In 2000, FedEx Express signed a seven-year contract to transport Express Mail and Priority Mail for the United States Postal Service. This contract allowed FedEx to place drop boxes at every USPS Post Office, and the contract has recently been extended until September 2013. USPS continues to be the largest customer of FedEx Express.

FedEx Express acquired the British courier company ANC Holdings Limited in 2006, adding 35 sort facilities to the FedEx network and direct flights from the UK to Newark, Memphis, and Indianapolis (rather than via its Paris hub). Caliber had been purchased in 1997, giving it a greater ground transport focus. More recent acquisitions were Flying-Cargo in Hungary and Prakash Air Freight in India both in 2007.

Its fleet at the end of May 2009 numbered 654 aircraft having retired some of its less fuel efficient aircraft such as the DC10 and A310 freighters. The 2008 slump forced it to postpone delivery of the new Boeing 777 freighter: four would be delivered in 2010 as previously agreed, but in 2011, only four would be delivered rather than the 10 originally planned. The remaining aircraft will be delivered in 2012 and 2013. FedEx is discussed in more detail in the case study in Chapter 12.

5.2.4 United Parcel Service (UPS)

UPS describe themselves as the world's largest package delivery company, with 426,000 employees worldwide (around 70,000 outside the US). Many of these are members of the Teamsters union, a key difference that it has with FedEx. They were founded in 1907 as a private messenger service in Seattle and expanded into the 'time-definite' package and more recently the supply chain and freight businesses, primarily within the US. International expansion started in the mid-1970s with the establishment of hubs in Canada and Germany and by 2008 it delivered packages to 6.1m consignees in over 200 countries. It operates a ground fleet of 107,000 vehicles and 570 aircraft, around 300 of which are on short-term lease or charter from other operators. Its licence to operate its own aircraft was granted by the FAA in 1988. Its reporting is focused on three distinct market segments:

- US domestic packages;
- international packages;
- supply chain and freight operations.

The first includes the delivery of letters, documents and packages throughout the US, and has been described as the 'cash cow' for the group despite strong competition in this market. The second covers the same types of products but delivered to consignees situated outside the US. This segment could include both shipper and consignee located outside the US. The third includes logistics and freight forwarding activities, both within the US and internationally. The latter segment was added in the late 1990s and required shipping larger consignments than hitherto.

The nature of the business has changed along with a change in the nature of the supply chain. In earlier days a US operator would be providing logistical support entirely within the US, most movements satisfied by truck services. Globalisation and outsourcing gradually developed such that US firms, both large and small, became more integrated into the world economy and international services were required using both ships and aircraft. To provide the latter, UPS Airlines was formed in 1985, with the acquisition of Fritz in 2001 and Menlo in 2004, increasing its capability in both trucking and ocean transport forwarding. International strengths came through the purchase of Lynx Express in the UK (2005) and Challenge Air in the US (1999) with an established Latin American network, and a joint venture with Sinotrans in China back in 1988.

UPS operates hub-and-spoke systems, as do the other major integrators. UPS's main hub is at its Worldport at Louisville, Kentucky. It also feeds shipments through regional hubs in the US at Columbia (South Carolina), Dallas-Fort Worth (Texas), Hartford (Connecticut), Ontario (California), Philadelphia (Pennsylvania) and Rockford (Illinois).

International hubs are located at Cologne (Germany) for Europe, Hamilton (Ontario) for Canada, and Miami (Florida) for Latin America and the Caribbean. No single hub can meet the needs of the Asian region, where flights are coordinated at Shanghai (China), Pampanga (Philippines), Taipei (Taiwan), Hong Kong and Singapore. A new hub was planned to open in 2010 at Shenzhen International Airport in South China. This would replace the Philippines hub. Distribution within China will use local airlines, for example the recent start-up, Shufeng Airways, that is owned by express and courier companies and has based two B757F aircraft at Shenzhen. UPS's largest ground vehicle hub outside the US was opened at Tamworth in the UK in 2009.

UPS strengthened its air transport capabilities in 1999 by acquiring Challenge Air, a US cargo airline with extensive Latin American traffic rights. Challenge's operating licence was taken over by Centurion Air Cargo, which continued to offer cargo flights with DC10 and later MD-11F freighters. Challenge's cargo and ground handling facilities in Miami and Latin America were included in the deal, as well as leases for ground and warehouse equipment, and information systems. Above all, UPS took over the airline's route operating authorities to 17 cities in 13 countries. Challenge's fleet of DC 10-40 and Boeing 757-200 aircraft were not included. It expanded into heavy freight by its acquisition of Menlo World Forwarding in 2004 (which it found hard to integrate with its existing businesses), and North American ground freight services with 'Overnite' in 2005.

Table 5.7 lists the major hub airports that UPS has established, the most recent being at Shanghai's Pudong Airport in 2009. Its major hub is the US airport of Louisville, Kentucky, where it is the major operator. The shaded area shows the other North American hubs and the remainder are in Europe and Asia.

Table 5.7   UPS US and international hub airports, 2009

	Size (sq.ft m)	Packages/ hour (000)	In/out bound flights/day	Aircraft parking stands
Louisville, KY	5,200	350	253	117
Philadelphia, PA	681	80	58	26
Ontario, CA	502	36	45	22
Dallas, TX	323	46	45	17
Rockford, IL	586	121	40	40
Columbia, SC	281	41	40	14
Hartford, CT	227	20	6	4
Miami, FL	36	7	29	9
Hamilton, Canada	31	6	24	n/a
Cologne, Germany	323	110	76	64
Pampanga, Philippines	64	8	17	n/a
Hong Kong	44	5	8	n/a
Shanghai, China	1,000	17	14	n/a

In 1999, UPS offered 10 percent of its shares or stock to the public for the first time. Up to then it had been wholly owned by its employees. The latter continued to hold UPS Class A shares that gave their holders 10 votes per share held, while the newly issued Class B shareholders were entitled to only one vote. The Class B shares were listed on the New York Stock Exchange and the Class A shares were fully convertible into B shares.

5.2.5 TNT

TNT was founded in Australia in 1946 by Ken Thomas. His company was named Thomas Nationwide Transport (hence today's TNT abbreviation), operating a single truck. From there it expanded, mainly by acquiring other companies, to become a global logistics and transport company, operating its own fleet of aircraft. Its interest in owning aircraft also goes back to its Australian roots with a joint venture in an aircraft leasing company, Ansett World Aviation Services, together with the now worldwide media company, News Corporation. Ansett was a domestic Australian airline that had placed a large order for British Aerospace 146s and wished to lease these to third parties. This helped establish TNT's European air network in 1987, resulting in a move towards it becoming a fully integrated carrier, at least in Europe. TNT no longer has its 50 percent investment in what became AWAS, having sold it to Morgan Stanley in 2000.[1] International expansion was helped by the purchase of Speedage in India (2006), Hoau in China (2007) and Mercurio in Brazil (2007).

TNT was acquired by the Netherlands PTT (Post Office) in 1996 in a friendly take-over. The government of the Netherlands had sold its shares in the national Post Office in two stages, and by 1995 it retained only a minority share and was effectively privatised. The new group continued acquiring smaller express and mail companies, mostly in Europe, and the corporate name (TPG) was changed to TNT in 2005 to reflect its strong international brand. TNT is a now a privately owned company, with 43 percent of its bearer shares considered to be owned by US and 25 percent by UK nationals. Only 5 percent are thought to be held in the Netherlands.

TNT is split into two main divisions, Express and Post. TNT's express division employed 62 percent of the group's full-time equivalent staff and accounted for 60 percent of its turnover. Just over half the division's employees were based in Europe, with only 4 percent in the Netherlands (compared to 69 percent of the mail division staff). Express carried 230m consignments in 2008 or 7.45m tonnes, equating to an average of 32 kg per consignment.

Its air transport operations are undertaken through 100 percent owned subsidiaries, TNT Airways based at Liège, and Pan Air in Spain. In 2008, TNT Express had access to a fleet of 46 aircraft (seven of which were chartered) and 26,610 ground vehicles. These were operated via an international air hub at Liège Airport, set up in 2004, and sorting centres and road hubs at Wiesbaden (Germany) and Brussels (Belgium), as well as an international road hub at Arnhem in the Netherlands. The aircraft that it owns include 12 BAe-146s, 10 B737-300Fs, two B757-200SFs, one B747-400ERF and four A300B4-600Fs. Additional capacity is wet leased or chartered from other operators such as the two Air Atlanta Icelandic A300-600Fs signed up at the end of 2009. Pan Air operates six BAe-146s.

In September 2009, it introduced a new service to Hong Kong from its Liège hub, with three flights a week using a B747-400 freighter. This complemented its existing flights to Shanghai Pudong via Singapore. In Europe, flights are operated to Amsterdam, Frankfurt, Goteburg in Sweden and Zaragoza in Spain, with Dubai served in the Middle East.

In 2006, TNT sold its logistics division to affiliates of Apollo Management, a leading private equity firm. This was a somewhat surprising development, given the growing focus of other major integrators on providing these services. However, TNT had decided to concentrate on its core competency of managing delivery networks. Also in 2006 it acquired domestic express companies in China and India, complementing its alliances with companies in many other countries.

---

1   Morgan Stanley subsequently sold AWAS to Terra Firma, a private equity firm in 2006, by which time it owned and managed more than 300 aircraft.

5.3 The Post Offices

In the UK the Royal Mail holds a licence to offer letter and parcels services within the UK subject to various delivery conditions and service requirements. The Royal Mail Group includes the Post Offices and Parcel Force, both run entirely separately from the mail services.

Overall in the EU, postal services are estimated to handle 135 billion items per year, reflecting a turnover of about €90 billion, about two-thirds of which is generated by mail services. The reminder is generated by parcels and express services which have already been opened up to competition.

Express Mail Service (EMS) is an international express postal service offered by postal-administration members of the Universal Postal Union (UPU). Currently EMS is offered by 153 of the 191 UPU member countries' postal authorities and an integral part of their normal postal services. An independent auditor measures the express delivery performance of all international EMS operators and each member is awarded a Gold, Silver or Bronze certificate depending on their yearly performance.

The United States Postal Service (USPS) provides Express Mail for domestic US delivery, and offers two EMS categories of services for Express Mail International. One is simply called Express Mail International and the other service is called Global Express Guaranteed (GXG). These two USPS International Mail terms are often confused with their service called Express Mail, which is a specific classification of mail for domestic accelerated postal delivery within the US. Special Delivery, a domestic accelerated delivery service, was originally introduced in 1885, initially with a fee of 10¢ paid by a Special Delivery stamp. It has been transformed into Express Mail, which was introduced in 1977 after an experimental period that started in 1970, though Special Delivery was not terminated until 1997.

Post Offices tend to send their international mail on the scheduled services of combination carriers which have the best range of destination and adequate lower deck capacity for mail items. They often charter small aircraft to take domestic mail to their main sorting offices. One postal authority that owned an airline was the French La Poste's Airposte airline, which operated B737-300 Quick Change aircraft on domestic and some intra-EU sectors. This was acquired by Irish registered Air Contractors in 2008 with the intention of using the aircraft to operate mail flights by night and European passenger charters by day.

5.4 Freight Forwarders and Consolidators

A freight forwarder is an intermediary who acts on behalf of importers, exporters or other companies or persons involved in shipping goods, organising the safe, efficient and cost-effective transportation of goods. Freight forwarders arrange the best means of transport, using the services of shipping lines, airlines, road and rail freight operators. In some cases, the freight forwarding company itself provides the service, taking into account the type of goods and the customers' delivery requirements. Forwarders vary in size and type, from those operating on a national and international basis to smaller, more specialised firms, who deal with particular types of goods or operate within particular geographical areas. The international market, however, is dominated by large global companies such as Deutsche Post DHL, DB Schenker and Kuehne + Nagel.

Figure 5.2 gives estimates for the development of the world freight forwarding market between 2003 and 2008. Growth averaged 10.6 percent over this period, and was forecast to increase by only 1.9 percent a year between 2008 and 2012 (taking into account the 2008/2009 downturn).

MergeGlobal estimated that freight forwarders accounted for 85 percent of the value of air freight market in 2007, excluding the express parcel market carried by the big four integrators (MergeGlobal, 2008). They also took 74 percent of the less than container load (LCL) sea freight value, but only 34 percent of the full container (FCL) sea freight. The rest in each case was carried by air and ocean carriers. The high share of air and LCL traffic results from their role in consolidation.

The world air freight forwarding market was estimated to have been 19 million tonnes in 2008 (exports only), with ocean freight totalling 31.7 million TEUs. The largest air freight operators were DHL, DB Schenker and Panalpina, while DHL, Kuehne + Nagel and DB Schenker took the top three positions in ocean freight. Contract logistics was estimated to have been worth €147 billion in 2008, with the top three players being DHL (8.5 percent), CEVA (2.4 percent) and Kuehne + Nagel (2.1 percent).

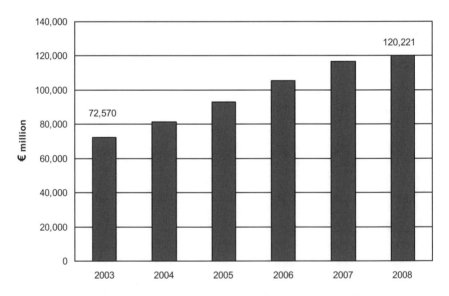

Figure 5.2   Global freight forwarding market size, 2003 to 2008

Source: Transport Intelligence in Logistics Management, November 2009.

It was estimated that 95 percent of LH Cargo's overall freight volume stemmed from large forwarding companies such as Schenker, Kuehne + Nagel and Danzas (Hellermann, 2002). The top four forwarders will be examined in more detail, noting the importance of Switzerland as a base for three of these.

Table 5.8 gives the top 10 forwarders ranked by the value or revenues of their forwarding business. Some such as DHL Forwarding and DB Schenker are part of larger groups, but only their forwarding activities have been included.

The top 10 were estimated to account for around 40 percent of total forwarding revenues in 2008, with concentration increasing in recent years. However, there are still a large number of small forwarders based in one country or specialising in certain kinds of freight. The largest companies are described in more detail below.

Table 5.8   Global freight forward value share by top 10 forwarders, 2008

	Percent
DHL: global forwarding	8.8
Kuehne + Nagel: sea and air freight	7.6
DB Schenker: air/ocean freight	5.8
Panalpina: air/ocean freight	4.2
Expeditors	3.3
Sinotrans: freight forwarding	2.8
Agility: freight forwarding	2.5
UPS SCS: forwarding services	2.4
CEVA: freight management	2.4
DVS: air/sea freight	2.1
Others	58.1
Total	100.0

Source: Transport Intelligence in Logistics Management, November 2009.

5.4.1 DHL: Global Forwarding

DHL Global Forwarding is the division of Deutsche Post DHL that is responsible for its traditional forwarding activities, further split into two business units: global forwarding and freight. Both operate under the DHL brand. The two other divisions are DHL Express (see section 5.2.2) and DHL Supply Chain. Global Forwarding is a purchaser of both air and ocean freight services, the latter using DHL aircraft on some routes (e.g. transatlantic) but more often contracted out to other companies. Global freight covers the European trucking services, while global mail is the German Postal Service (a separate division of the holding company). The express division deals with integrator activities while supply chain covers logistics solutions for larger multinationals. The ultimate holding company of these divisions, Deutsche Post DHL, is no longer majority owned by the German government: in February 2010, 63 percent of its shares were held by institutions, 7 percent by private individuals and 30 percent by the German government through its development bank.

In 2009, the global forwarding division had a turnover of €10,870 million, or 20 percent of group revenue of €54 billion, by far the largest parent of any of the other large forwarders. It only accounted for 9 percent of total group employment, which numbered over 400,000 full-time equivalent employees in 2009. Most staff are employed in the post and supply chain divisions. It estimates that it is the market leader in the world air and ocean freight markets and second to DB Schenker in the European trucking market. In 2009, air freight accounted for 50 percent of forwarding revenue, with ocean freight only 31 percent of the total. It handled 3.734 million tonnes of freight, down by 13 percent from the previous year compared to its 28 percent drop in revenues. Its ocean freight was 2.615 million TEUs,[2] down only 9 percent from 2008.

5.4.2 Kuehne + Nagel

The Swiss based Kuehne + Nagel's strategy focuses on providing integrated logistics solutions, a global expansion, and a stronger European overland presence. Its express products have expanded from 5 percent of shipments to 16 percent between 1997 and 2009. These 'promise' delivery within 1–3 days depending on distance, with next day for destinations of less than 800 km. It air freight averaged at around 14,400 tonnes per week, or 45,000 shipments (giving an average shipment weight of 320 kg). It uses a variety of airlines, in particular Lufthansa, Cargolux and Emirates. Its sea traffic uses such companies as Hapag-Lloyd, OCL and Maersk.

In 2009 it handled 2.546 million TEUs of ocean freight, down only 5 percent from 2008, while its air freight was 758,000 tonnes, down by 9 percent. However, turnover was down by 26 percent for ocean and 25 percent for air freight, broadly maintaining its share of air transport in total revenue. Air freight only accounted for 16 percent of its 2009 turnover, with sea freight taking 44 percent and contract logistics 25 percent.

5.4.3 DB Schenker

DB Schenker was formed following the acquisition of the global forwarder, Schenker, by the German railway operator Deutsche Bahn in 2002. In 2006 it added the US$2 billion turnover North American forwarder Bax Global to become one the world's largest logistics companies. The group is still 100 percent owned by the Federal Government of Germany although it was the intention to privatise it once conditions were right. These plans were put on hold following the global banking crisis in 2009. The combined group had a turnover of €15 billion in 2009.

---

2   TEU is an abbreviation for 'Twenty foot Equivalent Unit' and is used to describe traffic and capacity in container shipping. This 20-foot container has the dimensions 20 ft x 8 ft x 8.5 ft giving a volume of 1,360 cubic foot. There is no precise conversion to weight or mass, but a rough guide is a maximum gross weight of 24 tonnes or 21.6 tonnes net of the tare weight.

DB Schenker's business includes air, ocean, overland and logistics, with air freight traffic of 1.032 million tonnes and ocean 1.424 million TEU in 2009, down by 16 percent and 2 percent respectively from 2008. Its forwarding division also handled around 70m overland shipments within Europe. DB Schenker Logistics's 2009 revenues were €11.3 billion, or 39 percent of the group total of €29.3 billion. The group is thus a large operator, especially in Europe, but still only around half of the size of Deutsche Post DHL.

5.4.4 Panalpina

The other major Swiss forwarder, Panalpina, offers air and ocean freight as well as supply chain management. It targets in particular the following sectors:

- automotive;
- health care/chemicals;
- retail/fashion;
- high-tech;
- telecoms;
- oil and gas (logistics).

In 2009 it handled 731,000 tonnes of air freight and 1.103 million TEUs of ocean freight. It recorded a drop in air tonnage of 19 percent in 2009 compared with only 14 percent for ocean, confirming the trend of a modal shift towards sea. Panalpina is one of the largest sea-air operators, offering such multimodal transport from Asia to Europe and North America (see section 2.6). Its net revenue from air freight forwarding amounted to CHF 2,714 million in 2009 (US$2,502 million), compared to total net turnover of CHF 5,958 million (US$5,493 million), down by 33 percent from 2008. Net revenues are arrived at after deducting customs, duties and taxes. Air freight accounted for 45 percent of 2009 net revenues, ocean 40 percent and supply chain 15 percent. Its gross profit margin on air freight was 21 percent compared to 19 percent for ocean freight and 40 percent for supply chain management. Its staff costs were 64 percent of gross profit, which was the difference between net revenues and the cost of purchasing transport services, and is thus a relatively labour intensive business.

Historically, the Panalpina has purchased approximately 70 percent of its required total air transport capacity on a short-term basis without financial risk. About 25 percent of capacity has been contracted medium-term (up to six months in advance) with limited financial risk. The remaining 5 percent of the total air transport capacity has been contracted on a long-term (more than six months) basis, with the associated financial risk more than offset by the lower costs of the purchased capacity. At the beginning of 2009, due to the uncertain economic climate, it has significantly reduced the percentage of advance purchasing of air transport capacity.

In 2009, Panalpina renewed its charter contract with Atlas Air to fly a number of weekly B747-400F services between Luxembourg and Huntsville, Alabama, with connections in Mexico and an intermediate stop at Prestwick, UK, on some services. It also has connections to/from West Africa, which is justified by its significant oil and gas business.

5.4.5 Expeditors

Expeditors is a global logistics company based in the US. It offers international freight forwarding using both air and ocean transport, consolidation and customs broking. It does not own or operate aircraft (or ships) and does not compete in the courier or small parcels business. Its 2009 turnover was US$1.4 billion, 35 percent of which came from air freight, 24 percent from ocean and the rest from customs brokerage and other services. Its air freight share has remained almost unchanged over the three years to 2009, during which time its net margin on revenues averaged 18 percent. It is a very labour intensive operation, with labour costs just under 80 percent of total operating costs. Its customers tend to be either in the retail sector or involved in Just-in-time production and manufacturing.

5.4.6 Other Forwarders

There are a number of forwarders which are strong in their home country but have little global presence. One of these is, Sinotrans, a shipping company with a majority owned forwarder, Sinotrans Air Transportation Development Co. Ltd., founded in October 1999 and successfully listed on Shanghai Stock Exchange in December 2000. It has a large and fast growing home market and a number of joint ventures with global companies, namely DHL in the express business and Korean Air in Grand Star, a Chinese cargo airline (see Chapter 4).

Its main business is the provision of international air freight forwarding, air express and domestic cargo and logistics services. In 2009 it handled approximately 224,700 tonnes of air cargo, approximately 135,000 tonnes of which was imported.

Nippon Express is a long established transport and logistics company which has a strong market position in Japan and also operates internationally through over 50 subsidiaries. The Nippon Express Group claims to be the world's second largest international air freight forwarder but does not rank as high on air freight forwarding alone as it may have in the past. In 2009, the group's turnover was US$18,619 million, with air freight forwarding accounting for only $1.49 billion.

Another large Japanese forwarder is Kintetsu World Express (KWE) which traces its origins to the Kinki Nippon Railway Company moving into the international freight business over 60 years ago. It has always specialised in air freight, and in 2009 this accounted for 69 percent of its total revenues of US$2,656 million, with ocean freight having only 20 percent.

It can be concluded from the above that at least the larger forwarders are relatively profitable, with their air freight business often earning more than ocean shipping. Without needing transport vehicle assets they also report a good return on capital. Employee costs account for a high share of total costs, and these and other costs such as IT systems and purchase commitments for transport services, are relatively inflexible in the event of a major downturn. However, they can take advantage of lower shipping costs as airlines and shipping companies reduced their rates by as much as 30 percent during the 2008/2009 crisis. This means that forwarders tend to have higher and less volatile returns on capital than cargo airlines. The last 20 years has seen consolidation as forwarders have merged, acquired smaller operators and become part of total supply chain or logistics groups. This gives them an advantage when dealing with multinational firms. Smaller local forwarders can survive, especially where national regulations give them a competitive advantage, and their local knowledge is used to their advantage. They have also sought to link up with similar companies in other countries to be able to offer a better service to exporters.

5.5 Maritime Operators

Maritime operators compete at the margin with air transport and can be complementary through their role in sea-air shipment. It is the containership operators that are relevant here and the top 10 operators dominate the industry with 52 percent of TEU capacity offered in January 2010. The Danish Maersk Line is by far the largest with a fleet of 2.0 million TEU, followed by MSC (UK) with 1.5 million and CMA-CGM (France) with 1.0 million. The next largest is Evergreen from Taiwan with 559,000 TEU, closely followed by the Singapore based Neptune Orient Lines/APL, Hapag Lloyd (Germany), COSCO (China) and China Shipping. Both Maersk and Hapag Lloyd, two large European companies, have in the past owned passenger charter airlines, but these were not profitable and have been sold. The tenth largest, the Japanese NYK, now has a controlling interest in Nippon Cargo Airlines (see Chapter 12, section 12.2). Evergreen's parent company also owns the Taiwanese airline, Eva Air, a large air cargo carrier.

An example of a North Atlantic sea transport is Hapag Lloyd's Atlantic Express Shuttle from Antwerp to New York. The word 'Express' is relative since the voyage takes nine days, but it can take up to 2,200 TEUs or around 30,000 tonnes.

Mainline freight rates fell by 17 percent in 2009 for eastbound transpacific sailings while Far East to Europe dropped by 32 percent. These trends were similar to those experienced by air cargo operators. The Clarkson Containership Timecharter Rate index fell to its lowest ever level at the end of 2009. Shanghai has overtaken Hong Kong to be the second largest container port after Singapore, with the largest in Europe (Antwerp) and North America (Los Angeles) only a third of the leading Asia ports' throughput.

Chapter 6
Air Cargo Alliances and Mergers

This chapter will cover air cargo alliances and mergers, focusing on those that have been agreed between airlines, excluding forwarders and integrators. As on the passenger side of the business, mergers have been restricted to airlines based in one country to avoid upsetting ownership limits and thus putting into question traffic rights. Alliances have thus been seen as an alternative to mergers. Some of the benefits of cross-border mergers can be obtained in this way while remaining wholly owned and controlled by nationals of the home country. Alliances are, however, subject to governmental scrutiny to assess whether competition is impaired, and if this is the case conditions might be attached to the alliance.

Grönlund and Skoog (2005) argue that air cargo alliances are a response to marginal cost pricing and integrator power. However, it is difficult to see how alliances between airlines can consolidate their position in the door-to-door market, given even limited redress from the competition authorities.

Strategic alliances develop cooperation between airlines as far as possible without a merger. More and more of the world's airlines are now members of one of the three major groups. However, these alliances are principally designed to improve revenues and reduce costs of operating passenger services and not always the best way forward for the cargo subsidiaries or divisions of its members. These alliances and the cargo role in them will be discussed first, followed by the additional benefits of full mergers in the following section.

Some alliances are cemented with a minority stake exchanged between two carriers, and these will be addressed under alliances below. One-way minority stakes, which will usually be accompanied by some sort of alliance or joint venture between airlines, will also be discussed. Alliances or joint ventures with forwarders, integrators or Post Offices, which may involve setting up a joint company, are described in Chapter 5.

6.1 Air Cargo Alliances

6.1.1 Strategic Alliances

Regulatory restrictions on market access, ownership and control have pushed airlines towards the formation of strategic alliance groupings. Legislation aimed at protecting national interests has meant that it is virtually impossible to acquire a controlling interest in airlines in countries or trading blocs outside those in which an airline is owned and operated. As a result, over the years several alliance groupings have emerged, aiming to increase global reach, improve revenues, reduce costs and increase customer benefits.

Although there are many types of agreements and alliances between airlines, they tend to fall into three broad categories:

- Commercial: generally on a route-by-route basis and limited to some form of marketing agreement. They can include code sharing on a limited number of routes, block space agreements or joint venture flights (see below).
- Strategic: cover extensive code sharing and marketing agreements over the airlines' networks.
- Equity partnership: involve partners investing in each other through share purchases.

The extent of benefits to airlines and consumers derived from alliances very much depends on the type of agreement and the subsequent depth of members' integration of activities. The greater the depth of agreement, the higher is the possibility of alliances yielding tangible benefits. Closer cooperation is aimed at increasing revenues, and can also lead to cost reduction. For example a joint venture freighter service could save a considerable expense if the partner airline had a more appropriate aircraft type, say a B747-400 freighter. The main types of commercial agreement between airlines are discussed below.

Prorate agreement

A prorate agreement is a means of sharing the revenue generated from a multi-sector service involving more than one airline (a multilateral prorate is between more than two airlines). The revenue is divided between the operating airlines, normally on the basis of the general cargo rate for under 45 kg consignments, each airline's share calculated as the proportion of the rate for the sector it operated to the sum of the rate for the two sectors together. A special prorate is established where a different method of allocation is used, for example using great circle distances.

Code share

Code sharing refers to the use of an airline designator code of one carrier on a flight actually being flown by another carrier. It means that the non-operating airline can market the service as if it were its own, with the code-shared capacity appearing in booking systems. It can be route specific and not be a part of a strategic alliance. The carrier that sells the space will pay the operating carrier according to a net rate or on a commission basis. It can be used between the home country of an airline and the country of another airline, where that airline provides the service and it is uneconomic for the home country carrier to operate. For example, Korean Air may have a freighter service to a European country and the home country might code-share rather than fly the route itself. It can thus use its third and fourth freedom traffic rights without having to operate the service. Within alliances it is often used to connect with an airline's service using third and fourth freedom rights to/

from the point beyond the destination served, and in some cases also fifth freedom rights on the code-shared flight. This is much less common for air cargo since Road Feeder Services (RFS) can be used without the need for air traffic rights.

Block space agreement
A block space agreement is the purchase of an agreed capacity or space on the flight of another carrier. It would also involve code sharing. The arrangement could be 'hard block' whereby the purchasing carrier has to pay for the space regardless of whether it is sold, or 'soft block' where the purchasing carrier only pays for the space sold. An example of this is the Japan Airlines freighter service from Tokyo to London Heathrow, in which British Airways Cargo purchased 50 percent of the capacity, and marketed the flight under its code. This suited British Airways since it did not have much freighter capacity to spare and it preferred to use its valuable Heathrow slots for passenger services.

Capacity swap
Capacity swaps are similar to block space agreements but on a back-to-back basis. Each carrier takes block space on the flights of the other. China Airlines' and China Southern's strategic partnership signed in 2010 included such a swap, in addition to special cargo prorates.

Joint venture
Joint venture (JV) agreements are similar to what used to be called 'pooling agreements', which were very common in the 1960s and 1970s. A number of flights can be 'pooled' and included in the joint venture. Both carriers sell all the flights in the agreement and at the end of each accounting period the revenues and operating costs of the flights are divided between the two according to a pre-arranged agreement. Schedules and fares/rates are discussed jointly and thus JVs need approval from the competition authorities in both countries. Nowadays they usually form part of a strategic alliance that has anti-trust immunity for such activities.

The aim of commercial agreements or alliances is to increase revenues and reduce operating costs in the short to medium term and thus increase profitability. Each of these is discussed in turn.

Revenue enhancement
Airline alliances' initial focus appeared to be on increasing traffic, load factors and subsequently increases in revenue through:

- increased access to more destinations, and in some cases the only way to serve certain destinations (e.g. points in the US beyond gateways);
- establish presence in low volume markets with minimum capital outlay by exercising one way code sharing (where a larger carrier adds its code to the flight number of a smaller carrier), e.g. the code-sharing arrangements between network carriers and their franchisees;

- access to slot-constrained airports;
- obtain coordinated feeder traffic with minimum connecting times;
- exercise price leadership on members' hub-to-hub markets;
- better booking system display screen padding or priority over interline services, as the partners' codes under their code-sharing agreements are displayed twice for the same flight.

The extent of revenue benefits as a result of alliances has very much been dependent on the depth of members' operational integration. There appears to be evidence (from numerous press statements and articles) that airlines in global alliances have managed to improve their revenues through better traffic feed, rationalisation of their schedules and networks, better hub connectivity and code sharing. The provision of so called 'seamless travel' by alliances is also supposed to increase passenger loyalty which would have a positive impact on the level of traffic carried by the members. Joint marketing programmes such as targeted promotional fares or rates can potentially increase the attractiveness of the alliances services. However, most of these are more difficult to apply to cargo markets.

Reports of increased revenues from alliances should be treated with care. This is because it is very difficult to know how revenues would have developed in the absence of code-shares and the other alliance arrangements. These estimates are usually nicely rounded sums: United reported in 1996 that it generated US$100 million in revenue through its alliance member Lufthansa. Air Canada has reported that the Star Alliance members have gained US$300 million a year in incremental revenue from their link with Air Canada.[1] A study published in January 2000 by Airline Business and Gemini Consulting estimated revenue increases of $100 to $200 million a year for larger airline alliances with turnover of $7 billion per year, an increase of 1.4 percent to 2.8 percent in their revenue (not a very precise estimate).

Cost reduction
While alliances' initial focus appeared to be more on revenue generation activities, they have also moved towards cost reduction strategies. The cost savings through economies of scale and scope can be achieved from the following:

- Reduction of duplications in areas of sales, distribution and administration. This is likely to lead to a reduction in the number of employees and removal of duplicated roles in shared locations. This is almost impossible without a merger.
- Rationalisation of network and services could reduce costs. For example following the British Airways and Qantas alliance, British Airways reduced its service frequency from London to Jakarta via Kuala Lumpur and started a new service from London to Sydney via KL. Qantas ceased flying to

---

1   *British Airways News*, October 1999.

Kuala Lumpur from Sydney. Similarly JAL and Japan Air System (JAS) also announced in 1999 an agreement under which JAS would drop its own services to Seoul and code-share on JAL flights. Such policies can potentially allow partners to use their assets more effectively. Alliances also enable carriers to operate to new markets through code-sharing at a much lower cost than if they physically have flown to the same destinations.

- Coordination of slots amongst alliance members can also improve their operational efficiency. Wet leasing of idle aircraft amongst members can reduce costs and improve aircraft utilisation. A case in point was when in 1996 KLM wet-leased Northwest aircraft during their down time for its New York–Amsterdam operation.
- Provision of joint airport services could potentially reduce costs through sharing terminal and check-in facilities and handling each other's flights. For example, JAL planned to provide JAS with ramp and cargo support services. Services covered will include baggage handling, cargo handling, cabin cleaning and aircraft marshalling.
- Development of joint IT systems could also provide costs savings as the costs could be shared throughout the whole alliance, although harmonisation might initially involve changing to more compatible expensive systems.
- Joint purchasing, where partners can strike better deals with their service and product suppliers through bulk purchases. The suppliers could include aircraft manufacturers, catering, cargo handling services and equipment, fuel, aircraft maintenance and spare part supplier companies. For example, the A330 was ordered jointly in standard configuration by Qualiflyer members Swissair, Austrian and Sabena. BA and GB Airways, BA's franchisee, have jointly ordered 59 and nine of the A320 family of aircraft respectively. Such joint orders can provide the opportunity for prices to be negotiated down and also enable the partners to have more flexibility in utilising their aircraft. Acquiring the same types of aircraft also enables the alliance members to benefit from centralised engineering and maintenance facilities.

Another example of cutting costs through joint bids is an alliance between All Nippon Airways and JAS, aiming to share ground service providers at two domestic airports. ANA expects annual savings of US$375,000 as a result of such a joint bid policy.

A few studies have attempted to quantify the potential for cost reduction following airline alliances and mergers. Müller and Keuschnigg (1998) reported that Lufthansa has estimated that the potential savings resulting from their global alliances will amount to 10 percent of their operating costs. Another study estimated the cost savings as a percentage of total cost to range from 1.9 percent to 11.4 percent depending on the depth of integration.

The consultancy and specialist journal *Aviation Strategy* estimated a cost saving of total operating costs under full merger. Another study[2] estimated that hub-and-spoke operations by alliances provide the members with cost reductions such that break-even yields will decline by approximately 25 percent, compared to a series of point-to-point services offered by individual airlines on the same network.

It has to be noted that while airline alliances offer potential for cost savings it can also increase members' operating cost in the first few years due to the need to integrate areas such as IT (mentioned above), product features, pricing and other service provisions. In addition to these, there is the cost of management time involved in planning and executing joint alliance policies.

Consumer impact
The shipper or passenger interest is of concern to competition authorities when they consider applications from alliances for anti-trust immunity. Before deciding they look closely at the competitive situation in the relevant markets before and after the alliance. If two carriers with a considerable overlap to their networks are involved frequency might be reduced and rates increased to the detriment of the consumer. On the other hand two carriers might combine to form more effective competition with another (stronger) carrier. Because cargo alliance activity has been very limited, at least compared to passenger services, the impact on shipper or forwarder interest has not been evaluated much so far. Competition authority investigations of cargo operations have been almost entirely focused on pricing collusion, especially regarding fuel surcharges (see section 3.2.3).

6.1.2 Strategic Alliances with Minority Stakes

A few of the alliances described above were accompanied by one or both airlines exchanging minority stakes in each other. This may have been as a result of an airline privatisation, as in the case of KLM and Kenya Airways or British Airways and Qantas. In both these examples the two airlines cooperated through their respective strategic alliances, oneworld and SkyTeam. However, these rarely resulted in close cooperation on the cargo side.

6.1.3 Air Cargo Airline Alliances

The first section described the pros and cons of strategic alliances between airlines whose primary business is the carriage of passengers. It follows that the choice of partners is also based on passenger market criteria. The cargo part of those airlines sometimes cement closer ties with the members of the same strategic alliances but the fit is not always as good.

---

2   Airline alliances and competition in transatlantic markets. Final Report by PriceWaterhouseCoopers for the Association of European Airlines, 21 August 1998.

The 'WOW' alliance

The WOW alliance was founded by Lufthansa Cargo, SAS Cargo and Singapore Airlines Cargo in April 2000. JAL Cargo joined WOW in July 2002. The air cargo alliance could access a combined fleet of 43 freighters and the lower deck capacity of more than 760 passenger aircraft, many of them wide-body jets across a worldwide network of frequent flights. Until JAL joined this cargo alliance membership only included Star Alliance partners, but JAL was not (and still is not) in the Star Alliance. WOW was not an abbreviation: according to the Lufthansa Cargo website it stood for the alliance's values: "'Dynamism, Innovation and Vitality". An enthusiastic "WOW" is the customer response that the alliance aims to elicit with its services and quality'.[3]

In 2003 Lufthansa unveiled its first MD11-F in WOW livery, but SIA and JAL did not follow example. In April 2005, JAL Cargo withdrew its J-freight product from the WOW portfolio. As separate airlines they were not interested in selling capacity provided by alliance partners. The alliance started by harmonising four express products: 'J SPEED' from Japan Airlines Cargo, 'td.Flash' from Lufthansa Cargo, 'SAS Priority' from SAS Cargo and 'Swiftrider' from Singapore Airlines Cargo. Initially 10 percent of the cargo capacity that each offered was set aside for alliance bookings, and alliance standards for heavier and general cargo were to follow express products, although each retained its own brand.

Genuine cooperation between the WOW partners proved difficult, with each jealously guarding its own markets and capacity. As a result, in the mid-2000s Lufthansa lost interest in WOW, preferring to focus on bilateral projects with associates Jade and Aerologic and others. While it made no formal announcement that it would leave WOW its 2009 annual report made no mention of it at all.

SkyTeam Cargo

SkyTeam Cargo was set up about six months after WOW by four members of the SkyTeam passenger strategic alliance: Aeroméxico Cargo, Air France Cargo, Delta Air Logistics and Korean Air Cargo. Czech Airlines and Alitalia Cargo joined in 2001 followed by KLM Cargo in 2004 and Northwest in 2005. Since then it has lost two members: Delta Airlines left in 2008 and Korean Air in October 2009. However, rumours of the death of the venture were premature with the announcement in March 2010 that China Southern would join, following its acceptance into the SkyTeam strategic alliance in 2007. SkyTeam Cargo currently comprises the cargo arms of AeroMexico, Air France-KLM, Czech Airlines and China Southern. The SkyTeam Cargo website was re-launched in 2003 but by mid-2010 the latest information on it was from 2008. It linked to its members' cargo websites (including that of Delta) but this tended not to be reciprocated. SkyTeam members share cargo terminals at many airports and have developed four standard categories of product: Equation, Cohesion, Variation and Dimension.

---

3   Start-up passenger airline WOW Macau changed its name after Lufthansa complained it was too similar to that of its cargo airline alliance WOW.

Equation is for express cargo and offers the following:

- airport-to-airport express;
- top-loading priority: boarding on first available flight;
- no booking required: for weight per parcel up to 70 kg, for shipments under 300 kg;
- acceptance up to 90 minutes before departure;
- documents and shipment ready within 90 minutes of arrival;
- online shipment tracking available on the tracking section;
- money-back guarantee on selected routes;
- delivery time can vary from station to station;
- Equation Heavy is an option of Equation designed for parcels of greater than 70 kg on an airport-to-airport basis.

Cohesion offers fully customised shipping using a three-way contract between the shipper, the forwarding agent and SkyTeam Cargo. It also provides personalised information and handling guidelines specifically tailored to the shipper's freight needs. Its key features are:

- a specific contract is issued for a determined period between the shipper, the forwarding agent and the SkyTeam Cargo Alliance member;
- privileged access to the capacity on the chosen flight;
- loading priority;
- fixed rates for duration of the contract;
- dedicated monitoring through a computerised tracking system, which alerts customer service should an irregularity occur;
- recognition: individual customers receive personalised information;
- customisation: handling guidelines tailored to customers' needs;
- tracking: online shipment tracking with any SkyTeam Cargo member.

Variation is designed for any kind of freight, including items such as precious artwork, dangerous goods, perishable freight, oversized objects or live animals.

Dimension is the standard product any type of shipment of any weight that does not require special handling, and includes bulk and ULD allocations at special ULD rates.

oneworld
The other major global strategic alliance, oneworld, had 11 members in 2009 and total revenues of just under US$100 billion, of which only 2.5 percent was reported to come from interline billing between members. However, none of this came from cargo which is specifically excluded from the passenger alliance.

Qualiflyer

Another strategic alliance that ceased with the collapse of Swissair in 2001 was 'Qualiflyer'. This was composed of Swissair (later part of the SAir Group) and airlines in which it had a minority stake. Swissair's cargo was spun off into a subsidiary, Swisscargo, which in turn managed the cargo capacity for a number of Qualiflyer members including its sister company, Swissair. These included Sabena, Crossair and Citybird, as well as Cargolux (see next section). The plan was to build a global air cargo system with harmonised products and standards, an umbrella brand for all the airlines involved, but it was not put to the test.

One paper aimed at identifying and quantifying the impact of a major passenger alliance, between KLM and Northwest Airlines, on the development of cargo service characteristics for one of the alliance partners, namely KLM (Morrell and Pilon, 1999). The approach adopted was that of origin-to-destination city-pair matching based on the approach of previous research by Youssef and Hansen (1994). Freighter flights were not considered, because these tend to consist of consolidated shipments that entailed break-bulk activities, and consequently require more transfer time than the 90 minutes used for cargo transhipped in sealed containers principally using the lower decks of passenger services.

The network changes of KLM and NWA were examined from 1987 to 1998 although the effect of their alliance cannot be isolated. The number of theoretical markets (i.e. city-pairs) available to both passengers and cargo shippers appeared to have increased during the first three years of the alliance but fell (but remained higher than in 1991) between 1994 and 1998. More detailed analysis indicated that the number of non-stop exclusively served spokes increased significantly, reflecting favourable market conditions and increased traffic feed owing to the alliance.

The impact of the KLM/NWA passenger alliance on the transhipped cargo service characteristics was also analysed, focusing on how the quantity and quality of connections, through Amsterdam and Minneapolis (MSP), Detroit (DTW) and New York (JFK) with alliance partner NWA, and Chicago (ORD) with interline carrier United Airlines (UAL), have changed since the alliance. The period of analysis was between 1991 and 1998. As such the research centred on the impact of the passenger alliance on cargo services during the development of the passenger alliance. The hypothesis was that the passenger alliance had resulted in a deterioration in the quantity and quality of cargo connections, through both a reduction in transfer times to levels that were insufficient for cargo, and also less belly-hold capacity due to higher frequencies with smaller aircraft.

The quality of connections was measured in terms of cargo layover times and available belly-hold capacity. Minimum transfer time was doubled from 45 to 90 minutes to reflect additional handling activities for cargo. Four samples were used; one selected by the authors, the second focusing on code-shared flights, the third provided by cargo agents (via JFK) and the fourth connecting through ORD, KLM's existing cargo hub in the US, with interline carrier United Airlines.

Connecting services had gone up significantly for all samples, but JFK and MSP displayed the highest connectivity levels due to high service frequencies. Cargo layover times worsened during the first years of the alliance except for the samples connecting through JFK and ORD. Subsequent results depict significantly declining cargo layover times except for ORD, which showed declined connectivity. This highlights the fact that the KLM and NWA schedules now provided a better match than the KLM-UAL interline services. This can be considered evidence that effective schedule coordination requires a longer time-span than previous research indicated. However, the schedule remains primarily tailored to passenger services, as most flights out of AMS are around midday, whereas cargo is being built up during the day and would preferably be put on evening flights. This is a prevailing characteristic of combination carriers.

It should be emphasised that the above analysis is based entirely on supply characteristics. It thus does not consider cargo traffic volumes or consignment sizes, nor does it include possibilities for transfers between passenger and freighter services.

It is questionable whether a global alliance works for air cargo, at least as well as for passengers. Some cite the lack of economies of scale and scope, others cultural differences. Cargo is marketed more as a commodity and less as a brand. Airlines have problems promoting their own services as a brand and an alliance brand would be harder still. Lufthansa has switched emphasis to bilateral deals such as those that do not involve any financial commitment. In addition to its joint venture with DHL, it has a reciprocal cargo management arrangement with US Airways across the Atlantic, its investment in Jade Cargo in China and joint freighter flights with Air China, South African Airways and LAN Cargo. Forwarders dominate the distribution of air cargo and negotiate deals on service and price, with loyalty lower in terms of priorities. In contrast, the passenger business has been increasingly sold direct, with brand loyalty stronger and frequent flyer programmes well suited to strategic alliance cooperation.

6.2 Air Cargo Mergers and Acquisitions

6.2.1 Mergers and Acquisitions within one Country

Most air cargo merger and acquisition activity has taken place in the US, given its large cargo market already de-regulated since 1977. The first major take-over was Flying Tiger acquiring a large US cargo airline, Seaboard World Airlines in 1980. This was followed by CF Air Freight acquiring Emery Air Freight in April 1989 to form Emery Worldwide. Emery had purchased a large courier company, Purolator, two years earlier, but subsequently faced financial problems.

Flying Tiger, a US all-cargo carrier with a worldwide network, was in financial trouble towards the end of the 1980s and was acquired by Federal Express later in that year. Flying Tiger already had the extensive international network that Federal Express wanted, in addition to a long-haul freighter fleet and ground support facilities. In particular FedEx sought potentially lucrative routes to key Asian destinations such as Japan, which it was finding it hard to obtain under the ASAs in force at that time. Flying Tiger operated 30 weekly services between the US and Japan and these were transferred to FedEx after the take-over, with the approval of the Japanese government. It subsequently purchased Evergreen's route rights to China, a necessary step given China's restrictive policy at that time.

Federal Express purchased Flying Tigers in February for approximately $880 million, but took some time to integrate the two operations. FedEx had a younger workforce, employed more part-time staff and had a more formalised system of management (including strict dress code). Critically Flying Tiger was heavily unionised whereas FedEx was not. For example, none of FedEx's 1,000 or so pilots were members of a union and all of Flying Tigers' were. After the merger, FedEx tried unsuccessfully to de-unionise (decertify) the pilots of the airline it had acquired. Prior to the acquisition in 1988 FedEx carried 55,000 tonnes of cargo on international routes and 1.2 million tonnes within the US. In the same year Flying Tiger carried 490,000 tonnes in the US and 471,000 tonnes internationally. FedEx's internationally tonnage thus jumped to 451,000 tonnes in 1990, combining its own express parcels with Flying Tiger's heavier general cargo.

A large number of US network carriers have merged over the years from the acquisition of household names such as TWA (by American) to the recent merger of Delta and Northwest. Most of this concentration has not had a major impact on the air cargo industry since most of the airlines, at least on US domestic routes, operated narrow-bodied aircraft with limited cargo capacity. The Delta/Northwest merger had greater implications for cargo since both airlines had international routes operated by wide-bodies, and Northwest had its own freighter operations. Delta Airlines owned no freighters but operated a large number of Boeing 767-300 and -400 aircraft, as well as some B777-200s; Northwest owned 13 B747-200F freighters, all of which were grounded by the end of 2009. It is likely that these aircraft will be sold, leaving the merged airline with no freighters. In 2008 Delta carried 118,000 tonnes on domestic services and 184,000 tonnes internationally; Northwest carried a slightly lower tonnage on domestic routes but 338,000 tonnes on international flights.

Outside the US, Chile's national combination carrier, Lan-Chile, was privatised in 1989, with the airline's ownership transferred to private Chilean investors and the 50 percent government owned airline from Scandinavia, SAS, taking 25 percent. SAS and its partners were unable to improve its financial situation and subsequent sold it to the owners of a Chilean all-cargo airline, Fast Air, in 1994 for US$42m. Fast merged the cargo and passenger businesses under the Lan-Chile name and subsequently floated the airline on the US market, valuing the whole company at US$870m (Jofré and Irrgang, 2000). Thus a cargo airline took over a passenger carrier and the importance of air cargo is still reflected in the management of the airline today.

The Chinese government indicated in 2010 that it wished to encourage consolidation by Chinese airlines starting with their air cargo businesses. Two groups are planned: one combining the cargo operations of China Southern and China Eastern with Sinotrans Air Transportation Development (see section 5.4.5); and the other to combine Air China with Sinotrans Air Transportation Development. The latter may derail the joint venture between Air China Cargo and Cathay Pacific, which still needed Chinese government approval (see next section).

6.2.2 Cross-Border Mergers and Acquisitions

Cross-border merger activity has been limited up to now to within trading blocs such as the European Union. A number of passenger driven deals had taken place in the EU, the largest two being Air France's acquisition of KLM and Lufthansa's acquisition of Swiss and later bmi and Austrian. Lufthansa is a major cargo player with 8.3 billion tonne-kms carried in 2008 (see section 4.10.2). The airlines it bought did not carry much cargo, Swiss with 1.2 billion, Austrian 452 million and bmi 119 million FTKs respectively. Lufthansa decided to close Austrian's air cargo operations in early 2010, with 50 redundancies out of 200 Austrian cargo employees worldwide. It subsequently set up a company to market air cargo capacity to and from Austria, Austrian Lufthansa Cargo, in which the Lufthansa parent owns 74 percent directly. Swiss WorldCargo is still operated by Lufthansa as a separate operating company but has realised some synergies on the commercial side.

Air France Cargo and KLM Cargo were both sizeable cargo operations with established hub airports. These are still operated as two distinct divisions, one having its hub at Paris CDG and the other at Amsterdam Schiphol Airport. While they are both members of SkyTeam Cargo each has its own cargo partners, for example MNG Airlines (Air France) and Nippon Cargo (KLM). However, they intended to migrate KLM's IT system to that of Air France and a single sales team is envisaged. One of the earlier decisions in 2004 was to discontinue Air France's twice weekly freighter services from Paris to Singapore and to serve Singapore via KLM's flights. This Air France capacity was used to add frequencies to Atlanta and Bangkok. Overall, cargo synergies in the first year were estimated to reach €10 million.

Air France also took a 25 percent stake in the new Alitalia that emerged after the Italian government decided not to continue supporting its ailing flag carrier. The new airline combined what remained of Alitalia and another shareholder, Air One, and remained a member of the SkyTeam Cargo alliance, which appeared to have been relegated in importance by Air France-KLM.

The third of the EU network airline mergers was British Airways and Iberia, signed in April 2010. This will have a similar structure to the one between Air France and KLM with two operating companies. British Airways will have 55 percent of the combined entity and Iberia 45 percent. The airlines estimated that the synergies from the merger would reach €400m by the fifth year. The implications for cargo are mostly confined to the lower decks of passenger flights, with improved service and capacity to/from South and Central America. Unlike Air France and KLM, neither carrier operates many freighters: British Airways only three B747-400F and Iberia currently owns no freighters. Iberia's total FTKs were just over one billion compared to British Airways' 4.6 billion.

Turning to freighter specialists, Cargolux had for many years been around one-third owned by the Swissair group. Following the Swiss airline's collapse in 2001 Cargolux's ownership was in limbo pending the sale of these shares by the liquidator. Cargolux received interest from several potential investors but a screening process and unresolved legal issues prevented any sale taking place until 2009. It was then finally sold to the airline's existing shareholders pro rata as part of a financial restructuring. This resulted in the Luxembourg based passenger airline, Luxair, increasing its stake from 34.9 percent to 52.1 percent and Luxembourg based financial corporations BCEE, SNCI and BIP increasing their collective share to 37.4 percent, with the Luxembourg government taking an 8 percent stake. The remaining 2.5 percent is held by other shareholders, whose interest is unchanged.

Martinair was an unusual airline in that it operated a mix of passenger charters and cargo freighter flights. KLM had for some years held a 50 percent stake in the Netherlands based airline, with Danish shipping company A.P. Moller-Maersk holding the other half. KLM later became part of the Air France-KLM Group and at the end of 2008 A.P. Moller-Maersk sold their shares to its partner. The European Commission approved the sale after an in-depth investigation into the potential impact on transport between Amsterdam and Curaçao and Aruba in the Dutch Antilles. This makes Air France-KLM the largest air cargo operator in Europe. Given its lower cost base, Air France-KLM intends to use Martinair for some of its own cargo routes.

India relaxed the rules on foreign investment in air cargo carriers in 2008. The cap on Foreign Direct Investment (FDI) was raised from 49 percent to 74 percent, but investment by foreign airlines remained limited to 25 percent. Indian industrial groups may take an interest in cargo airlines, but a more likely partner is a global integrator. Foreign airlines have invested in joint ventures in China, with Lufthansa's 25 percent stake in Jade Cargo International, based in South China, China Airlines of Taiwan's 25 percent in Shanghai based Yangtze River Express, and Singapore Airlines 25 percent in Great Wall Airlines, also in Shanghai (see section 4.10.3).

Hong Kong based Cathay Pacific has bought into the cargo subsidiary of Air China, Air China Cargo.[4] Air China will control 51 percent and Cathay will hold 25 percent directly and 24 percent through its subsidiary, Fine Star. The company has the approval of the EU competition authorities but has yet to get approval from the Chinese government.

---

4   This is considered a cross-border investment, since Hong Kong is still a Special Administrative Region and has its own air transport relationships with third countries.

The integrators have been active in foreign acquisitions to fuel their expansion, especially in Europe and Asia. Their targets were usually logistics companies with local or regional truck distribution strengths, and they did not involve airlines. Airline capacity could more easily be purchased from other airlines, or wet leased. However, DHL is one integrator that has some important strategic joint ventures with airlines: in Europe with Lufthansa (Aerologic), in Asia with Cathay Pacific (Air Hong Kong) and in the US with Polar/Atlas Air.

In conclusion, neither alliances nor mergers have played an important role in the development of air cargo from the airline perspective. Airline passenger alliances have not been designed to give specific benefits to their cargo businesses, and attempts at airline cargo alliances have not been successful. Airline mergers, outside single countries or economic areas, have not been possible so far. At the same time, considerable merger activity has been taking place between forwarders and integrators and between both and other (non-airline) participants in door-to-door transport. While airlines cannot gain much from an alliance with a particular forwarder, the larger forwarders might increasingly charter or operate their own aircraft. On the other hand, the present approach of outsourcing this to a competitive airline industry might be preferred in the longer term. Integrators also realise that they are unable to provide the range of air services they require in-house and need at least the lower decks of passenger flights.

Chapter 7
Aircraft and Flight Operations

This chapter looks at how the capacity described in Chapter 1 is provided by airlines and the various types of aircraft that they operate. First the lower decks of passenger aircraft are examined, followed by the most common type of freighter, the converted passenger aircraft. Finally, new freighters will be covered, split into small, medium and large capacity, finishing up with a look at possible new designs for the future. It has often been said that the ideal fuselage shape for a freighter aircraft is rectangular rather than the ellipsoid that is required for aerodynamic reasons. One of the possible future aircraft in the last section meets that requirement.

Reference will be made throughout this chapter to containers and pallets that are loaded onto aircraft. These are described in more detail in Chapter 8 since it is in airports that these are handled, built and broken down. Measures of aircraft capacity will usually be given in terms of the maximum structural payload available. This can be transported over a certain range based on numerous assumptions such as fuel load required and runway length.

Aircraft are usually distinguished by a number such as Airbus's A320 or Boeing's B737. This defines the aircraft with different variants of the aircraft defined by an additional hyphenated number, e.g. B737-200, B737-300 etc. These are likely to be developments of the original design, whether stretched/shortened and/or equipped with a different powerplant. A freighter aircraft will usually have the letter 'F' attached to it, and an aircraft that can be switched from carrying passengers to cargo or back is given a 'C' for 'combi'.

Sometimes freighter aircraft have additional letters to describe whether it has a side cargo door (B747-200SCD) or was converted from a passenger aircraft (B747-400 BCF: Boeing Converted Freighter). The B757-200 could be a B757-200F as a normal freighter or B757-200PF as a freighter converted for an integrator carrying parcels. Boeing-authorised conversions from its passenger aircraft such as B767s to freighter versions are shown as B767-200SF, or Special Freighter.

ICAO also gives each aircraft a type designator of three letters/numbers. For example a Boeing 737-300 has the designator B733, irrespective of whether it is a passenger or freighter version. An Airbus A330-300 is A333.

7.1 Passenger Aircraft: Lower Deck

The introduction of wide-bodied passenger aircraft, led by the B747, in the 1970s resulted in a step change in the space available for cargo in the lower deck or 'belly-hold' compartments. The B747 offered 128m³ compared to only 48m³ for its predecessor, the B707[1] (although part of this would be needed for passenger baggage). Passenger flights, especially those operated by wide-bodied aircraft, offer up to 25 tonnes of payload for cargo shipments. For a large network carrier these have the advantage of frequent services to a large number of destinations. There are two main disadvantages: the timing of the flights is geared to passenger requirements, although on long-haul sectors they may also suit cargo shippers. Second, the lower deck hold will not accommodate larger shipments, whether due to space available or the size of the cargo loading door. Some passenger destinations will not attract much cargo, but there will usually be some shipments in the hold such as mail, airline stores and emergency items. Conversely there will be too much cargo for some passenger routes but freighters are likely to fill this gap.

Table 7.1   Typical payload, volume and density for lower deck cargo

	Payload with full pax load (t)	Volume for cargo (cu.m)	Max. density (kg/cu.m)
A320	1.0	3.6	277.8
B737-300	2.3	21.0	107.1
B737-400	2.9	24.0	120.7
B737-800	3.6	28.0	128.6
A330-200	14.1	61.8	228.2
A330-300	15.0	80.2	187.0
B767-300	16.5	63.0	261.9
B747-400	20.0	73.4	272.5
A380	20.0	68.0	294.1

Planning and booking cargo onto passenger flights is fraught with difficulty. This is because of the uncertainty as to exactly what payload and volume is available. The maximum structural payload defined by the difference between the maximum zero fuel weight and the operating empty weight might be reduced by the weight of fuel needed for the particular sector (after the Maximum Take-off Weight or MTOW is reached). This will only be determined on the day once the airport temperature, routing, headwinds and other operational considerations have been taken into account, in addition to the passenger weight and number of checked baggage containers (see section 7.5).

The maximum payload remaining has then to be allocated to passengers and cargo. The passenger load may vary up to the last minutes before departure with

---

1   The earlier Comet aircraft could only carry just under 1 tonne of cargo in its lower holds.

last-minute bookers and missed flights. Cargo planners therefore usually work on a full load of passengers. Even then the payload available for cargo is only known on the day of departure. The volume available in the lower deck will also depend on the amount of checked baggage and assumptions are needed for this, usually in terms of container positions occupied.

Table 7.1 gives some typical published cargo payloads for carriers such as British Airways, Lufthansa, Emirates etc. Airline specific variables that could alter these payloads significantly are:

- passenger seating density;
- passenger weights;
- estimated checked baggage;
- lower deck containers used (or bulk loaded).

Freighter aircraft are produced in many different configurations, and payload penalties may be experienced using converted aircraft or those with different engines. Weights may vary due to varying equipment or cargo doors. The next section will examine the more popular freighter and combi aircraft, focusing on those that were converted from passenger aircraft versus new production aircraft. Only those still operating will be covered, distinguishing between those still in production and those not.

Table 7.2   Top 10 most popular freighters

	Total	% unconverted
727-200	290	5
IL-76	288	100
747-400	259	75
MD-11	169	32
A300-600	157	71
757-200	152	53
DC-8	147	60
747-200	134	44
DC-10	125	11
DC-9	73	15
Total above	1,794	51
Total jet fleet	2,541	48

Note: The above aircraft are in operation or grounded.

Source: Flightglobal's ACAS Fleet Database, March 2010.

Table 7.2 shows that around half of freighters and combi aircraft were originally converted from passenger aircraft, or conversely not manufactured as new freighters. The best selling of all, the B727s, were almost all conversions from passenger aircraft, mostly for integrators who dominate the short-/medium-haul conversion market. Some passenger aircraft were operated as freighters or parcel carriers without any conversion, in the same way as the 'Quick Change' aircraft but without the ease of handling and cabin interior protection of the latter. These were mostly the B767-200s and DC9-41s flown by US carrier ABX, and B727s by a variety of operators.

7.2 Freighters: Converted from Passenger Aircraft

Around three-quarters of freighters were originally manufactured as passenger aircraft, if smaller propeller aircraft are included. Some of these will be retired from passenger service after around 18–20 years, converted into freighters and operated for a further 15–20 years. Some consider that passenger aircraft become candidates for freighter conversions as early as 12 years when their passenger appeal begins to decline.[2] However, the economics of conversion improve with older and lower second-hand value aircraft. Not all passenger models have good characteristics for conversion: cross-sections, cabin heights, cargo door potential and volume/payload ratio may work against a successful programme. Examples of aircraft that have not been good candidates were the Lockheed L-1011, the MD-80 series and, more recently, the A340.

The process of conversion takes approximately four months and involves the removal of all cabin fixtures and fittings, including the window blinds, and all other structural and system components that are no longer needed such as seats or floor structures. The new freighter conversion kits are then installed consisting of a cargo door and the related structural parts. The cabin floor designed for passengers is replaced by a new stronger floor structure. Ball mats and roller tracks are installed for the loading of containers. Windows are replaced by metal covers for ease of maintenance, reduced fire risk and to prevent damage to cargo from sunlight.

The main factors that determine the extent of passenger aircraft conversion are:

- the availability and price of suitable conversion programmes;
- the price of passenger aircraft suitable for conversion;
- the payload/range characteristics of the conversions;
- input prices, especially for fuel and capital.

The above are to some extent inter-related: for example, a high price of fuel might deter conversions of fuel inefficient passenger aircraft, but might boost the

---

2   Stephen Fortune presentation toAircraft Leasing and Finance Seminar, April 2009.

availability and reduce the price of these older passenger aircraft. Aircraft coming off lease and/or approaching their D-check would also be suitable for conversion.

Aircraft age is related to both the cost of used passenger models and fuel and maintenance costs. This means that candidates for conversion tend to be aircraft that are 15 years or older. However, one market with a huge potential for such aircraft, the Chinese, currently restricts the operation of freighters by Chinese airlines to those less than 15 years old.[3]

The cost of capital will partly depend on interest rates which, like fuel prices, tend to respond to global trends. It may also be country specific and thus affect some airlines more than others. New entrant or poor risk airlines might also have to pay a higher cost of capital which would favour lower cost conversions.

The intended use of the aircraft also plays a role: the longer range with full payload that a new freighter might offer may not be necessary for an airline that seeks to consolidate loads by operating multi-sector routings. And an integrator that plans mainly nighttime flights at low daily aircraft utilisation might prefer a low capital cost converted aircraft. This is evident from the fleets of FedEx and UPS which both contain large numbers of converted B727s and B757s.

Figure 7.1 shows the influence of the economic or industry traffic cycle on freighter conversions. The peak year in the latest cycle was 2007 with over 110 passenger aircraft converted to freighters before the sharp downturn in air cargo traffic kicked in towards the end of 2008. Of the wide-body conversions in that year, 26 were from B747-400 and 12 from MD-11 passenger aircraft. In 2005

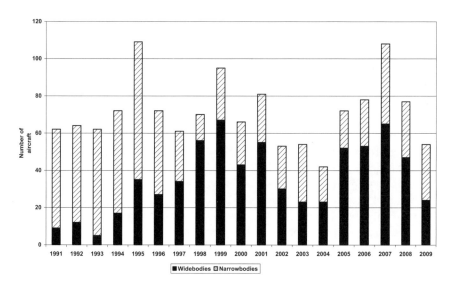

Figure 7.1   Freighter aircraft conversions, 2000 to 2009

Source: Ascend Worldwide, Viewpoint, March 2010.

---

3   *Freighter Operators' Guide*, 2009.

and 2006 between 70 percent and 75 percent of conversions were of wide-bodied aircraft. While aircraft for conversion can be purchased very cheaply at the low point in the cycle, there is also very little demand at that time, or for the coming 2–3 years, for additional freighter capacity. Furthermore, the right aircraft may not be immediately available and conversion programmes take time to set up. There also seem to be few interested in speculative investments in converted freighters.

Aircraft manufacturers (OEMs) are themselves (or through subcontractors such as Aeronavali or Singapore Technologies) offering conversions from their own passenger aircraft to freighters:

- Boeing B747-400BCF; B767-300BCF; DC10; MD-11BCF
- Airbus (EADS-EFW)A310-200; A300-600; A320.

Apart from the manufacturers shown above, the major companies authorised to carry out conversions are:

- AEIB737-200/300/400
- Alcoa-SIEB757-200
- IAI-Bedek B747-400; B767-200; B737-300
- Pemco (US): B737-300/400
- Precisions Conversions (US): B757-200
- Singapore Technologies: B757-200, MD-11
- TAECO (China): MD80/90; B747-400.

FedEx has in the past converted its own B727-200Fs, and some further conversions are planned or under development (such as IAI Bedek for the B737-400 and B/A Aerospace for the A300-600). Non-OEM specialists carry the product liability and must obtain the Supplementary Type Certificate (STC) from their aeronautical authorities. Some programmes are supported by the OEM but the work is contracted out to a cheaper company, for example in the case of Boeing with Singapore Technologies and TAECO in Xiamen. Non-OEM conversions are generally thought to carry more risk but be slightly cheaper. The risks are in product support and the possibility of the STC holder going bankrupt. The latter has happened to a number of conversion specialists in the past, notably GATX Airlog (B747-100/200), Rosenbaum (DC8) and Hayes (B727). Some operators such as FedEx now acquire all their conversions from OEMs.

Boeing had in the past provided free technical support to owners of its aircraft that had been converted to freighters by third party facilities. But it started charging for these services for aircraft conversions delivered after April 2009.[4]

---

4   Olivier Bonnassies, *Flight International*, 2–8 June 2009.

7.2.1 Short-/Medium-Haul Aircraft

The B727 conversion programme started at the beginning of the 1980s with the B727-100 and continued with the B727-200 from the mid-1980s until the early 2000s. A total of 477 aircraft were converted. The -100 series age at conversion ranged from 15–19 years and the -200 series mostly just over 22 years. A small number of -200s were converted between 2003 and 2007 at ages of 25–30 years.

The B737-100/200 aircraft were good passenger aircraft but did not provide the right payload and volume characteristics for use as freighters. Thus the next phase of conversions in the short to medium range category was the B737-300 and more recently B737-400. A total of 96 of the latter -300 series were converted between 1991 and 2007, over half of them since 2004. This aircraft had a maximum payload of just below 90 percent of the B727-100F.

The B727-100 was also manufactured as a 'combi' aircraft with 94 passengers or just under 30 tonnes of freight, between 35–40 percent of which could be carried on the main deck. A 'quick-change' aircraft was also produced, which like the combi and freighter had a strengthened main deck but which could be switched from passenger to cargo role and back. The roller bearing equipped main deck allowed palletised seats and galleys to be inserted and the whole process of switching it back to passenger operations was supposed to take only 30 minutes. In practice this was likely to be optimistic, but it allowed the same aircraft to offer passenger flights by day and cargo flights by night, achieving very high daily utilisation.

The B737-400 provides almost an identical payload and volume to the B727-100 (but still 25 percent less than the B727-200F) but so far few have been converted. The oldest B737-400s in passenger service were just under 20 years old in 2009, although over 100 were due to come off lease between 2008 and 2011 which were 15 years or more and suitable for conversion. Other aircraft in this size category, the A320s and A319s, are either too young or expensive.

The replacement for the larger B727-200F is the converted passenger B757-200. The same aircraft was also available new from the manufacturer. FedEx operated a total of 90 B727-200Fs, and has contracted with Singapore Technologies Aerospace to convert 87 B757-200s to freighters.

The A310-200F was only available as a converted aircraft from EADS-EFW. The first aircraft was introduced by FedEx in 1994. FedEx was also the launch customer for the longer range A310300F converted by the same Airbus/EADS company.

7.2.2 Long-Haul Aircraft

A total of 240 wide-bodied passenger aircraft were converted to freighters between 2004 and 2008 (Table 7.3). These were capable of operating long-haul sectors. The most popular models were B747-400s and MD-11s. The B747-200 had also been popular for conversion but most of these had already been converted by 2004 and by 2008 high fuel prices made it a much less economic proposition.

Table 7.3   Wide-bodied aircraft conversions to freighters, 2004–2008

	Indicative payload (t)	2004	2005	2006	2007	2008	Total 2004–2008
A300	39	2	3	8	13	8	34
A310	29	5	9	6	5	5	30
DC-10	65	2	5	4	1		12
B767-300	38	4	13	7	8	8	40
MD-11	58	10	19	17	12	9	67
B747-200	112		2				2
B747-400	124		1	11	26	17	55

Source: Freighter Operators' Guide, 2009.

7.2.3 Freighter Conversion Forecasts

Both Airbus and Boeing expect very similar numbers of freighter conversions to be carried out over the next 20 years (see Table 14.5 in Chapter 14). Airbus expect 60 percent of new aircraft deliveries to come from the largest category aircraft compared to Boeing's forecast of 75 percent. Airbus may have become more pessimistic following the market reaction to the A380F which had no orders as of July 2010. Boeing is presumably counting on strong orders for the B777F and B747-8F aircraft. The above forecasts excluded turbo-prop and piston-engined aircraft. Turbo-props are used extensively by integrators, especially for North American feeder flights.

OAG expect 756 freighter conversions between 2010 and 2019, with Boeing aircraft accounting for 74 percent of these, and almost half from just three aircraft types: the B757 (165 aircraft), B767 (107 aircraft) and B737 family (143 aircraft). The A320 family conversion is projected to begin in 2011 with the A320,[5] culminating in a total of 78 A320s and 46 A321s by the end of 2019. There are over 4,000 passenger versions of the A320 in existence so there should be no shortage of future aircraft for conversion. The long-haul category will be dominated by the B747-400 (94 aircraft), with 42 B777 conversions and 18 A340s.

Subsequent analysis in this chapter will take the Airbus jet freighter size breakdown of:

---

5   This may be optimistic since the certification date has already been deferred into 2012. This was because of the relocation of the cargo door to the rear to improve the centre-of-gravity.

Small:	B727, B737, A320, BAe146, DC9, Tu-204
Regional/long-range:	B707, B757, B767, A300, A310, A321, A330,
	DC-8, DC-10
Large:	B747, B777, A350, MD-11, A380

The regional/long-range category will be re-named 'medium'. As discussed in Chapter 14, these match closely the Boeing breakdown, with an identical large category of over 80 tonnes payload, and a medium range of 40–80 tonnes.

7.3 New Production Freighters

From 2010 to 2019, OAG forecasts the delivery of 116 B777F freighters, 94 B747-8Fs, 67 A330-200Fs, 32 B767F and eight B747-400F aircraft. These are the freighters still in production. It did not include any A380 freighters since the future of this programme appeared in some doubt at that time. In this section previous production freighters will first be discussed in terms of their capability since many are still flying today. Current production aircraft will be covered next within each aircraft size category (although it should be noted that there are no such programmes for small jet aircraft).

7.3.1 Small Jet Freighters

Boeing currently only manufactures its B737-700C in the small size category. This is a passenger/freight convertible aircraft that gives a maximum payload of just under 20 tonnes over a 5,300 km range fully converted to cargo configuration. The launch customer was Angolan airline, Sonair, originally formed by the national oil company.

In the past Boeing built only two B737-200 freighters but some 38 in combi version. No freighters were built from B737-300 or -400 versions, and only a few DC9s. British Aerospace built 23 new 146 freighters for TNT.

7.3.2 Medium Sized Freighters

Out of production (2010)
Of the aircraft in Table 7.4, the B757-200 and A300F4-600 were both very popular with the integrators, especially UPS (launch customer for the B757) and FedEx, hence the large number of aircraft that were built.

Only a small number of new A300-600F freighters were built, and EADS-EFW was the only provider of conversions from the passenger model. It was the replacement for the A300B4-100F and -200F, almost all of which were converted to freighters in the 1990s and will now be approaching 30 years of age.

Table 7.4   Medium-sized freighter aircraft: out of production in 2010

	Indicative payload (t)	Range (km)*	Total sold/ordered
B757-200F	27	6,051	80
DC8-61F	40	3,982	n/a
A300F4-600	54-64	5,378	72
DC10-30F and CF	70	5,741	37

Note: * With maximum weight limited payload.

Source: Manufacturers' estimates.

In production (2010)

Boeing's offer in the medium size category is currently the B767-300F. This is manufactured as a freighter aircraft that gives a maximum payload of 54 tonnes over a 5,800 km range.

Table 7.5   Medium-sized freighter aircraft: in production in 2010

	Indicative payload (t)	Range (km)*	Total sold/ordered
B767-300F	54	5,785	83
A330-200F	64	7,400	64

Note: * With maximum weight limited payload.

Source: Manufacturers' estimates.

The Airbus's slightly larger competitor, the A330-200F, was its first new freighter project for many years. However, its orders peaked at 77 in 2008 before the air cargo downturn resulted in some cancellations and deferrals. Of the 2010 total of 64 orders, 20 are from Intrepid Aviation and 12 from an Indian start-up freight specialist, Flyington Freighters (which as of mid-2010 had not commenced operations). Few established airlines were listed as customers of this aircraft, among them Turkish Airlines (two), Etihad (launch customer with only two ordered), with MGN Airlines taking four aircraft. Lessors feature strongly in the order book with Avion BOC, Guggenheim and MatlinPatterson ordering a total of 16 aircraft.

The Ilyushin company of Russia has been manufacturing aircraft from the days of the USSR in 1933 to the present. In the medium sized category it produces the Ilyushin Il-76, which carries a payload of around 50 tonnes over 3,700 km. From its introduction as a commercial freighter in 1967 increased payload/range versions have been developed, leading to the Il-78. This was ideally suited for transporting heavy machinery and military equipment to remote airports with short runways. Loading and unloading through its rear ramp makes it convenient for wheeled or tracked vehicles and it became a useful aircraft for disaster relief operations.[6]

7.3.3 Large Sized Freighters

Out of production (2010)
The major Western-built freights that are no longer offered as new aircraft are from Boeing (see Table 7.6). The MD-11 was launched as a freighter in 1986 with both FedEx and Lufthansa as the major customers. It eventually sold 53 aircraft until production was ceased in 2000. A convertible variant was launched in 1991 with an order from Martinair but only five of these were sold. Once the B777F was introduced the aircraft became uneconomic. It had a payload of 26 pallets (88" x 125") or 21,096 cubic feet and could take up to 91 tonnes of freight. The MD11F's predecessor, the DC10-30F, originally ordered by FedEx, was much less successful, selling only 11 production aircraft, although a large number were converted from passenger versions.

The 747-200F is the freighter version of the -200 model. It could be fitted with or without a side cargo door. It sold reasonably well for a freighter, with the attraction of a nose-loading door for faster handling and larger shipments. It first entered service in 1972 with Lufthansa. The 747-200C Convertible is a version that can be converted between a passenger and a freighter or used in mixed configurations. It was launched by World Airways but only 13 were built. The seats are removable, and the model has a nose cargo door. The -200C could be fitted with an optional side cargo door on the main deck. The 747-200M is a combination version that has a side cargo door on the main deck and can carry freight in the rear section of the main deck. A removable partition on the main deck separates the cargo area at the rear from the passengers at the front. Air Canada was the launch customer and 78 were built. This model can carry up to 238 passengers in a 3-class configuration if cargo is carried on the main deck. The model is also known as the 747-200 Combi.

Table 7.6   Large freighter aircraft: out of production in 2010

	Indicative payload (t)	Range (km)*	Total sold/ordered
MD-11F	90	7,222	53
B747-200F	95	8,150	73
B747-400F	110	8,150	166

Note: * With maximum weight limited payload.

Source: Manufacturers' estimates.

---

6 For example, two of the aircraft were flown to the US to assist in relief operations following Hurricane Katrina in 2005.

A stretched upper deck -300M version was built for launch customer Swissair, but only four were produced.

The B747-400F was a successful programme with 166 sold: apart from Russian built freighters it was the only commercial freighter of it size, and has a nose door for easier handling, not available on converted aircraft. Its last aircraft was completed in 2009.

The Ukraine (formerly USSR) has produced two large freighters, initially for military airlift but also for commercial operations: the Antonov 124 Ruslan and Antonov 225. The first has a payload of just over 120 tonnes with loading facilities for outsized shipments such as generators and helicopters. The larger An225 can carry the largest payload of any civil aircraft, up to 200 tonnes. Only one of these has been built. In 2009 it carried the largest commercial payload to date of 190 tonnes from Frankfurt/Hahn Airport to Yerevan, Armenia. The cargo was a thermal power plant generator, measuring 53 feet x 14 feet, and it first had to be carried by ship down the Moselle river to close to Hahn Airport.[7] The An225 was also involved in relief operations following the Haiti earthquake in 2010.

In production (2010)

Boeing offers a range of current production freighters from 100 to 150 tonnes of payload. The smallest (B777F) is a replacement for the B747-200F and a viable alternative to the slightly larger B747-400F. With the advent of the A380F Boeing stretched the fuselage of the B747-400 and sold its new model in both passenger and freighter variants: the B747-8F has so far been much more successful than the passenger version, and it is a direct competitor to the A380F in terms of payload but not range. However, the extra range of the A380 is not essential for many operators and the A380F currently has no orders. Previous launch orders from FedEx, UPS and ILFC for a total of 17 aircraft were withdrawn following the 2008/2009 sharp downturn in air cargo markets.

Table 7.7   Large freighter aircraft: in production in 2010

	Indicative payload (t)	Range (km)*	Total sold/ordered
Il-96-400T	92	5,200	6
B777F	103	9,065	73
B747-8F	154	8,130	78
A380F	157	10,400	0

Note: * With maximum weight limited payload.

Source: Manufacturers' estimates.

---

7   *Air Cargo World*, 14 August 2009.

The Il-96-400T is the cargo version of the Russian wide-bodied Il-96-300 aircraft first built in 1993. Its payload is significantly enhanced by being fitted with Pratt and Whitney engines. The passenger versions of the Il-96 are no longer built. Only three cargo aircraft are in commercial service with the Russian cargo airline Polet, with a further three on order.

The B777 freighter was first introduced by launch customer Air France in February 2009. It has to some extent shortened the economic life of the B747-400F, although Boeing now offers a larger version of this aircraft. It is very fuel efficient and also offers good range performance.

Unlike the B787, the B747-8F is manufactured with very little carbon fibre. It is 5.7 metres longer than the -400F, giving around 16 percent more cargo volume with the same nose door for accommodating large loads. Its wingspan is 4.1 metres greater than the -400, at 68.5m, still well under the 80m box. These dimensions are important for airport planning, and the A380 with its wingspan of just under 80m (and the Antonov 225 with 88m) pose problems for some airports. Tail heights and cabin widths are identical. It is much less noisy than the B747-400 and meets ICAO Chapter 4 and London QC2 noise standards, as well as being 17 percent more fuel efficient. The aircraft is the first freighter in Boeing's history to have been introduced before its passenger variant, which followed about one year later. It was launched with orders for 10 from Cargolux and eight from Nippon Cargo, and by mid-2010 it had 76 orders for the freighter (and only 32 for the passenger version).

Finally, mention should be made of two very large volume freighter aircraft specifically built by manufacturers to assist in their aircraft manufacturing: Airbus's 'Beluga' and Boeing's 'Dreamlifter'. The Beluga or A300-600 ST Special Transporter uses the A300 fuselage and cockpit to produce a two-engined freighter that has a payload of 47 tonnes and volumetric capacity of 1,210m³. Five were built to transport aircraft components from various subcontractors to the final assembly plants in Toulouse and Hamburg. It was introduced in 1995 and has operated some charters in addition to its work for Airbus.

Boeing's Dreamlifter or B747 LCF Large Cargo Freighter, on the other hand, is for the exclusive use of Boeing, having the same purpose although with a longer haul requirement. It is primarily for moving B787 components from subcontractors in countries such as Italy and Japan to the assembly line in the US. Four have been built in Taiwan, converted from passenger B747-400 aircraft. They have a volumetric capacity of 1,840m³. It was operated under contract by US cargo specialist, Evergreen, the contract moving in 2010 to Atlas Air under a CMI (crew, maintenance and insurance) contract.[8]

---

8 Who around the same time ordered 12 new B747-8F aircraft from Boeing with options for 14 more.

7.4 'Combi' and Quick Change Aircraft

These aircraft were mentioned already in the various sections above, since they are a part of the manufacturing or conversion process. Table 7.8 shows the aircraft that are available as combis, according to the Flightglobal database. This distinguishes between 'combi' aircraft that are permanently configured so that both freight and passengers can be carried on the main deck, and those that are not:

> Combi: multi-compartment aircraft configured for purposes of transporting passengers and freight together on the main deck.

> Converted Combi: aircraft models including combi models (converted or modified), rapid-change, multiple-change and convertible freighters used exclusively for freight transport.

Table 7.8   Combi, converted combi and Quick Change aircraft

	Combi	Converted combi	Total
737-200	38	9	47
747-400	30	17	47
747-200	0	41	41
727-100	1	23	24
DC-9	0	21	21
707-300	0	20	20
DC-10	0	16	16
747-300	6	6	12
MD-11	0	7	7
737-400	5	0	5
727-200	0	1	1
A300	0	1	1
737-700	1	0	1
Total	81	162	243

Note: The above aircraft are in operation or grounded.

Source: Flightglobal's ACAS Fleet Database, March 2010.

The DC-10-10CF is a convertible passenger/cargo transport version of the -10. Nine were built for Continental Airlines (eight) and United Airlines (one).

The DC-10-30CF is the convertible cargo/passenger transport version of the -30. Twenty-six were built, with deliveries to Martinair Holland (four), Overseas National Airways (five), Sabena (five), Trans International Airlines (three) and World Airways (nine). Sabena was the only commercial operator to fly both cargo and passengers at the same time with its DC-10-30CF.

7.5 Unit Load Devices for Aircraft

Unit Load Devices (ULDs) can be either pallets or containers. A pallet is a wooden or metal base of varying size to which cargo is secured. An aircraft container is an enclosed unit with solid base, walls, door and roof that can fit various aircraft types and be handled by its equipment. A multi-modal container is one that can be used on road, rail, sea or air transport, but one that is light enough for air transport and durable enough for other modes has not yet been designed. The airport handling aspects of ULDs are described in section 8.2.1. Here factors such as aircraft compatibility and operations are covered.

Before the introduction of wide-bodied aircraft, pallets were used for main deck freighters, and the lower decks of passenger and freighter flights were loose loaded and not containerised. With the advent of wide-bodied aircraft a large space needed to be filled in the lower decks of passenger flights and a quicker method of loading and unloading needed to be introduced. This led to the development of containers that were contoured to fit the shape of these holds. Containers were then also used on the main deck, and even on some narrow-bodied aircraft such as the A320.

There are two main systems of numbering or letters to identify the type of ULD. The IATA system of three letter codes was introduced in 1984, replacing the older system of LD followed by a number for lower deck ULDs and M followed by a number for main deck units. The IATA system replaced the widely used lower deck container LD3 with AKE. The first letter denotes a certified structural container (i.e. can interface directly with an aircraft's loading and restraint system), the second the dimensions and the third its shape. An additional refinement is the use of the letter 'N' as the third letter to signify the presence of forklift slots in the base. This adds some weight and reduces volume but is more convenient for handling. Special containers have also been developed for transporting horses and other livestock, and for items such as garments which can be hung on rails. Temperature controlled units are also available.

The major manufacturers of ULDs are SATCO, Driessen, Nordisk, Fylin, Amsafe and VRR. The dimensions, however, will be identical since they should be interchangeable across the fleet and between airlines, although the tare weights may vary.

Table 7.9   Description of most commonly used ULDs

Designator		Base width x depth x height	Useable vol. (cu.ft)	Tare weight (kg)	Max load (kg)*
LD3	AKE	62x60x64	153	80	1,587
LD3	AKN	62x60x64	145	100	1,587
LD9	AAP	125x88x64	270	381	6,033
LD11	ALP	125x60x64	240	185	3,175

Note: * Including tare weight.
Source: Airline websites.

Table 7.9 shows the dimensions and typical weights for the three most commonly used ULDs (see section 8.2.1). All are suitable for all wide-body aircraft types, including the B767. Some of the integrators have developed their own containers to suit their aircraft and meet the tight transfer times at their hub airports. One example of an airline's ULDs is British Airways which uses LD3s for the lower decks of its B747, B777, B767 aircraft and main deck of B757 freighter aircraft, LD9s for the lower decks of its B747s, B777s and B767s, and LD11s either as pallets or containers for the lower decks of its B747s and B777s. Because the B767 has a slightly narrower cross-section, loading it with LD3s wastes some space. Hence one of the design requirements of the B767's replacement, the B787, was for it to use the LD3, LD6 and LD11 family of ULDs to utilise fully the lower deck space.

7.6 Aircraft Operations

7.6.1 Operations Planning

Aircraft manufacturers publish standard operational characteristics for their aircraft that are based on standard operating conditions. These graphs, an example of which is given as Figure 7.2, give a rough idea of the trade-offs for planning purposes, but each airline will input its own assumptions based on company policy, and specific aircraft, airports and conditions at the time. The planning charts are usually based on a standard day in terms of ambient temperature, zero headwinds, standard climb out and cruise speed, and typical mission rules (e.g. fuel reserves etc.).

The shape of the graph in Figure 7.2 will differ for different aircraft type and engine combinations, and the initial flat line will be longer for long-haul aircraft. An airline will need to operate a particular network of routes that generate a given amount of revenue, and its fleet of aircraft are chosen to fly these routes in the most cost-effective way. This implies operating at point A in Figure 7.2, since a longer route will require some revenue payload loss, either passengers or cargo, and a

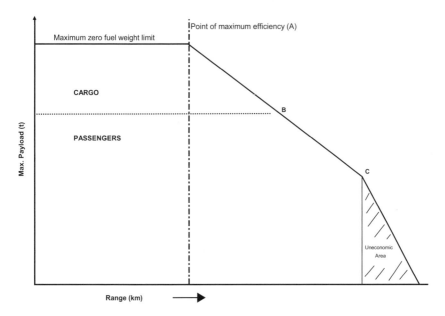

Figure 7.2   Payload-range trade-off

shorter route will not be using the aircraft's capability to the full. The network will include routes of varying lengths and so some compromise will be necessary, especially since it will also save costs to have as few types as possible.

Short-/medium-haul aircraft such as the B737 or A320 are often used on sectors that are much shorter than their design range (point A in Figure 7.2). They also carry little or no cargo and so they are paying for an aircraft the full capability of which they would rarely use. This is why LCCs such as Ryanair or easyJet have suggested that shorter range versions are offered at a lower price.

Another chart that is useful in fleet planning is one that shows runway take-off length for different take-off weights, up to MTOW. This could vary for say the B747-8F from around 2,000m for a take-off weight of 275 tonnes to 3,000m for MTOW at sea level. Airports that are situated at high altitude, for example Addis Ababa, could require a runway length of at least 4,000m to accommodate this aircraft at MTOW.

7.6.2 Air Routes

Freighter aircraft operations are relatively fuel intensive and thus operating more direct flights means lower block times and less fuel and other hourly-related costs. Non-stop flights often have to fly circuitous routes mostly because of military restrictions or to avoid sensitive areas. Intermediate stops can also add extra distance and need sufficient additional traffic and revenue to justify the higher costs.

China only allocates around 30 percent of its airspace for civil aviation operations and so international flights from East Asia to Europe often have to fly considerable extra distance. This was also the case with the former USSR, forcing these flights to take more southerly routes over India and Iran. However, in 2006 the efforts of IATA paid off with the opening of what was referred to IATA-1. This reduced flights times between China and Europe by 30 minutes with significant fuel savings. Just over 100 flights a week were affected but this has increased strongly since then.

Russia has also opened up more routes since the days of the former USSR but charges a high overflight fee for which limited navigation aids are offered (or now required). However, a diplomatic row was triggered by Russia's refusal to allow Lufthansa Cargo to use any of its airspace following the German carrier's decision to establish a regional hub in Astana, Kazakhstan instead of Krasnoyarsk in Russian Siberia. The latter hub was ruled out by Lufthansa due to a high incidence of low visibility weather conditions. Astana is around 1,500 km to the west of Krasnoyarsk and Lufthansa had to divert its 49 weekly cargo flights to/from Asia a considerable distance.

Flying non-stop between Europe and Asia may be of benefit to shippers of emergency items, but these may not be sufficient to fill a large freighter. Thus one or more intermediate stops might make more economic sense, as long as traffic rights are available and directional imbalances can be minimised. On the North Atlantic, an intermediate stop makes less sense, at least on the North American side since the departure airport can be fed by truck. On the European side, a stop in the UK en route to Europe may make sense, for example FedEx's Memphis/ London Stansted/Paris route. On the North Pacific, again an en route stop for traffic consolidation makes little sense, although a re-fuelling stop at Anchorage is often necessary due to the very long sectors involved.

On routes between Europe and Asia, a distinction can be drawn between North-east Asian countries, especially China, Korea and Taiwan, East Asia (Japan and Hong Kong) and South-east Asia (e.g. Singapore, Kuala Lumpur and Bangkok). An intermediate stop in the Middle East or India is close to the great circle route for South-east Asian countries such as Singapore but involves a much greater distance flown for carriers from North-east Asia.

Eurocontrol report that night operators are regularly given direct routings (especially cargo carriers). This supports moves to reduce emissions from air transport, but operators are not yet in a position to file these direct routings, which prevents them from optimising their fuel and freight carriage.

7.7 Future Freighters

Freighter aircraft have in the past all been derived from passenger or military models. As a result, from time to time proposals are put forward for new designs dedicated to freighters. The current high price of fuel and climate change concerns are also reinforcing the argument for new models sacrificing speed for increased payload, fuel efficiency and unit cost. Often proposals for radical new freighter aircraft go hand-in-hand with cargo dedicated airports. There has been no shortage of these in Europe as many large Air Force bases have been closed, leaving long runways and associated facilities. However, these are better suited to integrators than combination carriers that still carry a sizeable share of their traffic on passenger flights.

Three approaches are possible: developing existing fixed wing types, airships and 'ground effect' aircraft.

7.7.1 Conventional Designs

Proposals for future freighters using conventional designs and propulsion systems stress specific cargo airports and intermodal containers. They are to some extent inspired by the Airbus Beluga and the Boeing Dreamlifter (see section 7.3.3). Schmitt and Strohmayer (2001) list the basic requirements as:

- cruise Mach number not less than 0.7;
- payload not less than 250 tonnes;
- airfield runway length: ACN < 75;
- reduced noise for 24-hour operations;
- quick loading and unloading;
- pressurisation limited to cockpit area;
- good economics.

Such a concept was developed in 1999 by a consortium of three universities: Cranfield, TU München and ENSICA. It was subsequently called the Ecolifter and had a payload of 250 tonnes which it could carry over a range of up to 3,500 km. Its fuselage cross-section is greater than the A380 and similar to the Beluga described above. It would accommodate two 20-foot intermodal containers side-by-side on the main deck with two more on top, with a total of 40 of these heavier tare weight containers. The need for it to use cargo-only airports is partly dictated by its 85-metre wingspan and also because of the need for speedy handling for fast turnarounds. This would ensure that its high capital costs would be spread over a large amount of flying. It economics were estimated to be comparable to road transport, with unit costs of 10.3 US cents per tonne-km. This would make the diversion of cargo from road to air possible, although over its optimum 3,500 km range the amount of road freight available may be limited.

Others see the blended wing body as the path to a more fuel efficient future using designs that are already in military operation. This is the future that the CEO Fred Smith sees for FedEx, with the added advantage of flying an unmanned version (pilotless).

7.7.2 Airships

Airships are lighter-than-air aircraft that obtain their lift from gases such as propane, hydrogen or helium. The gas is contained in a balloon that can be flexible or rigid in structure. Helium is used today after previous disasters with inflammable gases. One project, the German based Cargolifter, was discontinued following bankruptcy in 2002. Its CL75 'Aircrane', which is filled with $100,000m^3$ of helium, was at one time on the verge of being sold to a Canadian company, and a larger $550,000m^3$ vessel powered by eight CT7-8L turbo-prop engines and designed to carry a 160-tonne payload was planned with a range of up to 10,000 km.

Airships have been proposed for carrying air freight for a number of years, but they have usually been better suited to outsized loads rather than regular traffic. The problem with airships is the relationship between speed and fuel efficiency. The latter deteriorates sharply as speed is increased to over 100 or 150 knots. Second, only very large payload airships can offer a significant improvement in fuel efficiency over, say, a B747-400F with a speed of 150 knots. This is still well below the 500-knot speed of current jet freighters, while needing up to 500 tonnes of payload to operate economically (Rawdon and Hoisington, 2003). This raises problems of market concentration and super-hubs before any infrastructure questions have been addressed. In this respect it is hard to see an airship fitting in with conventional air traffic management with its instrument arrival and departure paths.

There have been a number of Airship projects, usually with much smaller payloads than proposed above. The UK Airship Industries developed small airships with Porsche engines and a speed of around 50 knots. Another project was the Millennium Air Ship Inc from the US with its SkyFreighter. Another, from the Dutch firm Rigid Airship Design, proposes the RA-180 with a payload of 35 tonnes, suited for carrying, for example, flowers between the Netherlands and the UK, supplies to offshore platforms and even carrying passengers on short-haul routes.

The US E-Green Technologies was intending to make a test flight in summer 2010 with its Bullet 580 Airship. However, it carries only 7 tonnes at low altitude but a larger version could carry 50 tonnes at speeds of up to 80mph. Palma et al. (2010) compare airships with various existing modes, assuming speeds of over 100kph or 3–5 times faster than shipping. Compared to current fixed wing aircraft they rate airships much slower but with the advantages of increased capacity, more flexible loading and better economics. They do however draw attention to the vulnerability of airships to bad weather, especially in take-off and landing, although this has improved through technological advances such as fly-by light systems. Their survey suggested that only 32 percent would use airships for freight compared to 40 percent for passengers. Their restriction to shorter distances rules them out over the major air trade lanes, and their economics are much less favourable than trucks over shorter distances (assuming no significant physical barriers).

7.7.3 Ground Effect Aircraft

Ground effect aircraft can be sea- or land-based. There have been more proposals for the former in recent years. These take-off and land in water at high speed and cruise close to the water in order to make the most use of the ground effect. The very large wing frequently comes into contact with the water which is why land-based vehicles were until recently more feasible, but this has changed somewhat with improved flight controls. In earlier years most of the research and development took place in the USSR where huge distances over land with little or no population suggested an application. A land-based proposal, the Pelican ULTRA, has a maximum payload of just over 1,200 tonnes and a range of 18,000 km with a payload of around 700 tonnes (Rawdon and Hoisington, 2003). It can operate conventionally as well as using the ground effect. This source gives the total cost (including shipping, interest and depreciation) of US$0.30 per ton-mile for the shipment by air with a door-to-door delivery time of three days, versus a 30-day delivery by sea at $0.03 per ton-mile. The Pelican is estimated to deliver the shipment in three days at a total cost of $0.12 per ton-mile and will attract shipments of greater than $4.90 per lb ($11 per kg) compared to the present cut-off point of $15/lb ($33 per kg). Smaller Pelicans could also be built depending on the potential size of the market.

Chapter 8
Airport and Ground Operations

Airports provide the important interface between truck and occasionally rail delivery and distribution and the flight. Previous surveys have identified the airport as the location in the supply chain that often produces the most delays. This can compromise air transport's crucial advantage in getting goods to market in the shortest time. For this reason, integrators often prefer to operate from secondary airports with few passenger movements and little congestion. Network carriers, on the other hand, establish their cargo hubs where possible at their passenger hub location, assuming sufficient slots are available.[1] The airports with the largest throughput of international cargo are shown in Table 8.1, together with their main hub carrier.

Airport infrastructure needs to provide the runways, taxiways and aircraft parking areas to handle both freighter and passenger aircraft. This is the airside system that often extends to the first and last stages of the flight in terms of air traffic or approach control. The passenger terminal needs to be able to handle the cargo that is carried on passenger aircraft, with quick road access to the cargo terminal and in some cases a cargo transhipment unit at or below the passenger terminal. The cargo terminal(s) need their own aircraft parking stands, space for ramp handling equipment and the necessary handling and storage facilities within the building. Landside access is provided by truck parking and roads, preferably connected to major trunk roads nearby the airport perimeter. ICAO standards usually form the basis for designing and operating all these facilities.

In addition to the physical facilities needed to process the vehicles, aircraft and ULDs, data needs to flow between all the parties involved, records kept and authorisations given. This will be covered in this chapter because this is where information is vital to release cargo and allow aircraft to take-off and land. This will be addressed first, from the moment the cargo shipment arrives at the airport (and even at the forwarder's facilities close to the airport) to the time it leaves the destination airport on its way to the consignee.

The logistics chain for a typical air export involves the following steps:

1. a commercial deal between importer and exporter;
2. information gathered on the transport options;
3. air transport chosen and the flight booked;
4. the shipment is packaged, labelled and prepared for transport;

---

1 For example, British Airways is forced to operate its freighters from the London airport, Stansted, that is not its passenger hub due to slot restrictions at Heathrow.

5. the documentation is prepared;
6. the shipment is delivered to the airport (perhaps via a forwarder), within the latest acceptance time set by the airline (e.g. six hours prior to flight departure);
7. the flight is prepared with the following carried out:
   - planning
   - load building
   - departure control
   - customs and other inspections
   - loading aircraft
   - flight departure;
8. arrival of flight at final destination;
9. notification of arrival to importer/agent;
10. customs inspection and clearance;
11. collection from airport.

These steps involve the physical movement of shipments as they move from door-to-door and also the flow of information within and between the parties involved.

8.1 Information Flows

Previously much of the data and records moved between parties as hard copy, with the obvious risks of loss or delay. Today much of it is stored and transmitted in electronic form. According to the ICAO:

> In recent years the automation of the air cargo clearance process has been a high-priority item on the agenda of the customs services of the world as a means of managing the vast amount of data which is exchanged among the various parties involved, i.e. customs, shipper, consignee, air carrier, customs broker, agriculture and other interested government agencies. The need to enhance controls in the face of increased risks posed by drug trafficking, violations of intellectual property rights, smuggling of endangered species and other illegal activities, combined with the growth in international trade volumes, has made it increasingly difficult for government inspection agencies to perform their enforcement missions with finite resources. Moreover, studies of traditional air cargo systems have concluded that the average *dwell time* of an imported shipment (from its arrival to its release for delivery) is 4.5 days, a delay which to most air cargo customers is unacceptable. Automated solutions are sought by air carriers, customs brokers, and the authorities, to ensure better compliance with laws and faster clearance of low-risk cargo by managing the traffic more efficiently.

This is the challenge whose solution poses both political and technological problems. The latter has luckily been made much easier by the widespread adoption of the Internet, a platform that is ideally suited to allowing communication between each of the parties' own IT systems. The political problems occur at a company level with new policies needed to effect the necessary changes to manual systems that have been in place for years.

8.1.1 Parties Involved

Air cargo is mostly used for the export of goods to another country since mostly domestic or internal movements will go by surface transport. This means it needs to comply with customs regulations in terms of inspections and possibly the payment of duties. It may also involve special authorisation. It can also be looked at as an export from one country and an import into another country. This complexity means that the shipper of the goods, especially if they are small enterprises, can benefit by using the services of one or more agents. These could be one or more of the following:

- a freight forwarder;
- a cargo pick-up service;
- a consolidator;
- a customs agent.

These might be combined by a large forwarder who would also deal with the import side of the transport and who would contract with airlines and other parties to fill the gaps in the door-to-door transport. Alternatively the shipper might decide to choose an integrator who might use its own aircraft/vehicles to take care of every part of the journey. They could also use the national Post Office that may in turn contract its parcels business out to a forwarder or integrator, or deal directly with the airline.

8.1.2 Shipping Documents

Air waybill
The relevant shipping document is the air waybill, which does not give title to the goods but is an air 'ticket' and confirmation of receipt of the goods by the airline. In cases where a forwarder ships an individual consignment by air a 'House Air Waybill' or HAWB is issued. Where a forwarder consolidates a number of consignments (from different shippers) into a larger shipment a Master Air Waybill (MAWB) is issued. In the latter case the forwarder or consolidator becomes the shipper, with each of the individual consignments in the consolidation also having its own HAWB. These might be packed in customer loaded containers (or ULDs) off-airport, ready for loading onto the aircraft once they arrive at the airport.

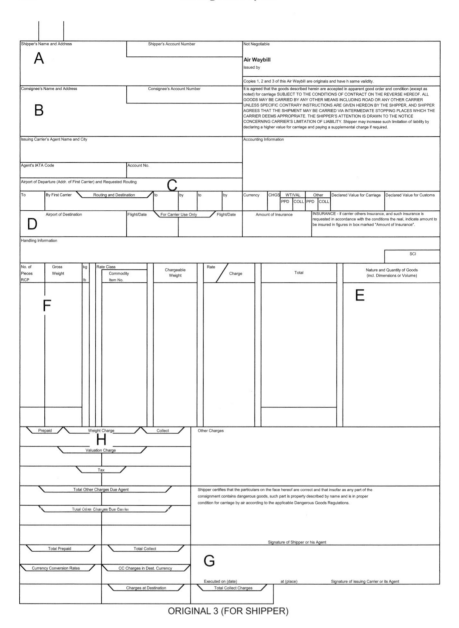

ORIGINAL 3 (FOR SHIPPER)

Figure 8.1   Example of air waybill

In the example in Figure 8.1 the following are the main items to be completed:

- the correct shipper (A) and consignee (B) must be shown;
- the airports of departure (C) and destination (D) must be shown;

- the goods description (E) must be consistent with that shown on other documents;
- any weights, measures or shipping marks (F) must agree with those shown on other documents;
- it must be signed and dated by the actual carrier (G) or by the named agent of a named carrier;
- it must state whether freight (H) has been paid or is payable at destination.

For the Master Air Waybill (MAWB) the following information is needed:

Shipper information: for consolidations, the name and address of the forwarder involved is sufficient. For non-consolidated shipments, the name and address of the actual shipper should be used.

Consignee information: for consolidation shipments, the identity of the forwarder, container station or broker is sufficient. For non-consolidated shipments, the name and address of the actual consignee should be used.

Cargo description: for all consolidated shipments, including those with only one house air waybill associated with the master, the description indicated in the *Nature and Quantity of Goods* box should read 'consolidation as per attached manifest'. For non-consolidated shipments, a complete and accurate description should be indicated.

Quantity: while the number of pieces tendered needs to be shown in the *No. of Pieces* box, the total number of internal pieces tendered (Shipper Load and Count, or SLAC), must also be shown in the *Nature and Quantity of Goods* box, below the Consolidation statement. For example, if two skids, each containing 25 pieces, are tendered, '2' would be entered in the *No. of Pieces* box, while the *Nature and Quantity of Goods* box would show 'SLAC – 50 pieces'.

Customer Loaded Containers (CLCs): for CLCs, the number of pieces contained in the container must be expressed as a 'said to contain' statement in the *Nature and Quantity of Goods* box. The shipper must also clearly indicate on the source document, consol manifest or pallet tag which HAWB, including number of pieces, is loaded in each CLC. For example, if a customer loaded LD3 containing 150 individual pieces is tendered, the entry in the *No. of Pieces* box would be '1', and, 'Said to Contain 150 pieces' would be entered in the *Nature and Quantity of Goods* box.

Cargo manifest

The airline manifest contains the details of both passengers and cargo carried on a particular flight. For cargo this would be the air waybill number, the ULD reference number, the number of pieces on each air waybill, the revenue weight, the actual gross weight, a description of the goods, and any special handling instructions. In other words a summary of the information contained on each air waybill. The revenue weight is the weight used for charging for low density shipments, and will be identical to the gross weight once the 167 kg per cubic metre cut-off is reached. The manifest data is transferred to the customs authorities in the destination (importing) country, preferably electronically in advance of the flight's arrival (see below).

Load sheet for weight and balance
The load sheet is required for both passenger and cargo flights to ensure that the weight and balance is correct, the centre of gravity of the aircraft is within the required limits and no specific loading limits are exceeded in any part of the aircraft. The load sheet gives the number of passengers and their weights, as well as the weight and hold positions of baggage, freight and mail carried. This is summarised as the total traffic load, which together with the trip fuel and other weights give the actual take-off and landing weights. This is separated into sections, but even then not in a very easy-to-read format:

1. flight information;
2. cargo information;
3. passenger information;
4. fuel and weight information;
5. balance information;
6. taxi information;
7. summary.

In order to avoid delays and ensure efficient handling, information needs to be exchanged between airlines, forwarders, shippers and customs authorities. Various links were developed first on an airport basis (through Community Systems or CCS) and then these were linked with other airports. A standard message format was used, Cargo Interchange Message Procedures (IMP), to send FWB information, status enquiries and updates, send and receive manifests, and booking. With the more widespread use of the Internet, some expect that Internet based systems will eventually replace the older systems.

8.1.3 Customs Clearance

Customs authorities need both the staff and space in order to carry out their inspections and process imports and exports by air (this has to be considered in planning the terminals covered in section 8.2). They are not present at smaller airports where special arrangements have to be made for customs clearance.

The term *import* means bringing goods into a country from another country for personal or commercial reasons. For EU countries this means outside the customs territory of the European Community. An import into the Community, as opposed to trade within the European Community, is treated differently from a legal standpoint. However legislation controlling the importation of goods such as firearms, offensive weapons or drugs into an EU country such as the UK also applies to goods from other EU Member States.

An *export* takes place when goods are sent from one country to a destination outside that country for any reason. Goods destined for a country within a customs union are not usually considered as an export, for example from the UK to Germany or another EU country. Many goods, for example military and paramilitary goods, radioactive sources, cultural goods and controlled drugs need a licence to be exported from the UK regardless of their destination. Customs have an interest in imports for a number of reasons. These include:

- correct payment of any duties and/or VAT due;
- trade statistics for both the UK and the EU;
- prohibitions and restrictions set in place by UK laws and EC Regulations.

Duties or tariffs and licences are determined by commodity, and each of over 16,000 commodities has a separate code to make processing easier. An electronic import declaration will have a commodity code which describes the goods and determines the tariff, and a customs procedure code which describes the purpose of the import to the country.

Customs declaration and clearance
Industry experts have noted that customs clearance procedures account for as much as 20 percent of average transport time and 25 percent of average transport costs of imports in many Member States. While expedited customs clearance is a crucial issue for the express delivery services industry, reductions in the time and cost of customs clearance will benefit all air cargo service providers (OECD, 2002).

Customs controls are designed to levy duties and taxes, enforce trade policy, prevent the movement of illicit drugs and collect statistical information. The procedures, involving identifying and checking thousands of different product categories, are slow and cumbersome in many countries and result in clearance times at airports of 15 hours or more. However, new EDI-based systems have been introduced in countries such as Australia and Taiwan that involve the electronic transfer of air waybill, manifest and entry information at the time the flight departs. This gives customs information sufficient time at the destination airport, especially for a long-haul flight, to decide on which shipments need inspection. This speeds processing time from 15 to four or less hours for the arrival of a fully loaded freighter aircraft.

The process of customs clearance starts with the importer's contract with the foreign supplier, followed by the arrangement for shipping (in this case by air), usually through a forwarder or integrator who completes the export declaration prior to the flight. The consignment details are sent electronically to the air cargo operator who makes a customs declaration to the relevant customs authorities of the destination country. Cargo manifest and air waybill data which are transmitted by the air carrier are matched in the customs system with entry data which has been transmitted by the importer or customs broker, and are reviewed by the inspector with the aid of databases to determine whether the goods can be released on the basis of the information or whether a physical examination needs to be made. If the information from both components of the system is transmitted early enough, this decision can be made before the arrival of the flight. Customs can then decide on which shipments they wish to inspect prior to the arrival of the shipment in its country. Once the flight arrives, those shipments that do not require customs inspection can be collected without any delay.

8.1.4 Flight Operations: Load Control

Before the departure of a flight it is necessary to calculate the take-off weights in order to calculate the amount of fuel that should be loaded onto the aircraft. This is needed for both passenger/cargo and freighter flights, although the process is more complicated for a passenger/cargo flight. Once the fuel load is known the loadsheet can be finalised and the final weights and their distribution known.

The weight of the aircraft is built up from the Basic Empty Weight (BEW) which includes the airframe and engines and all the fixed equipment. To this is added the cabin seats, IFE and other equipment (for a passenger aircraft), loading equipment (for a freighter), navigation equipment and ship's papers to give the Basic Weight (BW). The crew and their baggage weights are then added as well as the galley and its contents to form the Dry Operating Weight (DOW).

The traffic or payload on the aircraft is composed of the Dead Load Weight (DLW) which includes checked baggage, cargo (including the ULD tare weight) and mail, and the passenger weight. Standard passenger weights are used depending on whether they are male (88 kg), female (70 kg) or children (35 kg). Some airlines may use different weights on certain flights based on survey data.

The weight that is used for the fuel calculation for a particular flight is the Estimated Zero Fuel Weight (EZFW) which is the DOW plus the estimated payload. EZFW might be estimated five hours before the flight departure, with a better estimate two hours before, and the information finalised on the loadsheet six minutes before departure.

It is only in the final two hours or even hour that the number of passengers, checked bags and cargo will be known. The main uncertainties are:

- no-show (including missed connections) and stand-by passengers;
- checked baggage from passengers using online check-in;
- final cargo loads.

Fine-tuning is easier on the passenger side since each extra or lost passenger is only 100 kg compared to an extra pallet or container of 1,500 kg or more. The booking process for cargo is also less precise, with some loads differing considerably from their booked dimensions and a high percentage of loads arriving close to flight cut-off times.

From the Zero Fuel Weight (ZFW) the trip fuel and fuel reserves will be calculated taking into account diversion airport or allowance, temperatures, winds, etc. Take-off fuel and the ZFW will determine the Take-off Weight (TOW) which must not exceed the Maximum Take-off Weight (MTOW) that up to which it is certified.[2] The ZFW plus the fuel reserves give the Landing Weight (LAW) that must not exceed the Maximum Landing Weight (MLAW). There is also a maximum ZFW and a maximum taxi weight that is the TOW plus taxi fuel.

The above shows that, for a passenger flight, there is considerable uncertainty as to exactly what weight or even volume is available for cargo traffic. If the fuel load is small, because it is not a very long-range flight, there is less pressure to keep the cargo load within the limits discussed above, but the available space in the lower deck compartments is likely to be the limiting factor. On longer range flights there is the danger that the overall load factor could be improved or that too much fuel is carried and burnt. The economics of the flight can thus be improved by better estimation of the final load and coordination between the passenger and cargo planners.

Flights may be volume limited, also known as 'cubing out', or 'weighing out', when they reach their maximum payload before the volumetric capacity is totally used up. Longer sectors, where a full fuel load is needed, tend to weigh out first, but the average density of consignments might also be low and in these cases the flight is more likely to cube out. Research into international flights to and from India revealed that of the flights that reached either of these limits three-quarters cubed out from India, and 83 percent cubed out on flights to India (Klein, 2010). The use of pallets rather than containers also leads to weighing out before the volume is fully utilised.

8.2 Physical Facilities

The physical facilities or infrastructure at an airport are designed to expedite the movement of trucks, United Load Devices (ULDs) and their shipments, and aircraft. Aircraft have been described in Chapter 7 and a detailed look at trucks is beyond the scope of this book. ULDs and their handling will be examined before seeing how these processes are accommodated by the airside and landside infrastructure.

---

2   This maximum can be reduced in order to save money on airport or navigation fees in cases where the full payload or range will never be needed. DHL UK had its B757-200F aircraft maximum declared take-off weight reduced to 95.3 tonnes from the 115 tonnes at which it was originally certified.

8.2.1 Unit Load Devices (ULDs)

A ULD is the box or unit that is loaded onto the aircraft and unloaded at its destination. It may arrive at the departure airport ready for loading on to an aircraft or it may be assembled (built) in the airport cargo terminal. In the former case, the forwarder will combine packages from different shippers to one destination, and in the latter case the airline or its handling agent will do the same for shipments from various forwarders.

A ULD is a term than can apply to either a container or a pallet. The former is an aluminium box with a door, often of a shape that makes best use of the contoured sides of an aircraft. The latter is a solid wooden or metal base on which shipments are stacked, with a tarpaulin and netting cover. Aircraft ULDs are units that interface directly with an aircraft loading and restraint system. They meet all normal restraint requirements without the use of supplementary equipment, providing they are loaded in accordance with the specific Aircraft Load and Balance Manual.

The most popular standard container used for air cargo is the LD3 or AKE, which can be accommodated in the lower deck of both narrow and wide-bodied aircraft. Other popular containers are the LD9 and LD11. The most popular pallets are the PMC and PAG. One study estimated that PMCs accounted for around half the total ULDs used, AKEs 18 percent and PAGs 17 percent (Van de Reyd and Wouters, 2005).[3] The aircraft and types of ULD carried in each are discussed in more detail in Chapter 7.

Figure 8.2 shows a picture of the common half width lower deck LD3 container. It is contoured to make best use of the lower deck compartments. Its usable volume is a little less than $4.2m^3$, its tare weight around 72 kg and its maximum gross weight 1,588 kg. It is suitable for most wide-bodies including B747, MD11, B777 and B767 as well as A300, A330, A340 aircraft.

Because of damage, theft or demurrage airlines tend to overstock their ULD fleet. Location of containers becomes difficult once they move off airport to forwarder premises. Using lighter materials reduces tare weight and increases revenue payload potential, but they may be more susceptible to damage. This can take the form of forklift operator mistakes or exceeding 25mph speed limit when towed by tractors. Storage space is a problem in some airports and directional imbalances tend to leave ULDs in the wrong location. ULDs are valuable and carriers that frequently interline may lose them to partners or elsewhere. The IATA has thus set up a UKD Control Centre whose main purpose is to make sure that a unit is speedily returned to its owner, but, at the same time, he is compensated for the temporary absence of the unit by crediting him with a daily demurrage. Participating airlines pay an annual fee to take part.

---

3   LD3/AKEs would be nearer half the ULDs used in the lower deck of passenger aircraft.

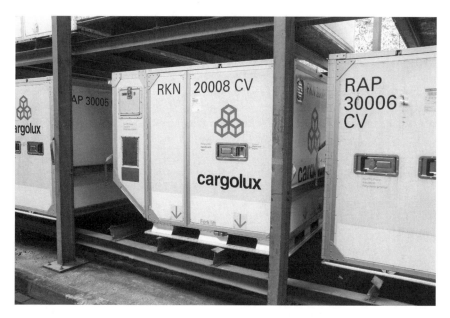

Figure 8.2   Cargolux containers

One manufacturer, Nordisk, has introduced the Ultralite AKE (LD3) container, which offers a weight reduction of around 25 percent compared to traditional aluminium containers. Together with DHL, it also developed an AAC container, which has a unique shape that fits both wide and narrow-bodied aircraft.

The advantages of pallets versus containers can be summarised as follows:

- lower tare weight and cheaper to buy;
- less costly to repair;
- arguably easier to handle;
- empty stacking (especially on-airport where space is at a premium);
- The disadvantages are as follows:more difficult to build and cover;
- warehouse staff resistance;
- problems with frozen or wet netting;
- cargo can be damaged by water.

8.2.2 Cargo Terminal Facilities

Combination carrier terminals
Cargo terminals or warehouses are needed on-airport to assemble and breakdown shipments. Even if cargo arrives in aircraft compatible ULDs storage space is needed before loading on to aircraft. Storage is also required before customs inspection or collection. These terminals can be owned and operated by the airport authority, by one or more airlines (usually involving the airline based at

that airport), or by a third party handler such as Menzies. It could also be jointly owned by one or more of these. Cathay Pacific Airlines had a 10 percent stake in Hong Kong Cargo Terminal Ltd (Hactl) which it sold in 2010 to other existing shareholders, along with the 20 percent held by its Swire Pacific parent. In 2008 Cathay was awarded a 20-year franchise to build the third terminal at Hong Kong International Airport in addition to that operated by Hactl and another by Asia Airfreight Terminal Co. Ltd (AAT). As part of that contract it agreed, together with Swire Pacific, to sell its holdings in Hactl, which it did to existing shareholders. AAT has a number of shareholders, notably Singapore Airport Terminal Services (SATS) with 49 percent and Federal Express 6 percent.

Some of the key criteria in designing terminal facilities are:

- on-airport land expensive: maximise building volumetric capacity or go off-airport;
- new cargo terminals are multi-storey and multi-level at Singapore (SATS 5), Chep Lap Kok and Evergreen at Taipei;
- air cargo terminal efficiency: peak at 15–18 tonnes per square metre per annum before automation required;
- aircraft pallets and containers easy to damage (e.g. by forklift trucks);
- as much as half of all air cargo handled is 'loose' (i.e. not unitised);
- employee health and safety issues.

Figure 8.3   Forklifting packages at Hong Kong International Airport

Source: Hactl.

Some have set targets of six hours' handling time from aircraft arrival to availability for customer collection of six hours, including container breakdown and customs inspection. Two hours or less are targets for express and perishable items.

Whether or not the terminal handling process is automated, tracking systems require some measure of automation. Bar coding and reading has been used for many years but this suffers from mis-reading, damaged labels and other problems. Radio Frequency Identification (RFID) promises to remove many of these problems, but is still quite expensive. Other means of automation are combined volumetric and weight scanners, high speed sorting and mechanising the build process and container delivery.

Radio Frequency Identification Tags (RFID) involve attaching a computer chip to the consignment or ULD, and installing a circuit that transmits data to radio antennae. These need to be mounted on loaders and sorters. DHL intended to put RFID on all its shipments by mid-2004, going for a system with a 2.7-metre range.

The cost of tags has been an impediment to its more widespread use, but this has fallen from US$1 in 2001 to around $0.20 each, with expectations of $0.05 to come. However, there is no agreement yet on one standard for data processing.

It is fairly common to find the ownership of cargo terminals to be split between the base carrier and the airport authority, with operations handled by the airline. One example is Lufthansa's joint venture at Munich Airport and another with Tianjin Airport in China. Forwarders also have their own terminals, for example the DB Schenker facility at Frankfurt Airport CargoCity South. This combined various import and export units that the forwarder had at various locations at the airport.

Emirates own and operate a cargo terminal at Dubai International Airport, the new 'Cargo Mega Terminal' opening in February 2008 with the following capacities:

- over 1.2 million tonnes' annual throughput;
- 43,600 square metres handling area (with 35,000 square metres footprint – floor area);
- 46 truck docks for acceptance and delivery of loose cargo;
- 78 airside ULD entry and exit gates;
- 133 workstations for cargo breakdown/build-up;
- 10,000 locations for loose cargo storage, with equal number of Large Storage Pallets;
- 2,064 general cargo ULD storage;
- 218 perishable ULD storage.

The terminal allows the automated retrieval, handling and location of consignments using the latest physical handling and wireless technology. Its perishables areas are separated into zones that are maintained at different temperatures and it has a freezer that can take up to 20 LD3 containers. It can handle up to 175,000 tonnes a year. Overall it can store up to 218 perishables and 2,064 general cargo ULDs.

Hong Kong Air Cargo Terminal Ltd (Hactl): Superterminal 1
Initial Investment: US$1 billion
Potential Handling Capacity: 3.5 million tonnes per annum
Total Floor Area: 328,702 square metres
Total Site Area: 171,322 square metres
Airside Facilities:
– Airside Transfer Frontage: 1,940 metres
– Number of Normal-Sized Pallet Dolly Positions: 938
Landside Facilities, in terms of number of truck docks:
– For bulk cargo: 226
– For pre-packed cargo: 53
– For perishable cargo: 60
– For empty ULD release: 14.

Hactl has a 95 percent target for the following service standards, which it reports to have been more than achieved in all cases:

> Landside services
> Truck waiting time (within 30 minutes)
> Cargo acceptance (within 15 minutes)
> Cargo release (within 15 minutes)
> Import cargo breakdown
> General cargo:
> Passenger flights (within 5 hours)
> Freighter flights (within 8 hours)
> Perishable cargo (within 2 hours)
> Express cargo (within 2 hours).

Integrator hub terminals

Integrators need very different airport facilities for their express parcels business. Items will tend to weigh less than 30 kg and automated sorting is the only way they can achieve the desired turnaround times for aircraft serving the hub and meet their delivery commitments. While they have developed aircraft containers, the sorting is applied to individual bar coded (and in a few trial cases RFID tagged) packages, and not ULDs. DHL entered into a franchise agreement with Hong Kong Airport to build, develop and operate a dedicated express cargo terminal, which opened in 2004.

Table 8.1   DHL Express hub at Leipzig/Halle Airport

Total investment	€345m
Total area	2m square metres
Distribution centre	48,000 square metres
Hangar	27,460 square metres
Administrative building	11,900 square metres
Freight turnover	1,500 tonnes per day (2,000 tonnes by 2012)
Sorting capacity	60,000 parcels and 36,000 documents per hour
Length of document sorter	900m
Loading/unloading air container positions	260
Employees inside hub	2,000

Source: *International Transport Journal*, 6 June 2008.

Table 8.1 shows the key parameters for DHL's major European hub at Leipzig which has taken over from its previous Brussels facility. This is services by trucks and flights operated jointly with Lufthansa Cargo.

Cargo West is a new complex developed jointly by East Midlands Airport and DHL Aviation with a 33,000m^2 sorting facility, office block and loading dock. The development can accommodate 16 aircraft of varying size.

8.2.3 Ground Handling

Cargo handling at airports is carried out either by an airline's own staff or by third party service providers. At a reasonably sized airline hub the airline probably finds it economical if they do their own handling. This almost always used to be the case but some are now questioning the economics due to the sufficient number of global ground handling companies that can provide a competitive service, not only at the hub but also at most outstations. Handling at outstations could never be justified if an airline did not have a sufficient number of flights there, since expensive equipment is needed as well as skilled employees and management. In those cases, before the advent of third party handlers the work was contracted to another airline, generally that having its main base there. This might be done on a reciprocal basis. As strategic alliances developed more joint activities to save costs, handling was contracted out to alliance partners as far as possible. It might also have been given to handling companies owned by the base airport, for example Fraport at Frankfurt/Main Airport or Aena at almost all Spanish airports.

The advent of sizeable ground handling companies is partly the result of an EU regulation that opened up larger airports to competitive service provision. Up to then the market had been controlled by airline and airport owned operations. The adoption of the Directive 96/67/EC in October 1996 forced EU airports which handled more than two million passengers or 50,000 tonnes of air cargo a year to open up their ground handling to third party suppliers. At least one of the suppliers at these airports was required to be 'independent of the management body of the airport and any dominant airline at the specific airport'. Both ramp handling and cargo handling were included in the scope of the Directive. There has been evidence since then of a reduction in contract prices for handling and possibly increases in service quality. Following the Directive, the number of third party cargo handling companies increased from three to four at Paris CDG Airport, from two to eight at Madrid, from three to six at Vienna, three to six at Dublin and from five to six at Amsterdam (SH&E, 2002). There was no change at Frankfurt, where there were already 22 companies, with London Heathrow adding one to 12. Opportunities to provide handling at North American and some Asian airports also arose, permitting the expansion of European based handling specialists into global companies.

Cargo handling companies offer a range of services from cargo warehousing to trucking. Cargo airlines negotiate contracts based on some or all of these together with the likely level of traffic and flights to be handled:

1. Warehousing:
   - acceptance, build-up and storage of shipments
   - ULD build-up and breakdown
   - inventory control
   - truck loading and unloading
   - handling of transit and transfer/transhipment freight
   - security services
   - express services.
2. Documentation:
   - acceptance and processing of import, export, transit and transfer documentation
   - sending of all cargo IMP messages
   - tracing.
3. Handling of dangerous goods, live animals, perishables and other special freight.
4. Transport to and from aircraft.
5. Air freight trucking services.

Even in highly automated cargo terminals in terms of storage and retrieval, the breakdown and build-up of ULDs is a labour intensive operation, and still makes use of forklift trucks to move pallets and containers to assembly areas. This can involve damage to containers and/or cargo. However, at some of the combination carriers' hub airports such as Frankfurt/Main or Paris CDG over half of the freight will be in sealed containers (some not full) that go from one aircraft direct to another or from truck to aircraft and vice versa (see also Chapter 1, section 1.4). These avoid the build/break operation. Another way of avoiding this (and reducing the need for expensive on-airport space) is to deliver ULDs direct to off-airport bonded warehouses where forwarders can do their own breakdown and building of units. In the UK these needed to be located within a radius of 10 miles of the airport and can transmit data direct to customs for them to designate the facility as an Enhanced Remote Transit Shed and thus have bonded status.

The IATA standard ground handling agreement defines the menu of services that can be offered including general cargo and mail handling, document handling, customs control, the handling of irregularities and ramp services.

Third party ground handlers tend to offer both passenger and cargo services and some are part of larger groups that offer trucking services or completely unrelated areas. Taking the passenger and cargo handling together, a study estimated that the third party handling market share increased from 24 percent in 2000 to 40 percent in 2005 (WTO, 2006). The total value of this market was around US$30 billion in 2005 with the airlines' own handling accounting for 50 percent and the remaining 10 percent from airport-owned companies.

Table 8.2   Major third party cargo handling companies

	Tonnes handled (000)	Locations	Customers
Worldwide Flight Services	3,500	n/a	n/a
Swissport Cargo Services	2,800	90+	300+
Menzies	1,400	44	n/a
AviaPartner	1,398	10	n/a
Penauille Servisair	900	40	600
Fraport Ground Services	410	n/a	50+
Aviance UK	160	2	40

Source: Company websites.

Some of the major third party cargo handlers shown in Table 8.2 are part of diversified groups. Servisair was acquired by a French environmental and business services group, Penauille, which was acquired by Derichebourg in 2005. Penauille had bought Servisair in 1999 and Globeground in 2001/2002. Its environmental services division works mostly on recycling for local authorities, while its business services includes contract cleaning. Swissport is owned by the Spanish toll road and airport group, Ferrovial, while Worldwide Flight Services was bought by a French group, Vinci, in 2001 and sold on to a French private equity firm in 2006. Menzies is part of a group whose major business is newspaper and magazine distribution, while AviaPartner is a family owned Belgian company. All are based in Europe, but most have become global companies.

Cargo handling companies will have to have various items of ground support equipment, some of which will depend on the aircraft types that it will be supporting. On the ramp alongside the aircraft the main items will be:

- The trolley or dolly is used to transport containers and pallets between the aircraft and the cargo terminal. These have in-built rollers or balls to make it easier to move the loads around. Trolleys for containers have a revolving deck to make containers turn to the direction of loading on aircraft.
- The loader is a platform that can be raised and lowered to enable the loading and unloading of cargo ULDs in and from wide-bodied aircraft and the main decks of all aircraft. It also has in-built rollers or balls to make it easier to move the loads into and out of the aircraft. There are different container and pallet loaders of different dimensions and capabilities (height). The A380F would have required special loaders to reach its upper deck cargo compartment.

- Belt loaders are vehicles with movable belts for unloading and loading of loose cargo (and baggage) off and on to an aircraft. A belt loader is positioned to the door sill of an aircraft hold for the operation. Belt loaders are used for narrow-body aircraft and the bulk holds of wide-body aircraft.
- Pushback tugs are used to push an aircraft away from the gate when it is ready to leave. They might also be used to position the aircraft on the apron if power-in is not possible. They might also tow an aircraft off the ramp to the maintenance or cargo terminal area. Different size tugs are required for different size aircraft.

8.2.4 Security

Security covers both the securing of shipments (and facilities) against theft, and more recently securing them and the aircraft against terrorist attack. Theft has been a problem in both baggage and cargo sorting areas and measures are available to deter theft, for example by placing CCTV cameras at strategic locations. Threats could come either from employees or from outsiders. Valuable consignments can be subject to special precautions, including their packing at the centre of containers rather than easily accessible places towards the outside. Insurance is usually available to cover these risks at a reasonable cost. Theft was estimated to have been worth around €170m for the Europe, Middle East and African region alone in 2008.[4]

'Aviation security' means the combination of measures and human and material resources intended to safeguard civil aviation against acts of unlawful interference. Since 9/11, very significant measures have been taken to address, and as far as possible prevent, terrorist risks. These initially focused on passenger aircraft and passenger processing at airports. Prior to 9/11 security measures were in force at most international airports through restricted access to the airside areas of the airport and security checks on passengers. Both these have been considerably tightened up and in some countries extended to domestic flights, which often connect with international ones. There is however a trade-off between effectiveness and cost and inconvenience.

Cargo is covered by these measures in relation to access to apron areas, but security screening has needed to be dealt with differently from passengers. This is because it is not practicable to screen every individual piece of cargo that moves through an airport.

The Transportation Security Administration (TSA) is responsible in the US for transport security which includes air cargo. It is the agency that ensures that legislation is enforced, in this case the *Implementing the 9/11 Commission Recommendations Act of 2007*, also known as the 9/11 Act. This requested the Secretary of Homeland Security to establish a system to enable industry to screen 100 percent of cargo transported on passenger aircraft at a level of security

---

4   *Air Cargo News*, 4 September 2009.

commensurate with the level of security of passenger checked baggage, within three years. In addition, the legislation set an interim milestone for industry to screen 50 percent of all cargo shipped on a passenger aircraft within 18 months of enactment, by February 2009 and 100 percent screening by August 2010.

In order to meet these targets, TSA has implemented three programmes: narrow-body cargo screening; the certified cargo screening programme (CCSP); and the international collaboration. The first became effective on 1 October 2008 and required that all cargo uplifted in the US on narrow-body aircraft (export or domestic flights) must be 100 percent screened individually at the piece level before it is netted, containerised, or shrink-wrapped. The CCSP enables freight forwarders and shippers to pre-screen cargo, avoiding any potential bottlenecks at the airport. Most CCSP shipper participants have been able to quickly incorporate physical screening into their shipping process at a small cost to their operation. Finally international collaboration has been initiated with the EU, Canada and Australia. By mid-2010 almost all domestic and outbound US cargo on passenger services complied with the Act, but inbound international air cargo looked as if it would not meet the deadline, due to the need to deal with foreign countries.

To qualify for CCSP shippers or forwarders need to purchase the necessary scanning equipment. This can be onerous for small companies as scanners can cost between US\$30,000 and \$100,000. Lufthansa recently invested in 1.8m x 1.8m tunnel scanners that can scan entire LD3 containers. It has introduced these at its Frankfurt and Munich bases, as well as Johannesburg.

The EU's Council and Parliament agreed a Regulation (EC) No 300/2008 on common rules in the field of civil aviation security in March 2008. This provided a framework that should be applied at the level of each member state. However, it adopted the known shipper/agent approach in the same way as the US. It made no distinction between passenger and cargo flights and gave a common standard for cargo and mail security controls as follows:

> All cargo and mail shall be subjected to security controls prior to being loaded on an aircraft. An air carrier shall not accept cargo or mail for carriage on an aircraft unless it has applied such controls itself or their application has been confirmed and accounted for by a regulated agent, a known consignor or an account consignor (Regulation 30/2008).

Who was to bear the cost of these measures was also left to each Member State to decide, with the various possible participants listed as 'the State, airport entities, air carriers, other responsible agencies and others'.

Some EU members such as the UK have already implemented a known shipper and forwarder scheme. In March 2010, Australia declared unannounced inspections of off-airport air cargo companies, whereas previously it had given 'reasonable' notice. In spite of tighter regulations, a survey of air freight distribution and handling companies in Europe revealed significant shortcomings. The majority of respondents argued that there was a lack of consistency in the application of the security regulations, insufficient security awareness among staff, and inadequate surveillance in buildings. It added that existing EU regulations have delayed urgent air cargo and increased costs by 'as much as 10 percent of total logistics costs'.[5]

There are generally stricter requirements for screening cargo carried on passenger flights than for freighters. This creates potential problems for transhipments between these two types of flights and may result in some switching from passenger to freighter services. The investment in equipment and trained staff could also result in increasing concentration of cargo traffic at larger hub airports where economies of scale can be exploited.

8.2.5 Dangerous Goods

The International Civil Aviation Organisation has produced detailed requirements for the international air transport of dangerous goods and these are in the Technical Instructions (see Chapter 3) which are incorporated into each country's aviation regulations, for example JAR-OPS in the EU. IATA also produces very similar requirements which most operators use. Handling staff are required by law to undergo prescribed training before being allowed to be involved with such shipments. It is the responsibility of the shipper to classify dangerous goods, which are defined with reference to the following categories:

Class 1: Explosives
Class 2: Gases
Class 3: Flammable liquids
Class 4: Flammable solids and reactive substances
Class 5: Oxidisers and organic peroxides
Class 6: Toxic and infectious substances
Class 7: Radioactive material
Class 8: Corrosive articles and substances
Class 9: Miscellaneous articles and substances

Specific instructions are given for packaging, labelling, storage and stowage and handling.

---

5 Report by the International Transfer Centre for Logistics and the Technical University of Berlin, summarised in *Air Cargo World*, 14 August 2009.

Chapter 9
Distribution and Marketing

Marketing generally includes distribution and is often divided in business school textbooks into the four Ps: Product, Price, Promotion and Place. The first refers to what is offered in the marketplace and covers physical attributes such as the colour, shape or size of what is being sold, or less tangible features such as quality of service and brand. The second is the price at which the product is sold, nowadays coming with a menu of additional features that are obtainable at an extra cost. This will be addressed in the next chapter. Promotion is the communication of the features of the product and the price to potential consumers and will include advertising. Finally, place is the means of making the purchase and is more commonly called distribution. These three 'Ps' will be taken in turn in this chapter, distinguishing between the airport-to-airport cargo airlines and the integrators.

Marketing strategies will depend on the type of transaction that is taking place and who the two or more parties are. Air cargo is a service that facilitates these transactions and a different approach may be needed depending on the parties involved. These can be divided into:

- business to business (B2B);
- business to consumer (B2C);
- business to administration (B2A);
- consumer to administration (C2A).

The first is focused on the elements that go into the production process, with firms subcontracting parts of this to other firms. Firms will also purchase final products such as office supplies or computers. It may also involve service industries such as advertisers, consultants and accountants. Agents may be needed for distribution and logistics specialists and air cargo carriers selected for transport and warehousing. What these producing entities all have in common is that they are either incorporated or in a partnership and decisions are made by their managers or committees. Their air transport needs can be met either by forwarder/airline combinations or integrators. If they have large volumes of air freight they might have a longer-term contract with a few service providers with exclusive use for all shipments exported to a given world region.

In contrast, in the second type one of the parties is an individual or family unit, with decisions generally made by only one or two people in the home rather than place of work. These types of transactions are not part of a supply chain and are usually described as retail sales. Traditionally goods were purchased in shops and transported to the home by consumers in their personal transport. Mail order from catalogues also took place but this was not a very large part of total retail sales. However, this has expanded rapidly in recent years with items such as books sold more and more through Amazon and other electronic outlets. Many other items such as groceries are also now purchased online and delivered to the home from the nearest warehouse. Many of these, for example groceries, are still a relatively local business with delivery undertaken by the store itself or a subcontractor. Air cargo is unlikely to be part of these supply chains. On the other hand, books, clothes, mobile phones and other items may be located far from the consumer and if a short delivery time is requested air cargo may be the transport taken. This type of transaction is more likely to choose an integrator for its air transport, mainly because these carriers have a retail service, including home delivery and collection, that is more appropriate than the use of a forwarder. Most transactions will also involve small shipments, which are the core express business of integrators.

The third and fourth bullet points identify administrations or governments as a different type of party. They behave in similar ways to businesses in terms of decision-making by government officials or committees, but with taxpayers' money at risk decisions can often take longer. Businesses sell to government departments in a similar way to other businesses, and governments increasingly 'sell' their services to consumers using such marketing tools as advertising and promotion. Governments also negotiate with and supply other governments in the joint provision of services or products, although the latter are now mostly delivered by means of state or privately owned corporations. These could also choose either forwarders or integrators in the same way as companies.

Customers can also be segmented according to their needs and the type of product and price is best suited to those needs. These were described in Chapter 2 in terms of their market characteristics. Here the most appropriate methods of selling and promoting an airline's services will be examined, keeping in mind that large forwarders may be the intermediaries that the airline will deal with for a wide range of market segments. Similarly, the airline may not be very familiar with the shipper or consignor since the forwarder often acts as an intermediary rather than an agent. Thus it may be of little concern to the airline whether the exporter or importer is responsible for selecting the mode of transport and carrier, since they have left these decisions to the forwarder. In some cases the exporter is in charge of the transport (cost insurance freight or 'cif') and in others it is the importer that needs to pay (free-on-board or 'fob'). But it is unlikely that either will be dealing direct with an air cargo carrier, except in the case of an integrator that also operates its own flights.

9.1 Marketing Environment

9.1.1 Global Trends

It is important to look at the environment in which supply chains have been developed and in which air carriers identify their marketing strategies. Some of these trends have been identified above, and others are expected to develop in the future. Technology has been the crucial influence shaping many of the types of transaction introduced above, above all the widespread use of the Internet in business, homes and government.

Open skies
The ability to carry air cargo traffic between any world airport is gradually being impeded by fewer restrictions. As these are further removed, cargo airlines will be able to base aircraft in foreign countries, operate circular routes and round-the-world flights and generally allow more economic operations. This will also give scope for more differentiated strategies and ways of marketing services. It will also raise new challenges in terms of selling in foreign countries with different cultures.

Globalisation and free trade
The word globalisation is usually used to describe the closer integration of countries and regions throughout the world by means of trade, tourism and communications. Of relevance here is trade, which could be in either goods or services which need transport, especially the former. The exchange of goods and services across borders has been enabled by the increasing removal of barriers, facilitated by negotiations through the World Trade Organisation (WTO). The various rounds of multilateral GATT negotiations have promoted free trade, especially through:

- the elimination of *tariffs*;
- the creation of *free trade zones* with small or no tariffs;
- reduced transportation costs, especially from the development of *containerisation* for ocean shipping;
- reduction or elimination of *capital controls*;
- reduction, elimination, or harmonisation of *subsidies* for local businesses;
- the harmonisation of *intellectual property* laws across the majority of states.

Multinational corporations
The emergence of very large international firms has been evolving over many years. These so-called 'multinationals' are often firmly rooted in one country (e.g. Coca Cola in the US) but their sales are global. This generally involves setting up local companies in many countries or certain regions, often with their own manufacturing capability. The key to their success has been the establishment of global brands such as McDonalds or Holiday Inn, some of which need to be adapted to suit the different cultural needs of the country.

Outsourcing and off-shoring

Another strong trend has been the shift of certain parts of the production or manufacturing process to other firms or countries. The first of these is described as 'outsourcing' and the firms contracted to do this may be in close proximity to the main production line. This was the original Japanese model for the Just-in-time (JIT) process that was adopted by US and other companies. However, moving production to other countries (off-shoring) has the added advantage of the potential for much lower labour costs. This a trade-off between lower wages, which many developing or emerging countries offer, and labour productivity, which may also be much lower than in the home country. In China, wages have been increasing quite fast, but so has productivity. Moving to other lower wage cost countries means that, at least initially, productivity is very low. Thus slower speed and lower quality might offset much of the wage rate advantage. Shipping costs also need to be taken into account and the need for increased stocks.

e-sales

More and more products are being bought and sold electronically, whether direct from manufacturers, through trading sites such as Expedia or Amazon, or from auction sites such as eBay. Two important drivers of these trends are secure means of payment and the more widespread use by consumers of credit and debit cards. Delivery or shipping costs can be borne by the seller but they are often passed on to the consumer, especially if the goods are needed more urgently and the consumer is prepared to pay the premium. Many of these sales generate air freight or mail revenues, usually in the first instance for integrators (but they may buy space on combination or all-cargo airlines). In cases where the goods turn out not to be suitable they may generate a return shipment and the delivery of a more suitable product, for example a shirt that fits better.

9.1.2 Transport and Logistics

Goods transported by air, land or sea can be moving from their factory of production to their final purchaser. The latter could be individual consumers from a shop or increasingly a distribution centre by email or phone order. It is more likely that they will be 'intermediate goods' moving from a factory to another company for incorporation into the final product. Intel's chips could have been manufactured in Mexico but first flown to laptop makers in Taiwan. The story doesn't end there because the laptop instructions might be printed in Singapore and shipped to a final assembly nearer the final market, say in Europe. This is the impact of globalisation, and the firms involved will range from large multinationals to small family owned production units. While countries such as Korea, Taiwan and China have become the engines for manufacturing worldwide and export huge quantities of finished goods, they also depend on imports of intermediate goods from Europe, North America and other Asian countries to survive. This is mainly to benefit from specialisation and economies of scale; but it is also because the 'emerging economies' such as China do not yet have access to some of the technology to be more self-sufficient.

Figure 9.1 is an example of a multinational car manufacturer outsourcing and off-shoring production of many different components. These all need to come together on the final production line, which for Ford will be in a number of regional centres. For Ford Europe a large number of components will be trucked from other European countries, but some will need reliable long distance transport so as not to delay the production line. Some companies such as Boeing have had to halt their production lines through delays in the delivery of key components, after introducing what is known as Just-in-time (JIT) production methods. As economies become more global and source production items further afield, competition is increasingly between supply chains rather than just between companies.

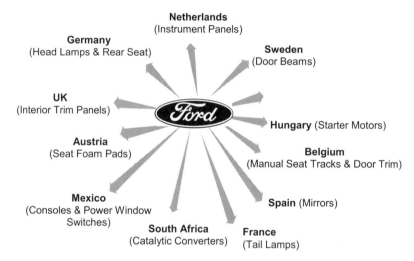

Figure 9.1   Example of multinational off-shoring of production

Source: Boeing.

JIT is said to have been invented by Henry Ford but it was Toyota in Japan that demonstrated its potential in a more modern context. The technique aims to simplify the production process by outsourcing the production of various parts to a small number of suppliers who are preferably located nearby, and buying their commitment with long-term contracts. Over time, however, it has become more complex, as the few suppliers became many, the suppliers in turn outsourced to other companies, and contractual relationships became fuzzier. This meant that the components were often produced in far off countries such as in Asia, with lower labour costs to some extent offset by more expensive air freight charges. Less costly inventory was needed and shorter lead times made planning and forecasting more accurate.

The speed and reliability of air cargo counted for nothing during the one-week closure of much of the northern Europe airspace following the Icelandic volcanic eruption in April 2010. Flower producers in Kenya suffered immediate damage with 'an estimated US$8 million worth of blooms destroyed and several thousand casual workers sent home'.[1] The potential to lose this market to ocean transport as a result of the future likelihood of such events seems small for these products, or even others. Lufthansa Cargo also reported that a shipment of 50 tonnes of flowers en route from Quito in Ecuador to Frankfurt had to be returned, although flights with emergency items such as insulin were getting special permission to operate.[2]

These production systems helped to turn the 2008 downturn in final demand (triggered by the banking crisis) into a sharp decline in international trade, especially air trade. Sales turned down in the lead up to Christmas when inventories were seasonally high. This triggered a cut in orders especially to Asian manufacturers, a fall in deliveries (Asian exports) and in turn a fall in intermediate products (Asian imports). The overall affect on world trade was thus severe. The same process, however, also works in reverse and the upturn was also magnified, once re-stocking started again in Western economies.

Logistics is another name for the movement and storage of goods in the production process or supply chain. The European Centre of Standardisation defined it as 'the planning, execution and control of the movement and placement of people and/or goods'. In the context of goods, in addition to transport, it concerns the management of inventory and warehousing. Losses can occur through obsolescence, as stored items can no longer be sold for a realistic price. Losses can also occur from theft or damage, and thus security and adequate packaging are also important. Both of these concern the transport part of the process as well as the storage of the goods in a warehouse or on the shelves of the final retailer. Air transport can be marketed as a more secure system, although such claims may not be borne out by past experience. However, the fact that the goods are in transit for a shorter time means that the risks should be lower. Surface transport handling may require more protective packaging than air transport, which could also be marketed as an advantage. Lighter packaging may in any case be essential for air transport to keep the freight cost down, but the same does not always apply to volume as goods are wrapped in lightweight plastic materials for shockproofing.

The time elapsed between manufacture and a cash sale involves a holding or carrying cost. This is borne by the manufacturer, an intermediary such as a distributor or the retailer, or more likely a combination of these. Costs have been incurred and the cash used to buy materials, labour etc. has an opportunity cost or needs to be financed. Financing costs could be the interest on borrowing and this will depend on the firm's average cost of capital. The sooner the goods are sold in the market the lower these carrying costs would be. This gives air an advantage assuming the shipper or consignee evaluates the total costs of alternative transport modes.

---

1   *The Economist*, 24 April 2010.
2   *Lufthansa Cargo Newsletter*, April 2010.

Inventory management is covered in many business school texts. Of most relevance here is the economic order quantity, and the re-order point, both of which favour air as the faster mode of transport. The latter has been reduced as manufacturers have moved to JIT approaches to ordering. Variations in sales from expected values mean a certain level of inventory is held to protect against loss of sales (and possibly customers). The main advantages claimed by air can be summarised as:

- lower packaging costs;
- improved cash flow and lower borrowing costs;
- smaller economic order quantities;
- reduced safety stocks;
- centralised warehousing.

These must be viewed in relation to the final price of the goods relative to its weight.

9.1.3 Total Distribution Cost Model

Most large freight forwarders use a mix of air and ocean transport based on the total costs of distribution, which include both transport and inventory-related costs. Transport costs cover the freight rates charged for the movement of goods from door-to-door, using a variety of modes but on the main trade routes most of this will either be air or sea. It also covers any related costs such as customs

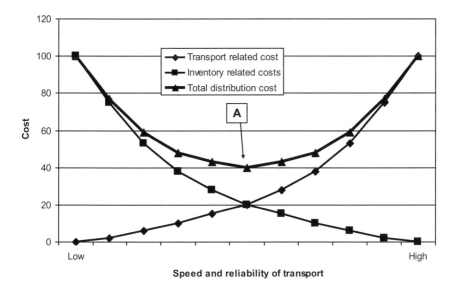

Figure 9.2   Total distribution cost model

inspections, documentation and special services offered by the carriers. Inventory costs cover the storage and handling of shipments between manufacture and final sale, as well as the financial cost of carrying the goods (and write down of spoiled or obsolete goods).

Figure 9.2 shows how these two categories of cost change as the speed and reliability of transport increases. Moving from 'low' to 'high' on the x-axis of this graph is going from a situation of all shipments travelling by surface transport to one of all moving by air. The y-axis shows the costs related to this range of transport speed, with transport costs increasing and inventory costs declining as more are choosing to go by air. The sum of the two costs is shown to fall to a low point before rising again as the transport costs accelerate and inventory cost advantages decline more slowly. The minimum point moves to the left when fuel costs rise significantly, and security costs can have a disproportionate affect on air transport, as occurred in the latter half of the 2000s.

Some commodities will always go by air, since the slower transit times by surface will result in lost sales and very high inventory costs. Others will never afford the high air freight rates and will not incur very high inventory costs. Some high-tech goods are initially shipped by air to exploit their advantage of being the first of a new product in the market (e.g. the iPhone). A high price can be charged initially but as the market matures and competitors arrive, the price will fall (or new expensive features will be added) and air freight becomes less affordable. Each mode attempts to shorten transit times to gain share: air by combining with LTL carriers and introducing faster ships, and air by cutting downtime at airports.

Maritime or sea transport consists of shipping containers as well as bulk commodities such as oil, coal and iron ore. This means that its share of total trade in terms of weight and distance travelled dwarfs that of air transport. Boeing estimated that in 2007 maritime vessels carried 60.9 trillion tonne-kms of traffic compared with only 193 billion for air cargo carriers. Sea transport still carried 17.9 trillion tonne-kms without bulk commodities (Boeing, 2008).

A more relevant comparison is between air cargo and dry cargo carried in containers. The latter amounted to some 6,400 million tonne-kms in 2007, growing at an annual average rate of 9.8 percent over the previous decade. Air cargo's share of the total market has been declining as a result of its slower growth of 4.1 percent over the same period (Boeing, 2008).

A US$5 billion investment is underway to widen the Panama Canal to enable it to accommodate the largest container ships of more than 12,000 containers (rather than the existing 4,500). This should be completed by 2014, and will improve the relative cost advantage of ships over air, but leave the relative speeds of the two modes unchanged. This is because it would still be quicker to get Asian manufactures to US east coast markets via Los Angeles using rail across the US (around 20 days from Shanghai to New York versus 25/26 days via the Panama Canal).[3]

---

3   'A Plan to Unlock Prosperity', *The Economist*, 5 December 2009.

The economic case for air freight can be illustrated by a simple example: assuming an article of clothing cost $5 to manufacture in Asia and shipping costs to Europe were, say, $1 by air and 20 cents by sea. Total costs would thus be $6 by air, increasing to, say, $7.50 if land transport and warehousing is included. Ocean costs would increase from, say, $6.70 to $7.20. Ocean's advantage (between 30 to 70 cents) would easily be reversed by stock-out and overstocking costs, which would be much higher for ocean due to the larger shipment size needed to justify the low transport costs in the example. Atlas Air has suggested that, if only 5–10 percent of shippers recognised this cost advantage, an additional 1.25–2.5 million tonnes of air freight would be generated.[4] However, those items of clothing with a high fashion content ('perishability') are the ones that would gain most from air and these probably already use air transport. They are the ones with retail prices that can cover the cost of shipping by air and also have a high cost in lost sales or inventory carrying cost. The items that do not use air are likely to have a low value to weight ratio, and thus be unsuitable for shipping by air. Furthermore, the shippers may not take the inventory costs into account in making their shipping decisions, either because they do not appear in their cost or profit centre, or the costs are not easily identified in their accounting system. Finally it should be noted that the relative profitability in the above example is much more sensitive to the air than the sea rate.

It should be added that container ships reacted to the very high fuel prices in 2008 by cruising more slowly (aircraft were already on cost optimisation cruise speeds). This may have enhanced the advantage of air. Certain sea ports also suffer from congestion which reduce speed and reliability, although some airports have similar problems. But rates remain the most important driver and these depend on the supply/demand position rather than the costs in the above example.

9.2 Air Cargo Marketing Strategies

Airline strategies with regard to air cargo will depend on their company's overall strategy and how far cargo is allowed to develop as a separate business. Many airlines are principally passenger carriers and cargo is seen as a by-product of this. Even airlines that carry a large amount of air cargo such as British Airways treat cargo as secondary to its passenger goals: its aim to be 'the world's favourite' refers to passenger rather than shipper choice. British Airways considered its key resource to be its network of passenger services and this could also be marketed to shippers and forwarders without addressing possible problems of limited capacity on some routes in relation to cargo demand and shipment size. McKinsey assessed BA Cargo's options in the early 1990s to be essentially continuing its existing by-product strategy or:

---

4   Atlas Air investor day presentation, July 2010.

- becoming a global cargo player;
- entering the retail express market;
- vertical integration (acquiring a forwarder);
- multi-modal transport.

A combination of the above would also be possible. The problem with the first is the large investment required with no clear benefits for shippers or forwarders. The second also requires funding and would bring it into direct competition with one of its main customers (DHL). The third risked retaliation from the other forwarders, and a large forwarder would need to be purchased to make any difference. The last option would imply a move into an industry in which BA had no experience, and one that was maturing and required a large fixed investment. It is perhaps not difficult to see why all four were rejected at that time, and have also been rejected by other cargo airlines.

Air cargo specialists such as Cargolux and Nippon Cargo Airlines (NCA) needed to address their strategic role head on, since they are not subsidiary to other business streams. NCA's Project Phoenix redefined its strategy at the end of the 2000s after some years of poor financial performance. Its vision was to be:

> A truly global, dedicated all-cargo carrier that provides diversified services and contributes to the development of society, the economy and the culture of the world:
>
> - A company that is financially healthy and that can anticipate steady growth in the future;
> - A company that can meet various needs of air cargo demands while maintaining safety and high quality service.

NCA's project Phoenix went on to define three pillars that would need to underpin its future developments:

- an appropriate cost structure;
- strengthen through simplifying and rationalising its scheduled services;
- improved profitability through attracting new business (including GSSA, handling, chartering and leasing out aircraft).

The target was to increase revenues and convert financial losses to break even over a three-year period. The project, however, was implemented at a time of a major downturn in air cargo worldwide and its success was likely to depend on the speed of global recovery.

A combination carrier, Air France-KLM, was also suffering losses on its air cargo operations at around the same time and also launched a new strategy, or at least a change of emphasis from freighter operations to selling lower deck space on its passenger aircraft. Its freighter capacity was reduced by 40 percent and number of aircraft to 14. The remainder of its freighter fleet was grounded, and could presumably be brought back into service once a permanent recovery was underway. Its charter cargo subsidiary, Martinair, was also integrated into the group, following the acquisition of the remaining shares from Maersk. It was also planned to take advantage of Martinair's lower costs by moving some freighter operations to this wholly owned subsidiary.

Marketing strategies at the major integrators focus on information systems that support the automated package delivery services. The customer is served with a portfolio of services that range from the small parcels to the heavy freight. They are also offered a relatively simple pricing structure with different time-definite delivery services for each type of package and destination.

9.3 The Air Cargo Product

9.3.1 Air Cargo Airlines

Air cargo airlines, whether they are combination carriers or all-cargo specialists, are offering an airport-to-airport service. Some, such as Lufthansa Cargo, have tried to enter the door-to-door market at least for home country collection and delivery but it has not been that successful.

The service offered involves a ground and an air transport component. On the ground the airline or its handling agent accepts shipments and prepares them for loading onto an aircraft. Documents need to be prepared, and the physical movement of consignments may involve combining a number of items onto a pallet or into a container and in some cases security screening. Quality of service here means reliability and security, including the avoidance of damage or theft.

Service quality means the ability to handle special products such as flowers, chilled goods, dangerous goods and animals. Temperature controlled shipments such as pharmaceuticals cannot be allowed to get too warm, and can also be ruined by freezing. Austrian Airlines noticed that the right hand side of the aircraft was several degrees warmer on a flight from Europe to Japan than on the left hand side. Putting such items as medicines one the cold side could lead to a temperature drop of up to 6°C, which would harm the shipment. So loading instructions are also necessary.

The flight part of the process includes the following aspects of the service:

- delivery time promise or guarantee;
- frequency of service;
- time of aircraft departure;
- aircraft type, especially loading restrictions.

The first aspect is only part of the total door-to-door time, and something that the forwarder or consolidator needs to take into account. Combination carriers may offer a tracking service on an airport-to-airport basis but this may not be especially helpful if the consignment is held up off-airport. The second and third items are not necessarily of interest if the first is offered, although it may be helpful if there is sufficient frequency to a particular destination for follow-up shipments. The last point could be critical for larger shipments.

Cargo airlines have introduced a variety of products targeted at the different market segments. Higher yield segments such as pharmaceuticals may need temperature control and a higher level of service (and cost). Lufthansa's products are heavily differentiated into special handling segments:

> Cool/td: temperature controlled such as medicines;
> Smooth/td: careful handling for shipments that could be easily be damaged;
> Safe/td1:   highly valuable shipments such as diamonds;
> Safe/td2:   theft endangered goods;
> Fresh/td: perishables such as fruit and flowers;
> Care/td: dangerous goods;
> Animal/td: animal transport.

Temperature control is also required for perishables but this may be either cooling or warming. Some flowers such as roses need to be kept at between 0 and 2°C, with orchids at 13–16°C. Fruits range from 0–2°C for strawberries to 13–16°C for lemons.

Different market segments have different priorities in terms of the product aspects discussed above. Emergency shipments will need a good choice of flight departure times and relatively high frequency of flights. Direct flights are preferred since that also increases the likelihood of fewer delays. Clearly flights that are scheduled should all, or almost all, be flown, and shipments booked on a flight should not be offloaded onto another flight. These segments will also have tough demands on the surface transport aspects of the door-to-door trip, but these could be provided by the shipper and consignee rather than the forwarder or integrator. Tracking systems have now become essential and delivery guarantees desirable. Routine perishable shipments are more price-sensitive with the rate being paramount, as well as their requirements for specific handling and storage facilities. They may be seasonal, and during this period flights should be of sufficient frequency to provide regular shipments to destination country supermarkets.

9.3.2 Integrators

Integrators are offering door-to-door delivery and take this overall responsibility even though they might have subcontracted part of the chain to others. However, they need to closely track every stage of the journey, frequently scanning shipments and entering their location into a central computer.

Some years ago most of their bookings were through call centres, and they set the standards for the industry (and others) for prompt response, friendly service and efficient booking. Calls were selectively monitored by supervisors and evaluated at the end of each day. Much of this has been lost, at least in other service industries, with the introduction of automated telephone answering routines. The integrators now use their websites for more and more bookings, and again boast that they set the industry standards in easy to use booking and tracking systems.

Table 9.1   Air freight rate structure for UPS, June 2010

Delivery commitment		Service
Air Freight within and between the US, Canada, and Puerto Rico		
Next Business Day	Guaranteed delivery by 12:00 noon or 5:00 p.m.	UPS Next Day Air Freight
Next Business Day	Delivery by 12:00 noon or 5:00 p.m.	UPS Next Day Air Freight NGS
2 Business Days	Guaranteed delivery by 12:00 noon or 5:00 p.m.	UPS 2nd Day Air Freight
2 Business Days	Delivery 12:00 noon or 5:00 p.m.	UPS 2nd Day Air Freight NGS
3–4 Business Days	Guaranteed delivery by 5:00 p.m.	UPS 3 Day Freight
3–4 Business Days	Delivery by 5:00 p.m.	UPS 3 Day Freight NGS
Air Freight for all other origins and destinations		
1–3 Business Days	Guaranteed delivery to door by end of day	UPS Express Freight
1–3 Business Days	Delivery to airport by end of day	UPS Air Freight Direct
3–5 Business Days	Delivery to airport by end of day	UPS Air Freight Consolidated
Less-Than-Truckload (LTL)		
Varies by Service Selected	Delivery based on destination and origin	UPS Freight LTL

Source: www.ups.com.

Table 9.1 gives an example of one of the integrator's product offerings, including guaranteed delivery times. FedEx has similar services, describing them as 'money back' guarantees. These they had to withdraw for packages sent to certain countries where they reckoned that customs inspections could significantly hold up deliveries.

9.4 Air Cargo Promotion

9.4.1 Air Cargo Airlines

With 90 percent or more of their business coming through forwarders, this is where promotional activity is focused. However, as in the case of Intel that sells chips to firms in the electronics industry advertising their brand to the final customers (e.g. purchasers of laptops or mobile phones) might also make sense. The final consumer might then insist on a product which contains an Intel chip or a shipper might request the forwarder to use a certain airline.

Airlines generally advertise in the cargo and logistics trade press, attend and/or offer stands at conferences such as those organised by The International Air Cargo Association (TIACA). Airlines may obtain a high proportion of their business from five or so very large forwarders and so promotion can be targeted at their key decision-makers by the airline cargo sales staff.

9.4.2 Integrators

Integrators need to promote their services both at the retail and wholesale level, and are conscious of maintaining a brand that represents good service, speed and reliability. Promotion is undertaken through the print and TV media, and some also sponsor various sporting events. FedEx sponsors football, basketball, motor racing and golf in the US as well as the French Open tennis tournament and Formula 1 racing. These appeal to both companies and individuals.

FedEx does a considerable amount of television advertising, especially in the US, where its advertisements are often humorous. DHL ran a famous TV advertisement in the US in 2004 which showed FedEx and UPS trucks held up on opposite sides of a railway level crossing while they watched a train carrying DHL delivery vans speeding to their destination.

9.5 Air Cargo Distribution

9.5.1 Air Cargo Airlines

On the passenger side travel agents used to provide the main distribution channel for airlines with some sales through their own city-centre offices and through call centres. The airline deals with a large number of individual passengers and some corporate travel departments. This made sense in terms of ticket delivery and payment, and booking was made by agents with the airline on behalf of the passenger. With the advent of the Internet, an ideal platform was developed to reach the final consumer direct at far lower distribution costs. Electronic tickets were developed and secure payment systems could be made with the growing number of debit and credit cards. Even online check-in could be available.

On the cargo side the airlines had also tended to deal through agents (forwarders), who could deal with air waybill preparation and arrange for payments from shippers. However, once forwarders started to consolidate loads they effectively became the final customer for the airline and bypassing forwarders to reach the shipper became less of an option. Airlines did not have the capability to consolidate shipments and, if they did, they might not do it as efficiently as the consolidators. No single airline risked trying to cut out the forwarder, and shippers were generally getting a good service from forwarders that could shop around for the best door-to-door option.[5] Furthermore, the equivalent of the ticket was slower to become 'electronic' perhaps also because there was less need for it to happen.

A survey of shippers carried out by AirTrade in 2000 estimated that only 4 percent used an airline direct, while forwarders only were the choice of 53 percent and integrator only for 31 percent. The remainder used both forwarders and integrators (12 percent). In Europe the forwarder only percentage was higher (63 percent) and the integrator lower (24 percent). This difference is reflected in the much higher integrator share in the US, which has a high weight in the total.

A large number of forwarder bookings with airlines still take place by telephone with data then entered into the airline's own computerised booking system. This would then be able to automatically prepare other documents such as load sheets and cargo manifests. By the turn of the century the only air cargo industry automation had taken place at the level of individual airports where Air Cargo Community Systems (CCS) were developed to link the computers of the airlines serving that airport or based there, the airport, handlers and customs authorities. Subsequently the CCSs were linked up through the help of systems such as Traxon, and the lines between these and portals became more blurred. In 2003, the Global Freight Exchange (GF-X) was introduced to provide a neutral online booking system for the cargo airlines (now owned by Descartes), followed by Cargo Portal Services from Unisys. Another system was set up by Cargolux and SITA, the airline telecommunications company. This has many of the functions of a portal, including consignment tracking and message switching. Some such as Cargomarkt only allow rate comparisons across air cargo operators, as does OAG's cargo portal that is more for information gathering and comparison, and does not allow transactions with airlines. Many airlines would like to simplify the current systems and move to an Internet platform that allows easier access by all parties.

Most major airlines have a cargo electronic booking system, accessed via the airline's website, via a portal such as GF-X or through a direct link with forwarders. One example is Continental Airlines that withdrew from the GF-X portal in 2010, saying it could no longer maintain the internal technical support resources needed. It had up to then offered booking through three channels: its own in-house Cocargo system, Cargo Portal Services and GF-X, and needed to prioritise its bookings through two systems.

---

5   Something the agents on the passenger side did not do because they were linked to a particular airline through technology and method of remuneration.

While the forwarders are retained by the shippers, airlines need representation in countries where they do not have a large presence and it is not worth their while assigning their own staff to these stations. These could be online which the airline serves with its own flights, and offline where it does not but still has some sales, and sales potential. In these cases they appoint a General Sales Agent (GSA) to market their services on their behalf, in return for a commission on sales. This provides an incentive to the agent and no fixed costs for the airline.

Another intermediary is the freight wholesaler who buys capacity from the airlines and sells it on to small and medium sized forwarders who are too small to obtain very favourable rates from airlines.

9.5.2 Integrators

The integrators offer their services to both the retail and wholesale or company sectors. They therefore need both direct website and telephone booking systems. For example FedEx stresses the importance of its technology infrastructure, including its computer system and website, for customers. Although the company is split into divisions, its website (fedex.com) provides a single point of contact for customers to access FedEx Express, FedEx Ground and FedEx Freight shipment tracking, customer service and invoicing information, as well as FedEx Office services. Similarly, by making one call to FedEx Expedited Freight Services, customers can quickly and easily evaluate surface and air freight shipping options available from FedEx Express, FedEx Freight and FedEx Custom Critical in order to select the service best meeting their needs.

Chapter 10
Pricing and Revenues

10.1 Cargo Revenue and Yield Trends

Cargo is defined as freight, mail and express and the ICAO financial statistics reporting system for the world's airlines requests that airlines include the following under 'freight revenue':

- Revenues for the carriage of freight, *including express and diplomatic bags*, after the deduction of applicable discounts and rebates, and interline prorated through-tariffs. It should also include express revenue and revenue from the carriage of diplomatic bags. Where the air carrier's staff has the privilege of sending personal consignments at reduced rates, such revenue shall be considered as normal freight revenue.

Mail should include all payments received from the carriage of all domestic and foreign mail at prevailing rates, irrespective of the fact that such rates may be fixed in advance or in arrears. Other definitions often add the fact that such traffic is limited to that of national Post Offices. Neither fuel nor security surcharges are mentioned here or under other items such as 'incidental revenue'. This means they could be netted from the relevant cost item, since the ICAO leaves it up to individual carriers, but carriers such as British Airways and Cargolux include revenues from passenger and cargo surcharges under their respective traffic revenues. This means that the yields also take into account changes in levels of surcharge.

Freight yields are normally calculated by dividing freight or cargo revenues by tonne-kms flown. Revenues normally included fuel and security surcharges, while the denominator is a measure of traffic rather than capacity. Some carriers also report yields per tonne or kilogramme, especially integrators who also publish yields per shipment.

Figure 10.1 shows how the passenger and cargo yields for world international and domestic scheduled services have developed over the past 20 years. These were totalled after conversion to US dollars, and then have been adjusted to constant prices by applying the US consumer price index. Both yields fell continuously until 2003 when increases were necessary, at least in part, to recover fuel price increases. Cargo yields turned down slightly following 9/11 but passenger yield appeared to decline further. Both yields declined by around 1 percent a year between 1990 and 2003, and by just under 4 percent a year in real terms. Both yields fell by about 14 percent in current prices in 2009 compared to 2008, this magnitude of fall not having been experienced for at least 20 years.

Moving Boxes by Air

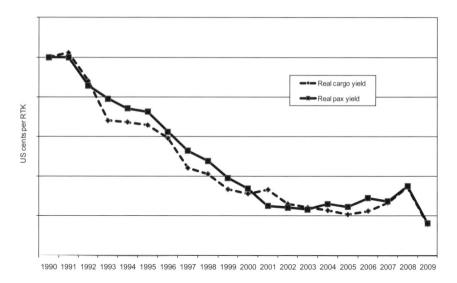

Figure 10.1   World airline passenger versus cargo yields, US dollars in real terms

Source: ICAO to 2007, IATA 2008 and 2009.

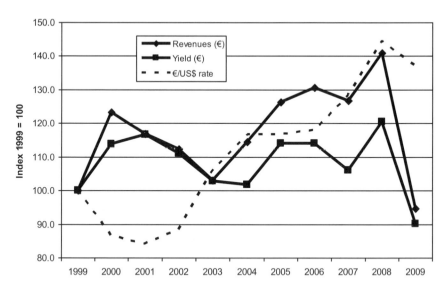

Figure 10.2   Lufthansa reported cargo revenues per RTK, and €/US$ exchange rate, 1999 to 2009

Source: Lufthansa Cargo Annual Reports.

Figure 10.2 shows the development of air cargo yields for Lufthansa over the recent 10-year period expressed in its local currency, the euro, per RTK. Total revenues in this period were highly cyclical, reflecting the two major downturns of the decade. The first followed the decline in international trade and subsequent 9/11 aftermath, while the second was triggered by the banking collapse and slump in international trade. The second was of shorter duration and greater magnitude. Yields, which along with traffic account for the revenue performance, were also volatile. These were largely determined by world market rates that tend to collapse at times when capacity is not reduced as fast as traffic declines. The rate of exchange between the US dollar and the euro is also shown, since this affects revenues earned in the US or countries whose rates are pegged to the dollar. An upward trend on the graph signifies a strengthening of the euro against the dollar, and this will reduce the euro equivalent of dollar earnings. Conversely, between 1999 and 2001, yields were boosted by a weakening euro. The large increase in yield in 2008 (which could have been larger without the exchange rate impact on some revenues) includes the impact of much increased fuel surcharges, which were removed in the following year.

Table 10.1   Lufthansa forecasts of yield by type of cargo (€ per kg), 2003 to 2009

Type of cargo	2003	2009	% change
Express	2.25	2.23	-0.9
Special	1.63	1.61	-1.2
General	1.42	1.40	-1.4
Weighted average	1.57	1.60	1.9

Source: Lufthansa Cargo Planet: Global Airfreight Outlook, 2004.

Table 10.1 gives Lufthansa Cargo's actual yields in 2003 by type of service. Express shipments commanded a 43 percent premium over general cargo, and the shipments that required special handling a 15 percent premium. These differentials were forecast to be maintained over the following six years.

The mail yield on total world scheduled services reported to the ICAO was consistently around 40 percent higher than the average freight yield until the year 2000, since which time it first declined relative to freight yields but then increased to around double. This may have been due to a reclassification of traditional mail traffic under 'express' and thus included under freight.

10.2 The Structure of Yields by Major Region and Type of Service

Yields may vary depending on the region of origin or destination and whether the cargo is carried on passenger or freighter services. They will also depend on the share of premium rated traffic in the total, and data that includes integrators will inevitably produce higher yields than those that do not, other things being equal. Since the major integrators, FedEx and UPS, operate many of their own long-haul services and are members of the IATA (and their government of the ICAO) their traffic and revenues are reported in international statistics.

Table 10.2 gives some idea of the difference in yields for the main long-haul world regions by type of flight operated. For the North Atlantic, freighter operations were distorted by one large integrated carrier reporting yields of between 80 and 90 US cents. Three carriers also reported high yields on freighters across the North/Mid Pacific but their importance in the total traffic was lower than for the North Atlantic.

Table 10.2   US cents yield per RTK by type of service, 2005

	Pax/combi aircraft	Freighter aircraft	Overall
North Atlantic (28)	17.5	69.6	30.3
Europe-Asia/Pacific (37)	24.1	24.2	22.4
North/Mid-Pacific (21)	24.8	34.0	27.9

Note: Number of airlines submitting data in brackets alongside three main regions of long-haul operation.

Source: ICAO Circular 316-AT/135.

On routes where there was little distortion from integrators from Europe to and from Asia it can be seen that there was almost no difference between yields on passenger and freighter services. This is contrary to popular belief that passenger service yields are lower because they do not reflect fully allocated costs. Previous IATA Cost Committee reports also gave little evidence of any differential. The most likely explanation is that the passenger service rates tend to pull down fully-costed freighter rates especially when there is plenty of capacity available in the market.

10.3 Air Freight Pricing

It is hard to find a comprehensive database of the rates charged for air freight and mail. More and more pricing is done under contracts between large forwarders and airlines and the rates agreed are confidential. Some countries publish indexes of various prices as these are often used in producing more composite consumer price indices. Germany is an example of this, and their price index for air freight is taken from the IATA CargoIS database for all air trade to and from Germany (see Table 10.3). This only goes back to 2006, but it illustrates the large increase in rates (including fuel and security surcharges) in 2008 of 20 percent globally as a result of the surge in fuel prices. A combination of a sharp reduction in fuel surcharges and a collapse in demand led to a very large decline in rates in 2009 of just over 30 percent worldwide.

One of the largest increases in 2008 was for China, which experienced similar pressures on oil prices as other countries but higher rates were also possible because of the shortage of capacity available out of China relative to demand at least until the last months of the year. Japan on the other hand, where demand was weaker, experienced a much lower increase. Japan and the UAE were the countries with the largest falls in rates in 2009 of 33–34 percent.

Figure 10.3 shows how maritime rates were more volatile than air freight rates over the three years to 2010. Both plummeted from a high in 2008, the maritime rate starting to fall one quarter earlier than air. If fuel surcharges had been included air freight rates would have showed a larger swing. The maritime index is based on those of the Baltic Exchange, while the air transport rates are from a sample of 418 markets and 19 airlines using CASS data.

Table 10.3   German air freight price index by region/country*

Region/country	2007	2008	2009
Total index	**98.5**	**118.4**	**82.2**
Asia-Pacific	98.0	125.6	87.8
China	99.3	134.5	96.2
Japan	90.9	109.7	73.3
Australia	102.7	120.0	95.7
Korea, Republic of	91.8	122.3	80.2
India	97.7	128.3	88.2
North America	96.9	111.1	70.0
USA	96.7	110.7	69.7
Canada	99.0	114.2	73.0
Latin and South America	99.9	112.0	81.7
Brazil	98.3	112.9	82.9
Mexico	100.2	105.6	70.3
North Africa, Middle East	99.9	124.2	89.8
UAE	101.3	134.1	88.0
Rest of Africa	100.4	113.9	84.4
South Africa	99.8	112.5	82.4
Europe	101.1	122.0	96.9

Note: * Average of four quarters; 2006 annual average = 100.

Source: German Federal Statistics Office from IATA CargoIS database.

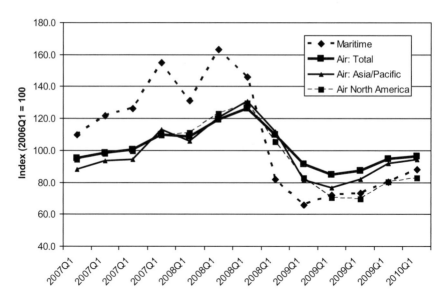

Figure 10.3   Quarterly index of French freight transport prices

Note: * Excluding fuel and security surcharges.

Source: Commissariat Générale au Développement Durable, Observation et Statistiques, No.125, June 2010.

Since the end of 2006, many airlines, integrators and forwarders have stopped publishing their fuel surcharge methodology and jet fuel index on their websites. This was as a result of the investigations by the anti-trust authorities in various countries and subsequent fines (see section 3.2.3). Airlines do, however, still issue press releases when they increase or decrease their own fuel surcharges and publish current levels, and Figure 10.4 shows these for British Airways World Cargo since their introduction in 2001 up to May 2010. The surcharges were probably originally meant to capture any extraordinary increase in one input to its production, albeit an important one. Once market prices settled down to their original trend they could be removed. Towards the end of 2008 they did come back to their mid-2004 price but not down to their pre-surcharges level, and then they started increasing again.

There are a number of questions that arise from the surcharges that airlines impose in their local currencies. The first is whether they adjust these for changes in the US$ to local currency exchange rates, since fuel is priced and paid for in US dollars? British Airways also published a dollar surcharge that was often far from the product of the UK pound surcharge and the dollar/pound exchange rate in the market. From Figure 10.4 it can be seen that the UK local currency surcharge tracked the fuel price fairly well once converted to dollars. This is not surprising given the method of determining the surcharge (see below).

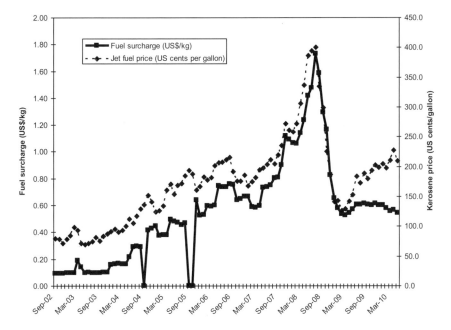

**Figure 10.4   British Airways fuel surcharge versus jet kerosene price
(September 2003 to May 2010)**

Source: British Airways press releases and OECD.

The second question is, if surcharges are staying for the longer term, whether fuel efficiency gains will be reflected, or whether a larger share of fuel costs will be covered by the surcharge? Airlines have tended to argue that the surcharge did not reflect the full amount of increase in costs and thus their profitability suffered. A final issue was raised by the freight agents that were paid on the basis of a percentage of the freight rate. Their commissions were not based on the freight rate plus the surcharge and thus remained at their original level while airline costs increased. They challenged the legality of separating certain costs, which made their commissions lower than they should be. The response to that argument is that the agents have no special right to this windfall, and are not involved in any additional work as a result of the cost increases. However, an Australian court ruled that the fuel surcharge is part of the ticket price on which commissions must be paid and thus Qantas (and other airlines selling in Australia) had to pay passenger agents on the higher price. Some airlines such as Emirates Cargo have discontinued the surcharge and covered all costs under the basic rate.

Other network carriers were more explicit about the way the surcharges were calculated. Up to 2006 airlines such as Lufthansa published the following fuel surcharge methodology, which still used by combination carriers, on its website:

- Fuel price index: 100 = 53.35 US cents per US gallon;
- Fuel price average of five most important jet kerosene spot markets;
- Fuel price index (3 June 2005): 291.

Example of fuel surcharge calculation methodology:

> Fuel surcharge = 0 for fuel price index of 100, then, for example:
> Fuel price index exceeds 240 for a period of two consecutive weeks:
> Fuel surcharge adjusted to €0.30 per kg
> Fuel price index exceeds 265 for a period of two consecutive weeks:
> Fuel surcharge adjusted to €0.35 per kg
> Fuel price index exceeds 290 for a period of two consecutive weeks:
> Fuel surcharge adjusted to €0.40 per kg
> Two weeks' notice for all changes.

Japan Airlines uses a similar approach to its fuel surcharges but uses the Singapore market spot price of crude oil as its benchmark. Under this system the surcharge is eliminated once this price drops below US$35 per barrel.

After the terrorist attacks of 9/11, all air carriers had to increase their security measures significantly. To cover these additional insurance costs, they implemented the Security Surcharge (SSC). Forwarders had to pay this to the airlines and passed the charge on to their customers in the form of a surcharge.

10.3.1 Network Airline Tariffs

Scheduled or network airlines are distinguished from charter airlines in selling the capacity of each flight to a number of different customers. Charter airlines sell the whole capacity to one customer at a negotiated price, but for scheduled airlines there is a standard tariff or system of prices available to a shipper or their agent. Scheduled airlines might also negotiate special rates with some of their large and frequent customers, and these are discussed below. Here we look at the system of rates available that has evolved over the years. These will vary by route, by size or weight of consignment and by type of goods or commodity.

In the past Air Services Agreements usually included a restrictive tariff clause that required the airline to submit its cargo rates (and passenger fares) to the authorities in both origin country (i.e. its own government) and the destination country for approval. Sometimes reference is made in the ASA to IATA Tariff Coordination requesting the agreement of tariffs whenever possible through the rate fixing machinery of IATA. That still occurs today but it is rare, since most governments now only concern themselves with rates if complaints are made related to restrictive agreements (e.g. on fuel surcharges) or predatory pricing (where rates are pitched well below cost to drive other operators out of business). Before governments used to have to approve rates, lengthy discussions needed to take place between airlines to agree freight rate levels and increases. These took place at the biennial IATA Cargo Tariff Co-ordinating Conferences.

Cargo Tariff Coordination is the means by which freight rates are established between airlines for multilateral interlining which enables cargo to undertake a journey involving travel on multiple airlines on a single air waybill. The IATA maintains that coordination is only required for interline rates, but these need to be based on actual point-to-point rates that are in force. Thus agreeing on the base rates such as the general cargo rate is also necessary. The *IATA Prorate System* provides a methodology for the sharing of revenue between airlines where the cargo is shipped at an agreed freight rate using more than one airline.

The Air Cargo Tariff (TACT) is the detailed record of all cargo rates and rules that are agreed by airlines and is published by the IATA three times a year. It contains the following rates:

> *general cargo* rates apply to the carriage of commodities that have not been allocated a specific commodity rate or commodity classification (class) rate;

> *specific commodity* rates relate to the carriage of particular commodities from a specified point of origin to a specified destination point; and

> *class rates (commodity classification rates)* are published for particular commodities from a specified point of origin to a specified destination point.

Table 10.4   Traditional air freight rate structure

London–Tokyo Cargo Rates (April 2001)

Classification	Min. kgs	£ per kg
N		£8.20
Q (NP)	5	£4.99
Q (BG)	10	£4.96
Q	100	£6.52
Q	300	£5.27
Q	500	£4.49
6		£2.42
386		£3.73
1024	100	£3.54
4402	100	£4.24
6006	100	£4.58
7119	250	£2.42

Class rates are applied to such shipments as live animals, valuable cargo, dangerous goods, perishable goods, baggage shipped as cargo, newspapers, and human remains. Specific commodity rates are designed to encourage certain types of cargo to be air freighted and are usually lower than general cargo rates. Class rates take precedence over general cargo rates. An example of the rates published is given in Table 10.4. 'N' is the general cargo rate, 'Q (NP)' a class rate for newspapers, and 'Q (BG)' another for baggage. Three quantity break-points follow, where heavier shipments can take advantage of lower rates. Various coded numbers follow, each representing a specific commodity such as flowers or medical equipment. In addition to these rates there are standard ULD rates which are shown per ULD and give lower rates per kilogram. Obviously much more attractive rates will be negotiated by larger forwarders direct with airlines.

The IATA Conference rates are agreed for shipment between three areas of the world. For example TACT Rules 3.7.7 give the rates for newspapers and periodicals. The minimum shipment size is specified for within and between the three 'areas' and a range of between 50 percent and 67 percent of the general cargo rate depending in which area the route is operated.

Aircraft lower decks tend to 'cube out' rather than 'weigh out': for example the B747-400 has only 70 cu.m. available for cargo in the lower deck,[1] but depending on length of haul (fuel load) and other parameters it could carry 20 tonnes of cargo or more on typical long-haul sectors. However, on a very long sector it might only lift 12 tonnes, such that it would 'weigh out' based on typical shipment densitites. The higher figure gives a 'volumetric payload' of 3.5 cu.m per tonne or 286 kg/m^3. Research by Van de Ryd and Wouters (2005) gave a range of densities for air shipments from 135 kg/m^3 for live animals to 495 kg/m^3 for metal products. However, most commodities shipped by air fell between 150 and 250 kg/m^3. They also looked at ULD densities and found that most lower deck ULDs were between 190 and 200 kg/m^3 but main deck ones were lower at around 160 kg/m^3. This was possibly because less care was taken in packing the ULDs for freighters, which as a result tended to cube out.

Low density shipments are converted to a *chargeable weight* using 6 cubic metres per tonne, or 167 kg/m^3. Thus any shipment with a density that is greater than this (or less than 167 kg/m^3) will be converted to a chargeable weight using this density and not its actual density. IATA proposed reducing this to 5 cubic metres per tonne (200 kg/m^3) from October 2003, but withdrew this in March 2005 following opposition from the US and other countries.

Shippers and forwarders therefore need to take care not to use voluminous packaging materials, but on the other hand pack goods sufficiently well to avoid damage. Over the past years the nature of shipments is thought to have changed somewhat from heavy machinery to DVDs, CDs and fresh produce, all of which are of relatively low density. There is also less lower-deck space available for cargo in latest versions of passenger B747s (more passengers and range/fuel) and cubing out is occurring more often.

---

1   Less than the first B747-100 which could carry less passengers over a shorter range.

Table 10.5 shows how consolidation can avoid high tariffs following the use of the chargeable weight for low density shipments. The example takes extreme cases of very low density pillows and very high density crane parts. The shipper of the pillows would face a cost of $1,804 through the application of the chargeable weight of 167 kg/m³ to its actual volume of 12 cubic metres. Based on its actual weight it would only have been charged $204.

Table 10.5   Charges reduced by consolidation

	Pieces	Volume cubic metres	Actual weight (kg)	Chargeable weightª (kg)	Costᵇ (US$)
Pillows	1,000	12	227	2,004	1,804
Crane parts	3	2	2,268	2,268	2,041
Consolidated	1,003	14	2,495	2,495	2,246

Note: a. Minimum density 6 cu.m per tonne (167 kg/m³) for conversion; b. At US$0.9 per kg.
Source: Letter from Robert Caton to *Air Cargo News*, 22 August 2003.

If, however, a consolidator combines the pillows with crane parts that need to be shipped to the same destination on the same day, the total shipment would have a density of 178.2 kg/m³ (actual weight of 2,495 tonnes divided by the total volume of 14 m³), which is above the cut-off. The consolidator will be charged $2,246 by the airline, as opposed to the $1,804 + $2,041 = $3,845 (or $4,175 under the higher chargeable weight that was proposed by the IATA airlines). It is then up to the consolidator as to how much of the saving is passed on to the shippers.

The above general and commodity rates have largely been replaced by contract rates by most major network airlines. ULD rates are charged on the gross weight of the ULD less the actual tare weight of airline-owned ULDs, and shipper or forwarder owned ULDs use the lower of the actual tare weight and the IATA specified weight for that ULD.

10.3.2 Network Airline Handling Charges

A large number of handling and administration charges will apply depending on the number of additional services required. These are often shown on airline websites but are also shown for all IATA airlines in TACT.

Network carrier air freight rates only cover the costs of shipping goods from one airport to another. Prior to departure from one airport and after arrival at the destination various handling and processing tasks are required for which the airline may charge a separate fee if it is carrying out these tasks. They might also be undertaken and charged for by a third party handling agent or the forwarder. Some examples of the various charges that were applied by British Airways World Cargo in October 2009 were as follows:

Exports

> Processing/handling loose cargo £0.08 per kg
> Security charge £0.08 per kg
> (With minimum charges)
> Dangerous goods £33.00 per Air Waybill

Imports

> Processing/handling loose cargo £0.12 per kg
> Storage £8.00 per 100 kg per day

10.3.3 Integrator Tariffs

Integrators combine handling, customs and other charges into one rate, but add a surcharge for their extra fuel and security costs. UPS uses an index-based surcharge that is adjusted monthly. Changes to the surcharge will be effective the first Monday of each month and posted approximately two weeks prior to the effective date. The surcharge will be based on the US Gulf Coast (USGC) prices for kerosene-type jet fuel reported by the US Department of Energy for the month that is two months prior to the adjustment. For example, the surcharge for January 2008 was based on the November 2007 USGC Jet Fuel Price (see Table 10.6). Unlike the surcharges applied by combination and freighter operators, these are expressed as a percentage increase to the rates in force rather than a monetary add-on to existing rates.

UPS's average air fuel surcharge in 2007 was 12.17 percent and in 2008 25.17 percent, coming back down to 10 percent in the middle of 2010. Fuel surcharge percentages and thresholds are subject to change without prior notice. If the fuel surcharge rises above 19 percent or there are changes to the thresholds, Table 10.6 would be updated. For the surface transport part of the trip, UPS apply a ground surcharge, on the same basis with percentages depending on the National US Average on Highway Diesel Fuel Prices reported by the US Department of Energy for the month. These surcharges averaged 7.97 percent in 2007.

10.4 Revenue Management

Cargo revenue management (CRM) is inherently more complex than for the passenger side, but its aim is similar, namely to maximise profitability by means of the management of price and capacity. The latter is also referred to as inventory, which for passenger bookings is largely known (except on very long sectors where weather conditions dictate more fuel and restricted passenger and cargo payload), but for the cargo carried on passenger flights highly uncertain, possibly even up to half an hour before the flight departs. Profitability is often taken to be synonymous with revenues if it assumed that the aircraft operating costs per weight unit are similar for different classes of passenger of cargo. This is to make things simpler

Table 10.6   UPS Air and International selected fuel surcharge calculations

At least	But less than	Surcharge
$0	$1.46	0.00%
$1.46	$1.50	0.50%
$1.50	$1.54	1.00%
....	....	....
$2.02	$2.06	7.50%
$2.06	$2.10	8.00%
$2.10	$2.14	8.50%
....	....	....
$2.50	$2.56	12.5%
$2.56	$2.62	13.0%
$2.62	$2.68	13.5%
....	....	....
$3.02	$3.10	16.5%
$3.10	$3.18	17.0%
$3.18	$3.26	17.5%
$3.26	$3.34	18.0%
$3.34	$3.42	18.5%
$3.42	$3.50	19.0%

Source: www.ups.com.

and in response to difficulties in evaluating such costs. This means that revenue management (RM) is only maximising revenues, and only in the short run.

As with passenger RM, key questions remain, for example: how much space should be reserved for express and urgent products? How much should be sold in advance? In both cases profitability or in practice revenue needs to be known, and such products tend to command premium rates due to their urgency. Mail also often gets priority due to its overall high yield.

Apart from the uncertainty in overall cargo capacity on passenger flights, cargo also suffers from a three-dimensional capacity problem: volume, mass or weight and container positions (Kasilingam, 1996). Capacity may be available in terms of volume but the shipments have hit the limit on weight, or vice versa. This is the 'cube out' versus 'weigh out' problem already mentioned. There might be both volume and weight payload available but no container position remaining. On the other hand freight has the advantage that it is not as route sensitive as passengers. This means if capacity is not available on one route, it can be sent on another as long as the agreed delivery day or time is met. This underlines the need for an origin destination approach for cargo. Fine-tuning is also easier for passengers, which come in units of one and sometimes more with families or colleagues travelling together. This makes fine-tuning easier, whereas with cargo the opportunity cost of turning away one container could be larger. Predicting the travel behaviour of a large number of single passengers is easier than that of a handful of very large forwarders who have a large number of competing alternatives.[2]

There are a number of reasons for the uncertainty, the main ones being:

- weather conditions en route and at the departure airport;
- passenger loads, especially where there are a high proportion of connecting passengers;
- number and weight of checked passenger baggage;
- variable tender behaviour.

The last point is the problem of shippers' and forwarders' deliveries of shipments to the departure airport that are significantly different in volume and dimensions than booked. If these are under guaranteed space contracts the space or weight available could change significantly, whereas if they are not they could be put on the next flight or sent on an alternative routing.

Capacity forecasts thus need to start with the payload available based on the expected weather conditions and the fuel needed to transport the aircraft and passenger payload to the destination with an allowance for diversion and holding at the destination airport. From this is deducted the passenger payload, the checked baggage weight and the priority mail weight. The passenger weight includes carry-on baggage, with industry standards of 70–80 kg often used (see section 8.1.3). Airlines have their own estimates for checked baggage, and these can vary significantly from route to route. Finally the extra fuel needed to take the cargo payload is estimated. The same procedure is done in terms of volume, and finally, for wide-bodied aircraft, the number of standard container positions (Kasilingam, 1996).

Guaranteed space contracts are also sometimes called 'allotments'. These are generally negotiated between an airline and its larger forwarder customers. Lufthansa Cargo's approach differentiates between two types of such agreement (Hellermann, 2002):

Guaranteed Capacity Agreement (GCA)
A contract between airline and forwarder that guarantees certain capacity on various flights over the next six months at a pre-agreed rate. The forwarder has the

---

2   'The Benefits and Failures of Cargo Revenue Systems', *Aircraft Commerce*, Issue 47, August/September 2006.

right to return capacity that is not required up to 72 hours before the flight or face penalties of 25–100 percent of the agreed rate. These penalties may not always be enforced, especially if the forwarder is a large customer of the airline.

Capacity Purchasing Agreement (CPA)

Non-returnable obligation by the forwarder to purchase fixed amounts of capacity on a particular route and day of week. The contract is over 12 months or more. An attractive price is obtainable due to the non-refundable commitment. This type of agreement is generally used on busier routes.

While the second type is effectively a block space agreement or allotment the first is not. Once the capacity has been estimated the allotment allocation will be deducted to give the capacity remaining. At this point an overbooking policy can be applied on the basis that some cargo will arrive too late at the departure airport or not materialise. This will in turn depend on what the policy on refunds is. Late arriving (and variable tender) cargo will be put on the next available flight. Some forwarders have been reducing the share of capacity that they commit to in advance, but others have tried to lock in low 2009 rates under a two-year CPA, something the airlines resist strongly.

The capacity left after allotments and sometimes mail is then allocated to the various market segments whose demand has been forecast, based on the profit or revenue contribution of each. As stated above, revenue is easier to estimate than profit, at least net revenue after subtracting special handling costs.

Close to the date of departure, if the volume (weight) limit was nearly exceeded Lufthansa would look for high density (low density) shipments at attractive rates (see Figure 10.5). The pricing structure and term of both GCAs and CPAs was changed in 2001, and overbooking was introduced. GCAs could now be shorter or longer than six months, and CPAs were uncoupled from particular routes or flights. This resulted in an increase in demand for CPAs.

Most of the RM applications to air cargo have focused on the capacity side. This comprises the estimation of the capacity for a particular flight that needs to be sold and the percentage of 'overbooking' that is added to the available capacity to allow for cancellations, no-shows and shipments that do not match bookings. Becker and Kasilingam (2008) stated that the first Cargo RM application was at American Airlines in 1991. However, this was only for capacity forecasting, one element of a complete RM system. They add that the first origin-destination CRM was developed by Sabre for Cathay Pacific Airways, used to determine long-term space allocations at the airline's online stations.

The capacity estimation process starts with the flight plan which is loaded into the booking system. As discussed above, this will depend on the passenger and baggage load, as well as priority mail. Average seasonal operational parameters will be assumed. This may be refined as the flight's time of departure gets closer. This capacity will then be allocated between long-term contract customers that usually get a lower rate for supplying the base load (and which may be guaranteed)

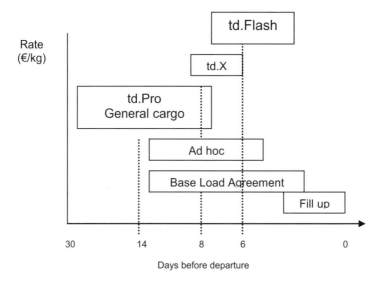

Figure 10.5   Spot market rates by product and advance booking

Source: Hellermann, 2002, using Lufthansa Cargo data.

and that which is sold on a first-come, first-served basis through the booking system. The latter should be at higher rates. The rates should also increase nearer the time of departure in the same way as passenger fares. The key is to keep back enough capacity to accommodate last minute bookings, which tend to be urgent and thus able to pay a higher rate.

The second part of the capacity estimation is the overbooking level. This is to reduce the 'spoilage' or loss of revenue when a cancellation leaves some spare capacity unsold. As stated above, air cargo demand tends to be 'lumpy' with cancellations having a larger impact on load factors than passengers. This is because bookings are larger and fewer customers are involved. This would tend to increase the potential revenue loss from one cancellation, with a greater impact on profit than the loss of one or two passengers from a booking. The optimisation process of revenue management is based on modelling that assumes that the show-up rate for each flight is normally distributed around a forecast value. For the passenger side that is a reasonable assumption but for cargo it has much less validity.

The overbooking level is the percentage of the estimated capacity of a flight (in both weight and volume terms) that will be sold. The higher the number and probability of cancellations forecast the higher this percentage could be. This overbooking level is determined by looking at historical data for each flight and evaluating off-load and spoilage costs for different overbooking levels.

Becker and Kasilingam (2008) stated that the cost of having to offload cargo if the overbooking percentage was set too high and the number of cancellations did not turn out as high as expected depends on:

- the cost of refunds;
- extra handling costs;
- extra storage charges;
- loss of goodwill.

Loss of goodwill might be minimised if other flights are available that get the shipment to the final destination without much delay or within guaranteed times. This will also lower refund amounts. Figure 10.6 uses hypothetical data to show how the offload costs increase exponentially with overbooking level. On the other hand the cost of spoilage declines with overbooking level, since each flight will operate with lower unsold space and higher load factors. The total cost is the sum of spoilage and offload costs and will decline up to the point that offload costs begin to increase exponentially and exceed any gains from reduced spoilage. Costs are optimised at that point and that overbooking level (around 110 percent in Figure 10.6).

The demand side of CRM is concerned with pricing and the rate at which bookings are accepted from well in advance to close to the time of departure. Accepting too many early bookings, or contract allocations at low rates, might result in insufficient capacity being available for a high rated urgent shipment close to the time of departure. Accepting too many bookings on one leg of a multiple sector flight may result in turning away high rated shipments that use this and other sectors of the flight. The aim is to achieve the best rate and density mix of shipments in order to maximise revenue on each flight (or better still across

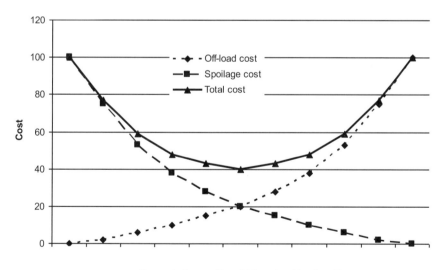

Percent of capacity sold (overbooking level)

Figure 10.6 Overbooking cost optimisation

Source: Adapted from Becker and Kasilingam, 2008.

the network), whether a passenger or freighter service. In order to do this it is necessary to forecast the demand at different rates by day for each flight segment up to time of departure. This may seem a tall order but some guidance should be available from historical data which can be used for statistical modelling and/or judgemental approaches.

Sabre of the US has developed the 'AirVision Cargo Revenue Manager', which previously known as CargoMax. Its key benefits were listed to be:

- provides key flight, customer and booking information;
- forecasts available cargo capacity by market, segment and equipment type; day of the week; and time of day to help accurately plan cargo loads for maximum revenue;
- ensures acceptance of higher yield shipments through optimal allotment of cargo space to stations and/or agents and online profitability evaluation;
- increases productivity and supports superior decision-making by supplying efficient data analyses via management reports and performance-monitoring tools;
- identifies revenue streams and potential service failures proactively through interactive flight-monitoring capabilities to improve earnings and service quality;
- considers booking behaviour during optimal overbooking of cargo capacity to capture additional revenue and reduce offloads.

Sabre said that revenues would be increased by up to 10 percent as a result of introducing its software, although other estimates suggest 2–3 percent higher revenue.[3] Another suite of programmes for CRM is Kale Consulting's CSP-RES using by Asiana. So far, however, the take-up of these software programmes is limited and the comprehensiveness of systems offered not as high as on the passenger side.

---

3   'The Benefits and Failures of Cargo Revenue Systems', *Aircraft Commerce*, Issue 47, August/September 2006.

Chapter 11

Airline Costs

This chapter will discuss the operating costs of carrying cargo by air. These can be divided into flight or aircraft operating costs, handling and marketing costs and overheads. First the operating costs of those airlines that operate only freighters will be examined, including marketing costs and overheads. Next a closer look will be taken of freighter aircraft operating costs by type of aircraft. A popular type of freighter use is on an ACMI and or wet lease basis and this will also be discussed.

Finally the problems of the joint costs of production on passenger flights will be addressed, whether using lower deck or 'combi' (lower and main deck) cargo capacity. Here the various ways of allocating joint costs to the passenger and cargo products are described.

11.1 All-Cargo Airline Costs

11.1.1 ICAO Cost Reporting

The operating costs of all-cargo airlines are published in more or less detail in the annual reports of some of these carriers, by the ICAO and some country aviation authorities. Airlines provide the data to their government authorities and they send it to the ICAO, which often means some delay before publication. ICAO data have the advantage of showing a breakdown of costs in a consistent way,[1] but some airlines are missing and some years are missing for the ones that do report. They can also be imported into Excel spreadsheets. This data will be analysed first, followed by examples of individual all-cargo airlines and integrators.

The ICAO data base was published as 'Air Carrier Financial Statistics' in hard copy until 2002 when it went digital and can now only be obtained through the Air Transport Intelligence and ICAO websites back to 1973. One advantage of the electronic publication is the inclusion of carriers as soon as their data is received by the ICAO, rather than the previous delay before a sufficient number had reported and the hard copy could be issued. The component parts of operating revenues and expenses are shown in US dollars, as well as non-operating items, to give the net profit for the year. Balance sheets are also shown in some detail. Unit revenues (yields) and costs can be calculated from traffic and capacity data for the

---

1   Although not all airlines follow the guidelines as strictly as might be hoped.

identical financial year. The financial year end is shown together with the average local currency to US dollar conversion rate.

Many but not all the major all-cargo carriers reported data for 2008. The major carriers missing were Nippon Cargo, DHL and Southern Air Transport. Atlas Air did report but its costs reflected a significant weight of wet lease and ACMI operations for which many cost items such as fuel would be paid for by their lessee customers. Unit costs are shown in Figure 11.1 by dividing total operating expenses by ATK capacity available. This is compared with the average sector distance operated since this is one of the crucial variables that will affect unit costs, regardless of any underlying efficiencies achieved. The FedEx data is included after removing a very large item under 'other operating expenses' since this must have related to its ground operations. Other distortions have not been addressed such as the inclusion in Cargolux's unit cost of provisions for payments of anti-trust fines.

Figure 11.1 shows a reasonable good correlation with sector distance, with UPS well below the level predicted by sector distance and Kalitta above. Since 2008 was a year of very high fuel prices, Kalitta's fuel inefficient B747-100/200F aircraft might have explained its higher unit costs, while UPS's airline costs are extracted from their US$46 billion total group costs (12 percent) and depend on overhead allocation methods. UPS's 'General and Administrative' costs in the graph are significantly lower than the other carriers and these would have been estimated from group data. Atlas Air's lower than expected costs, as stated above, reflect its mixed wet lease, charter and scheduled service operations. The operating

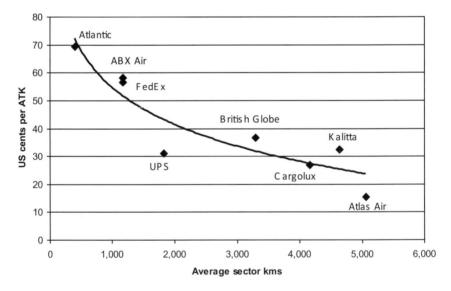

Figure 11.1   All-cargo airline unit costs versus average sector distance, 2008
Source: ICAO airline financial data and UK CAA.

Table 11.1   ICAO reporting form for collection of financial data, part 1

PART 1 – PROFIT AND LOSS STATEMENT
INTERNATIONAL CIVIL AVIATION ORGANISATION
AIR TRANSPORT REPORTING FORM
FINANCIAL DATA – COMMERCIAL AIR CARRIERS
FORM EF

OPERATING REVENUES
1. Scheduled services (total) . . . . _
1.1 Passenger . . . . _____
1.2 Excess baggage . . . . _____
1.3 Freight (including express and diplomatic bags) . . . . _____
1.4 Mail . . . . _____
2. Non-scheduled operations (total) . . . .
2.1 Passenger and excess baggage . . . . _____
2.2 Freight (including express and diplomatic bags) and mail . . . . _____
3. Other operating revenues (total) . . . .
3.1 Incidental transport-related revenues . . . . _____
3.2 Miscellaneous operating revenues . . . . _____
4. TOTAL OPERATING REVENUES *(sum of Items 1, 2 and 3)* . . . . ._

OPERATING EXPENSES
5. Flight operations (total). . . . .
5.1 Flight crew salaries and expenses . . . . _____
5.2 Aircraft fuel and oil . . . . _____
5.3 Flight equipment insurance . . . . _____
5.4 Rental of flight equipment . . . . _____
5.5 Other expenses . . . . _____
6. Flight equipment maintenance and overhaul . . . .
7. Depreciation and amortization (total) . . . . ._
7.1 Depreciation – flight equipment . . . . _____
7.2 Amortization of capital leases – flight equipment . . . . _____
7.3 Depreciation and amortization – ground property and equipment . . . . _____
7.4 Other . . . . _____
8. User charges (total) . . . . __
8.1 Landing and associated airport charges . . . . _____
8.2 Air navigation charges . . . . _____
9. Station expenses . . . .
10. Passenger services (total) . . . .
10.1 Cabin crew salaries and expenses . . . . _____
10.2 Other expenses . . . . _____
11. Ticketing, sales and promotion (total) . . . .
11.1 Commission expenses . . . . _____
11.2 Other expenses . . . . _____
12. General and administrative . . . .
13. Other operating expenses (total) . . . .
13.1 Incidental transport-related expenses . . . . _____
13.2 Miscellaneous operating expenses . . . . _____
14. TOTAL OPERATING EXPENSES *(sum of Items 5 through 13)*

Source: www.icao.org.

costs included in Figure 11.1 include a standard expense or cost breakdown (what is included is taken from the published ICAO reporting forms in Part 1), the form applying equally to passenger/cargo and freighter operators. Some of the cost items reported will only apply to passenger services, such as cabin crew.

Flight operations

Flight crew salaries and expenses (Item 5.1). Pay and allowances, pensions, insurance, travelling and other similar expenses (uniforms, etc.) of flight crews are included. Pay, allowances and other related expenses of cabin crews and passenger service personnel shall not be charged under this account but shall be included in the appropriate sub-item under Item 10. Include the training costs of flight crew (whether amortized or not).

Aircraft fuel and oil (Item 5.2). Throughput charges, non-refundable duties and taxes are included net of hedging gains or losses.

Flight equipment insurance (Item 5.3). Included is insurance against accidental damage to flight equipment while in flight and on the ground; insurance against liability occurring from operation of aircraft or, in the case of non-insurance, the resulting expenses for which the air carrier is liable.

Rental of flight equipment (Item 5.4). Included are expenses incurred for the rental of aircraft and crews from other carriers, such as in chartering, interchange and operating or short-term lease agreements.

Other expenses (Item 5.5). Included are those expenses pertaining to in-flight operation and related standby time of aircraft which are not classifiable under Items 5.1 to 5.4 inclusive.

Flight equipment maintenance and overhaul (Item 6)

Included is the cost of keeping aircraft, engines, components and spares in an operative condition, the cost of repair and overhaul and the certificate of airworthiness overhaul carried out under mandatory government requirements. Also include the pay, allowances and related expenses of all staff engaged in flight equipment maintenance as well as the cost of repair, overhaul and maintenance of flight equipment by outside contractors and manufacturers. The direct and related indirect maintenance cost of ground facilities should normally be included under Item 9. However, if that cost cannot be segregated, it should be included here with a note to that effect. If reserves are created for the maintenance and overhaul of flight and ground equipment, these reserves shall be charged to maintenance and overhaul each year in proportion to the use made of the equipment.

Depreciation and amortisation (total) (Item 7)

Included is the depreciation and amortisation charged to the current financial year. The amounts charged under this general heading are subdivided into:

Depreciation – flight equipment (Item 7.1). The normal annual depreciation of assets included in the balance sheet.

Amortisation of capital leases – flight equipment (Item 7.2). The amortisation of capital leases pertaining to assets included in the balance sheet.

Depreciation and amortisation – ground property and equipment (Item 7.3). The depreciation and amortisation of assets included in the balance sheet.

Other (Item 7.4). Charges for the amortisation of capitalised development and pre-operating costs and other intangible assets applicable to the performance of air transportation included in the balance sheet.

User charges (total) (Item 8)

Landing and associated airport charges (Item 8.1). Included are all charges and fees related to air traffic operations that are levied against the air carrier for services provided at the airport. These include landing charges; passenger and cargo fees; security, parking and hangar charges and related traffic operation charges, excluding fuel and oil throughput charges. The latter is a charge levied on a fuel supplier by an airport for access to the apron and usually passed on to the airline. Since the fuel supplier installs the fuel hydrant system or owns and operates refuelling vehicles it is more like a concession fee, and is charged on the amount of fuel uplifted. Landing charges are levied on both passenger and freighter aircraft by the airport and are usually based on the MTOW of the aircraft. A fee is charged per passenger to cover the costs of the passenger terminal, but this does not usually have an equivalent for cargo, since the cargo terminal is generally built and operated by one or more airlines or a third party. Thus the costs will be recouped from handling fees rather than airport charges. However, many African airports do have a cargo throughput charge, as well as Spanish, Swiss and Italian airports in Europe. The level varied between 1–2 US cents per kilogram in 2008. Canadian airports had an animal and plant health inspection charge of C$25 per arriving international flight in 2008. This covered the government agencies costs of inspecting garbage from arriving international flights and cargo manifests.

Air navigation charges (Item 8.2). Included are fees levied against the air carrier for the provision of en-route facilities and services, including approach and aerodrome control charges. Where a single charge is levied both for airport and air navigation services, the amount should be reported under Item 8.1, with a note to that effect.

Station expenses (Item 9)

Included are such items as: pay, allowances and expenses of all station staff engaged in handling and servicing aircraft and load, including flight supervisors, dispatchers and ground radio operators; station accommodation costs; maintenance and insurance of airport facilities, where separately assessed; representation and traffic handling fees charged by third parties for handling the air services of the air carrier; station store charges, including local duties on equipment, transportation, packing and materials, rental of stores, storekeepers' pay, allowance and expenses, etc. When the maintenance expenditures for flight equipment at outstations cannot be segregated for reporting under Item 6, they should be reported here with a note to that effect.

Ticketing, sales and promotion (total) (Item 11)
Commission expenses (Item 11.1). Included is the net commission payable to others for the sale of transportation on the reporting carrier's service less the commission receivable from the reporting carrier's sale of transportation on other air carriers' services.

Other expenses (Item 11.2). Include pay, allowances and related expenses of all staff engaged in reservations, ticketing, sales and promotion activities; accommodation costs; agency fees for outside services; advertising and publicity through various media, and expenses related thereto.

General and administrative (Item 12)
Included are expenses incurred in performing the general and administrative functions of the air carrier and those expenses relating to matters of a general corporate nature, whether separately assessed or apportioned in conformity with the air carrier's accounting practices. Overhead costs directly related to Items 5, 6, 9, 10 and 11 should be included under the expense items to which they are related and not under this item.

Other operating expenses (total) (Item 13)
Incidental transport-related expenses (Item 13.1). Included are operating expenses that cannot be assigned to Items 5 through 12 and those expenses associated with the revenues received and reported under Item 3.1. Payments made for capacity equalisation arising from pooled services are to be included here.

Miscellaneous operating expenses (Item 13.2). Included are all other operating expenses not covered under Items 5 to 12 and 13.1 above. The nature of such expenses should be shown under 'Remarks'.

It will be noted that labour costs are not separated out (as they usually are for the income or profit and loss statement in the annual report). They appear under the different functional headings. The second largest cost, or largest for many freighter operators, fuel, is generally arrived at after adding or subtracting hedging gains or losses.

11.1.2 Fuel Costs

Fuel costs have become a crucial determinant of airline profitability, since in the short-term little can be done to increase fuel efficiency in the face of large fuel price increases. Furthermore passing on all of such increases is not often possible. Fuel costs have also become important with the growing emphasis on environmental impacts, especially climate change. Burning fuel produces greenhouse gases, particularly carbon dioxide and greater fuel efficiency has become equated with a more environmentally friendly operation.

Fuel and other costs can be split into two components: fuel price and fuel efficiency. For airlines, it is the jet kerosene price that is paid and this reflects both the market price of crude oil and the so-called 'crack spread' or the margin above crude that airlines are charged. Fuel prices also include the cost of transport from the nearest refinery or storage facility and the cost of airport delivery to the aircraft. Airports sometimes levy a throughput charge for access to the ramp.

Figure 11.2 shows that during the escalation of crude prices in 2008 the crack spread remained fairly constant, unlike towards the end of 2005. This degree of price volatility suggests that hedging against sudden swings against an airline might be advantageous. Airline hedging activity has increased considerably during the mid to late 2000s, although following the rapid fall in prices in 2009 some airlines questioned whether they would be better off in the long term. Given that there might be a time lag between market price increases and additional revenues from fuel surcharges, it might be wise for weaker airlines to ensure against short-term liquidity problems that might trigger bankruptcy. However, the margin requirements for hedging operations might make it impossible for weaker airlines to obtain such cover.

The other element of fuel costs is fuel efficiency. These can be obtained through improved operational procedures such as slower cruising speeds and less waste. Some, such as continuous descent approaches to airports, need agreement from airport and ATC service providers; many such measures have already been taken, leaving less that can be achieved. Acquiring more fuel efficient aircraft will give larger improvements but may take time and will depend on the return on investment and the cost of retiring the existing fleet. Freighters provide very clear examples of this trade-off with the B747-400F versus older technology B747-200F aircraft. Table 11.7 below provides some comparative data, and airlines such

Figure 11.2   Trends in spot crude and jet kerosene prices, 2005–2008

Source: US Energy Information Administration.

as Atlas Air that operated both types highlight the need to retire the older B747-200Fs as quickly as possible, given current and likely future fuel prices.

11.1.3 Capital Costs

Capital costs are a combination of depreciation and rental costs; since rentals or lease costs include interest, interest charges on loans (a non-operating cost) can also be considered part of capital costs. Depreciation depends on the airline depreciation policy that determines the period over which the aircraft (and other assets) are depreciated and the residual value of the asset at the end of this period. Freighter operators generally assume a long deprecation period for new freighters especially when annual utilisation is not expected to be high. Converted freighter aircraft are often already plus or minus 20 years and thus realistically may only have a further 10–15 years left. The word 'amortisation' is often used interchangeably with 'depreciation' but the latter should be used only in conjunction with intangible assets such as slot values or goodwill.

Aircraft depreciation is obviously the largest part of total depreciation for an airline, and the longer the depreciation period and the higher the residual value of the fleet the lower this will be (and vice versa). Aircraft engines are often depreciated separately as are major airframe maintenance checks and overhauls, rotables and other equipment.

Table 11.2   Cargolux asset depreciation policy, 2009

	Life*	Residual**
B747-400 airframe	20	15%
B747-400 engines	12	10%
First maintenance D check	8	Nil
Subsequent D checks	6	Nil
Rotable spares	10	Nil
Equipment	5	Nil

Note: * Period in years over which asset is deprecated on a straight-line basis to its residual value; ** Residual value as a percentage of the initial cost of the asset.
Source: Cargolux Annual Report, 2009.

Table 11.2 shows the current depreciation of Cargolux's assets. Its fleet consisted of only one aircraft type with most purchased new from the manufacturer. Smaller, short-haul, types are sometimes depreciated over shorter periods of time, sometimes justified by the heavier wear that they might receive through a higher number of landings over the year.

Capital costs also combine the price of capital with the efficiency with which it is used. The price will depend mainly on the cost of new and converted freighters, as well as interest charges on the loans needed to acquire the aircraft and implicit in the lease rentals paid by airlines. The latter declined sharply in 2009 to historically extremely low levels, but at the same time the risk premiums for lending to airlines (and firms in other industries) climbed to improve bank profitability.

The value of most of the larger jet freighters currently operated are shown in Table 11.3. These are mid-range current values for aircraft as assessed at the end of April 2010. Current Market Value (CMV) is defined as the appraiser's opinion of the most likely trading price that may be generated for an asset under market circumstances that are perceived to exist at the time in question. Current Market Value assumes that the asset is valued for its highest, best use, and the parties to the hypothetical sale transaction are willing, able, prudent and knowledgeable and under no unusual pressure for a prompt transaction. It also assumes that the transaction would be negotiated in an open and unrestricted market on an arm's-length basis, for cash or equivalent consideration, and given an adequate amount of time for effective exposure to prospective buyers. It differs from the distress value which is a forced sale in a poor market.

Table 11.3   Freighter values (US$ million), April 2010

	Age of aircraft			
	New	**5 years**	**10 years**	**20 years**
A300F4-600R		42.9	32.6	
A330-200F	98.6			
B737-300QC			11.0	7.0
B747-400M			50.1	25.9
B747-400F	104.1	89.9	72.0	
B747-400ERF	107.8	94.4		
B757-200MPF			23.3	14.3
B767-300F	60.8	50.2	39.7	
B777-200LRF	151.1			
MD11C			27.4	
MD11F			36.4	

Source: Aircraft Value Analysis Company in Aviation Strategy, June 2010.

Aircraft manufacturers will also publish list prices for those still in production. Boeing's latest prices posted on their website are in 2008 US dollar prices. The B747-8F is listed at between $301.5 million and $304.5 million, the B777F between $252.5 million and $260.5 million and the B767-200F between $155 and $166 million. Large orders and launch customers will get a discount of up to 40 percent, and few airlines will actually pay these prices. However, they are used as a basis for the cost escalation formulae that apply between purchase contract and finally settlement at delivery.

11.1.4 All-Cargo Operator Costs

An all-cargo airline that has published consistent financial and operating data over a long period of time is Cargolux. Its fleet in 2008 consisted entirely of B747-400Fs, some of which were wet-leased from other carriers. It is thus a good example of a long-haul cargo airline with a single aircraft type fleet. Table 11.4 shows how each of the main cost categories has changed over the past nine years.

Table 11.4   Cargolux operating cost breakdown, 1999 versus 2008

	1999		2008	
	US$000	%	US$000	%
Personnel	98,685	16.8	213,980	11.3
Aircraft fuel and oil	104,539	17.8	934,074	49.3
Depreciation	45,061	7.7	56,185	3.0
Aircraft rentals	109,402	18.6	78,705	4.2
Maintenance and overhaul	39,716	6.8	101,832	5.4
Handling, landing and overflying	114,295	19.4	270,924	14.3
Trucking and related	43,512	7.4	116,754	6.2
Administration/other	32,873	5.6	120,712	6.4
Total	588,083	100.0	1,893,166	100.0

Source: Cargolux annual report and accounts.

Fuel costs have increased very significantly over the period, mostly in 2008. This resulted in a huge rise in the share of fuel costs in the total, making this a very fuel-intensive business. Aircraft rentals actually declined in money terms as the owned fleet was expanded. The average cost in US dollars of carrying one kilogram of cargo rose from $1.6 in 1999 to $2.7 in 2008. With rates scarcely above this level, break-even load factors had jumped to almost unachievable levels. It should also be mentioned that the average load factor moved up from 66 percent to 71 percent in this period and the average aircraft utilisation from 11.6 block hours per aircraft per day to 15.6 hours per day, examples of airline measures to increase efficiency and lower costs during a very difficult decade.

11.1.5 Integrator Costs

Some integrators separate out their airline operating costs, although this is not shown in their annual report. Both UPS and FedEx do in their submissions to the Department of Transportation and the ICAO, but as discussed previously the latter's data do not appear to follow the reporting requirement guidelines closely. TNT Airways reported limited cost data and no associated traffic or capacity figures. DHL did not report to the ICAO themselves although some of their feeder airlines did (but they did not operate exclusively for DHL).

FedEx depreciates its wide-body fleet over 15–25 years to zero residual value, with a shorter period of 5–15 years for narrow-body and feeder aircraft. TNT Airways applies 10–25 years to a residual value of 20 percent of cost depending on aircraft type. UPS re-evaluated the anticipated service lives of its Boeing 757, Boeing 767 and Airbus A300 fleets in 2006 and subsequently increased their depreciable lives from 20 to 30 years and reduced the residual values from 30 percent to 10 percent of original cost.

Table 11.5   UPS unit cost trends by cost item, 1999 to 2008

US cents per ATK	1999	2008	% change p.a.
Flight crew salaries and expenses	4.3	4.4	0.3
Aircraft fuel and oil	2.6	13.6	20.0
Depreciation and rentals	3.4	2.9	-1.5
Other flight operations	0.7	0.3	-8.2
Flight equipment maintenance and overhaul	4.5	5.3	1.8
Airport and ATC charges	0.8	2.1	10.4
Station expenses	1.5	1.4	-0.8
Ticket sales and promotion	0.1	0.1	-3.1
General and administrative and other	0.9	1.1	2.2
Total operating expenses	18.8	31.1	5.8
ATKs billion	10,850	17,481	5.4

Source: ICAO Financial database.

UPS's operating costs are shown in Table 11.5 for the same period as Cargolux. It experienced similar fuel cost pressures but kept its fuel costs to 44 percent of the total in 2008, compared to almost 50 percent for Cargolux. On the other hand its aircraft maintenance and overhaul costs were 17 percent compared to only 5.4 percent for Cargolux's newer fleet. FedEx's costs are discussed in the case study in Chapter 12, suffice it to say here that its costs (and revenues) include a large item for ground operations that UPS avoids.

11.2 Freighter Aircraft Costs by Aircraft Type

11.2.1 Converted Freighters

An example of an earlier conversion programme was Pemco World Air Services and the B737-200 aircraft. In 1998 the conversion was estimated to take between 75 and 110 days and cost US$1.4–1.6m. Another programme for the same type of aircraft was carried out by Stambaugh Aviation for STC holder AEI, with 100 days downtime and at a cost of just over US$1 million. More recent estimates were given by Airclaims in 2005, with conversion costs for the larger B737-300 estimated at US$2–3 million, US$4.65 million for a B757-200, between $6.0 and 9.5 million for an A300-600 and $17 and 22 million for a B747-400SF. The cost of acquiring the aircraft and perhaps carrying out a considerable amount of maintenance needs to be added to these figures.

Table 11.6   Cargo aircraft capital conversion costs, 2007

	Small jet	Wide-body	Large
New freighter cost US$m	35	70–90	140–180
Used aircraft for conversion US$m	8–12	7–20	35–45
Conversion costs US$m	4	13–14	22–28
Converted freighter cost US$m	12–16	20–34	57–73
Converted as % new cost	34–46	29–49	41–52

Source: IAI Bedek quoted in OAG, 2010.

A more recent estimate for a B757-200 conversion for FedEx by Singapore Technologies was US$2.6 million, but this was for a large order of 87 aircraft and used the experience of previous work.[2] The parent company of ABX Air that operated B767-300F aircraft on behalf of DHL had been considering acquiring used Qantas passenger aircraft for conversion to freighters. It was reported that the

---

2   Mary-Anne Baldwin, 'Buy New or Buy Used' in *Freighter Operators Guide*, 2009.

acquisition and conversion costs together should come to no more than US$28–30 million, although no conversion cost estimate was given.[3] A more recent estimate for the 2007 cost of converting a B747-400 passenger aircraft to a -400SF was US$25 million plus a further $5 million for the cargo loading system and other modifications.[4] Adding this to the cost of a used aircraft of $38–44 million gave a converted price of $68–74 million compared to the cost of a new B747-400F of around $130 million (see also Table 11.6).

Of course the new B747-400F is a slightly better aircraft in terms of the nose cargo door, a cleaner fuselage aerodynamically and its lower OEW. This should give it an advantage on cash aircraft operating costs but no data is available to compare a converted freighter with a newly manufactured one of the same type (with the same engine type).

11.2.2 Freighter Aircraft Operating Costs

The best and almost only data on aircraft operating costs in airline service are from the US DOT Form 41. These only cover US operators and the jet aircraft that they operate. They have the advantage of including associated operating data such as average stage length, size of fleet and hours, miles and sectors flown. Average payload is not shown for freighters in Form 41 data but it has been estimated for Tables 11.7 and 11.8. The data shows cost per block hour for the following aircraft related items:

- flight crew;
- fuel;
- maintenance and overhaul;
- depreciation;
- rentals;
- other expenses (including insurance).

Block hour costs are important but, if sufficient cargo is available to operate at a reasonable two-way load factor, cost per ATK is the most relevant yardstick. These unit costs have been calculated, after standardising fuel costs to US$3 per US gallon (and also US$2/gallon) and the aircraft ranked in order of increasing unit cost per ATK. Some anomalies arise and will be discussed for the short-/medium-haul and long-haul aircraft separately. The other approach to costing freighters is to take manufacturer's estimates for items such as fuel efficiency and maintenance man-hours and factor in specific wage rates or fuel prices. This will be examined after looking first at US cost comparisons for short-/medium-haul and long-haul aircraft in turn.

3   Lori Ranson, *Air Transport Intelligence*, 5 April 2001, www.rati.com.

4   Rene Schumacher, Presentation to Cranfield University Fleet Planning course, March 2010.

Table 11.7 Short-/medium-haul freighter aircraft operating costs, 2008

	UPS B767-300F	FedEx A310F	UPS A300F	FedEx A300F	UPS B757-200F	FedEx B757-200F	DHL A300F	DHL B727-200F	FedEx B727-200F
Average payload tonnes	46	37	44	44	27	27	44	24	24
Average stage miles	1,605	733	711	854	670	982	697	595	568
Average stage kms	2,582	1,179	1,144	1,374	1,078	1,580	1,121	957	914
Total block hours	101,962	53,241	73,696	87,284	93,166	1,895	5,318	23,073	72,832
Total aircraft miles (000)	45,316	23,477	27,266	39,235	34,815	735	1,765	8,109	25,148
Total aircraft kms (000)	72,913	63,129	43,871	63,129	56,017	1,183	2,840	13,047	40,463
Total ATKs (000)	3,354,018	2,335,777	1,930,324	2,777,681	1,512,468	31,931	124,955	313,137	971,115
Block hours per day	8.7	3.3	3.8	5.1	3.4	3.3	2.5	2.8	2.7
US gallons fuel/hour	1,478	1,502	1,507	1,543	1,052	1,321	1,828	1,344	1,243
US gallons fuel/ATK	45	34	58	48	65	78	78	99	93
US$ per block hour:									
Flight crew	1,787	2,168	1,769	2,164	3,516	135	3,319	2,496	2,742
Other flight costs	130	829	148	698	132	843	19	28	575
Fuel	5,117	4,299	5,064	4,582	1,840	2,255	5,491	4,031	3,457
Maintenance	1,514	4,520	1,497	2,690	2,015	3,908	4,565	2,189	3,227
Depreciation	792	1,305	1,223	697	1,073	0	322	1,009	421
Aircraft rental	278	816	89	1,994	131	328	1,370	73	953
Total operating costs/hour	9,618	13,936	9,790	12,825	8,707	7,469	15,086	9,826	11,374
Total op. costs/ATK (cents)	292	318	374	403	536	443	642	724	853
Fuel: US$ per gallon	3.46	2.86	3.36	2.97	3.34	1.71	3	3	2.78
Number of aircraft	32	54.2	53	56.7	75	1.6	5.9	22.8	74.1
Total op. costs/ATK (cents):									
Fuel price adjusted to $3	272	322	353	404	525	544	642	724	874
Fuel price adjusted to $2	227	288	296	356	491	466	564	625	780

Source: Airline Monitor, 2009 and author's estimates.

Short/medium-haul aircraft

All the operators of the short-/medium-haul aircraft types shown in the table are integrators. One or two others also provide data but they are for small fleets and not as comparable. As Table 11.7 shows the longer range B767-300F gave the lowest ATK cost but was the largest aircraft to fill. The A310Fs and A300Fs were next followed by the B757s and the B727s last. The latter tended to have high fuel and maintenance costs and a third cockpit crew member inflated those costs. Surprisingly these were not offset by very low capital (depreciation and rental) costs. Crew costs overall show some inconsistency given the fact that wages and seniority should not have been too different.

Long-haul aircraft

The operators of the long-haul aircraft types shown in the table are a mixture of integrators, ACMI, scheduled and charter operators. The MD-11F produced the lowest block hour costs and compared very favourably with the larger B747-400F on cost per ATK (Table 11.8). Not surprisingly the older DC10s and B747-200Fs came out worse, especially at what were historically high fuel prices. Fuel prices actually paid ranged from US$2.23 per gallon for Kalitta to $3.51 for Evergreen and at these levels fuel accounted for well over half of total aircraft operating costs for many carriers. The variation in price could have been due to the different volumes and fuelling points as well as the results from fuel hedging operations. Fuel efficiency in US gallons per block hour varied significantly for the same aircraft type, even over similar networks. Flight crew were fairly consistent apart from very low reported costs from FedEx, although its 'other flight' costs were significantly higher than for other airlines. Maintenance costs tended to be higher for the older aircraft as would be expected.

The lowest ATK costs aircraft were all operated over average stage distances of 4,000 km or more and had relatively high daily utilisation. The exception was UPS's cost efficient B747-400Fs which achieved only eight hours per day and had low capital costs per unit of output. The older technology aircraft were only operated 2–6 hours per day on average, either in charter or hub feeder roles.

Aircraft manufacturer's cost estimates

Aircraft operating costs are a key input to the fleet planning process, whether for freighters or passenger aircraft. US Form 41 might give some indications but an airline will need to forecast its own operating costs using manufacturers' estimates and guarantees and its own wage, price and efficiency assumptions. A short-list of potential freighters will be drawn up and detailed cost and revenue data determined under different scenarios. For example, Martinair's eventual decision to acquire B747-400BCFs to replace its B747-200/30F fleet started with a short-list of MD-11F and B747-400F aircraft, with new and converted aircraft considered for the latter. It is important to include the revenues that each aircraft type and version will generate, since these may vary according to payload or volume restrictions. Normally this investment appraisal process is focused on cash operating expenses

Table 11.8   Long-haul freighter aircraft operating costs, 2008

	UPS B747-400F	World MD-11F	Atlas B747-400F	Kalitta B747-400F	FedEx MD-11F	Atlas B747-100/200	World DC10-30F	Evergreen B747-100/200	FedEx DC10-F	Kalitta B747-100/200	UPS B747-100/200
Average payload tonnes	110	93	110	110	93	100	80	100	80	100	100
Average stage miles	3,408	2,833	3,367	3,284	2,367	2,412	2,778	2,586	1,034	2,816	889
Average stage kms	5,483	4,558	5,418	5,284	3,809	3,881	4,470	4,161	1,664	4,531	1,430
Total block hours	20,337	26,062	57,332	4,557	206,955	33,654	3,717	20,394	150,548	27,360	4,855
Total aircraft miles (000)	9,819	11,997	27,030	2,252	95,744	15,613	1,661	9,433	59,093	12,888	1,823
Total aircraft kms (000)	15,799	19,303	43,491	3,623	154,052	25,121	2,673	15,178	95,081	20,737	2,933
Total ATKs (000)	1,737,865	1,795,195	4,784,040	398,581	14,326,845	2,512,132	213,804	1,517,770	7,606,451	2,073,679	293,321
Block hours per day	8.0	11.5	17.5	10.5	10.6	15.7	6.1	5.3	6.3	4.5	1.6
US gallons fuel/hour	2,787	2,301	3,203	3,079	2,420	3,454	2,831	3,949	2,105	4,585	3,231
US gallons fuel/ATK	33	33	38	35	35	46	49	53	42	60	53
US$ per block hour:											
Flight crew	1,689	1,375	1,432	1,628	2,917	2,446	1,667	2,089	534	1,758	4,269
Other flight costs	123	128	45	182	876	78	155	88	699	149	398
Fuel	9,449	7,242	9,618	9,178	7,252	10,368	8,958	13,850	6,256	10,241	10,819
Maintenance	1,329	1,225	1,863	3,514	2,023	3,220	2,578	2,894	4,195	3,722	2,538
Depreciation	765	227	318	2,216	637	544	566	928	1,025	540	2,085
Aircraft rental	98	1,339	1,082	51	915	1,886	953	1,040	328	108	66
Total operating costs/hour	13,452	11,536	14,358	16,769	14,621	18,542	14,877	20,889	13,038	16,519	20,175
Total op. costs/ATK (cents)	157	167	172	192	211	248	259	281	258	218	334
Fuel: US$ per gallon	3.39	3.15	3.00	2.55	3.00	3.00	3.16	3.51	2.97	2.23	3.35
Number of aircraft	7.0	6.2	9.0	1.2	53.3	5.9	1.7	10.6	65.7	16.6	8.6
Total op. costs/ATK (cents)											
Fuel price adjusted to $3	145	162	172	210	211	248	251	254	259	265	315
Fuel price adjusted to $2	112	129	134	169	176	202	201	201	218	204	262

Source: Airline Monitor, 2009 and author's estimates.

which are initially compared with capital costs using a 'study' or best estimate price of the aircraft before serious negotiations. The cash flow streams for the various options will be compared in terms of Net Present Value (NPV) or Internal Rate of Return (IRR) to select the preferred type before consideration of financing. In order to get approval for the investment the NPV should be positive and therefore add to shareholder value or the IRR exceeds its target return or Weighted Average Cost of Capital (WACC). At this point financing and capital budgets play a role, and unquantifiable factors such as a need to diversify aircraft suppliers. In the Martinair example above, budgetary constraints led to the choice of the Boeing converted B747-400SF rather than the much higher capital cost B747-400F.

Cargolux needed to replace its older fuel inefficient B747-200Fs and faced a similar evaluation to Martinair. The disadvantages of the B747-200F over the newer B747-400F were essentially:

- higher fuel consumption (+15 percent);
- lower payload (-12 tonnes);
- augmented crew (one additional crew member);
- more technical stops;
- higher maintenance costs.

But the above were somewhat offset by the lower ownership cost of the B747-200F (Arendt and Wecker, 2007). The authors go on to examine the trade-offs between the -400SF conversion and the factory-built new aircraft. Their study indicated that the new aircraft offered a higher payload, lower fuel burn, lower maintenance costs, in addition to advantages of the nose door that gives access to very large shipments, easier loading and faster turnaround times.

Aircraft operating costs will also depend on whether an airline has commonality across its fleet. First, it would clearly give a cost advantage to B777F freighter operators if the airline operated the passenger version of the same type. Assuming the engines were the same there would be economies of scale in maintenance as well as crew costs. Trading up from a B747-400F to the new B747-8F would also give a 70 percent parts commonality as well as lower crew conversion costs. Airbus has also for many years offered a family of aircraft to airlines (at least on the passenger side), highlighting commonality across a fleet of different sizes.

Table 11.9 estimates aircraft operating costs of the main contenders for long-haul freighter operations. Their assumptions on payload are calculated using containerised volumes and a cargo shipment density of 7lbs per cubic foot (112 kg/m³). This results in a figure that is lower than the net weight payloads often quoted. It also means that some of the aircraft would be able to benefit from additional payload if the sector length had been set at the lowest (with full volumetric payload) of the sample. Cash operating costs are composed of fuel, maintenance and crew costs. Fuel costs have been calculated using manufacturers' estimates and a price per US gallon of US$2.05. Maintenance is based on estimates for direct maintenance cost per flight hour, while crew costs are built up from

Table 11.9   Large freighter operating costs, 2007

	MD-11F	B777F	B747-400SF	B747-400F	B747-8F	A380F
Volumetric payload (t)	65	73	82	85	95	104
Fuel cost/trip (US$)	60,000	48,000	n/a	69,000	n/a	96,000
Cash operating costs/trip (US$)	84,000	71,000	99,500	97,700	111,300	131,000
Aircraft capital cost/trip (US$)	15,107	37,185	21,662	33,446	42,588	44,258
Total operating cost/trip (US$)	99,107	108,185	121,162	131,146	153,888	175,258
Total operating cost per kg (US$)	1.52	1.48	1.48	1.55	1.62	1.69

Source: 'Large Wide-body Freighter Selection', *Aircraft Commerce*, No. 51, April/May 2007.

average salary and expense costs and an average of 700 flight hours per year.[5] Finally aircraft capital costs are estimated from lease rates for existing types and depreciation and interest for likely new prices for future types. The resulting total aircraft operating costs per kg are not very far apart, with the B777F and B747-400SF coming out just ahead, the former having very favourable fuel efficiency and the latter lower capital costs. The B777F also has good range capability while the B747-400F has a nose door for easier loading.

The above analysis contrasts with Boeing's estimate for the B747-8 having around 20 tonnes more payload than the B747-400F. This clearly depends on many factors, although in Table 11.9 the difference is only 10 tonnes and both are based on the same stage length (3,000nm). Atlas Air estimated the B747-8F to have 16 percent lower cash operating expenses per tonne-mile compared to the B747-400F (also with a fuel price of just over US$2 per US gallon) and 23 percent lower than the B747-400SF. Aircraft ownership costs will considerably reduce this difference, but the new aircraft advantage is likely to remain using Atlas's assumptions.

11.3 ACMI/Wet Lease Aircraft Operating Costs

ACMI is a specific type of lease arrangement between a lessor and an airline that gives the airline a dedicated aircraft in return for a guaranteed minimum level of operation. The main airlines offering this type of contract were identified in Chapter 4. It is ideally suited to air cargo services where the size of fleet that

---

5   All benefit from a two- rather than three-person cockpit crew.

the airline would need would be uneconomic. Furthermore the aircraft's owner and operator may not have the expertise to market the aircraft's capacity, and it may not have the traffic rights. In this respect it raises certain regulatory aspects (see Chapter 3) when, as often is the case, the owner and operator are located in different countries. It is also similar to other outsourcing arrangements where the party that is contracting the services (the lessee) gets the benefit of the efficiency of the airline providing the service. A choice of ACMI provider makes this process more attractive to the lessee and the various ACMI operators are described in Chapter 4. The duration of the agreement can range from five days to five or six years, sometimes with an early termination provision. Atlas Air reports longer 3–6 year ACMI contracts on its newer B747-400Fs and shorter periods for the older B747-200Fs. The minimum level of operations is guaranteed by means of a minimum level of aircraft utilisation, with payments or rentals based on the actual number of hours operated.

These contracts typically require the lessor, which is usually an airline, to supply aircraft, crew, maintenance and insurance, while the airline lessee generally bears all other operating expenses, including:

- fuel and fuel servicing;
- marketing costs associated with obtaining cargo;
- airport cargo handling;
- landing fees;
- ground handling, aircraft push-back and de-icing services;
- specific cargo and mail insurance.

There are variations on the basic ACMI contract model, including dedicated ACMI, cost provision split between the two parties (mostly relating to cabin crew on passenger services), Partial ACMI where an aircraft can be used by a number of different customers at different times, and Fractional ACMI where a number of different customers can take space on the same flight. A very recent addition is 'CMI' or the provision of crew, maintenance and insurance by the 'lessor' and the aircraft by the 'lessee', although this would no longer really be a lease, more the contracting out of the flight operations. In all cases the customer has to commit to using the aircraft or part of an aircraft for a given number of block hours per month or quarter. Penalties are payable if these minima are not reached. The minimum hourly commitment could range from zero to 400 hours per month, depending on the length of lease, whether it is just for a peak season, and whether an overcapacity situation means that the lessor is keen to do a deal. A typical hourly commitment would be between 300–400 hours per month.

Atlas Air provides operating cost data in its annual report but this consolidates ACMI, dry leasing, scheduled and charter operations, with ACMI accounting for only 22 percent of total revenues.

Table 11.10   Atlas Air segment contributions, 2008

	Revenues (US$m)	Contribution (US$m)	Contribution % of revenues
ACMI	358	81	22.7
Scheduled services	645	-43	-6.7
AMC charter	426	108	25.4
Commercial charter	127	10	8.1
Dry leasing	49	14	29.0
Total above	1,605	171	10.6

Source: Atlas Air Annual Report 2008, Form 10K.

Table 11.10 shows the healthy contribution that ACMI made towards Atlas Air group profits in 2008. Contribution was defined as income (losses) before taxes, aircraft retirement costs, gains on the sale of aircraft and issuance of shares, and unallocated fixed costs. US military charters were also good contributors, as was the dry leasing segment, which consists largely of B747 freighter leases to the UK Global Supply Systems which wet leases the aircraft on to British Airways. Scheduled services made a loss mainly due to the inability to pass on all the very large fuel cost increases in that year.

The ACMI rate charged to the airline customer will depend on the length of contract, type of aircraft and assumptions on the cost of inputs. Since the rate reflects crew, maintenance, insurance and a profit margin on top of the basic aircraft capital cost it will be expensive, although more attractive longer-term rates can be offered, with break points and penalties for early return of the aircraft. The

Table 11.11   ACMI rates by cost category and long-haul aircraft type, 1999

US$/flying hour	B747-400F	B747-200F	MD-11F	DC10-30F
Aircraft lease/finance charges	2,857	2,000	1,886	923
Aircraft maintenance	1,540	2,000	1,325	1,600
Cockpit crew	930	857	870	790
Aircraft insurance	298	160	179	80
Lessor's margin	1,375	283	740	607
Total	7,000	5,300	5,000	4,000
Lessor margin (%)	20	5	15	15

Source: *Aircraft Commerce*, Issue No. 6, July/August 1999.

data in Table 11.11 has been built up using standard assumptions for the four cost assumptions, such as crew hours per month, insurance rates and dry lease rates. While the older aircraft required a three-person cockpit crew the B747-400F and MD-11F only need two, although it was assumed that the latter needed a third due to the long sector lengths flown. While the data are no longer relevant today it shows the relative cost of the different long-haul aircraft types. It should be remembered, however, that the lower ACMI rates on older aircraft will today be more than offset by high fuel costs, paid by the lessee.

The total ACMI rate to the customer has been based on realistic prices obtainable in the market at that time, and the less efficient, large, B747-200F was less attractive to potential operators and thus the margin to the lessor much reduced compared to the other aircraft types.

Table 11.12 shows which of the two parties to the lease agreement are normally responsible for each operating cost category.

Table 11.12   Costs assumed by lessor/charterer

	Dry lease	ACMI	Charter
Aircraft capital		✓	✓
Cockpit crew		✓	✓
Aircraft maintenance		✓	✓
Aircraft hull insurance		✓	✓
Fuel			✓
Crew expenses			✓
Airport charges			✓
Air navigation			✓
Ground handling			✓
Marketing			

11.4 Problems of Joint Production on Passenger Services

Capacity for the carriage of air cargo is provided jointly with passengers and so the cost of operating the aircraft should be allocated between the two on a fair (but arbitrary) basis. However, it can be argued that the cargo carried in the belly-holds of passenger aircraft is a by-product of the main passenger operation and should therefore only meet the direct costs of marketing and handling cargo. On the other hand the argument that the passenger aircraft is designed solely for passengers and freight is only incidental is difficult to accept, and was rejected by an important study undertaken in the US at the time of the then Civil Aeronautics Board's investigations into regulated passenger fares and freight rates (Miller, 1973).

The by-product argument is no longer tenable when some frequencies are operated by combi- aircraft, where the volume allocated to cargo may exceed the passenger cabin volume. With freighter aircraft, the aircraft operating costs are obviously identifiable and only overheads need to be allocated between passengers and cargo. The by-product argument is also weakened by the fact that belly-hold capacity has an alternative use as galleys, crew rest areas or passenger lounges and cargo should therefore cover the opportunity cost of giving up these alternative uses.

In markets where passenger, combi- and freighter aircraft are operating the cargo rates will probably be determined by the lowest cost approach to pricing; some airlines are likely to operate only passenger aircraft and rates may be determined by the by-product approach, which may make it difficult for carriers required to allocate the full costs of cargo carriage, particularly freighter operators, to make a profit. Market characteristics might also be a powerful force in determining rates, especially where marked directional imbalances occur.

With the advent of the B747-300 and B747-400, with stretched upper decks, the space available for cargo in the belly-hold was reduced because of the additional passenger baggage, compared with earlier B747 versions. Ironically, Qantas employed their B747-300s in a less dense passenger configuration (398 seats) than their small B747-200s (up to 439 seats) and the move of a lower deck galley to the main deck actually gave an additional 3 tonnes payload on the -300 aircraft. The A380 extended the upper deck further with no significant increase in lower deck volume. Again, some A380 operators are offering more premium seats which reduces the impact somewhat on cargo capacity.

11.4.1 IATA Cargo Cost Allocation Methods

Under the IATA costing methodology, cargo operating costs on mixed passenger/ cargo services are determined by assuming that direct operating costs are common to both types of operation:

a) Common aircraft operating costs are apportioned between passengers and cargo proportionately to the usable volume allocated to each product.
b) The costs of ground handling and marketing are directly indentified where possible by the carriers in their data input.
c) Administration and overheads are split between passengers and cargo proportionately to the sum of all the other costs.

The above was the latest guideline issued by the IATA in 'Airline Financial Performance Benchmarks: Summary Report by the Airline Economic Task Force (AETF)', December 2004. Not many airlines participated in this collection of data and the AETF has since been disbanded.

Previously alternative methods of allocation were possible under IATA reporting guidelines. For example, under the revenue offset method, cargo revenue less cargo specific costs (such handling and marketing) is subtracted from the total cost of operating the service to give the net costs to be allocated to passengers. In other words, cargo is assumed just to cover all directly attributable costs of operating the service.

IATA recommend airlines to use whichever method produces the lower outcome between cargo revenue and cargo operating costs, a compromise which reflects arguments between member of the Cost Committee over many years. In the late 1970s, the argument came to a head when Lufthansa declared that the full cost allocation method only would be used, or they would no longer provide data. In response, British Airways said that they would not provide data if this proposal was adopted. Today, the compromise allows the two systems to co-exist. The allocation in a) above is carried out using various IATA rules of thumb:

1. Total usable volume for the passenger aircraft is taken to be the volume equivalent in all-cargo configuration. For example, a figure of 21,900 cubic feet is suggested for the B747-200 and 9,530 cubic feet for the B767-200.
2. This is then converted into an equivalent payload by multiplying by a suggested cargo density of 161 kg/m³ (4.56 kg/cubic feet) and into equivalent tonne-kms by multiplying by aircraft kms (see section 10.3.1 for more on shipment densities).
3. This is finally compared to bellyhold cargo available tonne-kms to arrive at the ratio for apportioning common aircraft costs flown.

Common aircraft operating costs are the difference between total aircraft operating costs and costs of passenger services (in-flight) and cabin attendants.

In order to determine cargo profitability, the costs computed according to the above methodology are compared with cargo revenues; included in these are freight and mail revenues, but not passenger excess baggage which is allocated to the passenger operation (it used to be combined with other revenues and not included in either passenger or cargo profitability analysis). Excess baggage revenue for IATA carrier international services amounts to around 1.5 percent of total revenues, a large percentage of which is likely to be from courier bags. A consistent approach needs to be taken to courier revenue and costs, depending on who is actually marketing the service, either including both revenues and costs in cargo, or passengers, with capacity costed accordingly.

Another potential problem arose with the commissions and discounts paid to freight forwarders. Revenues should exclude normal commissions, but be net of any discounts or override commissions. But it is not clear whether all airlines adhere to this method or reporting. Back in 1987 a discrepancy was discovered between British Airways and British Caledonian cargo yields; BA's yield was 24 US cents per RTK for all schedule services and BCal's was reported to be 28 cents. However, following the merger it transpired that BCal had not deducted overrides and discounts from gross revenues (and BA had), and a more comparable figure for BCal's yield was about 21 cents. Today it is much less common for forwarders to be paid on a commission basis and this problem has thus largely disappeared.

11.4.2 Boeing B747-300 Example

The various methods of cost allocation for passengers and cargo carried on passenger flights was clearly described in a Boeing paper that used a B747-300 combi flight as an example. The paper discussed by-product and joint product methods of allocation. First the various categories of cost are introduced, starting with the cargo specific costs:

- handling (loading/unloading/transhipment);
- sales, promotion and commissions;
- cargo insurance and other costs;
- additional fuel (due to cargo payload).

These are costs that would not be incurred if no cargo was carried on passenger flights, as in the case of some low-cost airlines. The additional fuel can be calculated from the extra weight of payload that is carried. The passenger specific costs are:

- handling (check-in, baggage, ramp, lounges);
- cabin crew and in-flight catering;
- airport passenger departure fees;
- sales, ticketing, promotion and commissions;
- passenger insurance and other passenger costs (e.g. delayed flight compensation);
- additional fuel (due to passenger and baggage payload).

The following joint costs can be allocated to each of the two products carried, passengers (and baggage) and cargo, depending on the method adopted:

- aircraft capital costs (depreciation, lease rentals, and possibly interest);
- aircraft insurance;
- basic fuel (without payload);
- aircraft maintenance and overhaul;
- cockpit crew;
- landing fees;
- air navigation charges.

Cost allocation can follow the 'by-product' (revenue offset) methods, the 'joint product' (fully allocated costs) methods, or no cost allocation. The last merely calculates the split of profit on the flight in proportion to the revenues earned. In the example in Figure 11.3 the profit per flight of $10,000 would be attributed to each product according to its share of total revenue of $75,900, giving cargo 31.2 percent or a profit of $3,123 and passengers the remaining $6,877 (rounded off in Figure 11.4).

The by-product methods are 'cargo break-even' and 'incremental cargo cost'. The first of these is shown in Figure 11.3, with the total cargo costs assumed to equate to the total cargo revenues. These costs would be the sum of the cargo specific costs of $10,300 and a further $13,400 of the joint costs, leaving $21,800 to be allocated to the passenger revenues to assign all the profit to passengers. The 'incremental cargo cost method' allocates to cargo only the cargo specific costs listed above, all other costs set against passenger revenues.

Joint product or fully allocated costs methods need to find a way to allocate all the joint costs both to passengers and cargo on a fair basis. The following methods are given in the Boeing study:

- volumetric capacity;
- weight (payload);
- zone;
- revenues;
- profit contribution;
- equivalent freighter.

The volumetric capacity calculation was described above. Weight payload takes the number of seats and assigns a weight to the passenger, their cabin baggage and checked baggage (some use an average of 90 kg, others slightly higher figures).

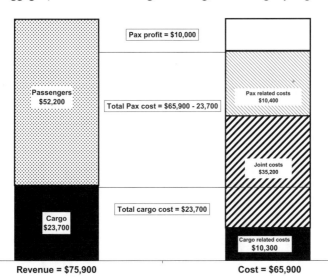

Figure 11.3   Cost allocation on passenger/cargo flights: cargo by-product

Source: Boeing, 1977.

The cargo payload will be the difference between the payload available for cargo after allowing for the fuel weight. The zone method determines the space taken by the cargo hold and the displacement of the seats on the main deck by the six pallets carried in relation to the total space available. The equivalent freighter method calculates the cost per tonne for a freighter of the same type at maximum payload and allocates the joint costs by multiplying the cost per tonne by the actual cargo tonnes carried on the 'combi'. The revenue and profit contribution allocate joint costs in the ratio of passenger and cargo revenues, and revenues less cargo or passenger specific costs respectively. A worked example is given of the volume capacity method followed by the weight payload method below. These two are the most frequently used of the fully allocated cost methods:

1. Fully allocated costs using volumetric capacity
Effective volume of passenger cabin: 360 passengers @ 36.1 cubic foot/passenger = 12,996 cu.ft (65.4 percent)
Cargo cabin volume:
6 pallets + lower deck (ex passenger bags) = 6,867 cu.ft (34.6 percent)
Total volume: 19,863 cubic foot (100 percent)
Costs allocated to passengers (65.4 percent x $35,200) = $23,000
Costs allocated to cargo (34.6 percent x $35,200) = $12,200
Passenger profit = $52,200 – 20,400 – 23,000= $8,800
Cargo profit = $23,700 – 10,300 – 12,200 = $1,200

2. Fully allocated costs using weight payloads
Weight payload of passenger cabin:
360 passengers @ 100 kg/passenger: = 36,000 kg (53.5 percent)
Cargo main and lower deck weight payload:
6,867 cubic foot x density of 4.56 kg/cubic foot = 31,314 kg (46.5 percent)
Total weight: 67,314 kg (100 percent)
Costs allocated to passengers (53.5 percent x $35,200) = $18,832
Costs allocated to cargo (46.5 percent x $35,200) = $16,368
Passenger profit = $52,200 – 20,400 – 18,832= $12,968
Cargo profit = $23,700 – 10,300 – 16,368 = ($2,968)

The profitability of air cargo on passenger flights can vary considerably depending on the allocation method used. This is shown in Figure 11.4 using the same data as the above examples. The payload weight allocation method loads the most costs onto cargo and is the only one to show cargo carried at a loss. The volume method was recommended by the IATA Cost Committee and this shows a small profit for cargo. Since for the same airline some flights will 'weigh out' and some 'cube out' there does not appear to be a simple answer to the question of a weight or volume allocation method. The main conclusion, however, would be to have a fully allocated method, especially for a combi aircraft with cargo taking up 47 percent of the payload and 35 percent of the volume. If cargo is not making a profit there is the option to reduce or remove the main deck cargo capacity available.[6]

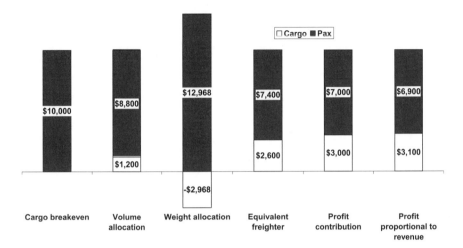

Figure 11.4   Product profit allocation on passenger/cargo flights

Source: Boeing.

6   If it not profitable to carry any main deck cargo the airline would be advised to replace the combi aircraft with a passenger version, thereby saving costs from the lighter structure.

Chapter 12
Air Cargo Financial Performance

The airline industry is not noted for its profitability and the cargo side of the business is no exception. In this chapter the profitability of carrying air cargo both on freighters and passenger flights will first be compared with passengers and other parts of the supply chain. Those airlines that carry only freight have often struggled to stay afloat financially and are faced with major industry downturns at frequent intervals. Many new entrants have failed in spite of often strict financial fitness tests by licensing authorities. This does not seem to deter potential new entrants and capital has been surprisingly forthcoming given the patchy financial performance, although operating leases reduce the capital required.

In order to discuss the financial performance of air cargo carriers, two case studies have been selected from two world regions: Asia and the US. The first is Nippon Cargo Airlines, an all-cargo carrier based in Japan, and the second Federal Express from the US. The first is an airport-to-airport operator, the second an integrator. Together these two typify the way the air cargo industry has developed over the past 30 years, reflecting regulatory and economic challenges along the way. Finally, air cargo subsidiaries of network, principally passenger, carriers are analysed using the limited data available.

12.1 Cargo Airline Profitability

12.1.1 Profitability by Type of Carrier

Cargo airlines have not been the most profitable type of carrier over the past four years, although they were not far behind the more profitable low-cost and regional airlines (see Figure 12.1).

Mainline airlines include regional subsidiaries and so the 'regional' category is mostly US independents, often with lucrative contracts with network or mainline airlines. Low-cost carriers are defined as new model point-to-point carriers, and leisure are travel groups or charter carriers. Mainline tend to be all those airlines that do not fall in the other categories, and include the old style flag carriers that are often highly unprofitable. They also have a high weighting in the total, accounting for 70 percent of 2009 revenues, compared to only 7 percent for the cargo carriers.

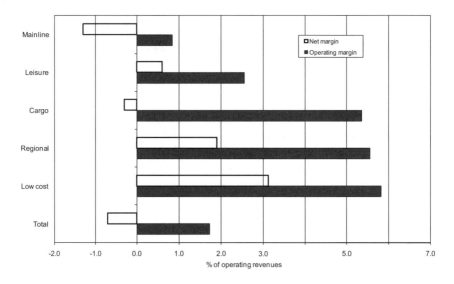

Figure 12.1   Airline profitability by type of carrier, average for 2006–2009 inclusive

Source: *Airline Business,* August of each year.

12.1.2 Profitability by Supply Chain Participant

Airlines often complain that low entry barriers, overcapacity and fierce competition prevent them making a higher enough profit margin over the longer term, resulting in an inability to earn a sufficient return on capital. This argument seems to contradict itself, since without a decent return on capital it is unlikely that capital could be found to make entry easy. Leasing helps and financiers often rely more on the asset than the profitability of the airline operating the asset. Some airlines also maintain that other participants in the industry make high profits at their expense, since they are mostly their suppliers. This notion is tested in Figure 12.2, which gives the average return on capital over an eight-year period.

Airlines indeed come out at the bottom with aircraft maintenance not far behind. This is partly because they are relatively capital intensive and higher returns are hard to achieve. Unfortunately the study did not separate cargo from combination airlines, which was performed in the previous section.

Freight forwarders are included in the figure, and performed fairly well over this period. They were helped by the fact that forwarding is not capital intensive and a reasonable return is easier to make. The freight forwarders included accounted for one-third of the global market, and 30 airlines featured with 64 percent of the world market.

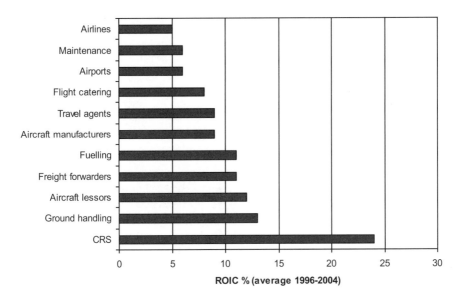

Figure 12.2   Return on invested capital by value chain participant

Source: McKinsey in IATA Economics Briefing No. 4, June 2006.

12.1.3 Profitability by Type of Airline Service

Section 12.4 examines the profitability of two cargo subsidiaries of network carriers. However, this does not answer the question as to the profitability of cargo on passenger services versus that of freighters. Clearly, the joint service profitability depends on the allocation of costs (see Chapter 11). The IATA cost committee used to collect data on the economics of these two types of service but this publication was discontinued in 2004. Generally the passenger flight cargo were unprofitable in every year while freighters made profits during the upswing of the economic cycle but made losses or broke even in the other years. This data included integrators such as FedEx but excluded non-IATA members, and a number of members not taking part in the data collection.

In the last year published (2003) cargo as a whole made an operating loss of US$0.2 billion, but no breakdown was given by type of service. The last pre-downturn figures available were for 1998. In that year North Atlantic cargo operations of passenger and combi aircraft produced a pre-interest loss of US$246m or an operating margin of -18.1 percent, with an actual load factor of 60.1 percent falling well short of the break-even level of 71 percent. This was based on fully allocated flight operations costs. All-cargo flights on the same routes produced losses of $88m, or a margin on revenues of -11.3 percent. The actual load factor on these flights was higher at 70.7 percent but the break-even level was 78.6 percent, mainly due to higher unit costs.

The picture was much better on routes between Europe/Middle East and the Far East: cargo generated an operating profit on passenger and combi services with a margin on sales of 0.9 percent. A small loss on freighters gave a negative margin of 0.1 percent. For the North and Mid Pacific (transpacific) cargo was not profitable on passenger flights (a margin of -42 percent) mainly due to very low load factors. Freighters were also unprofitable (with a margin of -3 percent).

12.1.4 All-Cargo Airline Profit Comparison

Specialist cargo airlines have not been especially profitable over time, but the year 2008 chosen for the comparison in Table 12.1 was not typical. That was the year that fuel prices soared and airlines were unable to pass all of this increase on to their customers. The two integrators in the small sample come out reasonable well, but they are less fuel intensive, with FedEx's fuel bill for 2007 of around 11 percent of total operating costs, compared to Cargolux's 37 percent, and have large ground operations, some of which cannot be excluded from the data (especially for FedEx).

Table 12.1   All-cargo airline profit margins in 2008 and previous years

	Operating margin 2008 (%)	Net margin 2008 (%)	Years to 2008	Av. operating margin (%)
FedEx	6.9	4.1	9 years	6.4
UPS	6.2	-1.1	9 years	6.4
ABX	3.8	0.2	3 years	3.6
Cargolux	0.7	-1.2	6 years	6.9
Atlas	0.1	-2.2	6 years	9.1
Southern	-1.6	-5.7		n/a
Kalitta	-3.8	-4.4	4 years	6.2
British Global	-9.2	-10.5		n/a

Source: ICAO Financial data and airline annual reports.

ABX was an airline that was contracted to operate flights for an integrator and thus less susceptible to the downturn. Cargolux has been consistently profitable over many years, but reported a small operating profit and net loss in 2008, partly due to provisions for anti-trust fines (taken as an operating cost that was around 4 percent of annual revenues). The operating margins looked better over a number of years prior to (and including 2008), especially Atlas Air which was also the most volatile. Cargolux was hit with its provision for fines for 2007 and 2008, but reported very healthy margins in the four years up to 2008.

12.2 Nippon Cargo Airlines Case Study

12.2.1 History

The arrival of B707 and DC8 freighters in the 1960s transformed the global air freight industry and provided the impetus for the establishment of a Japanese all-cargo airline. At the same time Japanese exports were increasing rapidly and the new freighters with their 30-tonne capacity and range made it possible to air freight goods directly and quickly to markets in North America and Europe. Initially it seemed impossible to form such an airline since the Japanese government designated only one international carrier and that was Japan Airlines. Airlines such as All Nippon were limited to domestic flights. However, the arrival in Japan of DC8F flights operated by Flying Tiger in 1969 intensified efforts to form a Japanese cargo airline.

Back in 1959 Nippon Yusen Kaisha, Osaka Shosen Kaisha and Mitsui Steamship Co. Ltd had decided to form an air cargo company with the support of Japan Airlines. However, four other companies, Kawasaki Kisen Kaisha, Yamashita-Shinnihon Steamship, Nippon Express and All Nippon Airways (ANA) decided to undertake a separate initiative to establish what, in November 1972, became Nippon International Cargo Airlines. The net result of these two plans was the formation of one all-cargo airline, what became known as Nippon Cargo Airlines, by six companies. Japan Airlines withdrew, having never been much in favour of the idea, presumably because of competition to its own cargo operations. The airline was registered as a company in 1978, after one of the participants, Nippon Express, had withdrawn from the consortium. The next step was to obtain a licence and air traffic rights and these proved difficult. Initially, the supply of aviation fuel was limited and the US/Japan air negotiations had broken down. These were vital to obtain the key transpacific traffic rights and gateways. In 1982 hearings were organised by the Ministry of Transport to evaluate NCA's route applications. At these, NCA was challenged on the three-crew transpacific operations that it planned (using ANA qualified employees) on the grounds that Japan Airlines employed five. A conference on the future of air cargo put further pressure on the Ministry to designate an international cargo airline, although Japan Airlines maintained its opposition to NCA's application, arguing that a situation of overcapacity would occur. The hearings concluded with a recommendation in favour of NCA's application and the Ministry granted its licence in 1983, six years after the formation of the coalition to establish the airline.

Plans then moved ahead to operate a B747-200F on the route Tokyo-San Francisco-New York, with two pilots and a flight engineer. The cost efficient crewing schedule was once again challenged, this time from within the consortium: by the ANA unions. ANA did not itself operate internationally at the time but provided technical and staff support to the new cargo airline. The ANA union argued that crew health could be at risk, although the use of licensed employees in this way did not conflict with international safety regulations.

While the international air transport system has changed significantly since then, management/union arguments have not.

Another problem that prevented the start of operations was the US/Japanese Air Services Agreement. Talks resumed at the end of 1984, one of its aims being to obtain fairer and more equal treatment for the Japanese. This meant the right by the Japanese to designate an all-cargo airline to match the US designation of Flying Tigers.[1] The US finally backed down after the Japanese threatened to retaliate, for example by reducing the number of flights that Flying Tigers could operate into Japan (which included supplies for US military bases). Agreement was given for NCA to start operating at the beginning of April 1985, but there was a last-minute hitch. The express parcels operator Federal Express wished to fly to Japan. A further round of talks delayed NCA's first flight, which finally got off the ground in May 1985.

With the mid-1960s shift of Japanese manufacturing production to lower labour cost Asia (just as is now occurring in Taiwan and China), NCA needed to add flights to other Asian points: thus two flights a week were introduced to Hong Kong in 1986. Singapore was also started in that year and a more direct route to New York via Anchorage (Table 12.2). In 1987/1988 the strong yen reduced fuel costs and US exports improved thus reducing the directional imbalance with the US.

12.2.2 Traffic and Operating Developments

Figure 12.3 shows that traffic increased steadily over the 15 years from NCA's first flight to the recession of 2001. This was despite the 1991 recession and Asian financial crisis in 1997. The freight traffic growth averaged 15.3 percent over this period but largely stagnated from the mid to end of the 2000s when it dropped to around its 1997 level. As might be expected from a start-up airline the average load factors in the first two years were below break-even but moved above 60 percent for the next few years, with an improved directional imbalance.

Its first services were operated using new B747-200F aircraft, with an order from Boeing for two aircraft, delivered from 1985 onwards. Some of these were converted from passenger models by Boeing, and many were on finance leases. Over the years these were expanded to 10 aircraft with the airline taking the last delivery off the Boeing production line in 1991 (it also took the last B747-400F). In 2003 with rising oil prices, the older B747-200Fs were becoming less cost effective and an order was placed for B747-400F and B747-400SF aircraft. However, by 2005 it had decided to substitute new aircraft for the -400SFs that were originally planned. The -400SFs were conversions from passenger to freighter aircraft that Taikoo (Xiamen) Aircraft Engineering in China undertook for Boeing. Once the new B747-400Fs started to be delivered in the second half of the 2000s

---

1   If the passenger flights were included there were five US airlines on transpacific routes and only one Japanese.

Table 12.2   NCA route development, 1985 to 2000

8 May 1985	Tokyo – San Francisco – New York
30 October 1986	Tokyo – Hong Kong
5 October 1987	Tokyo – Singapore
7 June 1988	Tokyo – Amsterdam
2 November 1989	Tokyo – Singapore – Bangkok – Tokyo
13 June 1990	Tokyo – Seoul
12 February 1991	Tokyo – Chicago – New York – Tokyo
2 April 1991	Tokyo – San Francisco – Los Angeles
22 January 1993	Tokyo – Amsterdam – Milan
6 September 1994	Tokyo – Osaka – Singapore – Bangkok – Tokyo
	Tokyo – Osaka – Singapore – Bangkok – Osaka – Tokyo
	Tokyo – Hong Kong – Osaka
31 October 1994	Tokyo – Osaka – Singapore – Kuala Lumpur – Tokyo
	Tokyo – Bangkok – Kuala Lumpur – Tokyo
8 November 1995	Tokyo – Osaka – Chicago – New York – Osaka – Tokyo
7 October 1996	Tokyo – Manila – Singapore
7 June 1997	Tokyo – Osaka – Anchorage – San Francisco – Los Angeles – San Francisco – Anchorage – Tokyo
12 September 1997	Osaka – Manila – Kuala Lumpur
4 October 1997	Osaka – Anchorage – Amsterdam – Anchorage – Tokyo
10 March 1998 (suspended 31 March 2002)	Tokyo – Osaka – Anchorage – San Francisco – Portland
	Tokyo – San Francisco – Los Angeles – San Francisco – Portland – Anchorage – Tokyo
8 September 1998	Tokyo – Anchorage – Amsterdam – London[*]
27 October 1998	Osaka – Shanghai – Tokyo
1 May 1999	Tokyo – Seoul[**] – Osaka
24 September 2000	Osaka – Frankfurt – Milan – Osaka

Note: * London discontinued in September 2006; ** Seoul discontinued June 2006.

Source: www.nca.aero (History).

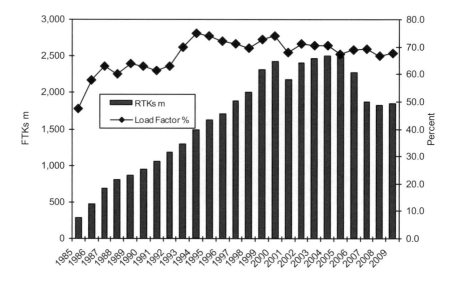

Figure 12.3   Nippon Cargo Airlines traffic and load factor trends, 1985 to 2008

Source: NCA (2010) and IATA WATS.

the problem was the disposal of the higher unit cost -200Fs.[2] It originally planned to retire its last 747-200Fs in August 2008 but it brought this forward to March. A number of these older aircraft were sold or leased to start-ups: Cargo B in Belgium and Jett8 in Singapore. By May 2009, the 10 747-400 were delivered, but the last two were placed with CargoB, a Belgian operator in which NCA bought a share. CargoB filed for bankruptcy in May 2009, and two 747-400 owned by NCA were subsequently stored in the US.

The earlier phase-out meant that additional aircraft were needed to replace the capacity lost and two more B747-400Fs were ordered in June 2006 for delivery in 2008. In the event traffic plummeted at the end of 2008 and this order turned out to have been unnecessary. The carrier currently operates five 747-200Fs and five 747-400Fs and has five more 747-400Fs on order with the manufacturer. It says Boeing has agreed to bring forward the delivery of its last 747-400F by two months, to March 2009, allowing it to complete the renewal of its entire fleet by the end of the next financial year.

NCA was the launch customer with Cargolux for the B747-8F with eight aircraft expected from 2010 onwards. The two airlines worked together on the aircraft's specification and intended to align 'their orders for buyer-furnished equipment

---

2   The values of the -200F had been declining since the beginning of the decade when prices of more than $50 million were being paid in some deals. A 1975 JT9D powered B747-200 freighter was advertised for sale at $8.2 million in September 2007 and this was considerably in excess of current values at the time.

and their planned operating practices' in order to benefit from standardisation and lower operating costs. In August 2007 it exercised options for six more Boeing 747-8 freighters, bringing the total of the type on firm order to 14.

Another key development to affect NCA was the sale of the All Nippon Airways' (ANA) stake of 27.59 percent to NYK Lines in August 2005, giving the latter control. The reason for the sale was ANA having a different view of the future strategic direction of NCA, and at the same time ANA had been expanding its own cargo operations through the acquisition of freighter aircraft (smaller B767s). NCA's losses were already becoming evident at a time when traffic growth was buoyant. ANA set up a joint venture with government-owned Japan Post with a view to leasing ANA's newly acquired freighter fleet to a new jointly owned airline.

In addition to its air services network, NCA also set up truck feeder services, first to feed its San Francisco hub in the early days and most recently the network established in China in 2003. Another truck network was centred on Amsterdam. These truck services carried air cargo at air cargo rates and were usually operated on an airport-to-airport basis.

12.2.3 Regulatory Developments

The problems that NCA faced in obtaining regulatory approval from the Japanese authorities were discussed in section 12.2.1 and further delays arose from the need to negotiate international route rights. The most critical of these was between Japan and the US and these negotiations were at times extremely acrimonious and reflected many similar battles often also involving the US. The backdrop to the problems during the 1980s and again in the 1990s was the original agreement between the US and Japan of the 1950s that was heavily weighted against the Japanese which at that time had a much weakened aviation capability.

A major dispute occurred in ASA negotiations between Japan and the US in 1995. As a result, Federal Express was forced to postpone the scheduled opening of its Subic Bay, Philippines, hub, and the US Clinton administration proposed retaliatory sanctions on Japanese air-cargo carriers. The sanctions would prohibit Japan Airlines and Nippon Cargo Airlines from carrying cargo from certain Asian markets on their scheduled all-cargo services from Japan to the US. FedEx and United Airlines were embroiled in similar disputes with Japan in 1993 and once again the matter was resolved before sanctions threatened against JAL were implemented. Nevertheless, fifth freedoms are the bigger issue. William Kutzke, a former US Department of Transportation lawyer, notes in his book on US-Japan aviation history: 'The US-Japan agreement retains the most extensive network of economically viable beyond rights for two US passenger airlines and one cargo airline that the US has under any agreement.' Edward Oppler, deputy director of the DOT's international aviation office, conceded in a speech: 'The subject of fifth freedom rights probably has been the largest irritant in the US-Japan aviation relationship' (*Airline Business*, August 1995).

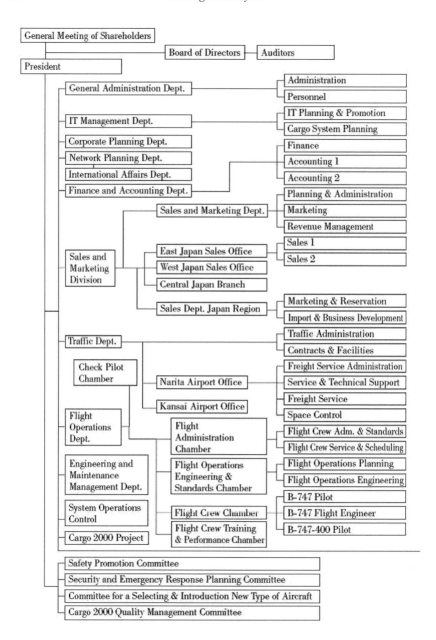

Figure 12.4   Nippon Cargo Airlines Organigram

Source: www.nca.aero.

The new cargo agreement in April 1996 gave Japan Airlines (JAL) the same unlimited fifth-freedom rights with the US as incumbent US cargo carrier FedEx enjoyed in Japan. JAL also receives unlimited co-terminal rights and three additional destinations in the US. In addition, Nippon Cargo Airlines (NCA) received 18 more weekly frequencies, up from 11, and unlimited beyond services. NCA's US destinations could be increased from four to seven. UPS Airlines, in return, was be given access to Kansai with up to 12 weekly flights and beyond rights to two other destinations. UPS was permitted to carry Japanese cargo to one of these beyond destinations six times a week. Incumbent US cargo carriers, FedEx, Northwest Airlines and United Airlines, also had increased flexibility to operate between any US city and three additional Japanese destinations, combined with their existing rights.

12.2.4 Economic and Financial Developments

The two key economic indicators for an airline are unit revenue or yield and unit cost. The ratio of the two gives the break-even load factor, which is defined to be the weight load factor required to equate total traffic revenues with total operating costs:

$= \text{Weight load factor} \div \text{operating ratio}$ .... (1)
$= \text{costs/ATKs} \times \text{RTKs/Revenues}$ .... (2)
$= \text{costs/ATKs} \div \text{Revenues/RTKs}$ .... (3)
$= \text{unit costs} \div \text{Yield}$ .... (4)

Equation (1) means that if the operating ratio is above 100 percent (i.e. in profit) the break-even load factor will be less than the actual load factor. Equations (2) and (3) reformulate and rearrange the terms in equation (1) and give the fourth equation's identity: the break-even load factor is unit costs divided by yield. These are the two key targets of airline management, with reduced costs and/or increased yields resulting in a lower break-even point.

Yields are heavily influenced by competitive pressures, especially on the major trunk routes that NCA served. These included the fuel surcharges that were imposed by all airlines after 9/11, although the amount passed on to and paid by shippers and forwarders usually fell short of the full additional cost of fuel. Figure 12.6 shows the three periods that experienced a sharp reduction in yields: the recessions of the early 1990s and the slump that occurred towards the end of 2008. The break-even load factor settled down between the mid to high 60s in 1990s but jumped to 74 percent in 2005 and 84 percent in 2006.

The first two economic downturns were also followed by periods of operating loss for NCA. The third, at the end of 2008, compounded NCA's financial decline which had already started in 2005 (see Figure 12.5).

NCA's profitability has been severely impacted both by fuel price spikes and international economic and trade downturns. Its financial success is also highly

Moving Boxes by Air

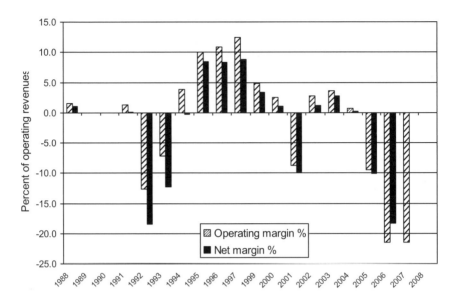

Figure 12.5   Nippon Cargo Airlines margin developments, 1988–2008

Note: Financial year end 31 March.

Source: ICAO and ATI.

dependent on the Japanese economy, and this has been in the doldrums since the late 1990s. Thus NCA did not experience the upturn in the 2003 to 2007 period that airlines with less Japanese exposure did.

Yields trends are largely dictated by international competition and overcapacity relative to demand, and NCA's trend between 2003 and 2007 was not sufficient to cover increased costs (see Figure 12.6).

In 2007 NCA established its own maintenance facility in order to bring in-house the major checks on its B747 fleet. This move was the reverse of the trend in maintenance and overhaul outsourcing that major US and other international airlines had experienced over the past 10 years. However, it has consistently operated a single aircraft type, staying with the Boeing 747 but moving to more efficient versions once they became available. Thus its fuel efficiency has improved significantly over the years, and its order for B747-8Fs will continue this trend. Its marketing emphasises quality of service and it will benefit from code sharing with JAL who are discontinuing freighters. In financial year 2008/2009 NCA invested US$480m in aircraft and associated assets, mainly progress payments on its new Boeing freighters.

NCA's staff numbers advanced from 284 in 1985 to 748 in 2000, and continued growing by 2.9 percent a year from then to 2008, despite serious financial problems. Average salaries increased by only 2.9 percent a year over the six-year period. However, staff productivity had declined by 40 percent from its high in 2000 to 2008, having increased at 8 percent a year in the 15-year period to 2000.

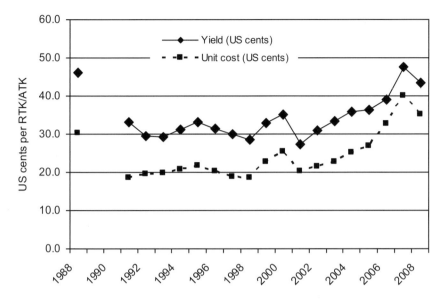

Figure 12.6 Nippon Cargo Airlines yield and unit cost developments, 1988–2008

Source: ICAO Financial Data, NCA (2010) and IATA WATS.

NCA's balance sheet looked reasonably sound at least up the financial year ending 31 March 2007. Both debt/equity ratio and current ratios looked no worse than many airlines. However, since that time the balance sheet was not available through the ICAO and the airline became consolidated with its controlling shareholder, NYK Lines.

The fortunes of NCA contrast with the financial success story of Cargolux, the other launch customer for the B747-8F. The latter benefited from its position in the centre of a growing EU market, while the former was tied to the stagnating Japanese economy, although it might have been able to take more advantage of the growing Chinese market. Both had a single aircraft type fleet but cost control was more evident at Cargolux than NCA who found themselves with an excess of capacity even before the recent downturn. NCA's future is highly uncertain and its fortunes to some extent linked to those of the Japanese economy. If this continues its poor performance NCA will have to rely on sixth freedom traffic via a relative high cost Japanese hub. At the same time it will face increasing competition from lower cost Chinese carriers and powerful multinational integrators.

12.3 Federal Express Case Study

Federal Express has been chosen as an integrator study first because it was the first to use airport hubs to distribute parcel traffic by air and also because its acquisition of Flying Tiger made it a major player internationally. Its path coincided with the first case study, NCA, in that it also wanted restrictions removed in the US/Japan ASA and the lobbying of their respective governments by both carriers resulted in a separate cargo bilateral agreement being signed.

The company is split into three main divisions: FedEx Express, FedEx Ground and FedEx Freight:

FedEx Express offers a wide range of shipping services for delivery of packages and freight. Overnight package services are backed by money-back guarantees and extend to virtually the entire US population. FedEx Express offers three US overnight delivery services: FedEx First Overnight, FedEx Priority Overnight and FedEx Standard Overnight. FedEx Same Day service is available for urgent shipments up to 70 pounds (32 kg) to virtually any US destination. FedEx Express also offers express freight services backed by money-back guarantees to handle the needs of the time-definite global freight market. International express delivery with a money-back guarantee is available to more than 220 countries and territories, with a variety of time-definite services to meet distinct customer needs. FedEx Express also offers a comprehensive international freight service, backed by a money-back guarantee, real-time tracking and advanced customs clearance. Express's highest revenue per package in 2009 was from international priority (IP) freight (US$57.81 in 2009) compared to an average for US domestic of $16.21. The yield on IP was $2.22 per pound or $4.88 per kg. The heavier international air freight achieved a yield of $0.99 or $2.16 per kg. The share of weight in total package volume (excluding international air freight) handled was US domestic 77 percent, IP 14 percent and domestic operations within non-US countries (i.e. the UK, Canada, China and India) with 9 percent.

FedEx Ground operates a multiple hub-and-spoke sorting and distribution system consisting of 520 facilities, including 32 hubs, in the US and Canada. FedEx Ground conducts its operations primarily with approximately 22,500 owner-operated vehicles and 31,500 company-owned trailers. It serves business and residential (home delivery) customers with guaranteed overnight services for packages of up to 150 pounds (68 kg) over sectors up to 400 miles or around 650 kilometres. It is estimated to have increased its share of this US market from 1 percent in 2000 to 22 percent in 2009, but it is still well behind UPS with a current share of 60 percent (and USPS with 18 percent). The yield per package for FedEx Ground in 2009 was $7.70 compared to the composite yield on Express within the US of $16.21.

FedEx Freight Corporation provides a full range of LTL freight services through its FedEx Freight (regional LTL freight services), FedEx National LTL (long-haul LTL freight services) and FedEx Freight Canada businesses. These shipments move largely by truck within North America. The average weight of each LTL shipment in 2009 was 1,126 pounds or 51 kg, with a yield of $0.38 per kg.

Table 12.3   Key Federal Express highlights

1971	Federal Express founded by Fred Smith
1973	Moved to Memphis International Airport
1978	Public listing of its shares on New York Stock Exchange
1981	Official opening of 'superhub' at Memphis International Airport
1986	Hub opened at Newark International Airport
1988	Hubs opened at Oakland and Indianapolis
1989	Acquired Flying Tiger and opened Anchorage hub
1995	Opened an Asia and Pacific hub in Subic Bay International Airport
1997	Opened hub at Fort Worth Alliance Airport
1999	European hub started at Paris Charles de Gaulle Airport
2006	Acquired ANC Holdings and introduced more direct flights to UK airports
2007	Acquired Flying-Cargo Hungary to support Eastern European expansion
2008	Started building new Central and Eastern European hub at Cologne Bonn Airport (due for completion in 2010)
2009	Closed Asia/Pacific hub at Subic Bay Philippines
2009	Opened new Asian hub at Guangzhou Baiyun International Airport in China; also announced start of Indian operations

Source: www.fedex.com.

Table 12.3 lists the major events in FedEx's history, especially the ones that are especially relevant to its air transport operations. It can be seen that the first, and major, US hub at Memphis was followed by other US hubs and later European and Asian hubs. Memphis was chosen for its central position in the US and the fact that there were few passenger flights, the weather was reasonably good and there was plenty of space for expansion. In 2009, FedEx accounted for around three-quarters of all passenger and cargo jet aircraft operations at the airport, and almost all its freight. The European hub in Paris was partly chosen because their preferred UK option was restricted under the Air Services Agreement at that time.[3] Paris is also more central for truck feed and lies next to a major autoroute (highway) system connecting it to France and neighbouring countries. However, it has a smaller presence in Europe than in Asia (the reverse being the case for UPS).

Its Asian hub was moved in 2009 from Subic Bay in the Philippines to south China. This is now much closer to one of the major manufacturing bases in fast

---

3   It has since been opened up under the EU/US open skies agreement.

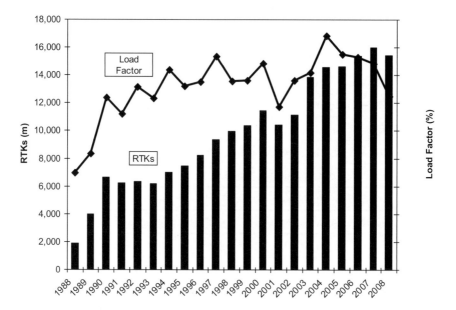

Figure 12.7   Federal Express traffic and load factor trends, 1985 to 2008

Source: ICAO Traffic data.

growing China, and it is also close to Hong Kong, whose airport is more congested and expensive. Additional major sorting and freight handling facilities are located at Narita Airport in Tokyo, for the Asian markets, London Stansted Airport in Europe and Toronto Airport for North America. The Miami Gateway Hub serves the South Florida, Latin American and Caribbean markets.

Figure 12.7 expresses FedEx's expansion in terms of traffic carried and average load factor. The jump in 1990 occurred following the acquisition of Flying Tiger, and this was followed by a period of consolidation and increasing load factors. The next step change occurred in 2003 when the recovery took place following the 9/11 slump.

FedEx has an agreement with the US Postal Service that runs to September 2013 whereby FedEx Express provides domestic air transport services to the US Postal Service, including its first-class, priority and express mail. FedEx Express also has approximately 5,000 drop boxes at US Post Offices in approximately 340 metropolitan areas and provides transportation and delivery for the US Postal Service's international delivery service called 'Global Express Guaranteed'.

At the end of May 2009, FedEx Express employed approximately 93,000 permanent full-time and 47,000 permanent part-time employees, of which approximately 16 percent were employed in the Memphis area, and around 26 percent abroad. Only the pilots are unionised, with attempts to form unions in other staff categories so far unsuccessful.

Table 12.4   FedEx Express fleet, end May 2009

Aircraft type	Owned	Leased	Total	Payload (t)
Boeing MD11	31	26	57	75
Boeing MD10-30 (2)	10	2	12	52
Boeing DC10-30	1	5	6	52
Boeing MD10-10	57		57	49
Boeing DC10-10	1		1	49
Airbus A300-600	35	36	71	39
Airbus A310-200/300	40	16	56	28
Boeing B757-200	24		24	21
Boeing B727-200	77	2	79	17
ATR 72-202/212	13		13	7
ATR 42-300/320	26		26	5
Cessna 208B	242		242	1
Cessna 208A	10		10	1
Total	567	87	654	

Note: MD10 series are converted passenger DC10s.

Source: Federal Express, Form 10K Report, 2008/2009.

In addition to the fleet shown in Table 12.4, FedEx Express had purchase commitments for a further 36 B757F, 30 B777F and two MD11F aircraft. The large number of small aircraft with only around 1 tonne of payload has been an essential part of the integrator's strategy since its early days, in order to feed the major and regional hub airports from small airports within range. This distinguishes them from UPS who rely on trucks, or DHL that operates more in international markets where ownership of aircraft by a foreign airline is difficult.[4] FedEx Express also operated approximately 51,000 ground transport vehicles, including pickup and delivery vans, larger trucks called container transport vehicles and over-the-road tractors and trailers.

Table 12.5 shows the large number of departures with the small feeder aircraft that FedEx operates over an average sector of only 222 km. Almost all the aircraft except the MD-11Fs are used on US domestic sectors, all at what would be regarded by combination carriers as very low average daily utilisation rates.

---

4   DHL tends to contract in such air services, but usually with larger aircraft, and also relies on trucking.

Table 12.5   Federal Express fleet productivity, 2008

	Departures	Stage km	Hours/day
Cessna 208	102,481	222	1.0
B727-200F	44,254	914	2.2
Airbus A310	32,049	1,179	2.7
Airbus A300B4-600	45,967	1,373	4.2
B757-200F	748	1,580	2.8
DC10-10F	43,072	1,588	4.9
DC10-30F	14,074	1,895	6.6
MD11F	40,448	3,809	9.7
Other	43,345	516	
Total	323,093	1,283	3.3

Source: ICAO fleet data.

This is because the aircraft are only used to feed the hubs and operate principally at nighttime (see section 1.6.3 for aircraft scheduling at the Memphis hub). The aircraft are mostly fully depreciated, and probably also purchased as used aircraft. Capital costs are thus low and variable costs are high, a combination that suits low utilisation operations. The B757-200F freighters are mostly converted passenger aircraft and therefore have relatively low capital costs. These are being phased in over the next few years to replace the ageing B727s. The B777F aircraft are new and will be operated over longer hauls and at higher utilisation.

Figure 12.8 shows the integrator's operating and net margins as reported to the ICAO. A large item was included as 'other revenues' and 'other expenses' in each year. Presumably this referred to ground operations. If these revenues and expenses were subtracted from the totals, the operating margin ranged between plus or minus 1 percent from 1990 to 2004 when it increased to 4–5 percent. This may show a better picture of the airline operations.

Figure 12.9 also tries to determine the underlying airline economics of FedEx, through the calculation of three key ratios with the ground revenues and expenses removed. It can be seen that the profitable period of the mid-2000s was achieved through increasing yields faster than unit costs were advancing. Fuel surcharges were applied during this period, and seemed more successful in covering increased fuel costs than all-cargo carriers. Thus break-even load factor dropped to the mid 50 percent range, having been close to 60 percent for most of the other years, except an increase to 64 percent in the year that the IT bubble burst.

Operating costs per ATK rose by 91 percent between 1990 and 2008 or by 75 percent to 2007. FedEx did not report all cost items in 2008 so the trends in each

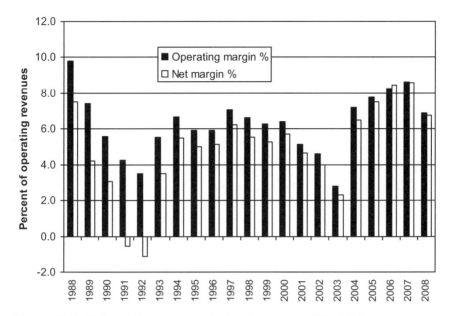

Figure 12.8   Federal Express margin developments, 1988–2008

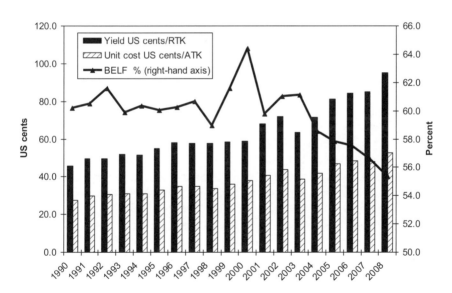

Figure 12.9   Federal Express airline yield, unit cost and break-even load factor, 1990 to 2008

cost item are only up to 2007: the only cost to fall was sales and promotion which declined by 57 percent. As expected fuel rose most evenly without including the steep increases in 2008: up by 127 percent per ATK over the 17-year period. Flight equipment insurance almost tripled, but still remained a small percentage of the total. Flight crew salaries and expenses were up by 43 percent, while aircraft ownership costs only rose by 13 percent (all per ATK). Overall the picture is one of cost control, combined with stable and increasing yields. The latter benefits from a strong retail sector, and the former from lack of unionisation.

12.4 Network Carrier Cargo Subsidiaries

In Chapter 4 attention was drawn to the combination carriers that had established cargo subsidiaries. Lufthansa was the first and the ones that followed tended to be from the same strategic alliance (Star). The two major ones, Lufthansa and Singapore Airlines, will be analysed below, leaving out the smaller ones: SAS Cargo with annual revenues of US$520m in 2008, and LAN Cargo (a member of oneworld) with US$747m. Others such as Air India and Aeroflot were formed more recently and little data is available.

12.4.1 Lufthansa Cargo

Almost half Lufthansa Cargo's 2009 revenues were earned on Asian routes despite the fact that these were most affected by the slump: Asia (48 percent), Americas (32 percent), Europe (11 percent) and the Middle East and Africa (9 percent).

The 50 percent share in Aerologic (the joint venture with DHL) started operations midway through 2009, resulting in the termination of previous chartering of aircraft to them.

Table 12.6 shows that Lufthansa Cargo expanded revenues in the four years to 2009, when its markets experienced a severe downturn. Yields had been fairly constant but fuel surcharges captured much of the cost increases, mainly from fuel, and the operating profit increased. Staff productivity had been improving but, with traffic down over the last part of 2008 and 2009, this declined sharply. Some benefit was obtained by staff going on short time, and all overtime and outside contractors were discontinued. The operating margin in 2009 was a negative 8.4 percent, with traffic down by 10.4 percent and yield by almost 30 percent.

Table 12.7 shows the breakdown of Lufthansa Cargo's main operating cost items. The fuel price dropped sharply and some of this flowed through to lower operating costs, depending on hedging loss allocations. Its share of operating costs also fell because of a decline in flights operated. Employee costs were also down, based on lower staff numbers and less hours worked per employee. Fees are the amounts paid for airport, ATC and ground handling services, which also depend on the number of flights operated. The majority of the item 'charter' covers the payments to Lufthansa passenger for space on their passenger flights, with the rest the chartering and wet leasing of freighters. Depreciation is on the MD-11F aircraft which are owned by the company, the grounding of some of these in 2009 obviously making no impact on these fixed costs.

Table 12.6 Lufthansa Cargo financial and operating data, 2005 to 2009

	2005	2006	2007	2008	2009
ATKs (m)	n/a	11,973	12,236	12,584	11,681
Freight tonne-kms (m)	7,829	8,103	8,451	8,283	7,425
Freight tonnes (000)	n/a	1,759	1,805	1,692	1,519
Cargo revenue (US$m)	3,408	3,589	3,765	4,270	2,715
Operating result (US$m)	134	103	187	241	-238
Operating margin (%)	4	3	5	6	-9
Net result (US$m)	n/a	n/a	213	277	-229
Cargo yield (US cents)	43.5	44.3	44.5	51.6	36.6
Load factor (%)	n/a	67.7	69.1	65.8	63.6
Employees (average)	4,768	4,671	4,607	4,568	4,619
RTKs per employee (000)	1,642	1,735	1,834	1,813	1,607
Average trip (km)	n/a	4,606	4,682	4,897	4,888

Source: Lufthansa Cargo website.

Table 12.7 Lufthansa Cargo operating cost breakdown, 2008 and 2009

	2008 (€ m)	%	2009 (€ m)	%
Fuel cost	573	21.9	365	17.0
Employee cost	327	12.5	311	14.5
Fees	291	11.1	238	11.1
Charter	923	35.3	820	38.2
Depreciation	123	4.7	123	5.7
Other	380	14.5	289	13.5
Total	2,617	100.0	2,146	100.0

Source: Lufthansa Cargo website.

Unfortunately no breakdown of revenue is available, for example between freighters and passenger flights. This might have shown how the company handled the slump in terms of transfer pricing between the two parts of the group. When the subsidiary was originally established it bought space from the passenger side at a somewhat lower cost than fully allocated according to the methods outlined in Chapter 11, with the cargo capacity based on full passenger loads. Freighter services were cut back with four MD-11F aircraft grounded (out of a total fleet of 18 aircraft). Utilisation was also down from an average of 14 hours a day to only 11 hours a day.

12.4.2 SIA Cargo

Singapore Airlines transferred its cargo business or division into a 100 percent owned subsidiary on 1 July 2001. Singapore Airlines Cargo Private Limited was the name of this company, which was responsible for operating the fleet of freighter aircraft and managing the cargo holds of the passenger fleet. Its freighters were leased from its parent company. Its revenues included revenues from cargo carried on passenger flights for which it paid the main operating company for the space. This payment amounted to S$1,347 million in FY2008-09 or 45 percent of its turnover, the same sum accounted for as revenue to arrive at the profitability of the passenger business. Load factors tend to be higher on freighter flights (see Table 12.8).

Table 12.8   Singapore Airlines load factors by product and type of flight, 2008–2009

	All-cargo flights	Pax flights (passengers + cargo)	Pax flights (cargo)	Passenger flights (passengers)
Available tonne-kms (m)	5,654	18,709	7,355	11,354
Revenue tonne-kms (m)	3,685	12,810	3,905	8,905
Load factor (%)	65.2	68.5	53.1	78.4

Source: Singapore Airlines Annual Report, 2008–2009.

SIA Cargo, unlike Lufthansa Cargo, does not publish separate accounts and generally provides less information on its subsidiary. Since 2005 its capacity and traffic has remained fairly constant, with some growth in revenues in the first part of this period (see Table 12.9). It has not been particularly profitable over the period, with losses in three out of the five years, with a sharp drop in 2008, with the increase in fuel prices. Staff numbers were finally reduced in 2009/2010, after a number of years of declining staff productivity.

In 2007 the cargo airline's loss led to a reappraisal of its strategy. One of the outcomes was to introduce greater flexibility in its freighter schedule, to take into account the fact that off-peak traffic was often 20 percent or so below peak levels. By reducing freighter capacity in the off-peak the airline could use the freed-up capacity for charters.

Table 12.9   SIA Cargo financial and operating data, 2005/2006 to 2009/2010

	2005/2006	2006/2007	2007/2008	2008/2009	2009/2010
ATKs (m)	12,379	12,890	12,788	12,293	10,510
Freight tonne-kms (m)	7,871	7,995	7,959	7,299	6,659
Freight tonnes (000)	1,249	1,285	1,308	1,220	1,122
Cargo revenue (US$m)	1,953	2,111	2,261	2,064	1,640
Operating result (US$m)	105	-21	90	-170	-104
Operating margin (%)	5	-1	4	-8	-6
Net result (US$m)	81	20	79	-107	-106
Cargo yield (US cents)	24.8	26.4	28.4	28.3	24.6
Employees (average)	987	1,086	1,096	1,073	937
RTKs per employee (000)	7,975	7,362	7,262	6,802	7,107
Average trip (km)	6,304	6,222	6,085	5,985	5,933

Source: ATI and airline annual reports.

This chapter has identified some of the factors that explained the air cargo industry's poor financial performance. Productivity and efficiency have often been increasing but such efforts have been negated by sudden increases in input prices, especially fuel, and the introduction of new costs for security. Anti-trust fines have hit some at a time when they are not in a financially strong position to pay them. On the other hand capacity has expanded too fast on the upswing of the cycle, and been cut back too slowly during the downturns. The barriers to entry by new airlines are not high. A recent book entitled *Why Can't We Make Money in Aviation?* puts much of the blame on government-owned airlines and attraction of the industry to rich industrialists (Pilarski, 2007). These aim to have some fun rather than make much money, and often succeed in losing much of what they have made elsewhere. The author also points out that there are some success stories such as Southwest, and this has also been true for air cargo with Cargolux. These are the role models for the new entrants but in air cargo there may not be too much room for many of these.

Chapter 13
Air Cargo and the Environment

13.1 Background

There has been a growing interest in the environmental impact of aviation, both in terms of noise and aircraft engine emissions. Discussions have included both mitigation measures and methods of internalisation of these external costs. Climate change has been the particular focus following the United Nations Framework Convention on Climate Change (UNFCCC) and subsequent Kyoto Protocol. The need for action at a global level has been further supported by more recent studies, for example from the UK Stern Report.[1] Air transport attracts attention far in excess of its current contribution to CO_2 emissions first because it is a high profile industry; and second because of its impact (still very uncertain) on climate change from NO_X and contrails at cruise altitude which result in a multiplier effect (so-called 'radiative forcing' effect).

Increasing concern has also focused on improving air quality around airports, although it is often hard to estimate exactly where the pollution comes from. NO_X is the worse pollutant in this respect and efforts to reduce this will also be discussed below.

Aircraft noise disturbance in the vicinity of airports has been reduced considerably over the past 30 years, and aircraft with high by-pass engines have been introduced. For example the 85 dB(A) noise contour produced at take-off by a B747-100 was 5.15 square miles, a B747-200 4.24 square miles and a B747-400 only 2.89 square miles (all at MTOW). The approach noise contour is much smaller and the B747-400's was half that of the first B747 model. Noise is still a concern as urban areas have crept up to and around large airports, and this will be discussed first, followed by emissions. Land use planning is another way to approach noise nuisance around airports, but this has not generally been very successful.

13.2 Aircraft Noise

13.2.1 Noise Certification of Aircraft

Reduction of aero-engine and aircraft noise has been achieved over the past 30 years by means of imposing stricter standards for the certification of new aircraft,

---

1 *Stern Review on the Economics of Climate Change.* Report to UK Treasury and Cabinet Office, October 2006.

the total ban by the EU and US on aircraft that do not meet certain standards, and locally by means of noise surcharges and night bans.

Noise certification standards have been agreed through the ICAO and implemented at the national level. These standards are contained in the Annex 16 to the Convention on International Civil Aviation described in Chapter 3. The first generation of jet-powered aeroplanes was not covered by Annex 16 and these are consequently referred to as non-noise certificated (NNC) aeroplanes (e.g. Boeing 707 and Douglas DC-8). The initial standards for jet-powered aircraft designed before 1977 were included in Chapter 2 of Annex 16. These included the Boeing 727 and the Douglas DC-9, some of which were later re-engined or hushkitted to meet later standards. Subsequently, newer aircraft were required to meet the stricter standards contained in Chapter 3 of the Annex. The Boeing 737-300/400, Boeing 767 and Airbus A319 are examples of 'Chapter 3' aircraft types. In June 2001, the Council adopted a new Chapter 4 noise standard, more stringent than that contained in Chapter 3. Starting at the beginning of January 2006, the new standard became applicable to newly certificated aeroplanes and to Chapter 3 aeroplanes for which re-certification to Chapter 4 is requested. In 2008, just under 20 percent of the world fleet did not meet Chapter 4 standards.

These standards were incorporated into national legislation, and, for example, became known in the US Federal Aviation Regulations as Stage 2 (Chapter 2) and Stage 3 (Chapter 3). This approach to noise reduction is slow, but once aircraft are replaced the effect is quite dramatic as the examples in the introduction showed. In order to speed up the phase out of Chapter 2 aircraft both the US and the EU introduced a ban on such flights, the US from the beginning of the year 2000 and the EU from April 2002.

More immediate relief can be obtained at a local level through either economic incentives or operational procedures which can also be more cost effective for an airline. These are discussed next, with most examples from European airports since it is these that are more often than not located in densely populated areas.

13.2.2 Noise Operational Restrictions

Landing and take-off noise abatement procedures are applied at many European airports. In all cases, these take the form of procedures for take-off and landing, in most cases there are also runways designated either for take-offs or landings, but in only a few cases are there limits on the maximum noise levels allowed.

Low noise approach paths usually take the form of a steeper descent during the first phase of the approach (5–6°), combined with a normal second phase (3°). The advantage of this two-segment approach is that noise is reduced, say, at around 3–5 nautical miles from the runway threshold, with the effect of higher altitude outweighing the greater noise from increased flap settings. Estimates of noise reduction using this procedure in the US ranged from 10 EPNdB at 5 nautical miles to 6 EPNdB at 3 nautical miles. Other procedures are low drag approaches with reduced flap settings, but this is not thought to give a very significant improvement. Continuous descent approaches also generate less noise from lower power settings, while at the same time being more economic for operators. Intercepting the ILS glide-slope further out and at a higher altitude will also give some relief to communities living closer to the airport, but may increase the noise impact somewhat on those living slightly further out. On balance, however, there might be a small net gain.

Procedures for lowering the landing gear closer to the runway threshold would also reduce noise somewhat. This has no significant impact on costs, but probably also has little impact in reducing noise nuisance. The use of reverse thrust on landing generates about 10 dB less noise than produced by the engines operated normally during take-off mode, but the noise is sudden and could cause nuisance to surrounding communities, especially at night. Thus a night ban on the use of this was found to be quite common at EU airports. The impact of this on airline costs was thought to be relatively neutral: the increased cost of maintaining brakes is balanced by the reduced costs of engine maintenance. In terms of safety, however, safety margins are likely to be higher using reverse thrust, with brakes still available as back-up. The use of brakes only, with reverse thrust as a back-up, is not as effective an option, since the seconds lost in getting engines from idle to full power would be critical in any emergency.

Noise can be reduced by cutting back power during take-off, once the aircraft has reached a safe operating altitude. Reduced power is then used until the aircraft is no longer over a populated area, when full power can be resumed. This procedure may result in some overall reduction in the noise impact, and will also re-distribute noise away from those living nearer the runway threshold to communities further away from the airport, who will be affected by aircraft flying at a lower altitude.

Low noise departures can also be made by increasing the angle of ascent. But there is a trade-off between the lower speed that is used in connection with the higher rate of climb, and the higher speed associated with the lower rate of climb. The same thrust is used in both cases. The first procedure imposes a higher noise nuisance over a shorter period of time, while the second a lower noise over a longer period of time. The precise impact will depend on the noise impact measure used, but this suggests that the net improvement may not be very large. Continuous descent approach reduces noise and gives cost savings to airlines: FedEx has been using these at its Memphis hub and has saved 2.5 minutes for each flight, which is equivalent to US$105 million between 2006 and 2009. However, busy airports may not be in a position to allow such approaches.

Noise preferential routes are also used at many EU airports, designed to minimise noise exposure to more densely populated communities. Short/medium haul aircraft tend to be more manoeuvrable, and thus find these routings easier to comply with, compared to heavier long-haul aircraft such as B747s that tend to be flown by cargo operators. The cost implications of such routes are difficult to estimate, since they would sometimes mean a greater distance flown and at other times a shorter distance.

Noise preferential runways are another way to reduce the impact of noise over more densely populated areas. A number of airports designate particular runways for either take-off or landings, so as to minimise the noise exposure experienced by more densely populated communities. The main examples of this in Europe are:

- Amsterdam (one runway used only for take-offs);
- Frankfurt (one runway used only for take-offs);
- London Heathrow.

At Heathrow, each of the two parallel runways is operated in either take-off or landing mode, so as to reduce the continuous exposure to both take-off and landing noise (segregated mode operations). The runway mode is switched every 12 hours.

These measures do not have any significant direct cost impact on airlines, but they do reduce the effective number of peak hour movements. Since some of these airports are also slot coordinated, this limits expansion and increased frequency possibilities, and also leads to greater congestion. Cutting down on the use of APUs at airports also saves fuel, and FedEx has saved 5.5 million gallons of fuel in this way.

13.2.3 Noise Penalties

Noise penalties or fines are levied at some airports, usually because an aircraft had deviated from the required flight path, and thus has probably caused a noise nuisance to a community that the flight path was designed to avoid. Penalties might also be levied on aircraft that exceed specified noise parameters, with a separate level for daytime and nighttime operations.

Noise penalties can only be applied where the airport has the necessary noise measuring equipment, and can link noise infringements to the radar track of identifiable aircraft and airlines. Some airports monitor noise on a 24-hour basis, but have not imposed penalties (e.g. Hamburg). Others such as Frankfurt do so, and publish lists of offenders, but also do not impose penalties. Other airports may be allowed to impose fines, but do not in practice do so.

Since 1990 a noise monitoring system has been developed around Brussels Airport. It consists of 21 noise-monitoring terminals (NMT) that continually register the aircraft noise as it is heard on the ground. The noise meters are connected to a central computer that receives and processes the noise data from the various NMTs. The same computer also receives and processes the flight data registered by the Belgocontrol air traffic control centre (CANAC) at the airport. Flight data include information on the type and route of each aircraft. The link between the individual flight data and the noise data makes it possible to map aircraft that deviate from the normal route ('corridor') or produce an abnormal amount of noise.

13.2.4 Noise-Related Charges

Some airports impose aircraft-related noise surcharges or discounts (incentives), usually linked to the aircraft weight based landing fee. This is sometimes structured as a surcharge or discount on the normal landing fee, and is sometimes incorporated in the landing fee calculation. Surcharges and discounts are usually designed to be revenue neutral, or not result in any net increase in aeronautical revenues. In some cases, however, additional revenues might be generated in order to finance noise insulation schemes in the surrounding community affected by the noise.

Airports generally classify aircraft for noise charging purposes according to their acoustical characteristics. Landing fees and night surcharges might be differentiated or different factors applied to the basic landing fee (see section 13.1.4).

It should be noted here that there is always the possibility that the normal landing charge or passenger departure fee might include a hidden amount that is required to cover environmental programmes. These might be noise insulation schemes, or such measures as airport garbage recycling, environmental impact statements or planning enquiries. Generally, it is unlikely that this would be significant, but new airports (e.g. Munich) or facilities (the second runway at Manchester) have certainly in the past incurred substantial environmentally-related costs.

13.2.5 Night Curfews and/or Restrictions

Around half of cargo flights in the Eurocontrol area occur at night, with the majority of long-haul cargo flights at night (Leleu and Marsh, 2009). Similar patterns of operation occur in North America and in parts of the world where integrators have a large presence. This type of operator has a need for small freighter feeder flights, often preferring night operation.

Many airports have some night curfews or restrictions. These might be a total night ban for all or noisier aircraft (with night defined as anything from seven to 14 hours), or operations limited to certain runways. In the UK, the London airports and Manchester Airport have night quota systems. Night restrictions might be one or more of the following:

- night quotas;
- night surcharges and discounts;
- night curfews and restrictions on aircraft movements;
- preferred runway use at night;
- reverse thrust restrictions.

All the above will be discussed here, with the exception of the night surcharges and discounts, which were covered in section 13.1.2.

The UK is the only country so far to introduce noise quotas, and these only apply at the three main London airports of Heathrow, Gatwick and Stansted. The detailed application of these, in terms of the system of aircraft classification, is similar to that shown in Table 13.1. The quota system places an upper limit for each summer and winter season on both air transport movements and noise quota (the product of an aircraft movement and its noise quota count). Very few aircraft have a quota count of zero (although there have been discussions about including very quiet aircraft types such as the BAe 146 in the zero class), with all jet movements at night contributing to the total.

At present, the night slot allocation system is not linked to aircraft noise. This is operated by Airport Co-ordination Ltd, in accordance with the EU regulation on slot allocation at coordinated airports. The three London airports which come under the night quota system are all slot coordinated. The allocation of night slots or movements is currently based on the overall usage of slots throughout the year, under a *local rule* provision. This means that short-haul commuter airlines have a high entitlement, for which they themselves probably have little need, whereas lower frequency charter operators have a smaller entitlement even though they have a far greater requirement for night movements.

Night curfews or restricted night operations are found at many European airports. The most common form that this takes is a night ban on Chapter 2 aircraft, a ban on some Chapter 3 aircraft over a more limited time period, or a total ban on landings with all aircraft types. Airports operating the system have a fixed quota for each of the summer and winter seasons. As each nighttime aircraft movement takes place, an amount of this quota is used depending on the classification of the aircraft. For example, the Boeing 747-400 is classed as QC/2 on landing and QC/4 on take-off, while the much larger Airbus 380 is rated QC/0.5 on landing and QC/2 on take-off. The quieter A380 aircraft therefore use up an airport's noise quota between a quarter and half of the rate of the 747, thus providing airlines with an incentive to operate quieter types of aircraft. Subject to some limited carry-over provisions, when the airport's quota has been fully used up, no more nighttime movements are allowed to take place. In practice, the airport spreads the quota so that it is used evenly across the season.

Brussels is another airport with a quota count system and is one of the strictest airports in Europe in terms of noise, especially during nighttime. In October 2009 its noise quota system became more stringent: at night (between 11 p.m. and 6 a.m.) and in the early morning (between 6 a.m. and 7 a.m.) the maximum authorised noise quota count was reduced from 12 to 8 and from 24 to 12 respectively. Quota count restrictions also apply during between 7 a.m. and 9 p.m. and in the evening, between 9 p.m. and 11 p.m. The overall noise quota of all individual movements during the total of nights is restricted per aviation season. The use of less noisy aircraft increases the possible number of flights.

Table 13.1 gives a range of quota counts for selected aircraft at Brussels Airport. These ranges depend on MTOW and engine type and include cargo aircraft. It can be seen that four-engined wide-bodied aircraft use a large amount of quota for each movement, particularly take-offs. On the other hand, the B777 is much quieter and compares favourably with some medium-haul aircraft.

Table 13.1   Quota Count (QC) for selected aircraft types at Brussels Airport, 2010

	QC departure	QC arrival
A300B	9.9–11.1	4.7–7.6
A319	1.5–3.5	0.9–1.3
A330-300	7.9–12.3	1.9–2.9
B767-300	6.3–10.6	1.9–9.2
B747-200	43.2–70.8	7.9–18.2
B747-400	18.5–27.1	4.3–10.2
B777-200	6.5–11.7	2.5–3.5
MD-11	10.7–11.9	10.2–11.7

Source: Brussels Airport.

13.3 Air Transport's Existing Contribution to Global CO_2 Emissions

13.3.1 Global CO_2 Emissions and Fuel Efficiency

Previous estimates of aviation's contribution to climate change from CO_2 emissions have not separated out air cargo from aviation in general. The widely quoted figure from the IPCC was an aviation contribution to total anthropomorphic emissions of 2.4 percent in 1992.[2] Aviation here includes a contribution of around 10 percent from military aircraft emissions.

More recent estimates for 2002 are now available, but these show little change in aviation's overall contribution: 2 percent (rounded from 2.3 percent).[3] This study did consider freighter aircraft, estimated at 7.6 percent of the civil aviation fleet, but converted their capacity into equivalent available seat-kms (ASKs) to apply to fuel efficiency data per ASK. Because the most recent year for global data is 2002, this will be used for the estimates below for the air freight industry.

In contrast, shipping is estimated to account for around 4 percent of global CO_2 emissions.[4] Furthermore, over the past 10 years world maritime dry cargo traffic has increased by 5.4 percent a year, compared to air cargo's growth of 5.1 percent a year.[5]

---

2 *Aviation and the Global Atmosphere*, Inter-governmental Panel on Climate Change (IPCC), 1999.

3 AERO2k Global Aviation Emissions Inventories for 2002 and 2025, QinetiQ/04/01113, 2004.

4 John Vidal, Environmental Editor, *Guardian*, 3 March 2007.

5 Boeing World Air Cargo Forecast 2006/2007, p. 5.

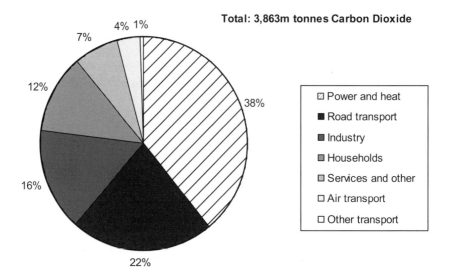

Figure 13.1   EU-25 CO₂ emissions by sector, 2004

Figure 13.1 shows the emissions by sector for the 25 countries of the EU. Air transport only accounted for 4 percent of 2004 CO_2 emissions, or 139 million tonnes, compared to 22 percent for road transport (859 million tonnes), or over six times the air transport contribution.

Previous studies have focused on the total air transport contribution to global emissions, but so far no estimates have been made for air cargo alone. This is addressed in the analysis that follows.

Table 13.2   Freighter flights by region of major airline base, 2002

	World	US	Asia	Europe
Total freighter ATKs* (m)	103,307	52,705	27,098	23,503
US gallons consumed (000)	4,608,730	2,470,865	1,206,510	931,355
ATKs per US gallon	22.4	21.3	22.5	25.2
Average load factor (%)	72	60	71	72
RTKs* per US gallon	16.2	12.8	16.0	18.3

Note: * ATKs is available tonne-kms or available capacity, RTKs is revenue tonne-kms or traffic carried.

Source: DOT Form 41, AEA and ICAO.

The coverage of Table 13.2 is larger in terms of revenue tonne-kms (RTKs) than the reported figures from the IATA and ICAO, and thus provides a very full account of world freighter aircraft movements.[6] Total world fuel gallons consumed by freighters is converted into Teragrams (tonnes x 10^6) in Table 13.3, where it can be seen that freighters represented only 6.4 percent of the total global consumption (and of course a similar CO_2 emissions impact).

Table 13.3   Global aviation fuel used by type of flight, 2002

	Fuel used (Tg)	% share	Fuel used (Tg)	% share
	Scenario A		Scenario B	
Civil aviation				
Passenger flights: passengers	113.0	64.4	139.5	79.5
Passenger flights: cargo	28.9	16.5	2.4	1.4
Freighter flights	14.1	8.0	14.1	8.0
Military aviation	19.5	11.1	19.5	11.1
Total	175.5	100.0	175.5	100.0

Source: QinetiQ/04/01113, 2004 and data from Table 1; A = fully allocated fuel; B = incremental fuel only.

Freighters were only 9 percent of civil aviation fuel used, although they accounted for 18 percent of passenger and cargo RTKs. This is because most jet freighters fly long-haul with above average fuel efficiency. The QinetiQ study quoted in Table 13.3 estimated that the overall fuel used per payload tonne-km in 2002 was 0.36. This is equivalent 8.5 RTKs per US gallon, well below the freighter average in all regions (see Table 13.4). The US region's average fuel efficiency was well below the other two major regions because of the greater use of smaller (short/medium haul) aircraft and also older aircraft (e.g. B727-100F), many of which have since been retired. Freighters used in Europe were mainly long-haul B747 and MD11 types with feeder sectors operated by trucks.

So far the fuel used to carry air cargo has only been estimated for freighters. However, 51 percent of air cargo traffic (freight tonne-kms) is carried on passenger flights, with this payload accounting for 20.4 percent of the total passenger and

---

6   Freighter flights operated by jet aircraft outside these three main areas have been excluded, but these are often ad hoc or seasonal charters, and only a small part of the world total; fuel efficient turbo-prop freighters have also been excluded, but these are mostly operated by integrators at very low daily utilisation and are unlikely to amount to more than 1–2 percent of the total in terms of fuel consumption.

Table 13.4   Jet freighter aircraft, estimated fuel consumption, 2002*

	Total block hours	US gallons used (000)	RTKs (m)	RTKs/ gallon
North America:				
B747-100/200F	180,461	644,338	8,267	12.8
B747-400F	26,667	77,474	1,590	20.5
B757F	111,158	122,528	1,596	13.0
B767F	101,937	161,727	2,300	14.2
MD-11F	163,750	403,674	7,085	17.6
A300F	109,550	175,301	2,104	12.0
A310F	63,242	98,708	908	9.2
DC-10F	179,420	400,585	5,084	12.7
B727-100F	43,230	43,647	207	4.7
B727-200F	159,720	220,901	1,151	5.2
DC-8-70F ·	56,934	92,748	879	9.5
DC-8-60F	29,234	29,234	369	12.6
Total/average North America	*1,225,303*	*2,470,865*	*31,540*	*12.8*
Europe:				
B747-100/200F	140,947	546,315	8,829	16.2
B747-400F	64,456	206,045	4,449	21.6
MD-11F	68,292	173,929	3,655	21.0
B757F	6,236	5,066	82	16.1
Total/average Europe	*279,931*	*931,355*	*17,014*	*18.3*
Asia:				
B747-100/200F	164,482	605,709	9,050	14.9
B747-400F	130,441	551,913	9,239	16.7
MD-11F	18,918	48,888	1,074	22.0
Total/average Asia	*313,841*	*1,206,510*	*19,363*	*16.0*
Total/average major regions	*1,819,075*	*4,608,730*	*67,917*	*14.7*

Note: * Some turbo-props operated especially in North America; for example FedEx-operated 247 Cessna 208B single-engined freighters, but only for an average of 1.3 hours per day totalling around 4.7m gallons (adding only 1 percent to the world total).

Source: US DOT Form 41, Association of European Airlines, IATA, ICAO.

cargo RTKs on those flights. A simplistic approach would be to allocate the 141.9 Tg of fuel used on passenger flights between the two payloads based on their 20.4 percent RTK share. This would give the combined air cargo share of global aviation fuel use of 24.5 percent (Scenario A in Table 13.3).

An alternative approach would be based on the fact that the passenger flights operated for the passenger travel market (and aircraft and schedules selected for this market). Many of these flights would be operated even without air cargo. Thus the cargo impact is the incremental fuel needed to carry the additional air cargo payload. This has been estimated using the B747-400 as a typical aircraft, with the resultant combined impact of 9.4 percent shown in Table 13.3 as Scenario B.

From Table 13.3, given aviation's 2002 contribution to global CO_2 emissions of 2.3 percent, the air cargo part of that would range from 0.3 percent to 0.6 percent. The climate effects of radiative forcing are still subject to a high degree of scientific uncertainty. The latest best estimate for the multiplier for aviation is 1.9,[7] which would increase air cargo's 2002 impact to between 0.6 percent and 1.1 percent.

13.3.2 Operational and Regulatory Constraints

Air cargo's current contribution to global emissions is inflated by both operational and regulatory constraints. Lack of airport and ATC infrastructure leads to congestion and the additional fuel burn associated with holding in the air and on the ground. Furthermore, many routes are flown less directly than they technically could be due to military zones and other governmental restrictions.

Regulatory constraints also affect the pattern of operations that airlines can offer to make most efficient use of aircraft capacity and thus fuel and emissions. In many parts of the world air traffic rights are still based on bilateral agreements between two countries, and an air cargo service that combined traffic rights between three or four countries (in the same way as for shipping) is often impossible. For example the eastbound transpacific route air cargo traffic is estimated to be almost twice the westbound flow (see Chapter 1). Thus operating on a strictly bilateral basis would severely limit the average load factor achievable over the route by up to 20 percentage points. Attempts to fill up the emptier directional flights, if at all possible, lead to significant yield dilution. Operating on a multilateral basis with round-the-world flights or triangular flights via Australia would improve load factors and fuel efficiency.

13.3.3 Future Global CO_2 Emissions Scenarios

Trying to estimate the future share of aviation emissions in the world total is a difficult task even over shorter timescales. Forecasting aviation emissions has been undertaken by a number of organisations, mostly taking traffic growth of around 5 percent a year and fuel efficiency improvements of between 1–2 percent a year.

---

7   Sausen et al. (2005) which updated the IPCC (1999) estimates.

The IPCC (1999) forecast an increase of aviation emissions' share from 2.4 percent in 1992 to between 2 percent and 10 percent in 2050, or between 4 percent and 17 percent with the inclusion of the radiative forcing effect. More recent forecasts of aviation's contribution were done by QinetiQ for the UK government, and for IPCC. These were for five cases for 2030, ranging from no improvements in technology to a US$100 carbon tax. Growth rates in world fuel burn ranged from 2.5 percent to 4.3 percent a year.

An even wider range of forecasts has been put forward for global emissions. These are generally expected to increase between 2002 and 2020 (by between 1.4 percent and 2.3 percent a year according to one report[8]), and, for some scenarios, then start to decline. For other scenarios increases continue well beyond that year, so aviation's share is subject to huge variation in both denominator and numerator. This gives an even larger range of final outcomes. It is thus possible to arrive at very large aviation impacts by judicious selection of assumptions to suit a particular viewpoint.

In general, however, if all polluters are required to pay for emissions, whether by tax or cap-and-trade (for example the EU Emissions Trading Scheme), it is likely that aviation's share will rise somewhat from present levels because of its higher rate of growth and since other industries will be faced with lower abatement costs at the margin.

13.3.4 Investment in Greater Fuel Efficiency for the Future

Around half of freight traffic is carried by air on long-haul freighters. Some short-haul freighters are operated by integrators for high priority shipments, but these aircraft tend to be operated on a low frequency basis. Other freight is carried on passenger aircraft which are selected and scheduled for passenger markets, but which provide cargo capacity on routes which could not support freighters.

Long-haul freighters tend to be already very fuel efficient. However, freighter flights also tend to be more fuel intensive than passenger flights because costs such as cabin attendants, catering and passenger-related airport charges are not incurred. For example, fuel accounted for 38 percent of cargo specialist Cargolux's 2005 operating costs compared to only 25 percent for a passenger airline with a similar average sector length, Virgin Atlantic (also in 2005). High fuel prices tend to force the retirement of uneconomic aircraft, as well as encourage airlines to operate as fuel efficiently as they safely can (e.g. continuous descent approaches, direct routings etc.).

Airlines will soon have replaced older DC-10s and B747-100/200s with much more fuel efficient B777 and B747-8 freighters. Further gains in both fuel efficiency and the emission of other greenhouse gases is expected from the use of bio-fuels, new engines, and blended-wing body designs. Much has been achieved by the larger air cargo specialists over the past decade or so. For example, Cargolux

---

8   IPCC Special Report of Working Group III, Emissions scenarios, 2000.

has moved from a fleet of two B747-400Fs and five B747-200F in 1996 to its 2006 fleet of 14 B747-400Fs. This has resulted in an increase in its fuel efficiency expressed in terms of ATKs per US gallon consumed across the fleet of around 40 percent, or just over 3 percent a year.

Some airlines have introduced fuel efficiency targets. One of UPS's Key Peformance Indicators (KPIs) is aviation gallons burned per 100 available ton-miles. This was reduced by 33 percent between 1990 and 2008, mainly by phasing out thirstier B727s and DC8s. The target is to reduce it by 38 percent between 1990 and 2020, or by a further 7 percent between 2008 and 2020. In other words, much of the original target from the 1990 Kyoto baseline had already been achieved by 2008, and thus what remained did not look too challenging. In any case the original target amounted only 1.6 percent a year, well below the growth in traffic. However, UPS was the launch customer for a low emissions version of the GE CF6-80C2 engine for its B767 freighters, and it is introducing alternative fuel ground vehicles at various hubs. FedEx plan to increase fuel efficiency of their air operations by 20 percent between 2005 and 2020, and supports the goal to move to 20 percent of aviation fuel from bio-fuels by 2030.

Lufthansa Cargo's average fuel efficiency per FTK declined from 237 grams in 1998 to 170 grams in 2009, a reduction of 28 percent, or 3.0 percent a year. A further reduction of 25 percent is targeted for 2020, when by which time it plans to use bio-fuels for 10 percent of its needs. British Airways had a target of a 25 percent reduction by 2025, although it is expressed in emissions per passenger-km, and is the IATA target. Cathay Pacific and Singapore Airlines also follow the IATA target.

13.3.5 The Air Cargo Network and Industry Fuel Efficiency

The ability to offer sufficiently high frequency of service and large enough aircraft to be cost effective is crucial to scheduled airline operations. Because many origin/destination markets do not generate sufficient volume for such operations, airlines combine various markets at a hub airport. This gives one-stop service to a large number of markets that could not otherwise be served. This is true of both the passenger and cargo business. Airlines thus offer a network of flights focused on one or more hubs.

On the passenger side, hubs are often served by feeder services with small aircraft. Convenient connections are provided to other short-haul and long-haul flights. On the other hand, cargo hubs tend to be fed by shorter haul truck services rather than flights. The reason for this is the lower unit costs of operating trucks, and also the somewhat lower time sensitivity of cargo in general. Especially in Europe, services are operated by airlines on an airport-to-airport basis by truck instead of aircraft. Connections are provided mostly to/from long-haul passenger and freighter flights. The dominant carrier at the world's busiest airports was discussed in section 1.4.

Air cargo traffic is carried by the 'combination' carriers that also carry passengers, the cargo specialists such as Cargolux, and the integrators such as FedEx, UPS, TNT and DHL. The latter tend to choose hub airports that are not passenger hubs and are thus less congested. This also reduces their environmental impact from stacking and long aircraft taxi times.

By feeding the hubs by truck and flying the long-haul sectors by air, the operators are able to optimise their fuel efficiency. They tend to use more fuel efficient B747-400F and MD11F aircraft combined with much more fuel efficient trucks.[9] The type of trucks used on these feeder services would generate just under 60–70 RTKs per US gallon, compared to 15–20 for a long-haul freighter aircraft and around 10 for a short-haul aircraft.

13.4 Environmental Taxes and Charges

Environmental taxes are difficult to introduce internationally because they tend to be prohibited under Air Services Agreements. The ones that are allowed such as the UK airport departure tax are not related to emissions and not levied on air cargo.[10] On the other hand, airports impose charges or surcharges/discounts depending on how noisy aircraft movements are, or based on their emissions during the landing and take-off cycle.

13.4.1 Noise Charges

Many countries currently apply aircraft noise surcharges and discounts, particularly in more densely populated regions such as Western Europe. Airports apply a percentage surcharge or discount on the MTOW based landing fee, depending on the aircraft acoustic category and for some the total landing fee varied according to aircraft acoustic noise category, such that it was impossible to separate out the noise element of the charge. For example, London Heathrow levies different landing fees depending on whether the aircraft is noise certificated as Chapter 4, Chapter 3 or Chapter 2 and non-certificated. The most common category three is split into QC1/0.5, being charged £698 and other Chapter 3 which are charged £776. There is also a night charge of £1,746 and £1,940 respectively. Thus a B747-400F (QC/2) would be charged £272 more than a B747-8F or B777F. Brussels Airports and Paris Charles de Gaulle impose a surcharge on the landing fee, which amounts to 1.7 times the fee for the noisiest aircraft at Brussels. Outside Europe there are noise surcharges at airports in Japan, Taiwan and Australia.

---

9   Recent high fuel prices are likely to lead to the phasing out of more B747-200F and older freighter aircraft.

10   The new coalition government that took office in May 2010 expressed the intention to move to a movement based tax that would also apply to cargo flights.

There are also variations in the structure of noise surcharges. Airport noise charges can be revenue neutral (in other words resulting in no net increase in revenues). Thus, increases in charges for noisier aircraft were balanced by reductions in charges for quieter aircraft. Where Chapter 2 aircraft operations are falling sharply, discounts for quieter aircraft need to be reduced to maintain income. Some have noise abatement investment programmes, but these are often funded from general revenues. The situation for Amsterdam Schiphol was more complicated, in that both airport and government levy noise surcharges, the revenue from which goes towards the noise insulation scheme (managed by the airport). While the airport scheme is revenue neutral, the government aircraft noise tax is not, but is ring-fenced for airport noise abatement investments.

13.4.2 Emissions Charges

Zurich Airport and other Swiss airports introduced an aircraft emissions based charge in 1995, with the stated aim of creating incentives to reduce emissions by promoting and accelerating the introduction and use of the best available technology in order to stabilise airport emissions without having to set limits to operations. Other airports have followed their lead, partly as a result of EU legislation on air quality and the focus on this in planning applications.

Emissions data for turbofan engines with more than 26.7 kN thrust is obtained from the ICAO document 9646-AN/943 (1995), which contains an engine exhaust emission data bank. Data for those engines not found in the ICAO data bank is taken from the FAA Aircraft Engine Emissions Database or from manufacturers.

Engines are allocated to the emissions classes, the most polluting being Class 1 and the least polluting Class 5. Class 5 incurs no surcharge on the landing fee, while Class 1 incurs a 40 percent surcharge. These are applied to the basic landing fee after inclusion of the noise surcharge. In order to achieve a neutral overall effect on landing fee revenues, there is a general reduction in landing fees to compensate for the revenue earned from the surcharges.

However, even though the emissions charge generates no overall additional revenue, the revenues from the surcharge are used for various environmental programmes at the airport, such as air pollution monitoring stations, ground power stations, additional taxiways and aircraft approach/departure systems.

Stockholm and other Swedish airports used to impose a surcharge on aircraft engine emissions, with a variable percentage applied to the landing fee depending on ICAO Annex 16, Volume 2, certificated emissions data. They changed to a system that applied a variable charge depending on NO_x emissions for the different stages of the take-off and landing cycle, with taxi times specified, and a charge which was SEK50 (€5) per kg of emissions in 2010. Frankfurt/Main applied a similar type of charge more recently, with a slightly lower charge per kg of €3.00, and London Heathrow levies £2.73 per kg NO_x.

13.5 Emissions Trading Schemes and Air Cargo

13.5.1 The Principles of the EU Aviation ETS

Following the proposal at Kyoto, the ICAO's Committee for Aviation (CAEP) considered and evaluated measures to reduce aviation emissions including the possible introduction of an ETS. It concluded that fuel taxes were impossible to introduce and encouraged regional emissions trading initiatives (subject to third country agreement). Thus nothing was likely on a global scale. In the meantime, the EU moved ahead with the incorporation of aviation into their existing ETS that was implemented for other ground based polluting industries from 2005.

The EU Directive for aviation was finally introduced in January 2009, and its provisions were expected to be incorporated into the legislation of each member country by the end of the year (European Parliament and Council, 2009):

- includes aviation in the existing scheme for greenhouse gas emission allowance trading;
- first year 2012;
- all flights to/from European Community airports;
- various exemptions including smaller aircraft, military, training and rescue flights;
- greenhouse gases cover only CO_2;
- cap based on actual emissions averaged across calendar years 2004, 2005 and 2006;
- cap set at 97 percent of baseline in 2012, and 95 percent for 2013 to 2020;
- emissions allocation based on benchmark;
- initially 15 percent of allowance to be auctioned;
- provisions for free allowance to be given to start-up airlines (with no operations in 2010) and those whose Revenue Tonne-kilometres (RTKs) are growing by more than 18 percent per year.

Some details were still to be finalised, such as the method of auctioning and the percentage of auctioning in subsequent years. The baseline 2004–2006 cap was published in 2011, and the actual amounts allocated to airlines will have to await the 2010 shares of RTKs.

From the time of publication of the European Commission's first proposal (2006) and the emergence of the Directive, there was considerable industry lobbying and studies, and the stronger role of the European Parliament is also reflected in the outcome. The latter proposed that the Commission's original proposal of a 100 percent cap was reduced to 90 percent, with all flights included from 2011 (not just the intra-EU flights in the original). The European Parliament Green Party was advocating 100 percent auctioning, with the Parliament settling on 25 percent. This crucial variable was initially set at 15 percent for 2012 but left open for 2013 to 2020, presumably dependent on how other industries in the scheme are treated. Given the state of the economy in general and the air transport industry in particular it would not be surprising to see little change in the auctioning share.

Taking British Airways as an example, 85 percent of its 2004–2006 aircraft emissions of around 16m tonnes CO_2 would be worth €544m at a CO_2 price of €40 per tonne. This gives an average of €16 per passenger, many of which are on long-haul sectors. New entrants might be deterred in a limited way by this free allocation. However, a fund will be established both for new entrants and those airlines growing by more than 18 percent a year. The Directive states that 3 percent of the total allocation of allowances shall be reserved for such applications, with a maximum of 1m allowances per airline. Since there are unlikely to be any fast growing airlines, all or most of this should be available to start-ups, with the upper limit allowing the new entrant up to between two and five million passengers a year, depending on business model and length of haul.

13.5.2 Benchmarking

There are two different approaches to the allocation of the free allowances: grandfathering and benchmarking. The former gives airlines allowances in proportion to their emissions in the base year or years, while the latter seeks to reward those airlines that have already taken steps to reduce their emissions through investment or improved operations. Benchmarking penalises those airlines that are less efficient than the 'average' and rewards those that do better. The 'average' can be formulated in different ways.

Benchmarking using a traffic rather than capacity metric has the advantage of rewarding airlines that have already introduced efficient aircraft, and those that achieve higher efficiency than their competitors. It is thus favoured by airlines that have high passenger load factors, e.g. low-cost carriers (LCCs) (Frontier Economics, 2006).

Benchmarking involves the determination of a baseline efficiency measure, say RTKs per tonne CO_2, which encompasses the traffic of both passenger and cargo operations, fixing an overall CO_2 cap, and allocating CO_2 allowances depending on an airline's share of RTKs. This was EU aviation ETS approach:

$$RTK_{total} = \sum_{i=1}^{n} RTK_i \qquad (1)$$

$$E_{total} = \sum_{i=1}^{n} E_i \qquad (2)$$

$$A_i = \frac{(E_{total})}{RTK_{total}} * RTK_i \qquad (3)$$

n   number of airlines taking part;

RTK_{total} total RTKs in the reference year (calendar 2010) for those taking part;

RTK_i total RTKs performed by the airline i in 2010;

E_{total} emissions assigned to all airlines in the base period 2004–2006 (average);

E_i emissions assigned to airline i in the base period times 97 percent (less amounts reserved for new entrants and fast growers) in the first year and 95 percent subsequently;

A_i emission allowances assigned to each airline for each of the years 2012 to 2020.

First, this method puts a smaller burden on those airlines operating with high load factors and over longer sectors. Second, those airlines flying shorter sectors would tend to be penalised, although Sentance and Pulles (2005) argue that this would encourage passengers to take less polluting forms of transport such as rail. The latter distortions could be addressed in alternative benchmark approaches, but with increased complexity (Morrell, 2007).

Figure 13.2 shows a hypothetical example of the difference in allocation using the EU ETS proposed method of benchmarking. The average fuel efficiency used in the allocation (assuming the base and reference year emissions are the same) is likely to reflect a relatively long sector length, given the inclusion of routes to/ from non-EU countries. Taking 1,000 nm or 1,852 km as the average, operators of identical aircraft types could get 1.4 tonnes of free CO_2 allowance more than it actually emitted over its longer than average sector length or 2.6 tonnes less than it emitted. A similar relationship would apply to the latest technology aircraft of

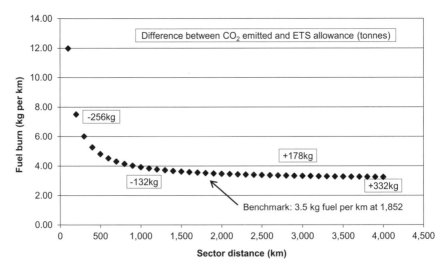

Figure 13.2   Impact of benchmarking on B737-400 flight with hypothetical average at 1,850 km sector length

this size (B737-700) and equivalent Airbus types (e.g. the A320 family). It should be added that for routes of this traffic density a more fuel efficient aircraft would not be currently available.

If these allowance shortfalls are monetarised using a CO_2 price of €40 per tonne, the extra costs incurred by the 230 km operator would be €103 per flight or less than one € per passenger.

The use of RTKs rather than ATKs might be considered to favour low-cost carriers (LCCs) at the expense of network carriers. LCCs would favour the RTK metric which would inflate their share of the reference RTK total used for allocation relative to the network, lower load factor airline. However, the cost of additional allowance required by the LCC would be a higher share of its average ticket price. Furthermore, the network airline would have fewer passengers to pass on the cost to, but more passengers that were less price-sensitive and the cost would be a lower percentage of the average ticket price. The network carrier is making a choice to offer fewer seats and operate at a lower load factor to encourage higher yielding (less price-sensitive) passengers.

Air travel markets are often served on a multiple sector basis, especially longer haul ones. Such markets can not always be operated non-stop, but a one-stop service can be attractive in terms of price, timing, earning frequent flyer awards, etc. An example given by EU carrier Finnair (Ihamäki, 2009) is the New York/Delhi market:

New York – Helsinki – Delhi (11,821 km) served by Finnair
New York – Dubai – Delhi (13,229 km) served by Emirates Airlines

There is no non-stop flight serving this market. The two sectors operated by Finnair would emit an estimated 294 tonnes of CO_2 while the Emirates flights 326t. Finnair would have to submit an equivalent amount of allowances under the EU ETS, while both Emirates sectors would be outside the ETS scope. Taking €40 per tonne CO_2 would result in Finnair paying €11,740 or €43 per passenger.

It should be added that the Finnair is serving the New York/Delhi market using more fuel efficient sector lengths. Fuel burn per kilometre flown generally declines up to around 4,000 km to 6,000 km in length and then starts to increase due to the additional fuel required to carry the larger fuel load (Peeters et al., 2005). This is more pronounced and at the lower end of this range for flights with very high load factors, as is often the case today. One estimate suggests that serving the market with one long non-stop flight might add 4 percent to total fuel burn, allowing for the landing and taking off at the intermediate stop (Green, 2002).[11] Thus in the above example an additional 13 tonnes of CO_2 is emitted due to this effect (+4 percent), the remainder due to the longer overall distance flow (+1,408 km).

---

11   The gain would be far higher if the long-haul aircraft were designed for a maximum range of, say, 7,500 km, since weight would be saved from lighter structures.

The inclusion of aviation in the ETS and its application to third countries was challenged at the end of 2009 in a UK court by the Air Transport Association and three US airlines, none of which have a very large cargo operation: American, Continental and United Airlines. The UK government obviously opposed the challenge but did not object to its referral to the European Court of Justice, and this took place in May 2010. The parties argued that the obligation to surrender allowances for emissions by third parties over the high seas, outside the framework of the ICAO, was illegal, contravening the provisions of:

- the Chicago Convention;
- the Kyoto Protocol;
- the EU/US open skies agreement.

The first argument rested on a clause in the Chicago Convention on the exclusive sovereignty over the airspace above its territory. Furthermore, it was alleged that the ETS would contravene Article 15 of the Convention relating to fees and charges. The open skies agreement has a similar clause exempting fuel uplifted for international flights from taxes, although the European Commission was advised that emissions allowance was not covered by this exemption. Finally Kyoto requires schemes to reduce emissions from international flights to be agreed through ICAO.[12] However, the US is not a signatory to the Kyoto Protocol, nor is the EU (as a whole) a signatory to the Chicago Convention. It thus seems unlikely that the challenge will be successful, and the aviation ETS will go ahead unless there is rapid progress in proposing a more comprehensive alternative through the ICAO.

Very little has so far been written about the allocation of emissions allowances between passengers and cargo on a joint service. Similarly passengers are now given the chance to 'offset' emissions when booking on an airline website, but nothing has been done on this front by airline cargo divisions. Air France-KLM Cargo may be the first combination carrier, having signed its first CO_2 offset agreement with four South-Africa-based agents specialising in perishable exports. Aviator Airfreight, Grindrod PCA, Morgan Cargo and Sky Services have agreed to offset at least 50 percent of the CO_2 emitted in shipping fruit in November and December this year. Contributions from the four agents will be invested in projects that create wind, water or solar energy with a Gold Standard certificate.[13] DHL has also introduced a voluntary carbon offset supplement for its international express customers (GOGREEN).

---

12   Clyde & Co.
13   *Air Cargo News*, 4 December 2009.

13.6 Air Cargo and Food Miles

The carriage of perishables such as fresh fruit and flowers by air has expanded fast in certain markets. For example, such exports are estimated to have accounted for 54 percent of air trade in 2005 between Latin America and North America. Worldwide, however, they took only 9 percent of air tonnages in 2005, unchanged from 1998.[14]

These commodities do not have very high value to weight ratios and cannot support high air rates per kilogram, and have lower values at times of year when importing country produce is available. They are also by definition unidirectional. As a result they need to be carried in the lower deck of passenger aircraft, where marginal cost pricing is often the norm. Alternatively, they can be carried on freighter aircraft, but can only be sustained where there is sufficient high rated traffic on the flight, especially on the backhaul.

Much has been made of the CO_2 emissions impact of food miles in the current climate change debate. As shown above, all perishables accounted for less than 10 percent of total air trade, and food is only one part of perishables. The share of air transport in the import and export of food to/from the UK was recently estimated to be only 1 percent of the 41.5 billion tonnes total, 62 percent of which was between the UK and EU countries.[15]

Finally, many of the fresh produce imports by air come from developing countries where they provide much needed jobs and export earnings. This is underlined by large differences in income between rich and poor countries, for example Kenya's average income per head in 2006 was US$540 compared to $39,700 for the UK. Many of the poorer countries are in Africa, and it is estimated that over one million people are supported by fresh fruit and vegetables exports from rural Africa just to the UK, most these going by air.[16]

Successful examples of this are Kenya and Peru. Peru's exports by air of fresh asparagus are currently 64,000 tonnes a year, and fresh flowers, fruit and vegetables make up 65 percent of all exports from Kenya to the European Union (EU), with most of this going by air. The UK's International Institute for Environment and Development estimates that if UK consumers boycott fresh produce air freighted from the whole of Africa, the UK's total emissions would be reduced by less than 0.1 percent.[17]

---

14   MergeGlobal estimates from *AirCargo World* May 1999 for the 1998 data, and *American Shipper* August 2006 for the 2005 data.

15   The validity of food miles as an indicator of sustainable development, a report produced for the UK government's DEFRA, July 2005.

16   'Fair Miles? The Concept of "Food Miles" through a Sustainable Development Lens', International Institute for Environment and Development, 2006.

17   'African Trade Fears Carbon Footprint Backlash', BBC News on-line, 21 February 2007.

13.7 Conclusions

There have been large reductions in aircraft noise over the past 30 years, but noise remains a problem at the local level. Air cargo operators are especially affected since freighter operations prefer night flights and these are the most sensitive to restrictions, especially in densely populated areas. Freighters are also often older converted passenger aircraft and are thus likely to be noisier than new ones.

Aviation emissions have implications both for local air quality and climate change. The former focuses on reducing NO_x emissions, and the latter has so far been applied mainly to CO_2, although NO_x is also a major problem. It is further complicated by the fact that there is a trade-off in engine technology between noise and fuel efficiency, and fuel efficiency or CO_2 and NO_x emissions. Previous estimates of aviation's contribution to climate change from CO_2 emissions have not separated out air cargo from aviation in general. The most recent estimate for this was 2.3 percent, excluding radiative forcing, for which the best estimate is a multiplier of 1.9. Around 10 percent of this contribution was from military aircraft emissions.

Air cargo's contribution can be split into the freighter aircraft impact, and cargo carried on passenger flights. Freighters accounted for only 9 percent of civil aviation fuel used, although they accounted for 18 percent of passenger and cargo RTKs. This is because most freighters fly long-haul with above average fuel efficiency. The freighter aircraft flights are thus much more fuel efficient than the average for all flights (16.2 RTKs per US gallon versus the overall average of 8.5 for passenger and freighter aircraft). Traffic is generally fed to/from the long-haul hubs by trucks, which are much more fuel efficient.

Two scenarios were used to estimate the fuel needed to carry cargo on passenger flights: the allocation of total passenger flight fuel between passengers and cargo based on their respective RTKs performed; and the incremental fuel required to lift the cargo payload. These two scenarios gave estimates for air cargo of 28.9 Tg of fuel or 16.5 percent of the global aviation fuel used in 2002, and 2.4 Tg or 1.4 percent respectively. This would give the combined air cargo share of global aviation fuel use of between 9.4 percent and 24.5 percent.

Of aviation's 2002 contribution to global CO_2 emissions of 2.3 percent, the air cargo part is estimated to range from 0.3 percent to 0.6 percent. The climate effects of radiative forcing are still subject to a high degree of scientific uncertainty. The latest best estimate for the multiplier for aviation is 1.9, which would increase air cargo's 2002 impact to between 0.6 percent and 1.1 percent. Aviation's (and air cargo's) contribution to future world emissions is the result of the ratio of two very uncertain figures. It is thus possible to arrive at very large aviation impacts by judicious selection of assumptions or scenarios to suit a particular viewpoint. Investment in more fuel efficient freighter aircraft is being driven by higher fuel prices, with B777 and B747-8 freighters replacing older DC10s and B747-100/200s. High fuel prices impact freighter more than passenger aircraft operators, since fuel is a much higher percentage of total operating costs.

Fresh produce is a small part of total air freight, and its boycott would have a negligible impact on developed country emissions. It would just damage developing country growth and employment. The air cargo industry also provides a ready source of essential transport for emergency food aid and medical supplies, as well as for time-sensitive regular shipments of pharmaceuticals and medical equipment.

Chapter 14
Air Cargo Forecasting

The air cargo industry lurches from periods of deep pessimism when large network carriers state their intention to discontinue freighter services for good to times of optimism and strong growth. The year 2009 was a time of a slump in world trade, a sharp downturn in almost all air cargo markets and the widespread grounding of freighter aircraft. By 2010, however, traffic had bounced back and the IATA was forecasting a healthier future.

The adage 'by all means predict a number, and by all means specify a date; but never do both' is apposite to the airline forecaster. If one has to do both, make sure the dates are well into the future. It is these longer-term prospects for the industry that still look reasonably good and is these that drive investment plans. These and shorter-term forecasts will be examined in the second part of this chapter.

There are a large number of reasons why airlines, airports, ATC service providers, regulatory authorities, governments and others need to make forecasts about the future level of activity. These include:

- plan company priorities and efforts;
- seek market opportunities;
- plan company resources in terms of equipment, people, capital, facilities and technology;
- set budgets, provide a basis for cost allocation and revenue generation;
- monitor internal activities and those of others;
- control performance and efficiency;
- determine and influence the business environment;
- prepare contingency plans.

Short-term forecasts meet many of the above needs, but longer-term projections are needed for facilities planning due to their long service life, and sometimes long lead time.

Forecasts are needed by airlines that carry cargo, airports that handle cargo and the various suppliers to these activities such as forwarders, handlers, investors, financiers, consultants and IT specialists. Some rely on the longer-term forecasts published by the major aircraft manufacturers such as Airbus and Boeing. Others are more interested in the shorter-term IATA or ICAO forecasts. Most, however, prepare their own forecasts or ask consultants to provide them.

The macro-economic framework has a strong influence on any forecasts of industry activity, with foreign trade, exchange rates and oil prices clearly some of the most important for air cargo. The key variables that would be expected to impact on future air cargo development are:

- international trade;
- GDP;
- exchange rates, especially the US dollar and other major currencies;
- interest rates;
- oil prices;
- banking and the availability of credit;
- corporate profitability;
- globalisation;
- manufacturing outsourcing and off-shoring.

Some of these are often used as explanatory variables in forecasting models that rely on statistical techniques such as regression. The 2008 banking crisis resulted in a massive stimulus to demand by most of the larger world economies, but it should be remembered that liquidity totally dried up for a time, and smaller operators will find it harder to borrow from banks for some time to come. This avoided a deep and long recession but carried the risk of inflation in some countries.

Micro-economic factors are related to productivity and investment in the air cargo industry itself, which would also depend on the health of the passenger side of the business. Examples of these are:

- regulation;
- productivity growth;
- aircraft fuel efficiency;
- distribution;
- industry concentration;
- environmental restrictions, taxes and charges.

These will be discussed as key issues in the next chapter, which looks at the future prospects of the industry in the light of possible changes in these key factors.

14.1 Air Cargo Forecasting Approaches

Before examining specific air cargo forecasts that are published by airlines, airport authorities and others it is helpful to discuss the various approaches to forecasting. These can be applied to cargo and passengers, airlines and airports, but the focus will be on air cargo. The forecaster should have a series of historical data for air cargo traffic and is asked to project these into the future. The horizon is likely to range from 5–10 years for an airline to 30–40 years for an airport. Airports will be using the forecasts to support long-term infrastructure investments so a long period is required. Airlines can lease assets for shorter periods and can be more flexible in adapting to market developments and thus need shorter periods. Traffic forecasting will be described here, although revenue, cost and other forecasts may also be required. However, these are generally based on traffic, which is the key driver of both capacity/investment and financial planning.

There are two main measures of traffic that may be forecast: tonnes and tonne-kms. Airports are more interesting in the former, while airlines the latter. Integrators may prefer to forecast the number of packages, since their sorting facility capacities may be defined in this way.

The ICAO *Forecasting Manual* describes in some detail the various forecasting methodologies;[1] its latest edition was published around 25 years ago, but it is still relevant today. It groups the approaches into:

- trend projections;
- econometric methods;
- market and industry surveys.

It also discusses 'bottom-up' approaches that build up totals from more detailed analyses. An example of this would be forecasting airport traffic for individual routes and combining them to give the total annual traffic. On the other hand, 'top-down' approaches forecast aggregate or total traffic, often based on an econometric model, and then allocate this total to the different traffic categories (e.g. domestic and international, scheduled and charter) and perhaps also to routes. Often both approaches are carried out and cross-checked against each other.

14.1.1 Trend Projections

Trend analysis techniques use time series and attempt to fit a trend line through historical data, whether on an annual or monthly basis. This line is then projected into the future depending on the equation that best describes the historical data. Statistical techniques can be used, ranging from simple averages to the more complex exponential smoothing. There is no attempt to understand the causes of traffic trends, and these methods are not reliable beyond five or so years into the future. Apart from these problems they work on the assumption that past trends will continue into the future. This has not been the case in the past especially with the average capacity of flights, which increased quite fast in the 1970s and 1980s only to flatten out in the 1990s. Similarly trend projections would not have taken into account the rapid growth in low-cost airlines over the past two decades in Europe.

Typical time series methods include:

- average annual rate of growth;
- moving average annual rate;
- exponential smoothing;
- simple trend linear;
- moving average trend.

---

1   ICAO Doc 8991-AT/722/2, Second Edition 1985.

The major problem with these methods is they do not attempt to obtain an understanding of the causes of past trends.

14.1.2 Econometric Modelling

This approach attempts to understand the key factors that affect and explain air traffic levels. It thus seeks to overcome one of the problems of trend analysis, although it introduces different challenges, notably those of statistical estimation. It has six main steps:

1. selection of explanatory factors or variables;
2. collection of historic traffic and explanatory variable data;
3. model specification;
4. forecasting explanatory variables;
5. forecasting air traffic using the model equation parameters and 4. above.

Some of the factors discussed in the opening to this chapter will be included, but the ones likely to feature in air cargo traffic models are:

- Gross Domestic Product (GDP) as a proxy for economic activity (value or growth rate);
- foreign trade volume or value, absolute amounts or growth rates;
- freight rates or yields (at current or constant prices);
- exchange rates;
- quality of service;
- surface transport competition.

Separate models might be developed to forecast directional traffic with directional trade flows more appropriate. Express, special handling and general cargo might also be forecast separately. International trade takes place as a result of a push by the exporter in one country and a pull by the consumer in another country. That is why the GDP of both countries might be included in the model, or a weighted average of the growth of each country. Values can either be expressed in current prices or the price levels applied in each year, or in real or constant prices, when current price values have been deflated by a suitable price index.

Sometimes a major political upheaval, war, terrorist attack or health scare can cause a sharp discontinuity in historical traffic resulting in problems with obtaining a good fit between the data predicted by the model and actual data. In these cases a 'dummy variable' can be used to give better results. This variable can be switched on or off, taking the value of '1' for the period or year of upheaval and zero for all other 'normal' years. Clearly these events are almost impossible to forecast so the dummy variable is normally switched off for future years for the base forecasts. Pessimistic scenarios, however, can be developed by switching it on in a future year and estimating the impact on traffic.

Model equations can be linear or non-linear, for example exponential. The statistical estimation makes use of linear regression, and thus non-linear models need to be transformed to linear form taking the logarithm of the explanatory and/ or dependent variables. For air cargo the model equation might take a linear form, in which case no transformation is necessary:

$$T = a + bX_1 + cX_2 \qquad\qquad \text{Equation 1}$$

Where: T is the air cargo traffic in tonne-kms
X_1 is real GDP
X_2 is cargo yield

Where historical data appear to follow a curved or exponential trends a logarithmic transformation is applied to the non-linear equation to give:

$$Ln(T) = a + b*ln(X_1) + c*ln(X_2) \qquad \text{Equation 2}$$

Linear regression can then be applied to Equation 2 to provide estimates of the parameters a, b and c. The logarithmic form has the advantage of making the parameters b and c identical to the elasticities. Fore example, c in Equation 2 would be the price or yield elasticity. It is assumed here that statistical tests have been done to give sufficient confidence to use the model equation for forecasting future values of traffic. These tests are described in numerous books on statistics. One problem that might arise is that some of the explanatory variables might be highly correlated with each other. The equation could still be used for forecasting but only on the basis that this relationship will not change over time. It would, however, not be possible to use the coefficients of each explanatory variable (i.e. the elasticities from log models) with any degree of confidence. If this assumption cannot be made, techniques are available to remove the 'multi-collinearity', for example by lagging certain variables or using other models to predict values of some of the explanatory variables. This becomes more time consuming and requires forecasts of even more explanatory variables. This highlights one of the problems of this approach: the result is only as good as the forecasts of explanatory variables and some of these are not easy to forecast.

It is easier to use econometric models for forecasting than to use them to understand the causal relationship between GDP, yield or other explanatory variables and the dependent variable, in most cases a measure of traffic. This is both because of statistical problems and uncertainty about spurious correlation. In other words is there any causation and do changes in explanatory variable cause changes in traffic or is it the other way round? This makes it dangerous using the elasticities derived from the regression equations. It is also not common to see a statistically sound regression model include yield or freight rates as an explanatory variable, even though this intuitively should cause more or less air freight traffic.

14.1.3 Market and other Surveys

Surveys of the type of commodities shipped by air and their value per unit weight can help estimate the share of total trade that could be carried by air. Thus surveys can be used in combination with forecasts of total trade or the exports of certain industries. The ICAO *Forecasting Manual* referred to a study of future air cargo demand on North Atlantic routes. This included an analysis of the share of each commodity group by value to weight ratio. Other surveys which might serve to support judgmental forecasts, especially by route, obtain views from cargo shippers and forwarders.

Other types of survey are those using the Delphi approach. This essentially involves the selection of industry experts to whom a questionnaire is sent seeking their views on specific forecasts or scenarios and their associated assumptions. These replies are summarised and sent to the same group of experts who are then asked to reconsider their answers in the light of the consensus view. This may be further refined in subsequent rounds until a final majority consensus is achieved.

14.2 Airline Forecasts

Air cargo carriers need both short-term projections to drive budget and cash flow estimates and long- or medium-term forecasts to provide the justification for decisions to invest in aircraft and other facilities. Chapter 10 discussed the forecasting needs for revenue management and these are generally the most detailed. Longer-term forecasts for fleet planning require much less detail, with traffic forecasts providing the basis for capacity and aircraft needs and yield and traffic for revenue forecasts. Capacity and aircraft will determine costs such that future profits and cash generated by each investment option can be estimated. Airlines such as British Airways and Lufthansa build their own cargo terminals and will also need forecasts for their investment evaluation, but these are discussed in the next section.

Air cargo traffic forecasts will have to be distributed between passenger and freighter flights. They could be crucial in the passenger aircraft investment decision, especially on long-haul routes. Payload penalties in terms of limited volume and/or weight in the lower decks of passenger services will reduce the potential revenue without any commensurate reduction in costs.

One of the airline industry medium-term forecasts is that of IATA, for example, over the five years from 2009 to 2013. The publication includes a first part summary, a second part covering passengers and the third part freight forecasts. Detailed 2008 freight tonnes and five-year forecasts for inbound and outbound freight are provided for 720 unduplicated international country pairs (1,402 country pairs by direction), including aggregated values for six world regions, 17 world sub-regions, 513 country to sub-region forecasts. These forecasts are a compilation of the forecasts provided by their member airlines.

The airline association AEA was asked by its member airlines to produce airborne trade forecasts for key trade lanes involving Europe for the years 1992 to 1997 (AEA, 1993). These are now very out-of-date but illustrate the type of econometric modelling that has been used in the past. The approach was taken to combine 10 major European countries together and forecast flows from the region to/from individual countries. This was because it was impossible to get data on the real origins and destinations of air freight at an individual country level. Models were produced for each air trade flow to and from 12 important trading partners: Australia, Brazil, Canada, Hong Kong, India, Ivory Coast, Japan, Saudi Arabia, Singapore, South Africa, South Korea and the US. The dependent variable was tonnes carried in total in each direction. The explanatory or independent variable in all but two directional flows was the GDP of the importing country, with private consumption expenditure (PCE) used instead for Japan to Europe. PCE of the importing country was also used together with exchange rates on Europe to Hong Kong, and exchange rates were also used with GDP on five routes. The country pair flows with the highest five-year growth rates were Europe/South Korea (17.2 percent), India (12.4 percent), Hong Kong (12 percent) and Singapore (10.5 percent). The forecasts concluded by stating that the real challenge facing forecasters is understanding the business environment and correctly anticipating some rather unpredictable variables.

14.3 Airport Forecasts

Airports provide cargo terminal space and the necessary infrastructure for aircraft to land, taxi, park and take-off. The latter includes both freighters, which may not be in significant numbers at large airports like London Heathrow, and passenger aircraft. While the airport itself may not build and operate cargo terminals (see Chapter 8) it needs to establish future air cargo flows so that a large enough area is available for cargo terminals and associated air and landside facilities. Forecasts would also be needed to provide the basis for concession agreements to others to operate and in some cases build cargo terminals.

The process of gaining planning approval for new terminals at airports can take many years in some countries. This highlights the need for good long-term forecasts. Even new passenger terminals have important implications for cargo throughput, as illustrated by the planning for London Heathrow's Terminal 5. Forecasts to support BAA's case were originally prepared in 1993, prior to the very lengthy planning enquiry leading eventually to approval and completion in 2007.

Table 14.1 shows BAA's air cargo forecasts with and without the new passenger terminal. Almost all of the airport's cargo was flown on passenger flights, and a large part of it on British Airways, which is expected to take up most of the capacity at the new terminal. Thus air cargo growth with the new facility was projected to grow at 3.3 percent a year over the 23 years compared to only 2.8 percent at the very constricted existing terminals. Crucially, transhipment traffic

Table 14.1   BAA forecasts of air cargo tonnes with and without Terminal 5

	Forecast traffic		Actual
x 1,000 tonnes	**Without T5**	**With T5**	**traffic**
1993	847	847	847
2000	1,150	1,150	1,307
2005	1,340	1,400	1,389
2008	1,434	1,516	1,483
2016	1,600	1,800	
Av.% 1993–2016	2.8	3.3	

Source: BAA, 1993.

between BA flights would be made much easier within one terminal rather than having to move between the existing Terminals 1 and 4 which involved using the tunnel under one of the runways. The table also shows that BAA expected the new terminal to be in operation by 2005, while in fact it was only open by 2008 (by which time the forecast was very close to the actual traffic). BAA also forecast cargo air transport movements (CATMs): these actually declined from 6,000 to 5,000 a year with the terminal, as airlines (especially British Airways) switched capacity to passenger flights.

Airports require annual forecasts of air traffic to provide the basis for estimating revenues, which combined with cost projections provide profit and Net Present Value (NPV) estimates. However, forecasts for shorter periods are essential for comparing with runway and terminal capacity, and determining when to bring additional infrastructure on-line. This in turn dictates the timing of additional capital costs and is the basis for forecasts of operating costs.

The period selected depends on the facilities that are being evaluated. Passenger terminal planning requires a busy hour measure to ensure that passengers are handled in the terminal at a specific level of service. In the cargo terminal, however, the average daily tonnage over the peak week would be sufficient. This is because cargo does not flow through the terminal in the same way as passengers and can be stored at various stages in the process. Examples of past patterns of cargo traffic are given in section 1.5. They can provide the basis for the projections, although changes may occur due to a change in the mix of traffic. Ideally imports, exports and transhipments need to be evaluated and forecast separately to enable sufficient capacity to be provided in each area of the terminal.

14.4 Air Traffic Management Forecasts

The US Federal Aviation Administration publishes annual forecasts of passengers, cargo and aircraft movements for the purposes of planning its tower and en-route ATC facilities. It does this mainly by means of a simple econometric model based on GDP. It has found that, historically, air cargo activity has been strongly correlated with GDP. It mentioned additional factors that have affected the growth in air cargo traffic including the global financial crisis, declining real yields and globalisation. It also cites a number of other changes that have affected the forecasts: air cargo security regulations by the FAA and TSA; market maturation of the domestic express market; modal shift from air to other modes (especially truck); increases in air fuel surcharges; growth in international trade from open skies agreements; use of integrated carriers by the US Postal Service to transport mail; and increased use of mail substitutes such as email.

Its forecasts of cargo traffic in terms of revenue tonne miles (RTMs) are based on several assumptions specific to the cargo industry: first, security restrictions on air cargo transportation will remain in place; second, most of the shift from air to ground transportation has occurred; finally, long-term cargo activity will be tied to economic growth. The forecasts of domestic cargo RTMs were developed with real US GDP as the primary driver. Projections of international cargo RTMs were based on growth in world GDP, adjusted for inflation. The distribution of RTMs between passenger carriers and all-cargo carriers was forecast based on an analysis of historic trends in shares, changes in industry structure and market assumptions.

Table 14.2   FAA air cargo traffic (ton-mile) forecasts, 2010–2030

	2009/2008	2010/2009	2011/2010	2010–2030
Domestic	-17.7	1.3	2.0	2.2
International	-23.0	4.7	6.6	6.4
Total	-21.0	3.4	5.9	5.1

Source: FAA, 2010.

The FAA forecasts published in 2010 are summarised in Table 14.2. This shows the steep decline in both international and domestic traffic in 2009, with a strong recovery particularly for the former in 2010. It also estimated that the US freighter fleet would increase from 854 aircraft in 2009 to 1,531 aircraft in 2030, or at an annual growth of 2.3 percent a year.

In Europe, Eurocontrol publishes short-, medium- and long-term forecasts of air traffic to plan its airspace facilities:

14.4.1 Short-Term Forecasts

Short-term forecasts are good at capturing recent trends month by month and projecting these into the immediate future of up to two years ahead. These are published four times a year.

14.4.2 Medium-Term Forecasts

Medium-term forecasts look seven years ahead and build on the short-term forecasts. The medium-term forecasts combine flight statistics with economic growth and with models of other important drivers in the industry such as costs, airport capacity, passengers, load factors, and aircraft size. The forecasts use a range of high and low growth scenarios, and are published in February and revised in September of each year. Medium-term forecasts include all-cargo flights that are modelled on an airport pair basis using GDP as the only explanatory variable (but these forecasts are not published).

14.4.3 Long-Term Forecasts

Long-term forecasts are published every two years. The long-term forecasts look at a range of distinct possible scenarios to determine how the air traffic industry might look in 20 years time. This allows a range of 'what if?' questions to be explored for factors inside the industry (e.g. the growth of small business jets, or of point-to-point traffic) or outside (e.g. the price of oil, or environmental constraints).

   The latest long-term forecasts of Instrument Flight Rules (IFR) movements cover the period from 2008 to 2030. These include freighter flights, which are modelled separately from passenger flights using 'a simplified approach to growth'. Only the forecasts of total IFR flights were reported in the latest publication.

14.5 Aircraft Manufacturer Forecasts

Air cargo forecasts are published by both Boeing and Airbus covering the next 20 years. These are published every two years by Boeing as a separate document and almost annually by Airbus (together with its passenger forecasts) and provide a regional discussion of traffic trends and estimates of the number of freighter (and passenger) aircraft that will be required over this period. That is the main purpose of the forecasts, which do not try to capture shorter-term cyclical traffic variations.

   The last Boeing forecast (2008–2009) was published in October 2008 and the next is expected in the fourth quarter of 2010. The latest period covered was 2007 (the latest actual year included) to 2027. It proposes four possible approaches to cargo forecasting:

- econometric modelling;
- judgmental evaluation;
- trend analysis;
- potential analysis.

Potential analysis is based on an examination of total trade flows and estimating the share that might be attracted to air based on value to weight ratios. The forecasts combine these approaches through both 'top down' and 'bottom up' forecasts.

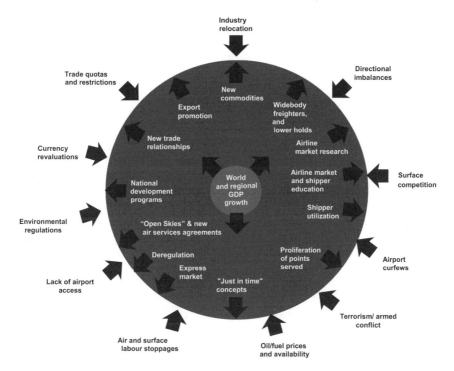

Figure 14.1   Forces and constraints for air cargo growth

Source: Boeing Commerical Airplane Co.

Figure 14.1 neatly encapsulates the positive and negative influences on air cargo traffic growth. Its core is world and regional economic growth without which international trade will not expand and few of the other positive factors such as network expansion and Just-in-time concepts will carry much weight. The constraints may also be weaker in times of economic downturn, for example the enthusiasm for introducing environmental measures. The chart does not attempt to capture the interrelations between factors, such as surface competition possibly having a greater cost advantage at times of high oil prices. However, these linkages are important and often reduce the effectiveness of econometric models.

Table 14.3   Boeing air cargo forecasts (RTKs), average annual change

	2003–2023	2007–2027	+/-% pts
World base case			
Cargo	6.2	5.8	-0.4
Regional flows			
Domestic China	10.6	9.9	-0.7
Intra-Asia	8.5	8.1	-0.4
Asia – North America	7.2	6.6	-0.6
North America – Asia	7.3	6.7	-0.6
Europe – Asia	6.8	6.7	-0.1
Asia – Europe	6.7	6.5	-0.2
Europe – North America	5.8	5.4	-0.4
North America – Europe	5.2	4.9	-0.3
Intra-Europe	5.3	3.6	-1.7
US domestic	4.0	2.6	-1.4

Source: Boeing World Air Cargo Forecast, 2004–2005 and 2008–2009.

Table 14.3 compares Boeing's long-term forecasts by major region of the world made in 2004, halfway through the post-9/11 recovery and in 2008, the start of the banking crisis recession. The picture was more pessimistic in 2008, especially in more mature markets such as Europe and the US. The least change was for the air trade between Asia and Europe. Airbus published their latest forecast in 2009 (Table 14.4), and did not publish one in 2008, so it is not comparable in period to Boeing's. As expected it is more pessimistic in terms of overall long-term outlook, but that was also the case for the previous 2003–2023 period which was identical to Boeing's forecast horizon.

Airbus has reduced its average growth rates substantially on all regional routes apart from within China, where it is more optimistic (and expects 2 percent higher average annual growth than Boeing). Its forecasts were made at the depth of the recent recession, but its views on Asia/Europe and Asia/North America (the two largest international region-to-region flows) are now well below those of Boeing. It should also be noted that Boeing is much more bullish on intra-Asia cargo flows, expecting 4.1 percent higher average growth rates over the 20-year period.

Both manufacturers are ultimately interested in the number of freighter aircraft that will be sold and converted over the forecast period. To estimate this it is necessary to forecast the lower deck hold capacity from the passenger forecasts, and subtract it from the cargo demand projections to determine the required

Table 14.4   Airbus air cargo forecasts (RTKs), average annual change

	2003–2023	2008–2028	+/-% pts
World base case			
Cargo	5.9	5.2	-0.7
Regional flows			
Domestic China	10.1	11.9	1.8
Intra-Asia	6.4	4.0	-2.4
Asia – North America	6.2	4.3	-1.9
North America – Asia	5.9	3.4	-2.5
Europe – Asia	6.2	3.6	-2.6
Asia – Europe	6.4	3.2	-3.2
Europe – North America	4.8	3.0	-1.8
North America – Europe	5.0	3.0	-2.0
Intra-Europe	5.0	3.2	-1.8
US domestic	4.2	1.7	-2.5

Source: Airbus Global Market Forecast, 2004 and 2009.

freighter capacity and thus number of aircraft. Neither of the manufacturers gives details of how the passenger lower deck capacity is calculated, or the share of cargo traffic carried on each type of service. However, Boeing takes account of recent developments such as:

- higher passenger load factors;
- the introduction of checked baggage fees;
- restrictive security procedures.

Boeing suggests that these all reduce the lower deck capacity available for cargo, although checked baggage fees are likely to have the opposite affect, at least in terms of space or volume. Its latest forecasts assume a very small rise in the share of traffic carried on freighters by 2027. This compares with a 2004 forecast from Airbus that forecast the freighter share to increase by seven percentage points by 2023. Table 14.5 compares the latest long-term freighter aircraft deliveries split into new production aircraft and those converted from passenger aircraft. Both the total aircraft requirements and the share of conversions are of very similar magnitude, but there are large differences by size category. This is partly because of the difference in definitions. The main difference between Boeing's 'standard-body' and Airbus's 'small' category is the inclusion of the B757F and

B707F by Boeing and not by Airbus. The B757 is operated in quite large numbers by integrators and this is a significant difference. In the 'large' aircraft category Boeing includes the large aircraft from the former USSR (An124 and Il-96T) whereas Airbus does not.

Table 14.5   Boeing and Airbus freighter aircraft delivery forecasts

	Production	Converted	Total	% converted
Boeing (2007–2027)				
Standard-body	11	1,323	1,334	99.2
Medium wide-body	211	711	922	77.1
Large wide-body	641	461	1,102	41.8
Total	863	2,495	3,358	74.3
Airbus (2008–2028)				
Small	0	786	786	100.0
Regional and long-range	340	1,285	1,625	79.1
Large	514	514	1,028	50.0
Total	854	2,585	3,439	75.2

Source: Boeing World Air Cargo Forecast, 2008–2009, Airbus Global Market Forecast, 2009.

Aero-engine manufacturers also publish long-term forecasts. Rolls-Royce's September 2009 outlook only gives passenger forecasts, although it includes freighter aircraft delivery projections (presumably new freighters): 419 between 2009 and 2018 and 378 between 2019 and 2028.

14.6 ICAO Forecasts

The ICAO produces short- to medium-term forecasts for total world air cargo traffic. These forecasts contribute to the ICAO's long-term planning functions and help its Member States in all aspects of civil aviation development. The ICAO has developed a comprehensive and robust methodology for forecasting air cargo flows, with its latest forecasts to be published towards the end of 2010. The method is shown pictorially in Figure 14.2.

The procedure begins with the data assembly in Box 1. The ICAO's member states provided detailed information on air cargo traffic flows by city-pair and nation-pair. This data expressed in units of cargo revenue tonne-kilometres (RTKs). The ICAO aggregated this data into nine region-pairs. Global Insight, an

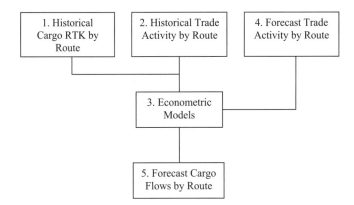

Figure 14.2 ICAO methodology for forecasting air freight

economic consulting group, provided historical country-by-country information on worldwide airborne commerce. These trade flows were expressed in value terms, because many countries do not assemble comprehensive weight-based statistics. By expressing the current value trade data in constant currency, the ICAO eliminated any distortions arising from inflation. The real country-pair trading value data was consolidated into region-pairs.

The econometric models of Box 3 express air cargo RTK flows by region-pair in terms of the value of bi-directional region-pair airborne trade. Each region-pair has its own unique model. The models are similar in form, although the values of the estimated parameters are unique. The models use a linear regression algorithm in which air cargo RTKs for each region-pair are expressed as a function of the corresponding value of airborne trade. When given the trading value data for any year, the models are sufficiently flexible to estimate the cargo tonne-kilometres for the corresponding year. Besides the specific coefficients, the regression algorithm also produces measures of the validity of each term in the models and of the whole specifications.

Global Insights provided both historical values and projections of future airborne trade activity (Box 4). The future estimates were consolidated by region-pair in the same manner as the historical data. The projections, when inserted in the appropriate econometric model, produced estimates of future cargo revenue tonne-kilometres.

This approach has the advantage of using a simple model, but it has a major drawback: forecasts are still needed of the future value or air trade which may be more difficult to forecast than traffic. It also misses any changes within the air cargo industry, whether from the supply side (and the capacity on passenger flights) and how air cargo yields might develop in the future.

14.7 OAG Forecasts

OAG produce medium-term air cargo forecasts over a 10-year horizon, taking the same trade lanes or major intra- and inter-regional flows to those taken by the manufacturers. In fact it takes 49 regional flows and forecasts using econometric models with regional GDP and exchange rates as explanatory variables. Their most recent results are shown in Table 14.6, prepared using historical data that included some of the major 2008/2009 downturn. Lower growth is predicted for the more mature North American and transatlantic routes, but it is relatively optimistic on intra-Asia and China.

Table 14.6   OAG medium-term air cargo traffic forecasts

	2010–2019
Total world	5.3
Intra-North America	3.7
Intra-Europe	5.4
Intra-Asia	6.2
North America/Western Europe	3.3
North America/Asia (ex China)	5.4
North America/China	8.0
EU/Asia (ex China)	5.9
EU/China	7.2

Source: OAG Analytical Services, 2010.

OAG also forecast aircraft deliveries split between new and converted aircraft. Their aircraft categories differ from both Boeing and Airbus but their estimates of the converted aircraft share are similar: 98 percent converted in the 'small' category (<45 tonnes), 70 percent in the 'medium' category (46–75 tonnes) and 50 percent in the 'large' category (>75 tonnes).

14.8 Other Industry Forecasts

Forecasts of air cargo traffic are also published (usually at a cost) by industry consultants. Avitas published these up to around 2006 but has since focused on its fleet valuations. Its 2006 Global Outlook for Air Transportation forecast world air cargo traffic to growth at 6.7 percent a year between 2006 and 2025. This was somewhat higher than Boeing and Airbus over a similar period. Like the manufacturers, Avitas also used econometric modelling, with GDP and yield as explanatory variables. However, its forecast of just over 2,000 freighter deliveries over the 20-year period was well short of the 3,000 plus for both the manufactures.

Consultants have also prepared forecasts under contract for government authorities, the resulting results often published. One such example was the May 2001 forecast by MDS and others for the UK Department of Transport (DETR). These consisted of medium-term forecasts (2000–2010) modelled using exogenous growth and price-induced growth from mode substitution. After rejecting GDP in favour of international trade, air cargo forecasts were prepared by applying an increasing air trade share to UK trade projections. This increasing trade share was based on historical evidence over only six years when the air share of the UK's non-bulk imports and exports rose from 1.5 percent to 1.9 percent, and was projected to increase to 2.5 percent in 2005 (MDS Transmodal et al., 2001).

The MDS/UK DETR long-haul air cargo forecasts were aggregated from forecasts for individual UK airports under various assumptions of runway capacity constraints. This tended to limit passenger services and thus the cargo capacity available in the lower decks of these flights. Pricing was also introduced to simulate competition between airports and resulted in diversion from the more constrained airports such as London Heathrow. The net result of these restrictive assumptions was an increase in the share of air cargo carried on freighters from 30 percent in 1998 to 57 percent in 2030 (and to 74 percent under an alternative scenario).

MergeGlobal publish short-term forecasts by major trade lane, together will some interesting analysis on mode share by commodity (MergeGlobal, 2009). This is in FTKs, consistent with most of the other forecasts discussed in this chapter, although a previous 2005 forecasts by the same consultancy was in tonnes. They expect the sharpest downturn in the most developed markets, with recovery led by intra-Asian routes (Table 14.7). The recovery assumes inventory re-stocking,

Table 14.7   Short-term forecasts by main region/routes, 2008–2012

	% total	% change in FTKs vs previous year				
	2007	2008	2009	2010	2011	2012
Europe-Asia	24.9	7.3	-10.0	3.6	5.7	5.4
Transpacific	11.2	-4.6	-14.4	6.2	4.1	5.1
Transatlantic	11.2	-4.6	-15.0	2.5	11.0	5.5
Intra-Asia	25.2	-6.3	-16.7	7.2	6.2	6.1
Rest of world	27.4	-11.0	-12.4	7.0	7.8	5.8
Total	100.0	-3.8	-13.3	5.5	6.7	5.7

Source: MergeGlobal, 2009.

stronger growth in short life shipments that need to get to the market quickly, and ocean shipping congestion. They also mention three major risks: first that the downturn is more severe than they expect; second the recovery is slower; and third some loss of traffic to ocean shipping.

The cargo division of consultants, Seabury Aviation, published short-term projections of air cargo on international routes to and from the US. This highlighted the strong growth in air exports and imports in 2010 compared to 2009, with transpacific routes experiencing 10 percent and 12 percent increases respectively. Some of this was accounted for by a switch of high-tech products from sea to air, but it was mainly driven by a recovery in US domestic sales and the resulting re-stocking. For the period 2010 to 2014, Seabury forecast an average annual growth of 4 percent of air trade, with transpacific growth of 5 percent for exports and 6 percent for imports with the Indian sub-continent slightly higher at 8 percent and 6 percent. Europe, however, is expected to experience 2–3 percent growth per annum.

14.9 Conclusions

The future for air cargo must certainly be closely linked to GDP and trade growth. Recent events have also suggested that competition with ocean transport can be intense for certain more mature products, and the higher longer-term growth of trade in some commodities could favour one mode of transport or the other. Many consumer products are often launched in the US and are introduced to other world markets a little later. Air transport is initially the main mode chosen but as sales of the product slow and its price is reduced air transport becomes less competitive.

Manufacturing is likely to continue to be spread between emerging countries with their relatively low labour costs and developed countries with their final markets, knowledge industries, assembly and marketing skills. As labour costs increase in China production will move to other countries but China will move more towards a consumer country. These developments will ensure continued growth in air trade, but directional flows will alter, some becoming more balanced and other less so.

A major problem for short- to medium-term forecasters of air cargo traffic has been the timing, duration and depth of cycles. Based on the latest cycle, they will be deep and relatively short. But sharp recoveries can be followed by a second dip (double dip) and the current recovery is far from assured. Econometric models are only as good as the forecasts of explanatory variables that are plugged into them, and these do not have a good record in tracking recoveries. It can be argued that if businesses and consumers believe the 'authoritative' forecast recoveries produced by such international bodies as the IMF, World Bank and OECD they will invest and consume more and the forecasts will be realised. But it is doubtful whether they do and most are more concerned with strengthening their balance sheets or reducing their consumer debt.

Forecasters such as Seabury (see the previous section) look to key ratios such as inventory to sales to find turning points that will guide the timing of air trade recovery. Sales, especially in the US, moved from growth to rapid decline in the last months of 2008, with inventories following after a lag of a few months at the beginning of 2009. It was this that caused the double digit declines in air cargo on the major routes in the first three months of 2009. In the same way, when sales started to recover in the second half of 2009, inventories started to look low and a delayed re-stocking was likely. They suggest a lead time of two months for this indicator.

A second indicator suggested by Seabury is the Composite Leading Indicator (CLI). The CLI, a derivative of key economic indicators published by the Organization for Economic Co-operation and Development (OECD), is developed to predict economic turning points and is available for 29 member countries, for six non-member economies and for seven country groupings such as the Euro zone. The data are available from the beginning of the 1960s for most countries.

CLIs are constructed from economic time series that have similar cyclical fluctuations to those of the business cycle but which precede the cycle by a number of months. Indices of industrial production are used rather than GDP because they provide a better proxy for turning points in economic activity and because data are available sooner than GDP. CLI growth is highly correlated to air trade growth, and it appears to lead by about four months. This is thought to make the CLI an excellent predictor of near-term developments in the air cargo.

On the supply side, the shorter-haul sectors will continue to be served by trucks where possible, and cheaper converted passenger aircraft where costs can be low enough to support feeder flights, especially by integrators with their higher yielding products and greater revenue. Here the A320/A321 conversion programme may satisfy demand for some years to come, assuming used aircraft can be acquired at a low enough price. This may be triggered by the advent of an A320/B737 replacement, something that has been expected for a number of years but inhibited by the strong sales of the existing production lines and lack of obvious new technology to give it attractive costs.

On the major long-haul trade lanes, a number of new, more efficient, freighters will be gradually introduced, for example the B777F, B747-8F and A330-200F. Larger aircraft from the former USSR are unlikely to move from their existing niche status and alternative technologies such as ground effect vehicles or balloons seem far from viable. However, the major impediment they face is the existing costs that have been sunk in the global airport and ATC infrastructure and the vested interests in the continuing use of these systems. Converting long-haul passenger aircraft to freighters is also an option and the current B747-400 programme is likely to continue, and be joined by other aircraft such as the B777 and A330.

On the negative side, high fuel prices will probably continue which would favour new, fuel efficient, freighters over some of the conversions. Fuel accounts for a smaller part of short-haul operations and would thus be less of an issue but on the long-haul high fuel prices made converted B747-200s (and productions models) uneconomic. Environmental taxes and emissions charges are likely to become more widespread, although some of the national ones such as the UK have in the past only applied to air passengers.

Chapter 15
Air Cargo Issues and Prospects

15.1 Air Cargo Issues

The cyclical nature of the industry was described in the first chapter and many of the problems and issues for air cargo operators are best viewed from the depths of the recession. Those that are strongly related to profitability receive the most attention: yields, overcapacity and fuel costs. Others such as over-regulation are also in evidence, followed closely by productivity and efficiency. These will be dealt with in turn. Finally, how will the future shape of the industry look? Will the present co-existence of airline, integrator and forwarder continue or will a few global brands emerge?

15.1.1 Air Cargo Yields and Capacity

Air cargo yields and capacity are closely linked, and when international trade and air cargo is in decline yields fall. This is because capacity is never reduced in line with the decrease in traffic, and indeed just under half the capacity is linked to passenger flights, which may not be subject to the same pressures. Air cargo often turns down one or two months before an economic recession affects air travel and thus, if passenger capacity is removed, it is often a few months after cargo.

Freighter capacity can easily be removed by grounding or storing freighter aircraft. Again there may be some months' delay before this occurs. This is because the downturn may initially be perceived as temporary and it is only when it is definitely considered as a major longer lasting recession that aircraft are taken out of service. The 2008 slump was a good example of this with airlines such as Cathay Pacific and Lufthansa announcing the withdrawal of freighters between four and 12 months after the first month of sharp traffic reduction. Two Cathay Pacific B747-400BCF grounded in January 2009 and two more in May 2009. Lufthansa decided in July 2009 to retire four MD-11F aircraft from its fleet 'for at least a year from 1 October 2009 at the latest'.[1] The IATA reported that 227 freighters, more than 10 percent of the global freighter fleet, were parked in 2009.

Once capacity has been reduced and traffic begins to pick up freight rates can move up again quite rapidly as shortages of capacity appear on some routes. The recovery may vary in different parts of the world, but eventually most of the more efficient freighters will be back in service. At this point grounded aircraft are brought back into service. Once the recovery is under way for 12 months or more,

---

1   In fact two of those aircraft were being prepared to re-enter service six months later.

the freighter conversion market also recovers, depending on aircraft availability and price. This could give a substantial boost to capacity after a delay to allow for the conversion work to be completed. This illustrates the complete air cargo capacity cycle which tends to accentuate upward and downward movements in yields. Within these trends the large air cargo carriers may have some longer-term contracts with forwarders but these will only give a small measure of stability, and the forwarders often have the market power to dictate terms.

It is difficult to argue that these pressures and trends will change in the future. What might be happening during the 2008–2009 downturn is a reappraisal of longer-term freighter economics by some of the combination carriers. Japan Airlines, Northwest (Delta) and SAS announced that they were discontinuing such services. British Airways considered a similar move as its lease contract for the three B747-400Fs came up for renewal, but decided to continue, upgrading to more efficient B747-8F aircraft. Lufthansa will continue operating its freighters, bringing its grounded aircraft back into service as the economy recovers. On the other hand, Finnair was considering converting its two passenger MD-11s to freighters, and various start-up ventures were described in Chapter 4.

15.1.2 Over-Regulation

Any industry is subject to various governmental regulations, and air cargo is no exception. These were discussed in Chapter 3. The main government departments imposing such regulations are 'transport/aviation' that designates operators and negotiates route and traffic rights, security agencies that impose controls and screening, and customs that limit some goods and impose tariffs on others.

Regulation from customs authorities has diminished over time as tariffs have been removed on more imports through the GATT and bilateral negotiations. However, there is still a long list of products that are subject to duties, and others that are licensed or banned. There was a risk that some of this liberalisation might have been reversed after the banking crisis as governments sought ways of reducing the impact of this on their economies, but this did not happen. Thus free trade seems to be set to continue into the future with more and more countries becoming convinced of its benefits and adopting similar policies. Where customs inspections are necessary the move to electronic documentation means that air cargo operators can release shipments more quickly and shippers benefit from less delays.

Liberalisation of Air Services Agreements is also likely to continue, albeit at a somewhat slow pace. Air cargo open skies often preceded the same freedoms for the carriage of air passengers, but a major constraint still applies to establishing a hub in a foreign country. This requires either fifth and seventh freedom traffic rights from the country of hub location and all the other countries that feed that hub or the relaxation of the ownership and control clause in the ASA. The second option is more likely and this may happen in the medium to long term, based on progress on agreement between the EU and US rather than any IATA or ICAO initiatives in this area.

Finally security regulations are unlikely to be totally removed, although they may be relaxed over time. Most of these stemmed from the aftermath of the 9/11 terrorist attacks and it has taken a number of years before a workable scheme has been introduced for air cargo. It is thus unlikely that this could be reversed very quickly, and the security situation worldwide is still thought to pose a sufficient threat to make screening necessary.

15.1.3 Productivity

Industries can only continue to prosper if productivity continues to grow and costs are reduced or controlled. This is not ranked highly as an issue in industry surveys but it is a continuing priority for most managers as they seek to cut costs further. Some of the gains from improved productivity need to go towards reducing rates and improving service in order to ensure a competitive industry in the future, but some need to flow through to shareholders and providers of capital.

One of the major sources of improved productivity in the past has come from freighter aircraft operations. Fuel efficiency has increased very significantly from the B707 freighters to the latest B747-8F. There was also a step change in pilot productivity as the crew needed for each flight dropped from four to two (apart from very long flights), and further gains were achieved as aircraft payloads increased. If sufficient traffic could be attracted to the larger aircraft other gains were available in landing, navigation and handling productivity and costs. Future emphasis may switch to environmental factors, but this will help achieve greater fuel efficiency, with fuel having a large share in freighter costs. Bio-fuels are likely to have a role, but some of the alternative aircraft ideas such as blended wing bodies or balloons seem unlikely for many years to come.

Future productivity may come more from e-commerce than physical movement of shipments. Many of the benefits that integrators have already adopted such as tracking are already becoming commonplace, and matching physical movements with information flows will be made much easier with RFID, once it becomes cheaper.

Future productivity in ocean transport is also relevant, especially in an era when fuel prices are likely to be higher. Various options of slower cruising and delivery time and enhanced fuel efficiency to faster cruising and more competitive journey times at the expense of fuel efficiency are likely to be offered. Air cargo needs to maintain or increase its position in terms of both costs and speed.

15.2 Air Cargo Prospects

The future for air cargo must certainly be closely linked to GDP and trade growth. Recent events have also suggested that competition with ocean transport can be intense for certain more mature products, and the higher longer-term growth of trade in some commodities could favour one mode of transport or the other. Many consumer products are often launched in the US and are introduced to other world markets a little later. Air transport is initially the main mode chosen but as sales of the product slow and its price is reduced air transport becomes less competitive.

Manufacturing is likely to continue to be spread between emerging countries with their relatively low labour costs and developed countries with their final markets, knowledge industries, assembly and marketing skills. As labour costs increase in China production will move to other countries but China will move more towards a consumer country. These developments will ensure continued growth in air trade, but directional flows will alter, some becoming more balanced and other less so.

Manufacturing is still considered to be producing goods in a single factory, but products now have a considerable amount of software embedded in them. This has led to a convergence of the goods and services markets, leading to further off-shoring as countries with strong and relatively cheap IT such as India become part of the manufacturing process.

A major problem for short- to medium-term forecasters of air cargo traffic has been the timing, duration and depth of cycles. Based on the latest cycle, they will be deep and relatively short. But sharp recoveries can be followed by a second dip (double dip) and the current recovery is far from assured. Econometric models are only as good as the forecasts of explanatory variables that are plugged into them, and these do not have a good record in tracking recoveries. It can be argued that if businesses and consumers believe the 'authoritative' forecast recoveries produced by such international bodies as the IMF, World Bank and OECD they will invest and consume more and the forecasts will be realised. But it is doubtful whether they do and most are more concerned with strengthening their balance sheets or reducing their consumer debt.

Forecasters such as Seabury (see Chapter 14) look to key ratios such as inventory to sales to find turning points that will guide the timing of air trade recovery. Sales, especially in the US, moved from growth to rapid decline in the last months of 2008, with inventories following after a lag of a few months at the beginning of 2009. It was this that caused the double digit declines in air cargo on the major routes in the first three months of 2009. In the same way, when sales started to recover in the second half of 2009, inventories started to look low and a delayed re-stocking was likely. They suggest a lead time of two months for this indicator.

Air cargo will be dependent on manufacturing with a sizeable and growing contribution from perishables exported from developing countries. Manufacturing will migrate to countries which combine low labour rates with high productivity. These are likely to continue to be in Asia, but there are opportunities in both Africa and South America. The latter also need air transport to take their fresh fruit, vegetables and flowers to markets in North America, Europe and increasingly Australasia. These will continue to demand low rates combined with regular long-haul flights on both passenger and freighter aircraft.

The current engine for growth in air freighted manufactured exports will continue to be located in China for some years, with lower value products migrating to other Asian countries with lower wage rates. China will move from what is principally an outbound air cargo market to a more balanced one, with its construction boom and increasing consumer spending power expanding the demand for imports. It will also move to more advanced technology industries such as aircraft and aerospace, integrated with subcontractors in other countries and international supply chains.

Manufacturing is still considered by some to be producing goods in a single factory, but products now have a considerable amount of software embedded in them (apart from being the product of plants in many different countries). This has led to a convergence of the goods and services markets, leading to further offshoring as countries with a strong and relatively cheap IT such as India become part of the manufacturing process. This may not result in India becoming a large exporter of manufactures, but exports of services will pay for a growing need for imported goods, many of which will need air freight, given the long distances involved.

Air cargo will continue to be carried by trucks on shorter sectors in Europe and North America, with integrators using small converted freighters to feed their hubs with premium traffic. In Asia, more intra-regional capacity is available from widebodied passenger flights (not much in evidence on such routes within the EU or US), and longer and over-water routes will provide a flourishing market for freighters, especially feeding major integrator and network carrier hubs. In addition to the large number of B737 family aircraft available, the A320/A321 conversion programme may satisfy demand for some years to come, assuming used aircraft can be acquired at low enough prices.

There will be some slowing down in the pace of application of technology to new aircraft: noisier prop-fans may have some potential, but not ideally suited to night cargo flights from big city hubs. New freighter programmes may emerge from lower cost manufacturers in such countries as China, Brazil and perhaps Russia. New concept freighters, whether using ground effect technology, airships or even blended wing bodied aircraft, may be a long way off. However, the potential for improving both the physical and information flows involved in shipping goods by air is large and hardly realised so far. These technologies include the greater use of e-commerce and the application of RFID to consignments. While security will remain a necessary part of the air transport system, tracking and enhanced availability of information will make spot checks possible with little disruption.

Fuel prices are likely to continue to be volatile, ratcheting up to higher levels. This will put the onus on producing more fuel efficient long-haul freighters, essentially using infrastructure that will not be greatly different from today. These aircraft will have to be produced in large enough numbers to bring their capital costs down, and will still need to serve passenger hubs, where lower deck holds will provide capacity to a large number of destinations at reasonable frequencies. Environmental taxes or cap and trade schemes will serve effectively to increase the fuel price, and ensure that it does not fall back too far. Noise in the vicinity of airports, especially passenger and cargo hubs, will increasingly constrain expansion and be a key requirement for the manufacture of future aircraft.

Finally, the future structure of the industry may not change significantly from the present co-existence between the various participants. The key question is whether the integrators decided to expand further internationally, perhaps by acquiring forwarders or airlines. One has done this already with Flying Tiger, and there are few suitable targets available. Buying more forwarders is perhaps more likely and outsourcing air transport to combination carriers and contract freighters. Control of every part of global logistics chains is very different from offering a global brand such as Coca-Cola.

Some see the future in terms of express products, with more of these shifting to the integrators, leaving the low rated business with the airlines. This scenario involves express taking an increasing share of the total market, a trend that may have its limits. How many people are prepared to pay the premium for next-day delivery of their book, mobile phone or shirt purchased through a website? If this market levels out at say a quarter of total air shipments, will the integrators move further into heavier items and acquire forwarders? Whatever happens it seems to leave the airlines with the provision of an efficient airport-to-airport service with fully integrated IT systems.

Definitions

A Checks
Low-level maintenance checks performed on aircraft at an interval of approximately 650 to 750 flight hours.

ACMI
A leasing arrangement whereby an airline (lessor) provides an aircraft, crew, maintenance and insurance to a customer (lessee) for compensation that is typically based on hours operated.

Air cargo
Air freight plus mail plus express/courier.

Air Cargo Guide
The official scheduling guide for scheduled air freight services, published by the Official Airline Guides (OAG). It contains current domestic and international cargo flight schedules, including freighter, wide body and combination passenger/cargo flights. Each monthly issue also contains information on air carriers' special services, airline and aircraft decoding, airport codes, a directory of air carriers and freight forwarders, customs information, a glossary of ULD terms and information, cargo charter airlines, interline air freight agreements, and aircraft loading charts.

Air Cargo, Inc (ACI)
A ground service corporation jointly owned by several US scheduled airlines. In addition to its airline owners, ACI serves over 50 air freight forwarders and international air carriers as associate participants. One of ACI's major functions is to facilitate the surface movement of air freight by negotiating and supervising the performance of a nationwide series of contracts under which trucking companies provide both local pickup and delivery service at airport cities and over-the-road truck service to move air freight to and from points not directly served by the airlines. ACI publishes a directory of these trucking services, listing points served in the United States and the applicable pickup and delivery rates. Other services include claims inspection, terminal handling, telemarketing service, group purchasing (equipment, supplies, insurance) and EDI services.

Air waybill
Shipping document used by airlines for air freight. It is a contract between the shipper and the carrier covering the transport of freight to a specified destination.

It includes the conditions of carriage, and also specific instructions for the airline, a description of the consignments included and the applicable transport charges.

Aircraft daily utilisation
Aircraft hours flown (block-to-block) divided by aircraft days available.

Airline Tariff Publishing Co. (ATPCO)
Publisher of airline industry tariffs setting forth rates and rules applicable to air freight. Tariffs are available on a subscription basis.

Asia-Pacific Economics Cooperation (APEC)
A forum for the 21 Pacific Rim countries to cooperate on regional trade and investment liberalisation and facilitation.

ATM or ATK
Available ton-miles (ATM) or available tonne-kms (ATK), which represent the maximum available tons or tonnes (capacity) and the distance flown (in miles or kilometres). It is calculated by multiplying the available capacity (tonnage) of the aircraft by the miles flown.

Block hour
The time interval between when an aircraft departs the terminal (from the start of taxi-out) until it arrives at the destination terminal (blocks placed in front of the wheels on the ramp).

Bottom-up approach
Analysis technique for forecasting air traffic that begins at the most detailed (micro) level and moves with less specificity towards the macro level only after considering complex, interrelated effects.

C Checks
High-level or 'heavy' airframe maintenance checks, which are more intensive in scope than A Checks and are generally performed at 18-month intervals.

Cargo declaration
Information submitted prior to or on arrival, or prior to departure by any means of transport for commercial use that provides the particulars required by the Customs relating to cargo brought to or removed from the Customs territory.

Cargo IMP message
Cargo Interchange Message Procedures. The Cargo-IMP messages have been developed by the member airlines of the International Air Transport Association (IATA) and the Air Transport Association of America (ATA) as Standard IATA/ATA Cargo Interchange Message Procedures. The purpose of these messages is to

ensure uniformity, mutual understanding, accuracy and economy in inter-airline data exchange and in data exchange between airlines and other air cargo industry participants including agents, brokers and customs. The messages are used in both manual and computerised environments.

Cargo position manifest

An electronic document containing the positions and weights of each pallet and container on the aircraft for each flight.

Cargo sales agent

An agent approved by the IATA to solicit and process international air cargo for shippers.

Cargo transfer

Cargo arriving at an airport on one flight and continuing its journey on another flight: using the same airline (on-line transfer) or using two airlines (interline transfer).

Chargeable weight

The weight of the shipment used in determining air freight charges. This may be the dimensional weight (using a conversion factor to go from volume to weight) or the actual weight. For ULDs it is the gross weight less the tare weight of the ULD.

City-pair

Two cities between which travel is authorised by a passenger ticket or part of a ticket (a flight coupon) or between which shipments are made in accordance with a shipment document or a part of it.

Combi (combination) aircraft

An aircraft capable of simultaneously carrying passengers and cargo on the main deck.

Consignee

The person or company whose name appears on the air waybill as the party to whom the goods are to be delivered by the carrier, or the receiver of the shipment.

Consignment

A shipment of one or more pieces, accepted in one unit by the carrier, and moved on one air waybill to one consignee at one destination.

Consignor

A person or company in whose name a contract of carriage has been concluded with a carrier.

Consolidator
A person or legal entity providing services relating to the carriage of goods by air to the public under its own tariff through the assembly of such goods from different shippers into one single consignment.

Container, aircraft
An enclosed unit load device with solid base, walls, door and roof that can fit various aircraft types and be handled by its equipment.

Contract logistics
Performance of complex logistics and logistics-related tasks along the value chain by a service provider. Services tailored to the particular industry and customer are provided under contracts lasting several years.

Customs
A government authority designated to regulate the flow of goods to and from a country referred to as imports into the country and exports from the country.

Customs declaration
A statement attesting to the correctness of the description, quantity and value of the goods imported into a country.

D Checks
High-level or 'heavy' airframe maintenance checks, which are the most extensive in scope and are generally performed on an interval of six to nine years or 25,000 flight hours.

Day Definite
Delivery of express shipments on a specified day.

Density
Weight to volume ratio of a shipment, usually in kilograms per cubic metre.

Design density
Relationship of an aircraft's payload to its available volume.

Dimensional weights
The conversion of the cubic space of a shipment into weight (kilograms or pounds); also referred to as the volume weight. Used for low density consignments.

Dry leasing
A leasing arrangement whereby an aircraft financing entity (lessor) provides an aircraft without crew, maintenance, or insurance to another airline (lessee) for compensation that is typically based on a fixed monthly amount.

Eurocontrol
The European Organisation for the Safety of Air Navigation (Eurocontrol) is an intergovernmental organisation made up of 38 Member States and the European Community. Its members in 2010 were the 27 EU countries plus Albania, Armenia, Bosnia and Herzegovina, Croatia, Moldova, Monaco, Montenegro, Serbia, Turkey, the former Yugoslav Republic of Macedonia and Ukraine.

Europe-Asia/Pacific
The Europe to/from Asia/Pacific or Far East/Australasia region is used for analysing specific air trade lanes along a group of routes. These refer to scheduled services between Europe and points east of the Middle East region, including trans-polar (direct and via Alaska) and trans-Siberian flights.

European Economic Area
Established at the beginning of 1994 following an agreement between the member states of the European Free Trade Association (EFTA) and the European Community, later the European Union (EU). Current membership: the 27 EU member countries, plus Norway, Iceland and Liechtenstein.

Express cargo
Air cargo shipments requiring door-to-door transport on a reliable, time-definite basis, with one carrier usually exercising integrated information control. Express carriers usually are characterised as 'integrated' because, in addition to carrying mostly airport-to-airport, time-definite cargo, they also offer many other services such as door-to-door pickup and delivery.

Flight stage
A flight stage is the operation of an aircraft from take-off to its next landing. A flight stage is classified as either international or domestic based on the following definitions:

International
A flight stage with one or both terminals in the territory of a state, other than the state in which the air carrier has its principal place of business.

Domestic
A flight stage not classifiable as international. Domestic flight stages include all flight stages flown between points within the domestic boundaries of a state by an air carrier whose principal place of business is in that state. Flight stages between a state and territories belonging to it, as well as any flight stages between two such territories, should be classified as domestic. This applies even though a stage may cross international waters or over the territory of another state.

Freight forwarder
To the airlines the freight forwarder is the shipper, and to the shipper an indirect carrier or agent. The forwarder receives freight from the shipper under his own tariff, often consolidating it into larger shipments, prepares the necessary documentation, and delivers it to the airline, sometimes in aircraft compatible ULDs.

Freight (or mail) tonne-kilometres performed
A metric tonne of freight or mail carried one kilometre. Freight tonne-kilometres equal the sum of the products obtained by multiplying the number of tonnes of freight, express, diplomatic bags carried on each flight stage by the stage distance. For ICAO statistical purposes freight includes express and diplomatic bags but not passenger baggage. Mail tonne-kilometres are computed in the same way as freight tonne-kilometres.

Freight (or mail) tonnes carried
The number of tonnes of freight carried is obtained by counting each tonne of freight on a particular flight (with one flight number) once only and not repeatedly on each individual stage of that flight. The only exception to this is for freight flown on both the international and domestic stages of the same flight, which is considered in computation both as a domestic and an international shipment or dispatch. The same principle should be used in calculating mail tonnes carried.

Freighter aircraft
An aircraft that carries only cargo, rather than both passengers and cargo. Some freighter aircraft have a few passenger seats next to the cockpit.

Full Container Load (FCL)
Shipments which completely fill a container.

Goods declaration
A statement made in the form prescribed by Customs, by which the persons interested indicate the Customs procedure to be applied to the goods and furnish the particulars which the Customs require to be declared for the application of that procedure. The persons interested may be the importer, the exporter, the owner, the consignee, or the carrier of the goods or their legal representative, according to the country concerned.

Handling agent
A company specialised in loading and unloading cargo from aircraft and building and breaking down ULDs.

House air waybill (HAWB)
The individual breakdown for each part of a consolidation.

Hub airport
Main transhipment base. Collection centre for the transhipment and consolidation of flows of goods onto flights.

Integrator or Integrated Carrier
They perform their own pickup and delivery services of smaller parcels, operate aircraft and trucks to support the door-to-door delivery operations supported by advanced information and communications technologies.

Intermodal transport
Transport chain integrating different modes of transport, often combining road and rail.

International flight
A flight that contains one or more international flight stages (see Flight stage, international).

Just-in-time
A manufacturing and distribution approach that meets immediate needs as opposed to relying on large inventories.

Known shipper or consignor
An entity that ships its own products, has a valid account with an airline, and is certified as secure by an accredited validator on behalf of the government agency responsible for security.

Less than Container Load (LCL)
Loads that will not fill a container by themselves and are therefore grouped for ocean transport.

Less than Truck Load (LTL)
A term used by road hauliers to designate smaller shipments handled as loose pieces as opposed to full truckloads.

Logistics
The process of planning, implementation and controlling the efficient, cost-effective, flow and storage of raw materials, in-process inventory, finished goods and related information from point of origin to point of consumption for the purpose of conforming with customer requirements.

Lower deck
One or more compartments below the main deck of an aircraft, available for the carriage of passenger bags and cargo.

Mail
All correspondence and other items tendered by and intended for delivery to postal administrations.

Master air waybill (MAWB)
Air waybill covering consolidated consignments showing the consolidator as the shipper.

Narrow-bodied aircraft
A narrow-body aircraft is one with one aisle in the passenger cabin, also known as a single-aisle aircraft. The typical fuselage diameter is 3 to 4 metres.

North Atlantic
The North Atlantic region is used for analysing specific air trade lanes along a group of routes. These refer to any scheduled service between Europe, the Middle East and Africa and North, Central and South America via gateway airports in the continental US (including Hawaii and Alaska) and Canada. The domestic sectors of long-haul flights are included.

Outsourcing
The subcontracting of tasks to external service providers.

Pallet
A wooden or metal base to which cargo is secured.

Payload capacity
Total payload capacity available (in metric tonnes), above and below deck, for the carriage of revenue load (passengers, baggage, freight and mail) taking into account payload restrictions, where applicable, and operational restrictions on the supply of capacity (see also tonne-kilometres available).

Perishable goods
A commodity possessing a quality or condition that makes it conducive to deterioration, spoilage or death. Includes seafood, flowers, vegetables and fruits. Also used for goods that may perish or lose value with time in the marketplace (e.g. newspapers).

Road feeder service (RFS)
Cargo that is transported by surface, usually by dedicated truck, on an air waybill. Carriage between origin and destination can be exclusively by air or surface. Also referred to as 'truck flight'.

Scheduled Service
The provision of scheduled airport-to-airport cargo services to freight forwarders and other shipping customers, for compensation that is billed by air waybill based on a rate per kilogram.

Sea-air market
Market in which cargo is transported from origin to destination by sea and air, taking advantage of the lower cost by ship between seaports and the speed of air over landmasses to balance time and cost.

Shipment
A unit of cargo that needs to be transported, mostly comprising a single commodity.

Shipper
Person or company that has issued the contract for carriage (the air waybill) of the goods.

Stage distance flown per aircraft
The average stage distance flown per aircraft is obtained by dividing the aircraft kilometres flown by the related number of aircraft departures.

Supply chain
A series of connected resources and processes from sourcing materials to delivering goods to consumers.

Tare weight
Weight of an empty container or pallet.

Time-definite shipment
Cargo services with a performance guarantee based on time. Often includes a refund of all or a portion of the payment made for same service if the advertised delivery time is not met.

Tonne-kilometres available
A tonne-kilometre is available when one tonne of payload capacity can be flown one kilometre (identical to ATK). Tonne-kilometres available equals the sum of the products obtained by multiplying the number of tonnes available for the carriage of revenue load (passengers, freight and mail) on each flight stage by the stage distance (see also payload capacity).

Tonne-kilometres performed
A metric tonne of revenue load carried one kilometre (identical to RTK). Tonne-kilometres performed equals the sum of the product obtained by multiplying the number of total tonnes of revenue load (passengers, freight and mail) carried on each flight stage by the stage distance.

Top-down approach
An analysis technique for forecasting air traffic that begins with a broader (macro) perspective and applies trends and conclusions to more specific situations.

Transpacific
The transpacific region is used for analysing specific air trade lanes along a group of routes. These refer to any scheduled service between North, Central or South America and the Far East or Asia (also referred to as North and Mid Pacific).

Truck flight
Also known as road feeder service (RFS). Cargo that is transported by surface, usually by a dedicated truck, on an air waybill. Carriage between origin and destination can be exclusively by surface or also may feed into airport-to-airport or surface.

Twenty-foot equivalent unit (TEU)
A unit of measure representing a standard, usually seaborne, shipping container approximately 20 feet long and 8 feet wide. Often transferred between surface modes of transportation. Can take up to 14 tonnes.

ULD (Unit Load Device)
An assembly comprising an aircraft container, an aircraft pallet and pallet net or an aircraft pallet and pallet net over an igloo. It is designed to store a number of packages or shipments, to be handled as a unit and to maximise the utilisation of available space in the upper or lower deck of an aircraft.

Weight load factor
Tonne-kilometres performed expressed as a percentage of tonne-kilometres available.

Wet lease
An arrangement that covers all facets of operating an aircraft on a carrier's behalf, including the provision of the airframe and engines, crew, and most, if not all, of the aircraft-related expense items.

Wide-bodied aircraft
A wide-body aircraft is one with two aisles in the passenger cabin, also known as a twin-aisle aircraft. The typical fuselage diameter is five to six metres.

9/11 Commission Act of 2007
Act of US Congress signed into law in August 2007 specifically implementing some 9/11 Commission recommendations including 100 percent inspection of all air and sea cargo entering the United States as well as redistributing anti-terrorism funding.

Sources: Deutsche Post, www.dp-dhl.com/reports/2010/annual-report/service/glossary.html; Van de Reyd and Wouters (2005); Boeing (2008); Groenewege (2003); Association of European Airlines Yearbook, 2007.

Bibliography

Achard, P. (2009). The Regulation of International Air Cargo Services. Master's thesis, Groupe d'Economie Mondiale, Sciences Po.

AEA (1993). *Airborne Trade Forecasts, 1992–1997*. Association of European Airlines, Brussels, April.

Air Transport Association of America (1988). *Air Cargo from A to Z*. Washington, DC.

Al-Hajri, G. (1998). The Impact of Sea-Air Mode on Air Cargo Transport. PhD thesis, Cranfield University.

Allaz, Camille (2004). *The History of Air Cargo and Airmail from the 18th Century*. Miami: Christopher Foyle Publishing in association with The International Air Cargo Association (TIACA).

Anger, A., Allen, P., Rubin, J. and Köhler, J. (2008). Air Transport in the European Union Emissions Trading Scheme. Study for the Omega Project, December.

Arendt, D. and Wecker, A. (2007). Large Cargo Freighter Aeroplanes: Current Industry Trends. *Airport Management*, 1(2), 146–150.

Ashford, N., Stanton, H.P.M. and Moore, C.A. (1997). *Airport Operations*, 2nd edn. New York: McGraw-Hill.

BAA (1993). Heathrow Terminal 5 Planning Application: Statement of Case, March.

Baird, R.W. (2007). Global Integrators, January, from www.rwbaird.com.

Becker, B. and Kasilingam, R. (2008). Success Factors for the Implementation of Air Cargo Revenue Management Solutions. *International Journal of Revenue Management*, 2(3).

Bloemen, M. (2009). Perishable Market Trends. Presentation for Cool Chain Association, 2 March.

Boeing (1977). Evaluation of Passenger and Cargo Profits in a Combi Operation. Sales and Marketing Department, Boeing Airplane Company, December.

Boeing (2008). World Air Cargo Forecast, 2008–2009. Available at: www.boeing.com/copmmercial/cargo.

Bolkcom, Christopher (2006). Civil Reserve Air Fleet. CRS Report for Congress, 18 October, Order Code RL33692.

Booz & Company (2009). Study on Consumer Protection against Aviation Bankruptcy. Draft final report for the European Commission DG TREN, 18 March.

Bowen, J.T. Jr. and Leinbach, T.R. (2002). Air Cargo Services in Asian Industrialising Countries. In *Strategic Management in the Aviation Industry*, edited by W. Delfmann, H. Baum, S. Auerbach and S. Albers (2005). Aldershot: Ashgate.

Clarkson (2010). *Container Intelligence Quarterly*. Clarkson Research Services, First Quarter.

Cranfield (1993). *International Air Express Report*. Centre for Logistics and Transportation, School of Management, Cranfield University.

de Jong, J.M. (2010). Modal Shift Study: A Quantitative Response to Anecdotal Evidence. Seabury Group.

Delfmann, W., Baum, H., Auerbach, S. and Albers, S. (eds) (2005). *Strategic Management in the Aviation Industry*. Aldershot: Ashgate.

Doganis, R. (2010). Chapter 11: The Economics of Air Freight. In *Flying off Course*, 4th edn. London: Routledge.

EC (2008). Regulation (EC) No 1008/2008 of the European Parliament and of the Council of 24 September 2008 on common rules for the operation of air services in the Community (Recast) Text with EEA relevance.

European Parliament and Council (2009). Directive 2008/101/EC amending Directive 2003/87/EC so as to include aviation activities in the scheme for greenhouse gas emission allowance trading within the Community, 19 November.

FAA (2010). FAA Forecast Fact Sheet: Fiscal Years 2010–30, 9 March, www.faa.gov/news/fact_sheets.

FIA International Research, Ltd. (2001). *Contraband, Organized Crime and the Threat to the Transportation and Supply Chain Function*. September.

Frontier Economics (2006). Economic Consideration of Extending the EU ETS to Include Aviation. Report for ELFAA, March.

GAO (2003). Foreign Investment in US Airlines, GAO-04-34R, 30 October.

Geloso Grosso, M. and Shepherd, B. (2009). Liberalising Air Cargo Services in APEC. Working Paper, SciencesPo & Groupe d'Economie Mondiale, October.

Gilbert, R. and Perl, A. (2008). *Transport Revolutions: Moving People and Freight without Oil*. Abingdon: Earthscan.

Green, J.E. (2002). Greener by Design: The Technology Challenge. *The Aeronautical Journal*, 106 (February).

Grin, B. (1998). Developments in Air Cargo. In *Handbook of Airline Marketing*, 1st edn. New York: McGraw-Hill.

Groenewege, Adrianus D. (2003). *The Compendium of International Aviation*, 3rd edn. Canada: International Aviation Development Corporation.

Grönlund, P. and Skoog, R. (2005). Drivers of Alliance Formation in the Air Cargo Business. In *Strategic Management in the Aviation Industry*, edited by W. Delfmann, H. Baum, S. Auerbach and S. Albers. Aldershot: Ashgate.

Grotius, Hugo (1609). *Mare Liberum*.

Harrison, A. and Van Hoek, R. (2007). *Logistics Management and Strategy: Competing through the Supply Chain*, 3rd edn. New York: Prentice Hall.

Hellermann, R. (2002). Lufthansa Cargo AG: Capacity and Dynamic Pricing. Case study reference no. 602-029-1, WHU Otto Beisheim School of Management.

Horst, M. (2006). The Role of German Regional Airports in Logistics Networks. MSc thesis, University of Westminster.

Hummels, D. (2009). Globalisation and Freight Transport Costs in Maritime Shipping and Aviation. Paper to International Transport Forum: Transport for a Global Economy, 2009-3, OECD.

IATA (2006). Value Chain Profitability. IATA Economics Briefing No.4, Geneva, June.

IATA (2009). Air Freight Timely Indicator of Economic Turning Point. IATA Economic Briefing, www.iata.org/economics, April.

Ihamäki, K. (2009). EU ETS: How Ready are the Airlines? Presentation to GreenAviation Airline ETS Masterclass, London, 1 June.

IPCC (1999). *Aviation and the Global Atmosphere*. Cambridge: Cambridge University Press.

James, George (ed.) (1982). Chapter 11: Strategic Cargo Planning. In *Airline Economics*. Boston: Lexington Books D.C. Heath & Company.

Jansen, G.-J. (2004). The European Perishable Market: Opportunities and Threats for South America. Presentation for YDL Management Consultants.

Jansen, G.-J. (2008). Shifts in Perishable Demand. Presentation to the 3rd Reefer Logistics Conference, 24–25 June.

Jofré, M. and Irrgang, M.E. (2000). Integration of Cargo and Passenger Operations. In *Handbook of Airline Operations*, edited by G. Butler and M. Keller. New York: McGraw Hill.

Kasarda, J.D., Green, J. and Sullivan, D. (2004). Air Cargo: Engine of Economic Development. Paper presented at the TIACA Annual General Meeting, April.

Kasarda, J.D., Appold, S.J. and Makoto, M. (2006). The Impact of the Air Cargo Industry on the Global Economy. Study commissioned TIACA and presented at the TIACA Air Cargo Forum, Calgary, Canada, 13 September 2006.

Kasilingam, R.G. (1996). Air Cargo Revenue Management: Characteristics and Complexities. *European Journal of Operational Research*, 96.

Klein, T. (2010). The Viability of Widebody Freighter Services on International Routes to and from India. MSc thesis, Cranfield University.

Leleu, C. and Marsh, D. (2009). Dependent on the Dark: Cargo and Other Night Flights in European Airspace. *Eurocontrol Trends in Air Traffic*, 5.

MDS Transmodal, Roger Tym & Partners, ACMS and RPS Clouston (2000). The UK Air Freight Industry. 13598_final dra_v2, for UK DETR, December.

MDS Transmodal, Roger Tym & Partners, ACMS and RPS Clouston (2001). UK Air Freight Study – 26199r_may2001, Final Report for UK DETR, May.

MergeGlobal (2006). Steady Climb. *American Shipper*, August.

MergeGlobal (2008). Forwarder Momentum: Opportunities for Value Creation in Freight Forwarding. *American Shipper*, March.

MergeGlobal (2009). Global Air Freight: Demand Outlook and its Implications. August.

Micco, A. and Serebrisky, T. (2004). Infrastructure, Competition Regimes, and Air Transport Costs: Cross-Country Evidence. World Bank Policy Research Working Paper 3355.

Miller, James C. (1973). The Optimal Pricing of Freight in Combination Aircraft. *Journal of Transport Economics and Policy*, September.

Morrell, P. (2007). An Evaluation of Possible EU Air Transport Emissions Trading Scheme Allocation Methods. *Energy Policy*, 35, 5562–5570.

Morrell, P.S. and Pilon, R. (1999). KLM and Northwest: A Survey of the Impact of a Passenger Alliance on Cargo Service Characteristics. *Journal of Air Transport Management*, 5(3).

Müller, J. and Keuschnigg, C. (1998). The Implications of Global Alliances for the EU Air Transport Market, a Case Study of the Star Alliance. Europa-Institut Universität des Saarlandes, July.

Neidl, R.E. (2000). A New Idea is Born and Developed by a Visionary: Atlas Air Inc. In *Handbook of Airline Operations*, edited by G. Butler and M. Keller. New York: McGraw-Hill.

OAG (2010). Air Cargo Forecasts.

O'Connor, W.E. (1978). Chapter 7: Air Cargo. In *An Introduction to Airline Economics*. Amsterdam: Praeger.

OECD (1999). Regulatory Reform in International Air Cargo, document DSTI/DOT(99)1, Paris.

OECD (2002). Liberalisation of Air Cargo Transport, document DSTI/DOT(2002)1/REV1, Paris.

Oxford Economic Forecasting (2005). The Impact of the Express Delivery Industry on the Global Economy. Oxford.

Palma, H., Pereira, L. and Silva, J. (2010). Airships as a Complement for Traditional Cargo and Passenger Air Transport: the Case for Portugal. Air Transport Research Society (ATRS) Conference, Porto, 6–9 July.

Peeters, P.M., Middel, J. and Hoolhorst, A. (2005). Fuel Efficiency of Commercial Aircraft: An Overview of Historical and Future Trends. NLR-CR-2005-669, National Aerospace Research Laboratory NLR, November.

Pilarski, Adam M. (2007). *Why Can't We Make Money in Aviation?* Aldershot: Ashgate.

Rawdon, B.K. and Hoisington, Z.C. (2003). Air Vehicle Design for Mass-Market Cargo Transport. American Institute of Aeronautics and Astronautics, AIAA 2003-555, January.

Sausen, R., Isaksen, I., Grewe, V., Hauglustaine, D., Lee, D.S., Myhre, G., Köhler, M.O., Pitari, G., Schumann, U., Stordal, F. and Zerefos, C. (2005). Aviation Radiative Forcing in 2000: An Update of IPCC (1999). *Meteorologische Zeitung*, 114.

Schmitt, D. and Strohmayer, A. (2001). Market and Design of a Dedicated Advanced Cargo Aircraft. *Air and Space Europe*, 3(3–4).

Seabury (2009). Perishable Market Trends. Presentation for the Cool Chain Association, 2 March.

Seabury (2010). International Air Freight 2009–2014: Riding the Rollercoaster. Seabury Cargo Advisory, June.

Sentance, A. and Pulles, H. (2005). The Initial Allocation of Permits at the Beginning of Each Year (Benchmarked Allocation). Discussion paper for Working Group 5 of the Committee on Aviation Environmental Protection (CAEP), ICAO CAEP 5 – WG5 WP5-5/3.

SH&E (2002). Study on the Quality and Efficiency of Ground Handling Services at EU Airports as a Result of the Implementation of Council Directive 96/67/EC. European Commission, October.

Shaw, S. (1993). *Effective Air Freight Marketing*. London: Pitman.

Shaw, S. (2007). *Airline Marketing and Management*, 6th edn. Aldershot: Ashgate.

Släger, B. and Kapteijns, L. (2004). Implementing Cargo Revenue Management at KLM. *Journal of Revenue and Pricing Management*, 3(1).

Smith, Peter S. (1974). *Air Freight Operations, Marketing and Economics*. London: Faber.

Stalk, George (2009). The Threat of Global Gridlock. *Harvard Business Review*, July–August.

Stern, N. (2006). *The Economics of Climate Change: The Stern Review*. London: HM Treasury.

Taneja, N.K. (1979). *The US Airfreight Industry*. Boston: Lexington Books D.C. Heath & Company.

Thomas, I. and Tan, A.K-J. (2007). Liberalisation of Air Services in the APEC Region, 1995–2005. The Centre for Asia Pacific Aviation for APEC Transportation Working Group and the Australian Department of Transport and Regional Services, January.

Tirschwell, P. (2007). Flying from Air to Ocean. *The Journal of Commerce*, 20 August.

UK DfT (2009). The Air Freight End-to-End Journey: An Analysis of the End-to-End Journey of Air Freight through UK International Gateways. UK Department for Transport, May.

UNCTAD (2010). Oil Prices and Maritime Freight Rates: An Empirical Investigation. Technical Report UNCTAD/DTL/TLB/2009/2, 1 April.

US General Accounting Office (2002). Aviation Security: Vulnerabilities and Potential Improvements for the Air Cargo System. GAO-03-344, December.

Van de Reyd, Jan and Wouters, Marnix (2005). Air Cargo Density Research. Delft University Thesis.

Vila, Carlos (2004). Logistica de la carga aerea (in Spanish). *Coleccion GESTIONA*, 1st edn. Valencia: LogisBook.

Wells, A.T. (1993). *Air Transportation*, 4th edn. Kentucky: Wadsworth.

Wensveen, John G. (2007). *Air Transportation: A Management Perspective*. Aldershot: Ashgate.

WTO (2000a). Communication from the European Communities and their Member States: the Review of the GATS Annex on Air Transport Services, document S/C/W/168.

WTO (2000b). Communication from Australia: the Mandated Review of the GATS Annex on Air Transport Services, document S/C/W/167.

WTO (2001). Developments in the Air Transport Sector since the Conclusion of the Uruguay Round, Part Seven: Background Note by the Secretariat, document S/C/W/163/Add.6.

WTO (2004). Logistics Services, Communication from Australia, Hong Kong China, Liechtenstein, Mauritius, New Zealand, Nicaragua, Switzerland, the Separate Customs Territory of Taiwan, Penghu, Kinmen and Matsu, document TN/S/W/20.

WTO (2006). Second Review of the Air Transport Annex: Developments in the Air Transport Sector (Part II). Quantitative Air Service Agreements Review (QUASAR) (Volumes I and II): Note by the Secretariat, document S/C/W/270.

WTO (2007). Second Review of the Air Transport Annex: Developments in the Air Transport Sector (Part III): Note by the Secretariat, Part E: Air Cargo Services, document S/C/W/270/Add.2.

Youssef, W. and Hansen, M. (1994). Consequences of Strategic Alliances between International Airlines: The Case of Swissair and SAS. *Transportation Research*, 28A.

Zhang, A. (2004). Air Cargo Alliances and Competition in Passenger Markets. *Transportation Research*, 40(2).

Zhang, A. and Zhang, Y. (2002). A Model of Air Cargo Liberalisation: Passengers vs. All-Cargo Carriers. *Transport Research*, 38.

Zhang, A., Hui, G.W.L.L., Lawrence, C. and Cheung, W. (2004). *Air Cargo in Mainland China and Hong Kong*. Aldershot: Ashgate.

Zondag, W. (2006). Competing for Air Cargo – a Qualitative Analysis of Competition in the Air Cargo Industry. Unpublished MSc thesis, Free University Amsterdam, Amsterdam.

Index

air cargo alliances
   consumer impact 122
   Qualiflyer alliance 121, 125–6
   SkyTeam alliance 123–4, 128–9
   types of alliance 117–22
   WOW alliance
Air Cargo Germany (ACG) 20, 88–89
Air France-KLM
   Cargo 2000 43
   CO_2 offset agreement 278
   fleet reduction 74
   freighter flights 20
   Martinair investment 76
   SkyTeam alliance 123, 128–9
   strategy 182
   traffic 8
      major hub airport 15
      regional traffic share 87
Air Services Agreement (ASAs) 55–65
air waybill 42–3, 73, 89, 155–60, 187, 197,
   200, 311, 314, 316–7
   definition 309–10
      house air waybill 314
      master air waybill 316
AirBridge Cargo 20, 74, 87–88
Airbus freighters
   A330 88, 131–2, 139, 162, 301
      characteristics 132, 140
      quota count 265
      value 215
   A380 138–9
      airport compatibility 143, 169
      characteristics 132
      noise 264
      operating costs 224
aircraft and equipment
   air routes 147–48
   combi and quick change aircraft
      144–5
   designators 131

freighter aircraft 3, 14, 18, 35–6,
   73–4, 76–8, 80, 83–7, 90, 103, 135,
   139–42
   definition 314
   future aircraft 148–51
   lower deck holds 1, 4–5, 8, 19, 34, 40,
      44, 73–5, 77–8, 90, 109, 123, 124,
      129, 131–3, 145–6, 161–2, 182,
      198, 207, 228, 279, 288, 294–5, 299
      definition 315
   narrowbodies 137, 139–41
      definition 316
   operating costs 200, 207, 219–25,
      228–29
   operations 146–47, 160–61
   passenger aircraft conversions 135,
      137–8, 142, 221, 298
   payload/range trade-off 147
   specialists in freighter conversions 136
   ULDs *see under ULDs*
   utilisation
   widebodies 137, 141–3
      definition 318
airline costs
   by type of airline 216–7
   by type of service 218–24
   capital costs 214–6
   fuel costs 212–4
   ICAO reporting 207–12
   lower deck cost allocation 227–33
   versus sector distance 208
   wet lease costs 224–7
   see also Nippon Cargo and FedEx case
      studies
airline profitability
   by supply chain participant 236
   by type of airline service 237–8
airport operations
   dangerous goods 172
   ground handling 167–70
   information flows 154–61

air waybill 155–6
  cargo manifest 157–8
  customs clearance 158–60
  load control 160–61
  load sheet 158
 security 170–2
 terminals 163–7
 ULD handling 161–3
All Nippon Airways
 directional imbalance 7
 JAS alliance 121
 JP Express 90
 Nippon Cargo 239, 243
Antonov freighters
 airline stake 81
 An 124
  passenger seats 77
  Volga-Dnepr fleet 81, 88, 142
 An 225 142–3
Atlas Air
 ACMI contract length 225
 air cargo cost advantage 181
 British Airways 87
 contribution by business segment 226
 cost versus sector distance 208
 defence support 36
 DHL joint venture 130
 Dreamlifter operation 83, 143
 Panalpina charter 114
 wet leasing 53–4, 80

bimodal transport
 rail-air 46–47
 sea-air 44–46
block space agreement 119
Boeing freighters
 B747–400F
  British Airways fleet 53–4
  characteristics 152
  cockpit crew complement 227
  costs 220–4, 226
  CRAF allocation 37, 85
  fuel efficiency 150, 268
  lower deck capacity 198
  passenger conversion 136–8
  quota count 265, 272
  ULD capacity 146
  value 215

B747–8F
 AirBridge Cargo 88
 Atlas Air 83
 B747–400F commonality 223
 Cargolux 80, 242, 247
 characteristics 143
 fuel efficiency 305
 future deliveries 139
 launch customers 143, 242
 list price 216
 Nippon Cargo 242, 247, 281
 noise charges 272
 operating expenses 224
 payload/range comparison 142, 147
B757 Freighter
 characteristics 140
 costs 220
 DHL feeder flights 106
 fuel efficiency 268
 intergrator flights 21
 launch customer
 passenger conversion 136–7, 218
 productivity, FedEx fleet 252
 UPS 139
 value 215, 218
 variants 131
B777F
 B747–200 replacement 142
 characteristics 143
 costs 223–4
 DHL introduction 102
 fuel efficiency 270, 280
 launch customer 143
 noise 264–5, 272
 Southern order 83
 ULD capacity 146
 value 215–6
British Airways
 ACMI lease 53–4, 83, 304
 airline ownership
  regional airline 76
  US airline 65
 Cargo 2000 43
 CO_2 emissions 275
 freighter flights 20, 119, *153*
 fuel surcharges 67, 194–5
 Iberia merger 128–9

operating costs 120, 229
price fixing fines 68
strategy 181
traffic
   directional imbalance 7
   Heathrow Terminal 5 289–90
   Indian traffic rights 51, 63
   regional traffic share 87
   transhipment share 15
   truck hub19

capacity
   integrators 21–2
   long-haul 19–20
   short/medium-haul 18–19
Cargoitalia 20, 88
Cargolux
   ACMI customer 83
   B747-8F launch order 143, 242, 247
   Cargo 2000 43
   financial results
      depreciation policy 214
      operating cost breakdown 216,
         218, 238, 270
      profit margin 238
   Italian subsidiary 87, 89
   Kuhne + Nagel 112
   management strategy 182
   ownership 80, 129
   price fixing fines 208
   Qualiflyer membership 125
   routes 19
   traffic 8
      international traffic share 81
      regional traffic share 20, 87
      traffic rights 57
Cathay Pacific Airways
   ACMI customer 83
   Air China
      Air China Cargo 128–9
      stake 92
   capacity management software 203
   capacity reduction 303
   Cargo 2000 43
   cargo terminal stake in Hactl 164
   DHL joint venture 92
   European flights 20
   forwarder action on price fixing 67–8

fuel efficiency target 271
traffic
   Asian share 91
   transhipment share 15
Channel Express 88
chargeable weight 156, 198–9
   definition 311
China Airlines
   ACMI customer 83
   China Eastern joint venture 90
   China Southern capacity swap 119
   freighter flights 20
   traffic
      export country base 90
      Indian traffic rights 63
      international traffic share 8
      major hub airport 15
      regional traffic share 91
   Yangtze River Express 91, 129
commodities carried
   animal transport 34
   by trade lane 25–30
   special handling items 31–2
competition
   price fixing and fuel surcharges 66–8
   regulation 65–8
consignee
   definition 311
consignment
   definition 311
consolidation 97, 100, 114–5, 128, 148,
      155, 157, 199, 314–5
consolidator 41, 98, 109, 155, 183, 187,
      199
   definition 312
consumers 34, 38, 72, 118, 122, 173–4,
      186, 279, 286, 300, 306
container, aircraft 14–15, 145–6, Fig 8.2
   animal transport 34
   definition 162, 312
   disadvantages 163–4
   forwarder/customer packed 98, 155,
      157
   handling 164–6, 168–9
   LD-3
      scanners 171
      ultra-light 163
   maritime 180–1

multi-modal 45–6, 145, 149
refrigerated 24, 32
valuable items, packing of 31, 40, 170
weighing out 161
costs
allocation on passenger/cargo flights
231, 233
breakdown into categories 207–18,
210, 216, 255
crew salaries 209–10, 217, 254
depreciation 151, 209–11, 214, 216–7,
219–22, 224, 230, 255
handling costs 15, 203, 205, 211
landing charges/fees 211, 225, 230,
263, 272–3
courier 97–101, 105–6, 114, 229, 309

Danzas 101, 111
DB Schenker 110–13, 165
defence support 36–7
density 132–3, 158, 161, 203, 205, 277
cost allocation, used for 229, 232
definition 312
minimum, for charging 198–9
payload assumption 223
DHL
Aerologic 254
Air Hong Kong 92
Airborne Express 85
aircraft container 186
aircraft operating costs 220
capacity 21–2
CO₂ offset agreement 278
CRAF allocation 37
description 100–104
DHL Air 88
forwarding 110–12
Polar Air Cargo 80
price fixing claim 67
traffic
European share 100
hub airports 14, 19, 166
international share 99
traffic rights 57
US operations 61
distribution cost model 179, 186
domestic traffic 1–5
DVS 7

economic cycle 10–12
Emirates Airlines 8, 13, 15, 46, 53, 58, 83,
93, 112, 133, 165, 195, 277
environmental impact
CO₂ emissions 265–8, 278
charges 273
EU ETS 274–8
food miles 279
noise
aircraft certification 259–60
night curfews 89, 263–4, 293
operational restrictions 260–62,
269
penalties and charges 262–3, 272–3
Expeditors 111, 114
express cargo 18, 124, 166
definition 313

FedEx
case study 247–54
CRAF allocation 37
description 104–5
DHL challenge 61
financial results
aircraft operating costs 220–22
depreciation policy 217
fuel costs 238, 262, 271
operating costs 208, 217
fleet 135–9, 141–2
MD-11 launch customer 141
pilotless aircraft 149
reduced noise approaches 261
shipment theft 40
sponsorship 186
technology 188
traffic
European share 100
hub traffic 13–15, 21
international share 99
North America 84–5
traffic rights 127, 245
finance lease 240
financial results
by supply chain participant 236
by type of airline service 237–8
Cargolux 238
FedEx 217, 220–22
Lufthansa Cargo 254–6

Nippon Cargo 245–7
    SIA Cargo 256
Flying Tigers 56, 61, 80, 104, 126–7,
        239–40, 247, 249–50, 307
forecasts
    airline forecasts 288–9
    airport forecasts 289–90
    ATM forecasts 291–2
    econometric modelling 286–8
    ICAO forecasts 296–7
    manufacturer forecasts 292–6
    trend projections 283–4
freight forwarders 109–15
    definition 314
freighter specialists 80–83
    charter and ACMI operators 82–3
fuel efficiency
    British Airways 271
    by type of aircraft 149–50, 195, 212–3,
        221, 224, 246, 265, 267, 269–72,
        280, 284, 305
    by type of airline 271–2
    Japan Airlines 271
    Virgin Atlantic 270
fuel surcharges 39, 66–8, 122, 191, 193–6,
        200–201, 213, 245, 252, 254, 291

Global Supply Systems 87–8, 226
Great Wall Airlines 15, 20, 81–2, 91–2,
        129

hub airport
        hub operations 1–2, 12–15, 17–19,
            21–2, 46, 58, 61, 69, 74, 86,
            89–90, 93, 99, 103–8, 120, 128,
            146, 150, 166–8, 243, 247–52,
            261, 271–2, 280, 304
        hub transhipment traffic 14–15
humanitarian aid 35–36

Ilyushin freighters 140
integrators
    airports, secondary 153
    containers, custom-built 146
    costs 217–8
    DHL 100–104
    distribution 188
    FedEx 104–5

foreign acquisitions 130
fuel surcharges 201
higher yields 18, 42
hub terminals 166, 272
industry standards 41, 305
market overview 99–100
Post Office ownership 68, 97
product features 184–5
profitability 238
promotion 186
tariffs 200
traffic 2–3
    European shares 100
    international share 73, 95, 99
    TNT 107–108
Transmile Air Services 82
UPS 105–7
US operations 5, 8
international traffic 1–10
    Korean Air 8
    Lufthansa 8
    Singapore Airlines 8
    transpacific 6–7
inventory
    management 40, 168, 177–81, 200,
        299, 301, 306, 315
    to sales ratio 11–12

Japan Airlines
    alliance with Lufthansa 101
    cargo division 79
    directional imbalance 7
    export industries 90
    freighter flights 20, 119, 304
    fuel surcharges 196
    Nippon Cargo 239, 243, 245
    Nippon Cargo merger 81
    price fixing claim 57
    traffic
        express product 123
        major hub airport 15
        regional traffic share 91
jet kerosene price 195, 212–3

Kuehne + Nagel 43–44, 110–12

LAN Chile 79, 94, 127

leasing 52–5, 63, 74, 83, 86–90, 95, 97,
    105–8, 121, 130, 135, 153–4, 160,
    207–11, 214–6, 224–7, 230, 235,
    240, 251, 256, 304, 318
    see also dry leasing definition 312
    see also finance lease and wet lease
Less than Container Load (LCL) 110
    definition 315
Less than Truck Load (LTL) 41
    definition 315
load factor 4–6, 19, 21, 119, 161, 204–5,
    216, 219, 237–8, 240, 242, 245,
    250, 252–3, 255–6, 266, 269,
    275–7, 292, 295, 318
low-cost airlines (LCCs)
    carriage of cargo 5, 75–6, 230
    CO_2 emissions 275, 277
    operations, 18, 75, 147
    traffic 4, 285
lower deck cost allocation 228–33
Lufthansa Cargo
    Aerologic joint venture 22, 79, 102,
        123, 130, 254
    airline ownership
        US airline 65
    B747–200F launch customer 142
    capacity reduction 303
    Cargo 2000 43
    DHL stake 91, 167
    financial results 254–6
    freighter flights 20–22
    fuel efficiency 271
    fuel surcharge approach 195–6
    Indian route rights 63
    Italian operation 89
    Jade (China) joint venture 82, 91, 129
    Kuehne + Nagel 112
    management structure 78–9, 254
    MD-11 launch customer 141
    mergers in Europe 128
    premium products 184
    price fixing investigation 66–7
    rate structure 204
    regional operations 76
    Russian overflights 148
    scanner investment 171
    shipment theft 41
    traffic

by segment 31–2
major hub airport 15
rail link to hub 46
regional traffic share 87–88
traffic rights, examples of 57
WOW alliance 123, 126
yields 191

mail
    definition 316
    Deutsche Post 101, 111
    La Poste (France) airline 109
    passenger flights, share carried on 77
    position in overall market 97
    regulation 68
    revenues 189, 209
    Royal Mail (UK) 100, 109
    security 171
    TNT (Dutch Post Office) 108
    traffic 1–3
    traffic rights 56
    US Postal Service (USPS) 109
    value, average in US 24
    yields 191–2, 201
    Zapmail (FedEx) 104
maritime operators 115
marketing
    distribution 186–8
    global trends 175–6
    logistics 176–81
        distribution cost model 179–81
    marketing strategies 181–3
    pricing 192–200
    product 183–5
    promotion 186
Maximus Air Cargo 93
mergers
    international or cross-border 128–30
    intra-country 126–28
modal choice 37–43
    quality of service 41–43
    security 40–41

network carriers
    management structure 78–80
Nippon Cargo Airlines (NCA)
    Air France-KLM partners 128
    B747-8F launch customer 143

Cargo B (Belgium) 89
case study 239–47
European flights 20
Japan Airlines, possible merger 79–80
management structure 244
ownership 115
profitability trend 246
route development 241
strategy 182
traffic
  international share 81
  trends 242
Nippon Express 81, 90, 114, 239
noise
  airports 259
  certification 259–60
  charges 263, 272–3
  curfews 263
  operational measures for reduction
    261–2
  quotas 263–4
  standards 143, 149

ocean transport 11, 27, 46, 49, 106,
    110–14, 175, 178–9, 300, 305, 315
  costs 181
  rates 38–39, 44
off-shoring 176–7, 284
operating lease 210, 235
outsourcing 83, 97, 106, 130, 176–7, 225,
    246, 284, 307, 316
ownership and control 65

pallet
  advantages 163–4
  bimodal shipment 44, 46
  cost allocation, zone method 232
  definition 145, 316
  freighter capacity 141, 146, 162
  handling 168–9
  seats and galleys 137
  security 40–1
  truck capacity 90
  weighing out 161
Panalpina 47, 100–11, 113–14
perishables 31–4, 39, 124, 164–6, 184,
    198, 278–9, 316

Post Offices 61, 76, 90, 97–98, 100, 105,
    108–9, 117, 155, 189, 250
pricing 192–200
  fuel surcharges 195–6
  rate structure 197–9
  regional differences 193–4
  Revenue Management 200–206
productivity 176, 206, 246, 252, 254,
    256–7, 284, 305
profitability 79–80, 92, 119, 181–2, 195,
    200–201, 206, 212, 215, 229, 232,
    235–8, 284, 303
  all-cargo airlines 238
  by type of airline service 237–8
  by value chain participant 237
  FedEx 253–4
  Lufthansa Cargo 254–6
  Nippon Cargo 245–7
  SIA Cargo 256
  see also airline profitability

Qualiflyer alliance 121, 125

radio frequency identification (RFID) 164
rail transport 29, 39, 44, 46–7, 109, 112,
    114, 145, 153, 180, 186, 276, 315
regulation
  Air Services Agreements 56–65
  future liberalisation 69–72
  ownership and control 65
  regional developments 59–65
  competition and price-fixing 65–68
  financial fitness 54–55
  mail regulation 68
  over-regulation 304–5
  technical oversight 50–54
Revenue Management 200–206, 288
Rutges 7

security 34, 39, 40–41, 56, 72, 168,
    170–72, 183, 315
  distribution costs, impact on 180
  regulations 291, 295, 304–5
  scanner investment 171
  surcharges 189, 193–4, 196, 200,
    211.257
Seventh Freedom traffic rights 57–8, 62–4,
    69, 304

Singapore Airlines
    cargo subsidiary 79, 256–7
    fuel efficiency 271
    Great Wall China 82, 91–2, 129
    price fixing claim 68
    traffic
        Asian share 91
        hub feed from exporter countries 90
        international traffic share 8
        major hub airport 15
        traffic rights 58, 63
    WOW Alliance 123
Sinotrans 92, 106, 111, 114, 128
Sixth Freedom traffic rights 57–8, 84, 247
SkyTeam alliance 122–4, 128
supply chain 12, 42, 115
    definition 317
    DHL division 100–101, 111–2
    global trends 175, 177–8
    Panalpina 113
    profitability 236–7
    UPS 105–6

tare weight *112*, 145–6, 149, 160, 162–3,
    199
    definition 317
TNT
    capacity 20–21
    depreciation policy 217
    description 107–8
    fleet 139
    mail regulation 68
    traffic
        European share 100
        hub airports 14
        international share 99
traffic variations
    directional imbalance 7, 26–27, 44,
        148, 162, 228, 240, 293
    monthly traffic 16–17
    weekly and daily traffic 17
truck 'flights' 90

Unit Load Devices (ULDs) 145–6, 162–3
    definition 310
    designators 146
    dimensions 146
    see also container and pallet

UPS
    capacity 21
    CRAF allocation 37
    description 105–7
    DHL challenge 61
    efficiency (KPIs) 271
    fleet 135, 139, 142
    freight rates 185
    fuel surcharges 200–1
    operating costs 208, 217–8, 220–22
    profit margins 238
    SCS forwarding 111
    shipment theft 41
    traffic
        European share 100
        hub airports 14–15, 22
        international share 99
        Nippon Cargo code share 81
        traffic rights 245
        US share 85
US Civil Reserve Air Fleet (CRAF) 37
US$ exchange rate 190

value to weight ratio 24, 38, 181, 279, 288,
    293
Varilog 94
Virgin Atlantic
    directional imbalance 7
    fuel surcharges 68
    Indian traffic rights 51
    regional traffic share 87
Volga-Dnepr Airlines
    AirBridge acquisition 88
    international traffic share 81
    ownership 81–2

wet lease 52–4, 83, 86–7, 88, 90, 108, 121,
    130, 208, 216, 224, 226
    definition 318
World Food Programme
    WFP Aviation 35
WOW alliance 123

Yangtze River Express 14, 91, 129
yields
    yield trends 189–91
    yields and capacity 303–4